Dedicated to the memory of my dear friend

K. Krishna Reddy

who motivated me to write this book, but left this world suddenly before it was published.

About the Book

The present book stands apart in the collection of books on Indian Society. Most of the books are either too complex for the lay readers or oversimplified and trivial. Starting with the historical moorings and formation of Indian Society, it journeys through the salient features and major components of the Indian Society – Caste and Caste System, Scheduled Castes and Other Backward Classes, Scheduled Tribes and Religious Minorities. Women and Society, Village India, Urbanisation and Social Movements are some other areas dealt with in detail. It also takes a hard look at the effects of globalisation on our society and issues of secularism, communalism and regionalism.

Inclusion of such current social issues as 'honour killing' of young women, social impact of Internet, development and displacement of people and other issues, usually not covered by other books, makes it special. A number of concepts being used, but not clearly understood by many – ethnicity, civil society, multiculturalism, diaspora, social exclusion and some others – have been explained in simple language.

Written in a lucid way, the book will be useful in Sociology, some topics of Anthropology, General Studies and Essay besides catering to the requirements of university/college students.

INDIAN SOCIETY
THEMES AND SOCIAL ISSUES

3e

For Civil Services and Other State Services Examination

Nadeem Hasnain · Aseem Hasnain

McGraw Hill

McGraw Hill Education (India) Private Limited

Published by McGraw Hill Education (India) Private Limited,
Registered Office: Anjana Complex No: 5/90 A, Butt Road, St. Thomas Mount, Chennai – 600 016

Indian Society: Themes and Social Issues, 3e

Print Edition:
ISBN (13): 978-93-6444-479-8
ISBN (10): 93-6444-479-5

E-Book Edition:
ISBN (13): 978-93-6444-204-6
ISBN (10): 93-6444-204-0

1 2 3 4 5 6 7 8 9 7101558 29 28 27 26 25

Printed and bound in India

Typeset at Transcend Content Solution, 163F Jaigirghat Road, Panchanantala, Kolkata – 700 063 and printed at Rajkamal Electric Press, Kundli, Haryana-131 028.

Image: Shutterstock
Designer: Anita Kanojia

Visit us at: www.mheducation.co.in
Write to us at: support.india@mheducation.com
CIN: U80302TN2010PTC111532
Toll Free Number: 1800 103 5875

APPEAL

COUNTER THE COUNTERFEIT & BUILD A STRONG FOUNDATION FOR SUCCESS

Books are our best friends, is the adage we have grown up with. However, the pirates of piracy are continuously forging 'our best friends'. Our books and their supplementary online resources are copyrighted, and we don't lend any right-to-copy. Piracy is synonymous to stealing books.

Knowledge comes real, let's not encourage its counterfeit. Therefore, we appeal all our readers to discourage pirated books and **choose authentic ones**.

HOW TO IDENTIFY THE PIRATED BOOKS?

1 Cover and Spine

- Look and feel (new or used book)
- Blurred images on the cover
- Hologram pasted on front
- Defective spine (wrinkles) or air pocket at its bottom
- Unclear ISBN/bar codes
- Missing/non-operational Unique Coupon Code for exclusive access to McGraw Hill Edge

2 Text/Printing/Binding

- Uneven inking of pages
- Poor quality or blurred photographs/images/charts
- Substandard paper quality and opacity
- Misaligned pages
- Missing pages
- Inferior binding quality

You can further watch this video on How to identify a pirated book

For more information about identifying piracy, visit **https://www.mheducation.co.in/piracy**

To report a pirated book, send 'Hi' on WhatsApp code given on the back cover or write to us at **support.india@mheducation.com**.

Reported pirated books are examined to combat their piracy.

Let's fight the Pirates of Piracy and resolve to go for original!

About the Authors

Nadeem Hasnain, a well-known social scientist, maintains a wide range of interests in his academic pursuits. He completed his Ph.D. from Lucknow University specialising in Social-Cultural Anthropology and taught in the same university. His area of interest and specialisation is marginalised sections of Indian society viz. the Dalits and backward communities, tribal communities, minorities as well as social change in Indian society.

As Fulbright 'Scholar in Residence' and later Visiting Professor at St. Lawrence University, New York, he taught in the departments of Global Studies, Religious Studies and Anthropology. He has also served as the Pro-Vice-Chancellor of Mahatma Gandhi International Hindi University, Wardha (Maharashtra) and Senior Fellow, Indian Council of Social Science Research.

Some of his well-known and popular books are *Tribal India, Indian Society and Culture: Continuity and Change, Handbook of Sociology, and Sociology of Marginalized Communities and Weaker Sections in India.* His latest book *Weaker Sections and Disadvantaged Groups in Indian Society* is like a ready reckoner for SC, ST, OBC and Minorities—Linguistic, Religious and Sexual as per the requirements of civil services examination.

Prof. Hasnain is a familiar name not only among the university students of Sociology, Anthropology and Social Geography but also among the civil services aspirants. He has been counselling and lecturing for the aspirants of Civil Services and State Services examinations for more than thirty years and his successful students are spread across the entire country. He is still very active academically and socially and known as an academic activist taking part in social issues and recognised as a public intellectual.

Aseem Hasnain is Assistant Professor of Sociology at California State University, Fresno, USA. He is a political sociologist with interests in historical, and mixed methods research.

He completed his Ph.D. at the University of North Carolina, Chapel Hill, USA, where he took graduate courses in Sociology, Religious Studies, and South Asian History. His research and teaching interests include: Ideology; Race, and Caste; Labor, and Environmentalism. His published works include research on identity politics, Indigenous social movements, comparative Human Rights, Politics of Food, and the sociology of Knowledge. He grew up in Lucknow, India where he studied Physics, Math and Finance before getting a postgraduate degree in community forestry from the Indian Institute of Forest Management, Bhopal. Before his Ph.D., he worked with non-profits in India. Presently Aseem lives in Fresno, California.

Why and How Is This Book Useful?

Indian Society, in one way or the other, figures prominently in Sociology/Anthropology, General Studies, Essay and Interview.

This book, perhaps, is the first and the only one available in the market that has been written to cater to the requirements of all the above-mentioned areas. Let us examine this claim.

SOCIOLOGY/ANTHROPOLOGY

The second paper of both Sociology and Anthropology deals with Indian Society. As for its usefulness in both, especially in Sociology, is concerned, it is stating the obvious. In view of the growing trend of not focusing mechanically on the syllabus, but going beyond it requires lot of supplementary information with critical examination. This aspect has been considered and the material is provided judiciously.

Moreover, a set of questions along with indicative answers give the readers an opportunity for self-assessment.

GENERAL STUDIES

The first paper of General Studies dealing with Indian Heritage and Culture, History and Geography mentions Indian Society once and in only one line, but it is very deceptive; it opens a Pandora's box.

See some of the questions asked and their range during the last few years:

1. Caste system is assuming new identities and associational forms. Hence caste system cannot be eradicated. Comment.
2. What are the two major legal initiatives by the State since independence addressing discrimination against the Scheduled Tribes?
3. Life cycle of Joint Family depends on economic factors rather than social values. Discuss.
4. Why are the tribals of India referred to as Scheduled Tribes? Indicate the major provisions in the Constitution for their upliftment.
5. Debate the issue whether and how contemporary movements for assertion of Dalit identity works towards annihilation of caste.

The book tries to tackle this problem (of peripheral issues) with utmost care and effort. Hence, the book will be a valuable source material. Moreover, questions and indicative answers also facilitate the selection of the most relevant information.

ESSAY PAPER AND INTERVIEW

Every year, at least one essay pertains to Indian Society. In Interview, questions, even opinion-oriented ones, are asked on the issues related to women, Scheduled Castes, Scheduled Tribes, Backward Classes, Minorities, Social Change, Impact of Globalisation on Indian Society, etc. Lots of information, including critical examination, has been provided to handle these questions.

Therefore, it may be honestly claimed that in the collection of available books, this book stands apart.

Happy and success-oriented reading!

Preface to the Third Edition

We are indeed delighted to write these lines for the third edition of this book. Three editions coming in four years speak for the acceptance among the readers and its popularity.

On the basis of feedback from the readers and analysis of examination papers over the years we have added some topics such as 'different perspectives on caste' and issues in 'challenges of social transformation' – crisis of development, ethnic conflicts, religious revivalism, disparities in education etc.

Readers will find the content in a new format and style. 'Chapter Outlines' for a quick overview, 'Quick Facts' for easy understanding of complex ideas, thought provoking questions under the tag 'What Do You Think' in every chapter to prompt the readers for looking at the content in a different perspective. Moreover, every chapter is followed by the questions asked during the past ten years while 'Focus Areas for the Exam' shall help the readers to identify areas to be studied more seriously.

We hope that the revision and additions in the content along with the innovations described above shall be more helpful to readers. As usual any suggestions and feedback are welcome to make the book more useful in the future editions.

Nadeem Hasnain
(nadeemhasnain@gmail.com)

Aseem Hasnain
(aseemhasnain@gmail.com)

Preface to the First Edition

The present effort goes back to my days as a student in Lucknow University. When I switched from Science to Social Science at the undergraduate level, I was fascinated by the story of society and culture. My coming to Anthropology was by a sheer accident. I did not confine myself within the narrow boundaries of disciplines, especially the wall between Sociology and Social Anthropology. I belong to both and vice versa. I have always, through my writings, tried to demolish this wall.

Before I write a book, I usually make a survey of the available books so that I may identify the glaring gaps and absence of important information and material.

On the basis of my involvement with the university students for four decades and civil service aspirants for three decades, I should admit that I enjoy an advantage over other scholars and authors – I write as well as teach and it helps me. I have always believed that teachers also learn a lot from their students. I am thankful to my students for raising questions pregnant with new ideas. It has helped me as an author and as a teacher.

I have tried to present a comprehensive and in-depth view of the present Indian society in a lucid and exam-oriented way and hope that my effort would benefit both civil service aspirants and university students.

Acknowledgements

For every edition of the book I (first author), wish to invoke the memory of my dear friend Late Krishna Reddy, who always motivated me to explore new fields in my academic pursuits.

We wish to express our heartfelt thanks to Rahul Banerjee, Associate Portfolio Manager and Mausumi Mukherjee, Content Developer for helping me bring this edition in record time. We are especially thankful to Mausumi, for coming out with innovative ideas and showing utmost patience with an impatient first author. Last but not the least, our thanks are also due to Suhaib Ali, Manager, Production Services and his associates for producing the book in its present form.

Nadeem Hasnain & Aseem Hasnain

Contents

CHAPTER 1

Introducing Indian Society: Historical Moorings

Chapter Outline

1. Understanding the complexity of Indian society and its historical evolution
2. Recognising the impact of fossil evidence, such as the Narmada Man, in understanding the prehistory of India
3. Comprehending the socio-cultural dynamics in India and distinguish between endogenous and exogenous changes
4. Identifying the significant influences of Westernisation on Indian society
5. Exploring the continuity and changes in Indian traditions, including the adaptation of caste and joint family systems to modern contexts
6. Analysing the interplay between Little Traditions and Great Traditions within Indian society
7. Evaluating the factors leading to modernisation in India, such as industrialisation, urbanisation, and the influence of Western values
8. The resilience of traditional structures like caste and religion in the face of modern societal transformations
9. Appreciating the cultural synthesis observed in Indian society – integration of different religious and cultural practices
10. Reflect on the challenges posed by cultural lag and the coexistence of traditional and modern values in contemporary India

It is believed, on the basis of fossil evidences, that man in India is around five lakh years old. But, it is difficult to identify the earliest inhabitants of India and their racial/ethnic affiliations despite the fact that several scholars have tried to solve this jigsaw puzzle on the basis of their classifications. It is only since the invention of script and the rise of the earliest known civilisation dating to around five thousand years that we have some concrete ideas about the formation of Indian society.

Quick Fact

Monistic activity

Monasticism entails withdrawing from worldly engagements to dedicate oneself to spiritual growth and religious devotion.

Pluralistic Activity

Pluralism refers to the coexistence and interaction of diverse religious, cultural, and philosophical traditions within a society. India, as a historically diverse nation, embodies pluralistic activity in various forms.

The very nature of the Indian society is highly complex. Indian society may not be described as 'society' in the strict sociological sense because it lacks in some of the basic attributes of 'society'. People residing in one geographical area under a state (it is only after independence that the dominion of India came into being) desire to perpetuate (it is **not a monistic activity of India, but a pluralistic one** till 1947) the social solidarity

(India has always been living as tribes, ethnic groups, *Jatis* and so on), a group of people bound by interrelationships, common institutions (except for warriors, pilgrims, traders, etc. This interaction and interrelationship were restricted till we became one Indian union.). Thus, it is 'societies in India' with a mind-boggling multiplicity that were living and the aggregate of which most of us prefer to describe as Indian society. All these hundreds and thousands of societies were hampered in their interactions because of lack of any commonly understood language and culture. Yet, perhaps, since 6th century B.C., different regions of India have been brought together.

Despite the immense cultural diversity, there has been a growing convergence of cultures because of the emergence of new forces and factors since the 19th century. Among these, common political structure, common legal system, uniform administrative system, uniform educational system, growing economic interdependence, a new kind of growing national awareness may be enumerated to have contributed to the making of an 'Indian society'. Of course, the technological and cultural impact of the process of westernisation such as modern means of transport and communication, new printing technology, English and Hindi languages, growing secularisation, etc. played a very important role in this whole process. Yet, Indian society has been **more of a cultural entity rather than a structural entity.**

Quick Fact

Cultural Entity

Cultural entities reflect the spirit of a society. India's diversity in languages, festivals, and cuisines forms a cultural entity.

Structural Entity

Structural entities provide the framework that supports a society's operations. The Indian Constitution, judiciary, and governance systems are a few structural entities of Indian Society.

Even today when one thinks of Indian society, religion immediately comes to mind as the basis of the traditional Indian social system. Hence, we find that the primary mooring of Indian society is religion. Hinduism or Hindu religion happens to be the oldest of all the religions whose followers inhabit India and the vast multitude of Indian masses live it. But, it is different from all these religions. It has neither fixed dogmas nor any centralised authority; rather it is a vast network of structures, institutions, beliefs, values, norms and so many other things scattered all over. The economic and educational systems were never totally divorced from the guidelines laid down by religion.

SOCIO-CULTURAL DYNAMICS THROUGH THE AGES

Socio-cultural dynamics refers to the changes in the social and cultural attributes of a society. Though social and cultural attributes are seen as an integral whole and hence inseparable, yet, social here refers to the structural aspects such as patterned interactions. We come across various social institutions. By cultural attributes, we refer to the collectively shared values, ideas and symbols which are associated with human groups. Thus, socio-cultural dynamics is a universal and timeless process. Since no society can be static, all societies at all times pass through this process of change.

Socio-cultural dynamics is a highly complex phenomenon. If the forces of change emanate within the social structure, it may be termed as endogenous. The rise of socio-religious ideologies such as

Buddhism or Jainism may be examples of **endogenous change** while the changes occurring through the advent of Islam or Christianity that came from outside may be placed under the category of **exogenous changes**. Changes within Indian society have occurred through both the processes.

> **Quick Fact**
>
> **Endogenous Change**
> Social or cultural change arising from within a society, such as the rise of Buddhism or Jainism in India.
>
> **Exogenous Change**
> Social or cultural change introduced by external influences, such as the advent of Islam or British colonialism in India.

IMPACT OF MODERN WEST ON INDIAN SOCIETY

Socio-cultural change in India under the impact of the modern west presents yet another important facet of socio-cultural dynamics. India has always been a highly traditional society and it is only through contact with the modern west that the process of modernisation, both technological and cultural, was initiated into Indian society. Sociologists have described these changes as a heterogenetic process of change. Though the Portuguese, the French and the Dutch had contacts with India, it is the British influence which had a profound impact on Indian society.

> **Quick Fact**
>
> **Rationalism**
> It emphasises reason and logic as the primary sources of knowledge and decision-making, over tradition or emotion.
>
> **Individualism**
> It prioritises the rights, autonomy, and self-expression of the individual over collective or communal interests.
>
> **Utilitarianism**
> It is the ethical philosophy that actions are right if they promote the greatest happiness or benefit for the greatest number of people.

To understand the socio-cultural dynamics with reference to the western impact, we must know the nature of Indian society and the western tradition. Indian culture was highly traditional while the western culture was a modernising one in terms of **rationalism, individualism** and **utilitarianism**. It also contained the elements of **egalitarianism** and **universalism** unlike the traditional Indian social system based on status and hierarchy with a strong religious orientation. With the advent of British rule, new structures developed in India, notable of which are educative, legal and military and these along with other factors of change introduced new criteria for stratification of which the criteria secular in nature played a very important role in the coming future.

> **Quick Fact**
>
> **Egalitarianism**
> The principle of equality, advocating for equal rights and opportunities for all individuals.
>
> **Universalism**
> The principle that all individuals are treated equally under a common set of rules, rights, and obligations, regardless of their caste, religion, gender, or social background.

A very important aspect of western impact was the introduction of English language and secular education. Before the advent of British rule, the official and administrative work in India were being carried out through Sanskrit, Persian and Urdu. They introduced English language and it provided a window to the outside world. It also facilitated exposure to a new value system based on egalitarianism, rationalism and secularism. Introduction of new and modern means of transport and communication contributed to an increase in spatial and social mobility. The new printing technology, postal services and radio helped in the dissemination of ideas. At the level of ideas, a new awakening began and it became the harbinger of radical social change. The introduction of a new penal code not only brought about changes in the legal system and distribution of justice, but it also directly attacked the traditional Hindu law, which was highly discriminatory and unjust, especially for the *Dalit* section of Indian society. The principle of '**equality before law**' was established along with a uniform legal system throughout India. Industrialisation and urbanisation – important factors of change – registered a sharp rise. The process of industrialisation facilitated new determinants and secular indicators of social status such as, material indicators were introduced to the Indian society. The concept of 'nationalism' gradually emerged and it played an important unifying role in the Indian society.

Quick Fact

Equality Before Law

The principle of 'equality before the law' and the establishment of a uniform legal system throughout India were initiated during the British colonial period. This was primarily introduced under the reforms of Lord William Bentinck, the Governor-General of India from 1828 to 1835.

Here, it is important to note that the impact of westernisation also facilitated the emergence of a new westernised elite that replaced the traditional elite of Indian society. This new elite, equipped and inspired by a new ideology and value system, looked at its own 'society' in a different way. It reinterpreted Hinduism and caste system in a progressive and more humane way and became the harbinger of a new social order. Thus, the impact of westernisation immensely contributed to the technological and cultural modernisation of India. Although 'how modern contemporary India is' has been a matter of debate, sociologists such as Deepankar Gupta (2014) have expressed scepticism about India's 'mistaken modernity'. But, the fact remains that the Indian society could never be the same again after it came under the influence of the west. At the same time, it is also true that these changes did not take place through the total replacement of traditional structures. The traditional structures in India have also shown an amazing resilience and have retained their basic features adapting to new roles. Caste and religion are two examples of this adaptation. Perhaps, that is why Yogendra Singh chose 'Modernisation of Indian Tradition' (1996) as the title of his very popular book. This title may sound very unusual or even contradictory to some people, but those who understand the socio-cultural dynamics of Indian society will agree with it.

What Do You Think?

In what ways has the influence of modern Western ideas, such as individualism and technological advancement, reshaped traditional Indian values, and how can India balance modernization with the preservation of its cultural heritage?

CONTINUITY AND CHANGE

Any society and every society is a continuation of the past, but a range of continuity is maintained even in the midst of change. This is how the identity of a society is maintained over a period of time. Even otherwise, some continuity is essential because human nature is immutable.

As S.C. Dube (1990) rightly suggests, the notions of **ascribed status**, hierarchy, ritual purity and impurity have been the basic ingredients of Hindu social structure. These have been attacked from time to time by social and religious reform movements, secularisation processes and a host of others. But, the system seems to have a remarkable resilience. It yields some ground, but returns again. For instance, when caste is sought to be dislodged from the religious (ritual) domain, it enters into the political process and caste consciousness comes back with a vengeance through urbanisation. In the face of scientific temper, religiosity and ritualism also increased and a substantial segment of the modern educated class shows latent and sometimes overt acceptance of the religious phenomenon that is occasionally steeped in irrationality and superstition. Moreover, even the religious ideologies that emerged outside India, such as Islam and Christianity, accept some of these attributes and become 'Indianised'. The joint family norms instead of fading away in the face of urbanisation and industrialisation have adapted to the process of democratisation and acceptance of dissent. The joint family today is more democratic and the traditional autocratic authority of the *karta* (head of the joint family) has become a thing of the past. All these examples point to the fact that what is being continued is a transformed version of the past. When a Clifford Geertz talks about 'Old Societies, New States' (1963) he has a point.

Quick Fact

Ascribed Status

It refers to the social position or rank that an individual occupies based on characteristics determined at birth, such as caste, family lineage, ethnicity, or gender, rather than personal achievements or choices. It contrasts with achieved status, which is based on personal effort or merit.

Another dimension of continuity in the Indian society may be explained through the continuity of **Little Traditions** with **Great Traditions**. Even among the modern, educated urban people, during sickness in the family, a modern physician visits the patient in the morning and the same family takes recourse to sorcery *ganda* and *taveez* (amulet) *bhabhut* from the so-called godmen, *swamis* and *babas*, *Pirs* and *faqirs*. A common sight in any Indian village is the puja for the tractor bought by a farmer, invoking the blessings of the local deity, performing *aarti* and applying *sindoor* to the tractor, a product of modern technology. Not only the continuity between the Little Traditions and Great Traditions, even two different Great Traditions may go together or get fused into one another. For the vast multitudes of the Hindu masses, paying respect to the *mazar* of a Sufi saint along with praying in a temple is not unusual or mutually contradictory. It does not dilute their *Hindutva*. The contribution of a number of Muslims to *Shastriya* Sangeet is well known and a number of these musicians have been paying their respect to goddess Saraswati before starting their daily *riyaz* (practice) of music, both vocal as well as instrumental. Ustad Bismillah Khan playing Shehnai on the threshold of Kashi Vishwanath temple immediately after performing Haj at Mecca is a pleasant sight to many. It tells us that there is something inherent in Indian civilisation which facilitates cultural continuity.

Quick Fact

Little Traditions

Localised, community-specific cultural practices often found in rural areas or tribal societies.

Great Traditions

The overarching cultural practices and beliefs shared across larger regions or societies, such as classical Indian traditions.

Among the factors of change in Indian society discussed above, independence from British rule, democratisation, **adult franchise**, constitution as a vehicle of change (state-sponsored change), industrialisation and urbanisation, modern education and increase in education and legislative and administrative means may be the most important factors of change. At the grassroot level, industrialisation and market economy have led to the breakdown of the *Jajmani* system. Urbanisation has contributed to increased occupational mobility and disorganisation of joint family at least structurally. A new system of stratification based on achievement rather than ascription has emerged. But, as pointed out elsewhere in this chapter, these changes have not taken place through wholesale replacement of traditional structures. However, the craving for retaining and strengthening traditional social institutions such as caste and religion along with modernisation poses a threat of breakdown or '**cultural lag**' to the process of modernisation. The increasing level of communalism and casteism along with violence, use of modern technology like television to promote religious animosity and growth of separatism may be cited as examples. Increased ritualism, religiosity and religious consciousness and an upbeat economy, democracy and declining levels of tolerance of dissent, an open polity with atrocities on the weaker sections, high spiritualism with increasing vulgarisation of values is alarming to students of contemporary Indian society. As S.C. Dube (1990) remarked, contemporary Indian society is undergoing a trauma of change and is confronting a series of dilemmas and paradoxes. While some aspects of tradition will survive because of their vitality and usefulness, many of the prejudices of the past will have to be eradicated and structures of exploitation and tyranny demolished. The road ahead is long, the process may be painful, but every citizen of India has a stake in this future.

Quick Fact

Adult Franchise

Adult franchise established the principle of one person, one vote, ensuring that every individual had an equal say in electing representatives and shaping governance. It was a transformative tool in post-independence India.

Quick Fact

Cultural Lag

The delay in the adaptation of societal norms and values to technological or social advancements.

Questions and Indicative Answers

1. Describe the impact of the modern West on Indian society.

- Introduction of English language as the window to the western world;
- Rationalism, individualism and individual rights;
- Egalitarianism and gender equality;
- Secular education;
- Technological modernisation, modern means of transport and communication, new printing technology, radio and postal services, etc.;
- Spatial and social mobility;

- Principle of equality before the law, against caste system's discriminatory attitude towards Dalits; and
- New English-knowing westernised elite.

2. Discuss the continuity and change in Indian society.

- Continuity (ascribed status, hierarchy, ritual purity/impurity);
- Religiosity despite promotion of scientific temper;
- Non-Indic religions becoming 'Indianised';
- Change: Joint family disintegrating;
- What is being continued is a transformed version of the past;
- Continuity of Little traditions with Great traditions; and
- Democratisation of polity.

3. What are the important factors of change?

- New western values through British rule;
- Industrialisation and urbanisation; and
- Modern education.

Previous Years' Questions

1. How does Indian society maintain continuity in traditional social values?

(GS Mains Paper I, 2021)

Focus Areas for the Examination

1. Continuity and recent changes in Indian Society

CHAPTER 2

Perspectives on the Study of Indian Society

Chapter Outline

1. Understanding various approaches to study Indian society – Indological, Structural-Functionalist, Historical, Culturological, Marxist, and Subaltern
2. The strengths and limitations of the Indological Approach
3. Exploring the significance of empirical fieldwork in the Structural-Functionalist Approach
4. Importance of cultural analysis in the Culturological Approach
5. Analysing the role of the Marxist Approach in understanding socio-economic structures
6. Comprehending the contributions of the Subaltern Approach in highlighting the experiences of marginalised and oppressed groups – Peasants, Tribals, and Dalits

There have been several perspectives or approaches to the study of Indian society ranging from the **Indological Approach to the Subaltern Approach**. Some of these have been used by different scholars over a period while some others are new additions. Taken together, the following approaches may be enumerated to understand and study the Indian society. However, there is a certain degree of overlap between the two or more approaches:

1. Indological Approach
2. Structural-Functionalist Approach
3. Historical Approach
4. Culturological Approach
5. Marxist Approach
6. Subaltern Approach

Quick Fact

Indological Approach

An approach to the study of Indian society based on textual sources. It relies on a 'book view' rather than an empirical field view, often criticised for presenting a static and romanticised image of Indian society.

Subaltern Approach

A post-Marxist approach studying marginalised and oppressed groups in society. It highlights the lived experiences of groups like peasants, tribals, and dalits.

INDOLOGICAL APPROACH

Indological Approach has been quite popular among scholars of Indian society. Indology is the academic study of history, culture, languages, etc. of the Indian subcontinent which may include the modern-day states of India, Pakistan, Bangladesh, Sri Lanka and Nepal; all coming under the Indian or South Asian Civilisation. Thus, Indology may be understood as a systematic study of Indian society and culture. The justification behind the Indological Approach is that the Indian civilisation is too unique to be 'fitted' into the framework of western sociology and the Indian society can be understood only through the concepts, theories and frameworks of Indian civilisation.

Quick Fact

Empirical Field View

An approach that collects data through direct fieldwork and observation, contrasting with textual or book-based methodologies.

The major drawback or weakness of the Indological Approach is its reliance on texts or textual/book view of Indian society rather than the **empirical/field view**. Thus, it presents a stereotyped and static image of Indian society and culture. It is also to be noted that the Indological Approach is deeply influenced by Indology, but should not be taken as coterminous with Indology. Most of the Indologists were the products of different schools of indological tradition such as Indological Research Centre of Pune, Lucknow and Asiatic Society of Bengal founded by Sir William Jones. Significantly, the founding fathers of Indian Sociology were influenced by the Indological Approach and they included G. S. Ghurye, B. K. Sarkar, Radhakamal Mukherjee, K. M. Kapadia, P. H. Prabhu and Iravati Karve. G. S. Ghurye was more influenced by the works of Indologists of the Bhandarkar Institute, Pune. Being a student of Sanskrit, Ghurye primarily used Sanskrit texts to understand Indian society and culture. His understanding of caste, tribe, Indian Muslims, Indian values and knowledge was hotly contested by other sociologists and anthropologists on the ground that it was biased and unidimensional. The critics of Ghurye are of the view that he failed to recognise the rise of modern India and the contribution of Islam and British rule. Moreover, his approach romanticises India which lived within inequality and exploitation. Thus, other approaches arose as a reaction to the view promoted by scholars of the Indological Approach.

Quick Fact

Indology is older than Sociology

It traces its origin back to 1784, when Sir William Jones established it in Kolkata. In 1787, he founded the Asiatic Society of Bengal, where he introduced two disciplines – Sanskrit and Indology.

STRUCTURAL-FUNCTIONALIST APPROACH

Structural-Functionalist Approach is, perhaps, the most popular of all approaches to the understanding of Indian society. Significantly, it gives more importance to the empirical structure than to the normative framework of culture. Inspired by A. R. Radcliffe-Brown, this approach promotes a very systematic and rigorous fieldwork.

Followers of the structural-functionalist approach never take 'truth' for granted. They believe that it happens in the social context that requires empirical investigation as opposed to the textual view followed by scholars of the Indological Approach. Thus, one must go to the field for first-hand information. It rules out the glorification of the past on the basis of available texts. For a structural-functionalist, social structure is an empirical reality present at a given point of time. Radcliffe-Brown was of the view that any scientific study of culture should be undertaken as a dimension of social structure. Thus, social structure is the central concept of this approach. This approach became very popular after India's independence was spearheaded by M. N. Srinivas. It was used for the study and analysis of rural community, caste structure, family structure, kinship structure, religious structure and political structure.

M. N. Srinivas not only used the structural-functionalist approach, but also inspired his colleagues and students to apply it in understanding the Indian society. His classic study of 'Religion and Society among the Coorgs', 'Rampura Village' and 'Social Change in Modern India' are important examples of application of the structural-functionalist approach. S. C. Dube's study of 'Indian Village' is another important example. All of these and similar studies used the field study approach to understand the Indian society. Though the major strength of this approach is its strong empirical foundation, its critics are of the view that it suffers from its limitation of neglecting the cultural and historical dimensions.

Quick Fact

Criticism of the Structural-Functional Theory

This theory has been criticised for various reasons. The most popular reason says, it oversimplifies complex social phenomena. It can't adequately explain social change somewhat because of its circular nature.

HISTORICAL APPROACH

Historical Approach is another important approach to study Indian society. Its uniqueness lies in the fact that it gives more importance to the historical process of development than to the 'synchronic' structures of the social phenomenon. Like **Marxists and Weberians**, it is primarily concerned with the process of social development. It focuses on the historical processes of industrialisation, urbanisation, democratisation, modernisation, etc., thus aiming to understand various processes of development within the historical framework. Though G. S. Ghurye and R. K. Mukherjee also used historical approaches, their works are classified under the Indological Approach.

Quick Fact

Marxist and Weberian Theory

Marxists and Weberian are two significant schools of thought in sociology, each offering distinct perspectives on society, power, and class. According to the Marxists, society is shaped by economic structures and class struggles. According to the Weberians, society is influenced by multiple factors beyond economics, including culture, ideas, and individual actions.

CULTUROLOGICAL APPROACH

Culturological Approach is a relatively minor and 'non-standardised' approach because it encompasses a variety of viewpoints. However, what is common to all these viewpoints is the emphasis on the primacy of culture as the object of study relegating social relationships and social structures as the secondary manifestation of culture. It looks at person as a cultural being. This approach evolved mainly under the influence of cultural anthropologists rather than sociologists. This emphasis on culture may bear similarity with the Indological Approach, but unlike this, it takes the field view, rather than the book view practiced by Indologists. Moreover, the method of cultural analysis and theories of culture have played an important role in this approach. The works of such important anthropologists as Clifford Geertz, McKim Marriott, David Schneider, Milton Singer and others bear testimony to this fact.

MARXIST APPROACH

Perhaps no other approach to study Indian society has had a more profound impact than the **Marxist Approach**. It came out of the historical approach being used in historical sociology. The Marxist Approach helps to understand social reality through production, the techno-economic division of labour involved in operating the instruments of production and social relations of productions or what was more precisely characterised property relations. The Marxist Approach gives central importance to property structure in analysing society. It recognises the dialectics of evolutionary as well as revolutionary changes of the breaks in historical continuity in the transition from one socio-economic formation to another.

D. D. Kosambi, A. R. Desai and D. P. Mukherji are considered as exponents of the Marxist analysis of Indian society. Desai made an attempt to develop a historic-sociological model to understand the Indian society. As a Marxian scholar, he considers that the foundation of Indian history is based on the modes of production that evolved during different points of time – pre-colonial stage, colonial stage and post-colonial stage. Among his seminal contributions are the study and analysis of social, economic and cultural structure of rural India and the changes coming into it. His 'Social Background of Indian Nationalism', 'Rural Sociology in India' and 'Rural India in Transition' are invaluable contributions to Indian sociology.

SUBALTERN APPROACH

Subaltern Approach to the understanding of Indian society is perhaps the youngest of all these approaches. It is often seen as a post-Marxist movement because many of its protagonists combine Marxist theory with a variety of other influences. The subaltern school of historiography emerged in the 1980s in the study of South Asian societies, especially India. Influenced by the Marxist philosopher Antonio Gramsci, the concept of subaltern includes all marginalised people in a society. This approach was prompted by the fact that the Marxists were reluctant to accept the ideology of caste and religion as crucial factors in Indian history. They were thus, according to the subaltern scholars, totally unable to gather and use vital historical data for the 'lived' experiences of various oppressed classes, which were submerged in religious and social customs.

A galaxy of eminent scholars such as Ranajit Guha, Partha Chatterjee, Gyan Prakash, Shail Mayaram and Shahid Amin did pioneering work using the subaltern approach. The subaltern concept is now being used regularly in various disciplines such as history, literature, anthropology, sociology, etc. This is largely used in post-colonial theory. Though subaltern studies emerged in the 1980s in India, it now has a global presence as an area of academic specialisation. With reference to the Indian society, this approach documents the lives of all the marginalised, deprived and oppressed people such as the exploited peasants, workers, tribals and Dalits whose voices were rarely heard in history.

Questions and Indicative Answers

1. What do you mean by Indological approach?
- It is based on textual sources.
- It takes the textual view of Indian society.
- Most of the Indologists were products of different traditions of Indology.
- Founding fathers of Indian sociology were influenced by the work of indologists of Bhandarkar Institute of Pune.

2. Explain the structural-functionalist approach.
- Perhaps it is the most popular of all approaches in the understanding of Indian society.
- It gives more importance to empirical view rather than normative framework of culture.
- It was inspired by Radcliffe-Brown and it promotes a very systematic and rigorous fieldwork.
- Social structure is the central concept of this approach.
- M. N. Srinivas spearheaded this approach followed by others.

3. Explain subaltern approach.
- This is the youngest of all approaches.
- It is seen as post-Marxist movement.
- Its protagonists combine Marxist theory with a number of other influences.
- Subaltern school of historiography emerged in the 1980s in the study of South Asian societies.
- It was influenced by the Marxist philosopher Antonia Gramsci.
- The subaltern includes all the marginalised people in a society.
- It was prompted by the fact that the Marxists were reluctant to accept the ideology of caste and religion as crucial factors in Indian history.
- With respect to Indian society this approach documents the life of all the marginalised, depressed and oppressed people such as peasants, workers, tribals and Dalits whose voices were rarely heard in history.

Previous Years' Questions

1. Write a note on G S Ghurye's Indological Perspective of understanding Indian Society.
(UPSC CSE Mains Sociology, Paper II, 2018)
2. Critically examine GS Ghurye's Indological approach to the understanding of Indian Society.
(UPSC CSE Mains Sociology, Paper II, 2022)

Focus Areas for the Examination

1. Indological Approach
2. Structural Functionalist Approach

CHAPTER 3

Salient Features of Indian Society

Chapter Outline

1. Understanding the historical events that shaped Indian society such as the Aryan advent and the anti-colonial freedom struggle
2. Analysing the factors contributing to the diversity of Indian society, including geography, culture, and historical migrations
3. Identifying the racial and ethnic classifications of the Indian population and the related debates
4. Exploring the linguistic diversity of India
5. Examining the structure and dynamics of Indian social institutions, such as kinship, family, and marriage, and their evolution over time
6. Assessing the impact of urbanisation, industrialisation, and women's empowerment on traditional family structures
7. Contemporary challenges and legal frameworks related to marriage, divorce, and live-in relationships in Indian society

As demonstrated in the previous chapters, Indian society is the product of a long and complex historical process. T.K. Oomen (1998)[1] identifies seven major events that contributed to the formation of this process:

- The Aryan advent;
- The emergence of the Indian 'protest' religions – Jainism, Buddhism and Sikhism;
- The entry of non-Indic religions – Islam, Judaism and Christianity – into the subcontinent as 'immigrant' religions;
- The Muslim conquests;
- Western colonialism;
- The anti-colonial freedom struggle; and
- The partition of the subcontinent in 1947 on the eve of the British exit.

Any narration or analysis of salient features of Indian society is not possible without initiating it with **Diversity**. To a great extent, the continental dimensions of India account for the amazing variations and diversities. Look at the vastness of the land and varying geography and ecological conditions. As theorised by the culture ecologists, 'Culture is the human response to the local ecological conditions'. This implies that the way any human group responds or adapts to its environment defines

[1] Oomen, T K, Citizenship, Nationality, and Ethnicity: Reconciling Competing Identities, Polity Press, 1997

its culture/way of life. Thus, geography is largely responsible for the diversities in food, clothing, housing, etc. On the other hand, the vastness is also responsible, in the absence of viable means of transport and communication, for lack of intermingling of people living in far off places. India, since ancient times, has been a favourite destination of outsiders including the westerners because of abundance of natural resources and moderate and diverse climatic conditions.

Any casual observer of the Indian Society may notice diversity in the following aspects:

Racial/Ethnic Elements, Religions, Sects and Cults, Schools of Philosophy, Family Structure, Marriage Types and Rituals, Ways of Greetings, Festivals, Cuisine and food habits, Clothing, Language and Literature, Epics, Dance, Drama, Cinema and Theatre, Music, Painting, Sculpture, Architecture, etc.

Among these diversities, racial/ethnic and linguistic diversities and marriage, family, kinship and religion have been selected for special treatment along with caste, tribe, minorities and women.

SECTION A

▸▸ Racial/Ethnic Diversity

The identification and description of various racial elements in India has been a difficult task. India has always been a place of attraction for a variety of immigrants from various parts of the world. Whether it was religious persecution or harassment on other grounds or mere attraction towards India because of economic factors, waves after waves of people have been coming into the subcontinent. Most of them never went back to their original habitats. In this way, people having different racial elements have been coming and settling down in India and the process of admixture has been taking place with the local populations. This has resulted in the colourful mosaic of human affairs that the Indian society is today.

What Do You Think?

How can we move beyond celebrating diversity as merely a cultural display and instead ensure it creates equitable opportunities for all in education, employment, and leadership?

Unfortunately, we have been getting only stone tools in the name of archaeological evidence; skeletal remains have rarely been found. Because of these constraints, it is very difficult to construct a racial history/map of India. Even during historic times, the paucity of skeletal remains is the major reason for the glaring gaps in our knowledge about the racial history of India. The last one hundred years have seen some spurt in archaeological researches leading to fossil finds. But, the situation is still hazy.

Herbert Risley may be considered as the first scholar to have attempted the racial classification of India on a scientific basis. He was a civil servant who, in 1890, conducted this study based on **anthropometric techniques**. He was appointed

Quick Fact

Anthropometric techniques involve the systematic measurement (height, weight, body circumference, limb length, and skinfold thickness) and analysis of human body and its dimensions. These methods are widely used in Anthropology, Health and Nutrition, Ergonomics and Sports Science.

by the then Government of India as census Commissioner for the 1901 census. He presented his conclusions in the report of the census and in 1915 in his path-breaking work, *The Peoples of India*, he classified Indian population into seven racial types.

The second important attempt in this direction was made by Haddon. He divided India into three main geographical regions which, according to him, cover the entire racial groups present in the Indian population. These three geographical regions are:

(i) The Himalayas
(ii) The Northern plains of Hindustan
(iii) The Deccan

In this crowd of scholars **B.S. Guha** stands apart. He presented his racial classification basing it on scientific criteria. This classification is based on anthropometric surveys conducted as part of the 1931 census. It was for the first time that a study of racial types was done using the then developed anthropometric techniques. By virtue of being based on a sound scientific method, it is regarded as the most recognised and acceptable racial classification till date. It is invariably used in any study of Indian population. This classification is as follows:

(i) Negrito
(ii) Proto-Australoid
(iii) Mongoloid
- (a) Palaeo-Mongoloid
  - (1) Long headed
  - (2) Broad headed
- (b) Tibeto-Mongoloid

(iv) Mediterranean
- (a) Palaeo-Mediterranean
- (b) Mediterranean
- (c) Oriental type

(v) Western Brachycephals
- (a) Alpinoid
- (b) Dinaric
- (c) Armenoid

(vi) Nordic

Quick Fact

B S Guha's Racial Classification

1. **Negrito Features:** Short stature, dark skin, curly or woolly hair, broad nose), found in Andaman Islands and some tribal groups in South India
2. **Proto-Australoid Features:** Long head, dark skin, broad nose, and prominent supraorbital ridges, found in Central and southern India, especially among tribal populations like Gonds, Bhils, and Santhals
3. **Mongoloid Features:** Broad face, flat nose, and slanting eyes, found in Northeastern India and parts of the Himalayan region
4. **Mediterranean Features:** Long head, medium stature, fairly light skin, and straight or wavy hair, found predominantly in North and South India
5. **Western Brachycephals Features:** Broad head, robust build, and medium complexion, found in Western India, parts of Gujarat, Maharashtra, and Rajasthan
6. **Nordic Features:** Tall stature, long head, light skin, and sharp facial features, found in Northwestern India, especially among upper castes

Among the conclusions of Guha's survey, the most important is that the Brachycephals (broad-headed people) dominate the Indian population. This was not the general belief before Guha's classification. Guha's classification has received the maximum approval of scholars in this field. Since no other study or survey based on scientific line of this magnitude has been conducted, this classification continues to be the most recognised and acceptable. The two points on which Guha has been criticised most are the undue importance to Negrito elements and that the sources of all racial groups in India have been traced outside India.

On the basis of intensive study of racial elements in Indian population, three most important racial types may be described. These are Negrito, Proto-Australoid and Mongoloid. It is the general belief that the people with Mongoloid racial elements came last.

In fact, the main difference of opinion is with regard to Proto-Australoid and Negrito. Guha and before him De Quarterefages in 1877 had expressed the view that the people with Negrito racial elements are the earliest inhabitants of India. He expressed the view that a certain submerged Negrito race had come to India perhaps from Malaysia; this Negrito racial element seems to be present among the Veddas of Sri Lanka and Kadar, Irula, Kurumba, etc. of South India.

Some Proto-Australoid racial features have been noted from the skeletal remains found from Mohenjo-daro. A number of scholars have expressed the view that the Australoid and Proto-Australoid racial elements are present throughout the Indian population. If the Negrito racial element had ever dominated the Indian population, then some definite and clearly visible Negrito features should be there in the North Indian populations. Serological studies tell us that the Negrito features are almost absent even among the most primitive tribal communities of India. The primitive tribes of India have rarely demonstrated the predominance of B-blood group as is the case with Negroids. Australoid groups have a predominance of A-blood group; many primitive tribes of India have predominance of A-blood group. Another interesting and significant point in this discussion is that though the tribes like Bhil and Munda show a high frequency of B-blood group like the Negrito, they lack other physical features of the Negritos. Even otherwise no final conclusion can be drawn on the basis of only serological facts, especially under the conditions when not many serological studies have been conducted in India. There is a lot of scope for research in this direction. Based on the present status of knowledge, we can conclude only that, perhaps, the Proto-Australoids were the earliest inhabitants of India who experienced the admixture of African or Negrito blood in several parts of the subcontinent. Though not the final word, it will continue to be the most acceptable conclusion until further research.

▶▶ Linguistic Diversity

India occupies a unique place in the world for its amazing linguistic heterogeneity; that is why it has been a subject of great interest among linguists. The inhabitants of India speak many languages and dialects because this subcontinent has been, for quite some time, the destination of diverse racial groups. Any linguistic group contains within it several features of social importance. One of the important features is the sentiments of social integration between speakers of the same language or dialect. Common language also promotes **emotional integration** in the society. Diverse languages and dialects come into existence because

Quick Fact

Emotional integration refers to the process of fostering unity and harmony among diverse groups by building mutual understanding, empathy, and shared emotional connections.

of a prolonged geographical isolation of a group. In this way language plays an important role in the understanding and identification of a regional identity.

The magnitude of India's linguistic diversity may be estimated from the fact that here more than 200 languages are spoken by different groups. Half of these languages are spoken by less than 10,000 people each and the speakers of 23 languages only constitute about 97% of the total population. Amongst these 23, 15 (including English) are in the Eighth Schedule of the Constitution of independent India.

The languages spoken by Indian population may be divided into four language families:

(i) Austric family (*Nishad*)
(ii) Dravidian family (*Dravid*)
(iii) Sino-Tibetan family (*Kirat*)
(iv) Indo-European family (*Aryan*)

The languages included in these four language families demonstrate a great diversity. The speakers of Aryan languages are around 73%, of Dravidian languages about 20%, of Austric languages 1.38% and of Sino-Tibetan languages are around 0.85% only.

In the Austric language family, mainly the languages and dialects of central Indian tribal belt are included. The Santhals, Munda, Ho, Koraku, etc. belong to this language family. Speakers of the Sino-Tibetan language family are generally the tribal populations of the north-eastern region. Telugu, Tamil, Kannada, Malayalam, Gondi, etc. are prominent Dravidian languages. Speakers from the Indo-Aryan language family constitute the majority. In this category are included, on the one hand, languages like Punjabi and Sindhi and, on the other, languages such as Marathi, Konkani, Rajasthani, Gujarati, Marwari, Mewati, Hindi-Urdu, Chhatisgarhi, Bengali, Maithili, Kumayuni, Garhwali, etc.

In the presence of such an amazing variety of languages and dialects, one may conclude that such a great linguistic heterogeneity may prove to be disruptive for national integration. Such an apprehension may largely be deceptive. Side by side with this linguistic diversity, one may also witness the pleasant development of an all-India common vocabulary. Sanskrit, Persian and English languages have been the state or administrative languages at one time or the other. Sanskrit has not only acted as a bridge between different Indo-Aryan languages, but has also served as a communication link between Indo-Aryan and Dravidian languages. During the medieval period of Indian history, Persian influenced a number of Indian languages like Marathi, Kannada, Telugu, Tamil and Bengali. The role of English language has been especially significant during the modern times. During the last few decades Hindi-Urdu has contributed significantly to the linguistic unity of India, perhaps that is why Mahatma Gandhi promoted the idea of *Hindustani* language that contains words from different languages with the predominance of Hindi-Urdu. In this context, we should not forget the role of movies in Hindi-Urdu (*Hindustani*) language. The mainstream cinema of Bombay may not deserve laurels because of generally poor quality, but its immense contribution to the linguistic integration and the development of an all-India vocabulary cannot be minimised. The amazing popularity of Hindi-Urdu movies in all the corners of the country bears testimony to the fact that the dialogues and the songs are being understood at least minimally and people are enjoying them. The growing influence of the neighbouring communities on the primitive tribes, who have been leading a life of relative geographical isolation till some time ago, reveal that the journey of linguistic unity in the country continues at an increasing pace. Now most of the tribal communities are bilingual and even trilingual – speaking their mother tongue, official language of the state and Hindi/English being taught in schools.

SECTION B

Among the social institutions of Indian society, marriage, family, kinship, religion and caste occupy the most important place. Even in this aspect lot of diversity may be seen.

▸▸ Kinship, Family, Marriage and Divorce

The social structure of the Indian society is based on caste without which it cannot be understood. With the proclamation of equality by our constitution, caste inequalities have received a severe blow, but in the day-to-day life of the people it continues to occupy an important place in peoples' consciousness and the overwhelming majority continues to live in the universe of caste system in a variety of ways. As social institutions, kinship, family and marriage along with religion are integral to Indian social structure. Through kinship, the individuals as members of the society relate with one another. The family as a unit is given much importance in Indian society. Marriage is considered largely as a social obligation and carries lot of sanctity. Indian society is strongly patriarchal with the exception of a couple of small communities which continue to be matrilineal-matriarchal. All these social institutions are undergoing change and as M. N. Srinivas (1992) rightly comments, 'we are living in a revolution'. The following narration and analysis try to explain not only the concepts, but also gives a brief account and trends of change in all these social institutions.

▸▸ Kinship and Family

Kinship is a system by which individuals as members of society relate themselves with one another. Members of every society create a network of relations through which one leads one's life. On the basis of type, kin may be of two types:

1. Consanguineous kin
2. Affinal kin

Both these types of kinship bonds are very important. Consanguineal kin are related by blood ties while affinal kin come into existence as a result of marital bonds. Thus, the kinship bonds between the parents and the children and beyond that with all the blood-related kin, whether primary, secondary or tertiary, come under consanguineal kin. The kin who come into existence as a result of the establishment of marital alliance such as husband–wife and their kin are the affinal kin. Kinship system is not the same throughout India, for instance the kinship system in North and Central India. Even this region is characterised by variations. But, by and large, in this region people marry outside the village as they consider members of the caste living in the same village as brothers and sisters. It is also a strongly patriarchal system. But, in terms of the range of kinship (inclusion/exclusion of different degrees of kin – primary or direct, secondary or the primary of the primary kin and tertiary or secondary of one's primary kin) local and regional variations may be observed. Among the majority of Hindus of different regions, the range of kinship along with the kinship expectations is very broad while most of the Muslim communities in India exhibit narrow kinship range. This may be seen when the list of invitees/participants is drawn and gifts given along kinship expectations. Because of urbanisation and industrialisation and the growing trends of individualism, the kinship range even among Hindus is shrinking.

Family may be understood as a group of individuals living together during different phases of lifetime and bound with each other by biological, social and psychological relationship. Procreation also takes place within this unit and thus it is the most important social institution for bearing and rearing and socialisation of children. In the Indian society family bonds are very strong and the family serves as the valuable support system socially, economically and psychologically. The organisation of family also exhibits variations. In the northern region it is patriarchal, patrilineal and patrilocal, which means that the authority in the family rests with the male, lineage is traced through the male and the bride resides with the husband and his family. In some regions such as north-eastern parts, the Khasi and the Garo have been following matriliny while in the south the **matrilineal family** system may, to an extent, still be observed such as among the Nayars of Kerala whose matrilineal household is popularly called a *Tharavad*.

Quick Fact

Matrilineal Family

A family system where lineage and inheritance are traced through the mother.

Patrilineal Family

A family system where lineage and inheritance are traced through the father.

Joint family system, popularly called Hindu joint family, has not only been the hallmark of the large Hindu populations, but has also been popular among Muslims, Sikhs and others in a slightly different form and for that matter with a large number of agrarian communities though not enjoying the same amount of sanctity as a tradition. In this type of family structure members belonging to three or more generations live together. The characteristic features of the joint family are:

1. Generational depth
2. Common residence
3. Common hearth or kitchen
4. Common or jointly shared property
5. Authority of the *karta* or the eldest male member of the family

Evolved in a non-mechanised agrarian set-up requiring a common pool of labour and other resources, it continued for several centuries. However, with the passage of time, factors of change emerged with the changing situations and joint family was left with no other option, but to disintegrate or make adaptation with the changes and survive. Several studies show that the traditional joint family has almost disintegrated, at least structurally, in the urban areas and crumbling in the villages too. The following are the main factors of change:

1. Spread of modern education and emergence of multiple new occupations providing new options to the people;
2. Fast pace of urbanisation and large-scale migration of people from villages to towns and cities;
3. Small and limited housing in urban areas;

4. Increased individualism and individual rights;
5. Growing assertiveness of educated women for their rights, not submitting meekly to all the dictates of the head of the family; thus, the educational, economic and political empowerment of women contributed to the erosion of patriarchal power; and
6. Role of the state in coming out with legislative measures and amenities facilitating the empowerment and self-sufficiency of women. Thus, state-sponsored schemes also played an important role in changing the power structure within the joint family as well as the nuclear family.

Because of the above-mentioned and other factors of change, the winds of change started blowing and the omnipotent joint family could not be the same again. Women's education and the resultant empowerment was greatly supported by state agencies and such facilities as hostel for working women, crèches for kids of working women and maternity leave with full salary and other benefits went a long way in empowering women, no more living as dumb cattle. When she started asserting her rights, the omnipotent patriarchal joint family was shaken, though patriarchy as a value remained strong. Most of these changes picked up after independence. These familial changes resulted in the redistribution of power, a new division of labour and increased democratisation within the family. The institution of joint family had realised that if it had to survive, it must be democratic in its functioning. Though nuclear families (consisting of couple and the unmarried children) are fast becoming the norm in towns and cities, a sense of belonging and mutuality of obligations, which is the basis of the 'jointness of the joint family', is still surviving to a great extent even with the structural disintegration of the joint family. Further, the number of female-headed nuclear families is rising fast mainly because of failed marriages. Thus, the power structure in the family is undergoing changes because of changes in power distribution, marital norms and role of women.

▶▶ Marriage, Divorce and 'Live-in Relationship'

The institution and idea of marriage is universally present in all human societies in one form or the other. Marriage may be described as the socially sanctioned union between a male/males and a female/females. In Indian society too there is a wide variety and types of marriage. Moreover, wedding traditions vary across religion, region, caste, ethnicity, etc.

Though monogamy (marriage between one male and one female) is followed by the overwhelming population, other types are also prevalent in small numbers such as polygyny (one husband and two or more wives), polyandry (one wife and two or more husbands), bigamy (one husband and two wives), etc. Moreover, among several tribal communities, multiple ways of acquiring mates through various modus operandi are followed such as marriage by probation, marriage by ceremonial capture, marriage by elopement and several others. Moreover, the status of premarital and extramarital sex relations also varies from group to group and so is the ways of dissolution of marriage. Caste endogamy (marriage within the same caste group) is still a strong norm among Hindus, Muslims and Sikhs, though in cities inter-caste marriages have begun, but in most of the cases these are arranged by the couple with or without the consent of the parents. Child marriages still occur in small numbers.

Kinship groups in Indian society demand a strong social loyalty and hence marriage, to a large number of people, is an affair deeply impacting the entire family and kin. Thus, traditionally speaking, marriage is not merely an alliance between two individuals, but between two families. In the so-called arranged marriage, criteria of caste, horoscope, physical appearance and family background are very important. But, the criterion of dowry is equally and now for many most important. With the rise of growing materialism, consumerism and consumer culture, the craving and amount of dowry has been rising phenomenally. Arranged marriages were being settled through matchmakers such as a Pundit, the family-attached barber or other middlemen. Biodata and pictures are exchanged and after the scrutiny of various criteria and negotiation for dowry, the marriage is fixed. Notwithstanding the legal ban on seeking dowry, it continues and there is only a small minority of people who forego or refuse to accept any dowry in either cash or kind. The evil of dowry among Muslims was confined to the lower castes/classes only, but now it has engulfed almost the entire population. Among the educated classes, previously there was also a practice of giving matrimonial ads in newspapers and magazines of particular caste associations, but with the advent of the Internet, during the last two decades or so, several matrimonial websites have emerged and millions of marriages are being fixed through it. This is equally popular in all castes and communities.

With the increasing education, social mobility, freedom and the resultant empowerment of women, the number of inter-caste marriages has increased manifold. These are self-arranged, popularly called as 'love marriages', but such marriages are mostly confined to cities and towns. In many instances, these are solemnised in an Arya Samaj temple in a simple and austere ceremony. Despite the promulgation of the Special Marriage Act, 1955, facilitating interfaith/inter religious marriages, the society at large is still very hostile and prejudiced to such alliances. In villages and towns, in most of the cases, it may create even a law and order problem, but in cities, especially in metros, it does not attract much attention. As several couples entering into wedlock under this provision narrate, the state is secular, but the persons who have been assigned the responsibility of implementing it create unnecessary hurdles. The marriage is supervised and registered by a designated Special Marriage Officer, usually a magistrate, in each district. Under special circumstances, he or she is authorised to perform the formalities even outside the premises of his or her office.

▶▶ Live-in Relationship

The traditional system of marriage faced the first big challenge from inter-faith marriages, but now has to reconcile even with the 'live-in relationship', which may or may not result in a formal, legalised marriage. Live-in relationship may be described as an arrangement of living under which the couples who are unmarried live together to conduct a long-lasting relationship similar to that in marriage; such couples cohabit rather than marry for a variety of reasons. In many cases, it is just to assess mutual compatibility; in gay/lesbian relationships, for financial reasons and so on. Some of them claim that such cohabitation was permissible even during Vedic times. For that many of our tribal communities have been liberal enough to allow it in the form of '**marriage by probation**'. Though the Indian society too is opening up in some ways, for the overwhelming majority, this is socially unacceptable even in metros where it just 'tolerates' it, but does not accept it by heart.

Quick Fact

Marriage by probation is a system or practice where a couple agrees to live together as husband and wife for a trial period before formalising their union through a permanent marriage. While formal 'marriage by probation' is not a widely recognized practice, its principles are reflected in modern concepts like cohabitation or live-in relationships.

Economic boom in big cities coupled with women's empowerment has facilitated the 'acceptability' of certain practices. Urban anonymity in metros gives courage to a number of aspiring couples to adopt a live-in relationship and get away with it. In smaller cities, especially in towns and villages, one cannot live in anonymity and may get punished or socially ostracised because of such relationships. In metros such as Delhi and its neighbouring suburbs like Noida, Ghaziabad and Gurgaon, in Bengaluru and Mumbai people do enjoy much more freedom to indulge in practices the traditional-orthodox society term as 'deviant' and 'corrupt'. Better standard of living and avenues offered by the big cities have lured young men and women from all over India to settle in these areas whose substantial population consists of 'migrants' who may not be concerned and interested in the affairs of others.

In May 2013, in a landmark judgement, the Supreme Court observed that if a man and a woman in love decide to live as a couple, it will be within their 'right to life' and by no means can be deemed as a criminal offence. It provided the much-needed legal protection to such couples. Obviously it has not gone down well with the traditional and conservative people. It is a part of right to life to go away with someone you love, the bench remarked.

In the light of the Supreme Court's verdict, the government willingly or unwillingly has been taking various measures for the past few years to protect the interests of live-in partners. In one such move, the government extended economic rights to women in live in relation under the Protection of Women from Domestic Violence Act, 2005. Similarly, the Maharashtra state government in 2008 granted a proposal suggesting a woman involved in cohabitation for a 'reasonable period' should be given the status of a wife.

In the same year, the Ministry of Women and Child Development was urged by the National Commission of Women to include female live-in partners in the definition of wife as described in Section 125 of the Code of Criminal Procedure (Cr PC). The objective of this recommendation was to harmonise various other sections of law with the Protection of Women from Domestic Violence Act, 2005. Justice Malimath Committee[2] of the Supreme Court recommended that this be turned into a law by all states. The committee had observed that "if man and woman are living together as husband and wife for a reasonable long period, the man shall be deemed to have married the woman." The Malimath Committee also recommended that the word 'wife' under Cr PC be amended to include any "woman living with a man like his wife". All the judicial verdicts apart, the fact remains that the larger society is just not prepared to accept it, but in the future it has to accept it as part of an individual's right which has to be respected.

▶▶ Divorce

In Indian society, marriage carries a lot of religious-social sanctity and hence there has always been a great impact of religion and culture on the practice of divorce. Marriage is a religious sacrament among Hindus and a civil contract among Muslims. Since marriage carries religious sanctity among Hindus 'solemnised with *Agni* as witness and blessings of gods and goddesses', its dissolution was never considered desirable and it continued like this for centuries. Dharma forces one to remain married even if it does not work. Moreover, being divorced carried a strong stigma and one had to bear the cross of unhappy marriage to protect their image as an 'ideal Indian family'. It was only with the promulgation

[2] Justice Malimath Committee Report, Govt. of India, Ministry of Home Affairs, Parliament Digital Library, New Delhi

of the Hindu Marriage Act, 1955 that dissolution of marriage became permissible under the law, but it is still considered undesirable socially. However, community disapproval is stronger for divorced women than it is for divorced men. That is why remarriage for men is much easier than women. That is not the case with the Dalit (both Hindu and Muslim) communities and tribal communities who take divorce normally because women in these sections of the society enjoy much more cultural autonomy and unlike the higher castes the strongly patriarchal value of *Pati Parmeshwar* (husband the highest god) and gender discrimination are not that much strong and women do not have to face sexual harassment and character assassination the way they face among the higher castes.

All major religious communities in India have their laws governing divorce. Hindus, Sikhs, Jains and Buddhists are governed by the Hindu Marriage Act, 1955; Christians by the Indian Divorce Act, 1869; Parsis by the Parsi Marriage and Divorce Act, 1936; and Muslims by the Dissolution of Muslim Marriage Act, 1939. Unlike western societies, there are only few grounds for seeking divorce, the most important of which are adultery, desertion, cruelty, impotence, mental derangement, conversion to another religion and chronic diseases. It was only in recent times that through an amendment in the Hindu Marriage Act that non-compatibility in temperament was also allowed as a valid ground for divorce. Among Hindus, divorce is a difficult process while among a large section of Muslims it is relatively much easier. However, among Shia Muslims, the instant *Triple Talaaq* (pronouncing three times in one go by the husband) is not permissible. It is to be pronounced in three sittings with a substantial time interval, in the presence of witnesses, to give to the couple sufficient time to reflect and introspect and make the possible reconciliation. Among Muslims it is much more difficult for a woman to seek divorce, though it is permissible. The obnoxious practice of *triple talaaq* has already ruined the life of millions of Muslim women and the progressive sections of Muslims have been demanding a total ban on this practice the way some Muslim countries have already done. However, it has another aspect. The cases of bride burning/killing and dowry-related atrocities are much less among Muslims as they can divorce the wife much more easily and go for another marriage unlike among Hindus where it is not easy to get divorce and hence, the aggrieved and greedy husband finds it easier to eliminate the wife and go for another marriage. Thus, the plight of women is almost the same. However, the Supreme Court of India in response to a petition by a Muslim divorcee woman has declared the practice of instant divorce invalid and a criminal offence. Following the verdict, the Parliament enacted Muslim Women (Protection of Rights on Marriage) Act, 2019.

Questions and Indicative Answers

1. What are the major events that contributed to the formation of the historical process of Indian society?

- Aryan advent, emergence of the Indian protest religions – Jainism, Buddhism and Sikhism, entry of non-Indic religions – Islam, Christianity and Judaism;
- Muslim conquests, Western colonialism;
- Anti-colonial freedom struggle; and
- Partition of subcontinent in 1947.

2. Give factors or reasons for the diversity of Indian society.
- Vastness of land and varying geographical and ecological conditions;
- These gave rise to diversities in food, housing, dress patterns, customs, traditions, etc.; and
- Absence of viable means of transport and communication was responsible for the lack of intermingling of people living in far-off places.

3. Give a critical description of racial/ethnic elements in the Indian population.
- Mention Risley's and Haddon's classification;
- Reject these for their shortcomings;
- Describe Guha's classification as the most acceptable; and
- Mention difference of opinion on Negrito element in Indian population.

4. Give a brief description of linguistic diversity of the Indian population.
- Give reasons for the emergence of different languages and dialects.
- Describe the four language families and their distribution.
- Comment on the status of English.
- Emergence of an all-India vocabulary through Hindi-Urdu/Hindustani cinema.

5. Mention different types of families and describe joint family and its decline.
- Give a brief description of nuclear family, matrilineal family, polyandrous family, etc.
- Define and describe the joint family.
- Discuss the factors responsible for the decline of the joint family such as urbanisation, industrialisation, rise of individualism and individual rights, growing assertiveness of educated women and role of the state.

Previous Years' Questions

1. Write on the following in about 150 words:
   Linguistic clements in Indian population. **(UPSC CSE MainsAnthropology, Paper II, 2016)**
2. Give a critical assessment of Negrito problem in India. **(UPSC CSE Mains Anthropology, Paper II, 2016)**
3. Discuss the contemporary trends in family as a response to social change in modern society. **(UPSC CSE Mains Sociology, Paper I, 2016)**
4. What makes Indian society unique in sustaining its culture? Discuss. **(GS Mains Paper I, 2019)**
5. Do you think marriage as a sacrament is loosing its value in modern India? **(GS Mains Paper I, 2023)**

Focus Areas for the Examination

1. Live-in Relationships and its impact

CHAPTER 4

Population of India and Indian Population Policy

Chapter Outline

1. Analysing demographic data to understand trends in India's population growth over the decades
2. Identifying factors influencing population distribution
3. Exploring causes for the imbalanced sex ratio in India and its socio-cultural implications
4. Identifying the distribution, literacy, and economic conditions of Scheduled Castes and Tribes in India
5. Examining the multi-religious fabric of India and its impact on demographic and literacy patterns
6. Assessing India's Population Policies to understand the objectives and measures outlined in the National Population Policy (NPP) 2000

Although India was one of the first countries in the world to have an explicit population policy, the Indian performance so far is more of a failure than a success. India accounted for approximately 22% of the estimated population of developing countries. At present it has nearly 17% of the total world population, while it accounts for only 2.5% of the world's surface area. In any demographic miscellany, growth of population occupies the most important place. The following table gives us a clear idea of growth in India's population over the years.

Census Year	Population (in Crore)	Average Annual Exponential Growth Rate (in %)
1901	23.83	0.30
1911	25.20	0.56
1921	25.12	0.03
1931	27.89	1.04
1941	31.85	1.33
1951	36.10	1.25
1961	43.91	1.96
1971	54.82	2.20
1981	68.52	2.22

Census Year	Population (in Crore)	Average Annual Exponential Growth Rate (in %)
1991	84.63	2.16
2001	102.87	1.97
2011	121.01	1.64

The first formal census enumeration was taken up in 1881 and since then the decennial census enumeration exercise has been a regular feature involving a high degree of expertise and substantial manpower. The offices of the census Commissioner and the Registrar General of India have been responsible for providing the demographic profile of the country. As per the 1991 census, the total population of India was about 85 crores, an increase of about 24% over the 1981 census. It rose to around 122 crores in 2011. According to demographers, the major cause for increase in population is the rapid fall in death rate. According to the 1981 census, birth rate in the country was 33.3 per thousand and death rate 12.5 per thousand population while the figure for the same duration in the next decade is 30.0 and 10.0 per thousand population. In 2011, the birth rate and the death rate were 19 and 7, respectively, while the life expectancy rose to 68.8 years. Thus, the birth rate as well as the death rate have registered a fall, though marginally. But, this marginal improvement is not enough because of the gigantic level of population India has achieved over the years. The following table gives us the idea of birth and death rates and helps us to understand the population problem of the country.

Year	Birth Rate per 1000 Persons	Death Rate per 1000 Persons
1901	—	—
1911	49.2	42.6
1921	48.1	47.6
1931	46.4	36.3
1941	45.2	31.2
1951	39.9	27.4
1961	40.9	22.8
1971	41.1	18.9
1981	33.3	12.5
1991	30.0	10.0
2001	25.4	08.4
2011	19.0	07.0

When we take up the density of population in India, we come across significant findings. Density of population means the number of people living per sq. km. Density of population of the present area (adjusted for partition of India in 1947) increased from 7 persons per sq. km. in 1901 to 267 persons per sq. km. in 1991. Thus, it shows an increase of almost 3.5 times. The following table gives the density of population in India in different census years.

Census Year	Density of Population per sq. km.
1901	77
1911	82
1921	81
1931	90
1941	103
1951	117
1961	142
1971	177
1981	216
1991	267
2001	325
2011	382

The table shows that the rate of increase was faster in the later decades. However, it varies from state to state depending on several factors:

1. The lowest density was found in Arunachal Pradesh, where only 10 persons inhabit per sq. km. Other low-density states are Mizoram, Andaman and Nicobar Islands, Sikkim, The Union Territory of Jammu and Kashmir, Meghalaya, Nagaland, Manipur and Himachal Pradesh. All the eastern states except Assam and Tripura have low density and so do the hilly states like Himachal Pradesh and Jammu & Kashmir.
2. National Capital Territory (NCT) of Delhi, Chandigarh and Puducherry have the highest density.
3. States which have population density of three times the national average are Daman and Diu; states which have two times or more are Kerala and West Bengal.
4. States which have population density above the national average are Assam, Bihar, Goa, Haryana, Punjab, Tamil Nadu, Uttar Pradesh and Dadra and Nagar Haveli & Daman and Diu.
5. States which have population density lower than the national average are Andhra Pradesh, Gujarat, Karnataka, Maharashtra and Tripura.

The sex ratio in India has always been a topic of discussion and debate. The sex ratio has increasingly been favourable to males over the years, rising from 1029 in 1901 to 1076 in 1991. It means that there was a shortage of 30 females per thousand males in 1901 which has now increased to 71 females per 1000 males as per the 1991 census. It was 933 in the 2001 census while it showed some improvement in the 2011 census when it was reported as 943 females per 1000 males. Various causes could be attributed to this phenomenon. Higher mortality rates at infancy and later, relatively more neglect, higher mortality rates among women in the childbearing age, female infanticide and foeticide may be some of the reasons for this increasing disparity. Sometimes female births are also not reported by the parents. As per the 2011 census, Kerala has the best sex ratio where there are 1084 females per 1000 males followed by Puducherry 1037, Tamil Nadu 996, Andhra Pradesh 993 and Chhattisgarh 991. The worst sex ratio is reported from Haryana and Rajasthan because of high rates of female foeticide and infanticide resulting in 'import' of brides from poverty-stricken areas of Jharkhand, Odisha, Assam, Bengal, etc.

The least explained fact in the issues involved with unequal sex ratio is related to this growing imbalance in the face of decreasing discrimination against females and decreasing rates of infant mortality. One probable reason is that many couples having a few sons do not want to have one or two daughters as well; they may opt for sterilisation. Kerala is the only state where the sex ratio is higher for females. This may be due to over-migration of males from the state in search of jobs.

Another feature of population is literacy rate. Based on the definition of literacy being the ability to 'read and write a post card', 52.11% is the percentage of literacy in India according to the 1991 census. The rate of literacy among males is 63.86% and for females, it is 39.42% – a conspicuous gap. It has risen to 74.04% (2011 census) – 82.14% for males and 65.46% for females. Kerala with 94% literacy enjoys the first position followed by Lakshadweep (91%), while Bihar has the lowest (61%) literacy rate. This is one of the factors accounting for economic backwardness of the country. Notwithstanding the fact that literacy rate has gone up in the post-independence period, the number of illiterates has also gone up in absolute terms. Kerala became the first state of the country where almost 100% literacy was achieved. However, schools were not the only means for education and literacy for everyone. Generally, Hindi-speaking states are very unprogressive in terms of achieving literacy and female literacy. Madhya Pradesh, Chhattisgarh, Uttar Pradesh, Bihar, Jharkhand and Rajasthan had very low female literacy rates. Better care must be taken to improve the quality and condition of children's literacy and education. Studies have shown that even free education is of little help as long as children continue to contribute towards family economy. The phenomenon of child labour has to be overcome. Apparently, poverty of the parents is the root cause of the lack of education and the high rate of dropout of children. Significantly, wherever Christianity has been used as an agency of welfare, the rate of literacy shows an upward trend. This is apparent in states like Mizoram, Meghalaya, Nagaland and parts of Bihar.

SCHEDULED CASTES AND SCHEDULED TRIBES

The **Scheduled Caste** population constitutes around 18% of the total population of India. This population is divided into around 1000 castes distributed all over India.

Scheduled Tribes constitute about 9% of the total population of the country (84.32 million). They are among the weakest sections of the society. They speak different languages and dialects and inhabit virtually all the geo-climatic regions of the country. About 55% of the scheduled tribe population is concentrated in the eastern and central tribal belt including West Bengal, Bihar-Jharkhand, Madhya Pradesh-Chhattisgarh, Odisha and parts of Andhra Pradesh; about 28% are in the Western tribal belt consisting of Gujarat, Maharashtra, Rajasthan, Goa, Dadra and Nagar Haveli & Daman and Diu; only about 6% of the scheduled tribe population are found in the south consisting of parts of Andhra Pradesh, Karnataka, Kerala and Tamil Nadu; about 10% are in the north-east, 0.83% are in Himachal Pradesh and 0.10% are in Lakshadweep and Andaman & Nicobar Islands. There are four states, Meghalaya (80.58%), Nagaland (83.99%), Arunachal Pradesh (69.82%) and Mizoram (93.55%) and two Union Territories, namely Dadra and Nagar Haveli & Daman and Diu (78.82%)

and Lakshadweep (93.82%), where 70% or more of the population belong to the Scheduled Tribes category. There are also five states where more than 20% of the population are tribal. These are Madhya Pradesh (22.97%), Manipur (27.30%), Odisha (22.43%), Sikkim (23.22%) and Tripura (28.44%).

Among the major tribes, the population of Bhils is about 6 million followed by the Gonds (about 5 million), the Santhals (about 4 million) and the Oraon (about 2 million). Among the minor tribes, the Great Andamanese have been reduced to just 32 souls because of severe depopulation. The Sentinelese, the Jarwa and the Onge of Andaman & Nicobar Islands are within 200 numbers in terms of population. It is estimated that the tribal areas comprise about 17% of the total geographical area of the country, but these areas contain about 70% of the forest and mineral wealth of the country. A number of tribes are polyandrous such as the Toda of Nilgiri Hills and Khasa or Jaunsari of Jaunsar Bawar (UP) while some tribes like the Khasi of Meghalaya are matrilineal. There are about 70 tribes who are still food-gatherers/hunters and are concentrated mainly in Andhra Pradesh, Tamil Nadu and Kerala. The tribes practicing shifting cultivation mainly inhabit the North-Eastern region while about 70% of the tribal population depends on settled/plough cultivation. A few tribes still earn their livelihood as artisans. The percentage of literacy among the Scheduled Tribes is around 59%. However, interstate variations are quite considerable ranging from 8% in Andhra Pradesh to about 60% in Mizoram.

RELIGIOUS COMPOSITION

India has always been a multireligious and multiethnic society. Followers of almost all the major religions of the world inhabit this great land. They are Hindus, Muslims, Christians, Sikhs, Buddhists, Jains, Zoroastrians *(Parsees)* and Jews. The Hindus are the majority community comprising about 80% of the total population of the country followed by Muslims (about 14%), Christians (about 3%), Sikhs (about 2%), Buddhists (about 1%) and Jains (about 0.5%). The Parsees and Jews are microscopic minorities. Among the major religious communities, Hindus, Muslims and Christians inhabit virtually all the geo-climatic regions of the country and speak local languages and dialects.

In terms of ratio, Muslims are in majority in Lakshadweep and Jammu & Kashmir, whereas Christians are in majority in Nagaland and Meghalaya, Sikhs are in majority in Punjab and Buddhists in Arunachal Pradesh.

It has been reported that the religious minorities show a greater percentage of literacy and education than the majority community. Parsees, Jains, Jews and Christians have shown this pattern. Among Muslims, the Shias, an important minority within a minority, may be cited as a case in point. They show a very high rate of literacy, comparable only with the Parsees and Christians. The most plausible explanation of this phenomenon is that in a multireligious democratic society every intelligent minority knows that it cannot influence the society or enjoy leverage through its sheer number. That is why it goes for excellence to have its due place in the society and through their contributions they tend to command influence and respect.

What Do You Think?

How does India's religious diversity shape its national identity, and what challenges and opportunities does it present for fostering social harmony?

POPULATION POLICY

India was the first country to launch a national programme of family planning in 1952. It emphasised the necessity of reducing birth rates to stabilise the population. The National Health Policy, 1983 stated the replacement levels of Total Fertility Rate (TFR) should be achieved by the year 2000. A stable population is an essential requirement for promoting sustainable development with more equitable distribution. In pursuance of this goal, the National Population Policy 2000 (NPP 2000) was launched. It affirmed the commitment of the government towards voluntary and informed choice and consent of citizens while availing reproductive healthcare services. The immediate objective of NPP 2000 is to address the unmet needs for contraception, healthcare infrastructure and health personnel and to provide integrated service delivery for basic reproductive and child healthcare.

In pursuance of this objective, the following national socio-demographic goals were to be achieved by 2010:

- Address the unmet needs for basic reproductive and child health services, supplies and infrastructure;
- Make school education free and compulsory up to age 14 and reduce dropouts at the primary and secondary levels below 20% both for boys and girls;
- Reduce infant mortality rate below 30 per 1000 births;
- Reduce maternal mortality ratio to below 100 per 10,000 live births;
- Achieve universal immunisation of children against all vaccine-preventable diseases;
- Promote delayed marriage for girls, not earlier than age 18 and preferably after 20 years of age;
- Achieve 80% institutional deliveries and 100% deliveries by trained persons;
- Achieve universal access to information/counselling and services for fertility regulation and contraception with a wide basket of choices;
- Achieve 100% registration of births, deaths, marriage and pregnancy;
- Contain the spread of AIDS and promote greater integration between the management of reproductive tract infection and sexually transmitted infections and the National AIDS Control Organisation;
- Prevent and control communicable diseases;
- Integrate Indian system of medicine in the provision of reproductive and child health services and in reaching out to households;
- Promote vigorously the small family norm to achieve replacement levels of TFR; and
- Bring about convergence in implementation of related social sector programmes so that family welfare becomes a people-centred programme.

If the NPP 2000 is fully implemented, we anticipate a population of 1107 million (110 crore) in 2010, instead of 1162 million (116 crore) projected by the Technical Group on Population Projection.

FACTORS INFLUENCING THE STRUCTURE AND GROWTH OF INDIAN POPULATION

- *High fertility due to unmet need for contraception*: Urgent steps are required to make contraception more widely available and affordable. The accessibility of contraceptives is still relatively more difficult in remote rural and tribal areas.
- *High infant mortality rate*: Because of high infant mortality rate in rural areas of the Hindi belt, people are not sure about the survival of their infants and hence opt for more children.
- *Early marriage of girls*: Over 50% of girls marry below the age of 18 leading to 'too early, too frequently, too many children'. A high percentage of births occur at intervals of less than 24 months, which also results in high infant mortality rate.
- *Widespread son preference*: Across all religious communities, there is a widespread preference for a son because of social, economic and religious factors. With increased empowerment of women – educational, social, economic and political – this may be curbed to a great extent. The social evil of dowry is also a contributing factor behind this preference.
- *Poverty and educational backwardness*: It is now universally accepted that in conditions of poverty and deprivation, children are considered an asset and not liability because from a younger age they start contributing to the family economy. Wherever children contribute to the family economy, they may not be sent to schools or it may result in a higher rate of dropout. Moreover, it has been proved that a higher rate of female literacy and education lead to better management of small family norm.
- *Religious beliefs and traditions*: India is a strongly religious and traditional society. Among large sections of people across religious lines, it is believed that children are a gift of God and their birth should not be curbed. But, the same society also resorts to female foeticide and infanticide. The same people are comfortable with this contradiction and hypocrisy.

What Do You Think?

How do socio-economic factors like education, healthcare access, and cultural practices influence the population growth and age structure of India, and what implications does this have for the country's future development?

Questions and Indicative Answers

1. What are the possible reasons for the disturbed sex ratio in India?

- The population of females has been declining especially since the 1971 census.
- The growing materialism, consumerism and consumer culture have contributed for the increasing demand for dowry.
- Many parents, especially coming from middle class, look at the birth of daughter as a liability.

- There is insecurity of women coupled with eve-teasing, sexual assault and acid attacks on young women.
- Haryana, Punjab, Rajasthan, Bihar and some other states now feel the shortage of brides for eligible bachelors.
- Girls from poorer regions of India are now being bought and sold and taken to the villages of grooms.
- It is reported that many of these brides serve as domestic and sex slaves.

2. What are the immediate objectives of the national population policy?

- India was the first country to launch a national programme of family planning in 1952.
- By 2000, national population policy focussed on certain objectives and goals to be achieved as soon as possible.
- Make school education free and compulsory up to age 14 and reduce dropouts.
- Reduce infant mortality rate below 30/1000.
- It is seen that a high infant mortality rate brings insecurity among parents and they go for more children.
- Reduce maternal mortality rate drastically.
- Achieve universal immunisation of children.
- Achieve 100% registration of births, deaths and marriages.
- Family welfare should become a people-centred plan.

3. Explain the main factors influencing growth of the Indian population.

- High infant mortality rate;
- Early marriage of girls;
- Son preference across castes and communities;
- Poverty and educational backwardness, especially of women; and
- Religious beliefs across castes and communities that children are gifts of god and He is responsible for the sustenance of children.

Previous Years' Questions

1. What are the various factors influencing population growth in India?

(UPSC CSE Mains Anthropology, Paper II, 2018)

2. What were the salient features of India's population policy? How far its goals have been achieved?

(UPSC CSE Mains Sociology, Paper II, 2020)

Focus Areas for the Examination

1. Factors Influencing the structure and growth of India's population

CHAPTER 5

Caste and Caste System

Chapter Outline

1. Understanding Social Stratification, particularly focusing on caste, estate, and class
2. Analysing how caste operates as a form of social hierarchy, its origins, and its evolution in Indian society
3. Exploring Sociological Perspectives – perspectives of G.S. Ghurye, M.N. Srinivas, Louis Dumont, and Andre Beteille
4. Functions of Caste System
5. Role of Ritual Purity: Examine the binary opposition of pure/impure within caste hierarchies as a basis for social order and discrimination
6. Recognising the socio-political implications of untouchability
7. Understanding how caste-like structures have influenced non-Hindu communities in South Asia
8. Exploring the intersection of caste and politics
9. Studying social and occupational mobility within the caste system
10. Investigating the factors contributing to changes in the caste system – urbanisation, industrialisation, and state interventions

Social stratification as a field of study and research occupies an important place in disciplines such as sociology, anthropology, political science, economics and psychology. Further, the most appealing of all utopias is (total) equality and hence study of **social stratification** has been and still is one of the most fascinating fields of study in different social sciences.

Quick Fact

Social Stratification

The division of society into hierarchical layers based on various factors such as wealth, power, and social status.

The term 'stratification' has been borrowed from Geology and it refers to the layers/strata of earth being vertically arranged. But, this geological metaphor has its own limitation. As rightly pointed out by Andre Beteille (1987)[1], "the arrangement of persons in a society is enormously more complex than the arrangement of layers of the earth; and social strata are not visible to the naked eyes in the way that geological strata are." When we talk of social stratification, we draw attention to the unequal positions occupied by individuals in the society. Broadly speaking, social stratification refers to the division of society into a number of strata, hierarchically arranged groupings. These groupings have assumed numerously

[1] Beteile, Andre, The Idea of Natural Inequality and Other Essays, Oxford University Press, New Delhi, 1987

historical and cultural variations, of which castes, estates and classes are the most familiar. From the 1960s onwards, attention also turned to ethnic and gender stratification.

Though there is no unanimity on this issue, the dominant opinion among sociologists and social anthropologists definitely believes in the universality of social stratification yet the bases of inequalities vary from time to time and society to society. David Jary and Julia Jary in their Dictionary of Sociology (1991)[2] write that "since there are very many bases on which human inequalities may be understood and upon which exploitation and oppression may be produced and reproduced, it is important to recognise that these variables are not mutually exclusive." In simpler terms, social differences become social stratification when people are ranked hierarchically along some dimension of inequality, whether this be income, wealth, power, prestige, age, ethnicity or some other characteristics.

Explaining the mechanism and dynamics of social stratification, Andre Beteille (ibid) tells us that everywhere power plays an important part in the maintenance and reproduction of social stratification. First, there is the use of the apparatus of state for enforcing the privileges and disabilities of superior and inferior strata, as in South Africa (till recently). Violence may also be used for the same purpose outside the framework of the state as in the case of **lynching**, whether of Blacks by Whites in the United States or of untouchables by caste Hindus in India. Whereas power is important in upholding the existing order, the extent to which force is openly used to the advantage of superior strata against inferior strata varies.

Quick Fact

Lynching

An extrajudicial killing of a person or group by a mob, often as a public spectacle to punish someone who is alleged to have transgressed or to intimidate others.

IMPORTANT FEATURES

(i) It is a process by which individuals and groups are ranked in a hierarchy of *status*.

(ii) It involves a more or less enduring hierarchy which means that the inequalities are *institutionalised* and legitimised by the society.

(iii) Stratified societies have been and still are a universal phenomenon.

(iv) The bases of inequalities vary from society to society.

(v) Stratification is social in nature and it does not include biologically caused inequalities.

(vi) Stratification is found in *simple* and *complex* types of societies. In simple or primitive societies, it was based on age, sex, physical strength, etc.

(vii) In members of various strata which constitute each level of the stratification, hierarchy tends to have common life chances and lifestyles and may display an awareness of communal identity and these characteristics further distinguish them from other strata.

(viii) Sociologists normally identify three major types of stratification: *caste, estate* and *class*.

(ix) The *functional theory of stratification* asserts that in all societies there are positions that objectively have more functional importance than others and need special skills, if they are to be performed adequately. So there *must* be adequate rewards to induce the right

[2] David Jary & Julia Jerry, Dictionary of Sociology, Harper Collins, Glasgow, 1991

people to develop their skills. Such rewards are typically a mix of monetary inducements and high social status or prestige.

CASTE

'Caste' has come to be associated with a social science concept. The phenomenon which we now call 'caste' was named by western observers of India at an early stage in the colonial period. The phenomenon of caste has probably aroused more controversy than any other aspect of Indian life and thought. Some scholars see India's caste system as the defining feature of 'Indian culture'. Caste is such a complex phenomenon that it is difficult to define and the definitions pose lot of problems. Yet, in order to use it for practical purposes, some of the following definitions may be used:

Caste is a collection of families, bearing a common name, claiming a common descent, from a mythical ancestor, human or divine, professing to follow the same hereditary calling and regarded by those who are competent to give an opinion as forming a single homogenous community.

... Herbert Risley[3]

When a class is somewhat strictly hereditary, we may call it a caste. ... C.H. Cooley[4]

When status is wholly predetermined so that men are born to their lot without any hope of changing it, then the class takes the extreme form of caste. ... Maclver and Page[5]

Caste is a closed class. ... D.N. Majumdar[6]

Caste system is a form of social stratification in which castes are hierarchically organised and separated from each other by rules of ritual purity. ... Penguin's *Dictionary of Sociology*[7]

Historically, the most developed form and some would argue the only true form, of caste stratification occurred in India in association with Hinduism. The origins of this system are obscure. They probably lie in the twin bases of ethnicity and occupational specialisation. The system which the Brahmins perfected was founded on five main divisions: four caste groups (*Varna*) and an outcaste group (*Pancham Varna*), the untouchables. The four caste groups were the Brahmins, the priestly class having religious authority; the *Kshatriyas*, the secular and military ruler and landlord caste; the *Vaishyas*, the mercantile middle class; and the *Shudra*, the servant and slave class. The untouchables performed only the most degrading and ritually impure/polluting tasks.

Caste has been described as the fundamental social institution of India. As Andre Beteille (1996)[8] points out "sometimes the term is used metaphorically to refer to rigid social distinctions or extreme social exclusiveness wherever found. But, it is among the Hindus in India that we find

[3] Risley, Herbert, The People of India, Oriental Books Reprint Corp, Delhi, 1969

[4] Cooley, CH, Social Organization, Routledge, 1983

[5] Maciver & Page, Society, Farrar & Rinehart, New York, 1941

[6] Majumdar, DN & TN Madan, An Introduction to Social Anthropology, Asia Publishing House, Bombay, 1960

[7] Penguin Dictionary of Sociology, Penguin Books, London, 2006

[8] Beteile, Andre, Varna and Jati, Sociological Bulletin, 45:1, 1996

the system in its most fully developed form, although analogous forms exist among Muslims, Christians, Sikhs and other religious groups in South Asia."

PERSPECTIVES ON THE STUDY OF CASTE SYSTEM

A number of sociologists and social anthropologists have studied caste system and some of them have really done outstanding and somewhat pioneering work. In the process of looking at caste system they developed different perspectives. Among them, G S Ghurye, M N Srinivas, Louis Dumont and Andre Beitelle and some others stand apart. Let us briefly have some idea about their different perspectives.

G S Ghurye published his landmark and pioneering work *Caste and Race in India* (1932). Deeply influenced by the indological and historical approach, he also came under the influence of 'diffusionist school' of cultural evolution propounded by anthropologists. He puts both caste and race on the same pedestal and believes that both are related to each other. He believed that the entire Indian population and society is based on the caste system. Interestingly but significantly, he includes the tribes too in this system. Following this line of argument, he described tribal population as 'Backward Hindus' who needed to be assimilated in the mainstream Hindu society. For this, he did not enjoy the support of many other sociologists and anthropologists. Ghurye maintained that kin and caste networks in India parallels in some other countries too. Moreover, kinship and caste in Indian society served as integrative frameworks. He looked at the evolution of Indian society in terms of integration and deep inter-relationship between racial groups and kin and caste network.

Being a follower of indological approach laced with historical approach he made several speculations. With the rise of empiricism and field-based studies his over dependence on text became a target of severe criticism. Despite many of his ideas becoming obsolete and 'Hindu centric' instead of being totally objective, he will be remembered as the first sociologist to have challenged the colonial notion of caste.

M N Srinivas added a very significant dimension to the caste studies by talking about mobility in the caste system. He pointed out that any social institution may be seen through two views – Book view/Textual view and Field view/ Empirical view. The textual or theoretical view rules out any change or mobility in the caste system as if it is frozen in time. Through his and path breaking work *Religion and Society among the Coorgs of South India* (1952) he presented the empirical situation in which the lower castes were seen emulating the values, customs, traditions, food habits etc. of the Brahmins to move upward in the caste/status hierarchy which he termed this process as Brahminisation. He gave up this term when confronted by cases from elsewhere in which any higher caste (later the local dominant caste) might serve as the 'reference group' to be emulated. Then he coined the term Sanskritisation to describe this phenomenon. Through his perspective on the caste system, he opened new windows for the study of mobility in the caste system of different parts of India.

Louis Dumont, an eminent French sociologist, developed a new perspective on the caste system by laying emphasis on the 'ideology of caste system'. He was concerned with the attributes of caste and hence his approach was called 'attribution approach' to the caste system. In his path breaking and highly philosophical work *Homo Hierarchicus,* he laid out his understanding of caste and caste system. He understands caste as a set of relationship of economic, political and kinship systems sustained by certain values which are mostly religious in nature. Dumont maintains that caste is not a form of stratification but a special form of inequality whose essence has to be deciphered by the sociologists. He is of the firm view that caste divides the whole Indian society into large number of hereditary groups. These groups are separated by the strict rule of endogamy and ritual distance between these groups. Moreover, because of elaborate division of labour each group was assigned an occupation which was hereditary in nature and any group could not deviate from it under the force of custom. No two groups can be equal and in this gradation of status/hierarchy these will be superior or inferior to one another. He moves on to describe caste system as a system of values and his analysis is based on the binary opposition between the pure and impure. Dumont's *Homo Hierarchicus* builds a model of Indian civilisation based on non-competitive ritual hierarchical system. No other sociologists before him looked at the caste system from this perspective and hence Dumont's contribution to the study of caste system is still considered very significant despite fifty-five years of the original publication in French and forty years after its English translation came through.

Andre Beitelle's perspective on the caste system is refreshingly new. He moved away from the Indological, theoretical and abstractional model to a model of ethnographic and theoretical analysis. His understanding is largely based on the relationship between caste, class and power in the context of change. Caste system has undergone substantial change during the British rule, but the post-independence period has witnessed the distribution of power in a non-traditional way. His major work *Caste, Class and Power: Changing Patterns of Stratification in a Tanjore Village* (1966) analyses the change in the caste system in the wake of democracy, land reforms and empowerment of non-Brahmin castes. He has empirically demonstrated that the traditional relationship between caste and power has been radically changed. At the micro level, village Panchayat in the village Sripuram is controlled by non-Brahmins and the traditional elite has been pushed to the background. He observes that the "power has also become independent of class to a greater extent than in the past. Ownership of land is no longer the decisive factor in acquiring power. Numerical support and strategic position in the party machinery play an important part". Thus, for the first time the relationship between the caste structure, the class system and the distribution of political power has been theorised on the basis of ethnographic research.

FUNCTIONS OF CASTE SYSTEM

Caste system may be seen traditionally as performing the following functions:

(i) It minimises economic competition by determining the occupation of various caste groups.

(ii) By restricting and limiting the range of choosing spouse, it helps its members in their endeavour of choosing a life partner. The rules of **endogamy** are, traditionally, very strict and violations are taken seriously with punishments.

> **Quick Fact**
>
> **Endogamy**
>
> A custom that requires individuals to marry within their own caste or social group.

(iii) The economic basis of the caste system is the jajmani system. It is an elaborate division of labour governed by a well-defined system of exchange of goods and services.

The higher landed castes and the lower occupationally specialised castes or 'service castes' are traditionally bound by certain Jajmani obligations. The patrons *(jajmans)* or higher castes who control land ownership exchange the land produce against the services provided by other castes.

(iv) Caste may also be seen as a social and psychological resource for its members. Because of a sense of solidarity and common consciousness, the members of a caste come to the rescue of fellow castemen.

RITUAL ASPECT OR BINARY OPPOSITION BETWEEN PURE/IMPURE (POLLUTION)

1. The opposition between pure and impure has been regarded by Louis Dumont (1980), as the fundamental principle underlying the Hindu caste system.

2. The principle is implicit in the three predominant features of the caste system, which were systematically spelt out by Bougle and later endorsed by Dumont. According to Bougle (1968), the caste system comprises a series of hereditary groups (the socially relevant *jatis*) characterised by (i) 'hierarchy' or gradations according to ritual status; (ii) 'mutual repulsion', implying rules governing contact, ensuring their separation; and (iii) division of labour and consequent interdependence.

3. Dumont shows that the opposition between the pure and the impure is implicit in all the three attributes: in 'hierarchy' because the pure and impure must be kept separate; and in the division of labour because pure and impure occupations have to be segregated.

4. Following from this, the caste system is viewed as a 'whole' which is founded on the necessary and hierarchical coexistence of the opposites (the pure and impure). This represents a view point of caste according to which both the pure and the impure have their rightful place in the system and each has its privileges and coexists with the other.

5. One way of assigning rank to castes in terms of their relative purity and impurity is to study their attributes and accordingly order them in relation to one another. The attributes of purity include features such as wearing sacred thread, veneration of cow, vegetarianism, teetotalism and prohibiting widow remarriage. Pollution is associated with human emissions, death, disrespect of cow and consumption of meat and alcohol, to mention the principal elements.

6. The attributes of purity and pollution discussed above may be used to identify the two broad extremes in the caste hierarchy – the Brahmins and the untouchables. But, the precise determination of the highest and the lowest among Brahmins and untouchables respectively is conditioned by local interpretations of the pollution concept. Thus, while scavenging and beef eating would make a caste group untouchable almost anywhere, it may still be able to establish its precedence over some other groups through fine distinctions of behaviour. The fact that the empirical referents of the pollution concept are subject to local interpretations highlight the point that caste hierarchy, when viewed as a specific phenomenon, is confined to a given local area. Hence, caste *(Jati)* hierarchy shows regional variations.

7. The tendency which results in the hierarchical arrangements of castes in a given locality is often replicated within a caste and leads to the grading of segments both in the same local community and over a wide territorial area.
8. The operation of local interpretations of pollution explains various regional differences in the evaluation and ranking of castes. However, even within a given locality and multiplicity of attributional criteria, the necessity of evaluating them in relation to one another renders it difficult to grade all the castes in a fixed hierarchical order.
9. Dumont attempts to show how these attributes may be used to establish a series of divisions, each more precise than the other, between superior and inferior castes. For example, the vegetarian castes may be placed above the non-vegetarian ones; among the vegetarians those who prohibit widow remarriage would be superior to those who permit it. Similarly, among the non-vegetarians further dichotomies may be established between beef eaters and non-beef eaters; and among the later still further gradations may be made between those who eat only mutton or birds and who eat pig (pork) raised by lower castes and fed by garbage. Dumont argues that such dichotomies, which establish distinctions of relative purity and impurity, reaffirm the importance of the hierarchical principle.
10. At the same time, it is difficult to explain that any particular village hierarchy solely depends on the basis of attributional criteria. A vegetarian caste, in some cases, may actually rank below a non-vegetarian caste. It is also not clear how the various attributes of pollution combine together to form an unambiguous hierarchy of values. For example, are the attributes of diet more important than those of occupation? Among certain occupations, such as butchering goats, cutting hair and tapping toddy, which would be lowest?
11. Such difficulties led McKim Marriott to propose an interactional theory of caste ranking based on inter-caste relationships as manifested in the 'ritualised giving and receiving of food and the giving and receiving of ritual services'. He considers food transfers more decisive in establishing rank than the receiving of ritual services, but the two are connected since the services are paid for partly in food.
12. The circulation of food is one significant index of rank because a caste which receives more of the purer kinds of food than it gives to other caste groups may be regarded as the recipient of relatively more ritual honour in relation to the others. Following the same principle, a caste which receives more ritual services from other castes than it gives to them ranks higher. It is lower if it gives more ritual services than it receives or renders these to lower castes.

UNTOUCHABILITY

The notion and practice of untouchability is a direct product of the caste system. Most of the historians are of the view that the earliest Vedic text *Rigveda* makes no mention of untouchability. Perhaps, it developed with the establishment of the present-day caste system during the Gupta period. Here we are not concerned with the debates on this issue among historians. Sociologists and anthropologists are more interested to know the dynamics of caste-based discrimination manifesting in social, economic and political exclusion and segregation and how it is, in present times, considered as a gross violation of human rights.

As already mentioned, untouchability is the by-product of the notion of purity/impurity or ritual pollution and how the caste hierarchy is based on ritual hierarchy, i.e. degree of ritual purity gone downwards up to the zone of impurity/pollution. In order to maintain ritual purity, the 'pure' castes are supposed to maintain ritual distance manifesting itself in physical and social distance.

Those sections of the society who were made to adopt ritually impure occupations for their livelihood and to serve the rest of the society are considered 'untouchables' whose physical touch makes the persons of higher castes 'impure' and 'polluted' requiring a purificatory bath. Even in the present- day settlement pattern in villages in India, in most of the cases, the castes considered as untouchables are made to live on the fringe of the village while the central place is inhabited by Brahmins and other higher castes – even those relatively lower castes not considered untouchable. Those people engaged in leather work, handling dead animals, scavenging and a variety of other such occupations being considered as 'polluting' are declared as untouchables. Till recent decades, in several parts of the country, persons of the so-called untouchable castes were supposed to carry a small drum around their necks and beat it to warn others to maintain distance with them. In several other instances, some untouchable castes enjoyed only limited or restricted mobility and they could use the public roads only during stipulated hours of the day or night. Things have changed a lot, especially after independence and promulgation of the Constitution through which the practice of untouchability has been abolished and made a cognisable, criminal offence. It has almost disappeared from urban centres, largely because of urban anonymity and secularisation of social life; village India lags behind. Thus, untouchability may be seen in practice in varying degrees, in thousands of villages and small towns in different forms.

The following are some of the widespread practices of untouchability despite the presence of such legislative measures as Protection of Civil Rights Act, 1976 and Scheduled Castes and Scheduled Tribes (Prevention of Atrocities) Act, 1989, amended in 2015:

1. Separate utensils for these castes in tea stalls and eating joints and at several places they have to wash their utensils, mugs, etc. to get tea or food;
2. Denial of right to fetch water from the common source of water;
3. Denial of entry into the houses of upper castes;
4. Segregation in seating arrangement in schools;
5. Denial of right to the wedding procession with musical bands to pass through the locality of higher castes;
6. Resentment and opposition to the practice of a Dalit bridegroom coming to the bride's place riding a horse;
7. Denial of service from barber and washerman;
8. Denial of entry into temples;
9. Discrimination in health services; and
10. When the state/central governments introduced the practice of providing midday meal to school children, upper caste children were instructed by their parents not to accept meals if cooked by a Dalit woman, thus, creating a lot of problems for this scheme.

Thus, we see that social, economic and political exclusion continues in varying degrees in villages and small towns. On the basis of past experiences and to a lesser extent even present, one may say that to be untouchable did not merely mean to be untouchable, but to enter a futile world devoid of hope. Though the past had witnessed a number of social and religious reform movements such as the Arya Samaj movement, the practice of untouchability continues in one way or the other. Similar to apartheid in South Africa till some decades back, it is a gross violation of human rights.

CASTE SYSTEM AS VIEWED BY CONTEMPORARY SOCIAL ANTHROPOLOGISTS

Since the late 1940s, a number of British and American social scientists have taken a new approach to the Indian caste system. The dominant features of this approach are inspired by contemporary social anthropology. Pauline Kolenda (1984), a keen observer of the Indian scene, in a sharp analysis, has tried to identify the important features of this new approach. According to her, the first important feature is the collection of information about the caste system by residing in a village and observing. According to her:

1. Caste as a system operates only within a limited locality, a single village or a few linked villages.
2. A village or local population is composed of a series of mutually exclusive castes, usually numbering anywhere from a handful to a score or more.
3. A dominant caste or a dominant family or set of families, typically has preponderant political and economic power over everyone else in the locality. Dominance is rooted in monopolistic control over arable land and in physical force.
4. Each caste has an occupational specialty and offers this to other castes in exchange for food, products or services. Especially important is the food grain provided by the land-controlling dominant caste or families to the landless servant, artisan and mendicants caste. This exchange of food, goods and services is a ritual system concerned with purity and pollution as well as an economic system called the *jajmani system*. It functions so that the highest castes remain pure while the lower castes absorb pollution for them.
5. Castes within a local caste system tend to be mutually ranked according to their respective degrees of pollution in this ritual system.
6. Efforts to improve caste rank in this local caste hierarchy are made by middle and lower castes, especially by means of discarding polluting customs and by emulating the customs of the higher purer castes.
7. Political power is monopolised by the dominant caste, family or families or occasionally by a pair of competing dominant castes. Non-dominant castes tend to support their patrons within the dominant segment. Such support may be important if there are *factions* contending for power within the dominant segment.
8. Disputes may be settled either by council within a caste segment or by one or more elders of the dominant caste or family.
9. The caste segment itself is an endogamous descent group. The local contingent of a caste is usually composed of kinsmen, ideally related unilineally, though often actually related cognatically. (Patrilineal descent refers to a line of males related through father–son links, going back to a common male ancestor. Matrilineal descent refers to a line of mother–child links, going back

to a common female ancestor. Cognatic descent refers to a line related through either male or female links, going back to common ancestors.)

10. Each caste segment tends to live in its own quarter. Universally, untouchables (who are unclean) live in isolation from those of purer caste, either in a separate hamlet or on the outskirts of a village.

CASTE: CULTURAL AND STRUCTURAL VIEW

Caste is a system of stratification. To be more precise, caste system is a system of social stratification in the Indian society. It represents the basic idea or notion or ideology of social stratification in the traditional Indian society. Sociologists, sometimes, take divergent views of caste. Two most popular views are the (i) cultural view and the (ii) structural view. The differences in these two views lie not in the basic content, but in the levels of analysis.

Those who tend to take the **cultural view** of caste treat it as a system of ideas and values. It may also include beliefs and norms. In this view, the most important factor is hierarchy, which forms the basis of ranking of persons or groups. The prominent protagonists of this view are Louis Dumont, G.S. Ghurye, Edmund Leach and M.N. Srinivas. They look at caste as a social or cultural phenomenon peculiar to the Indian society, more precisely to the Hindu society because among the non-Hindus it does not constitute the religious ideology despite the fact that they have also developed 'caste-like' stratification. Treating caste as a cultural phenomenon within the general principle of social stratification, they pinpoint the hierarchy of hereditary groups as its basis. These hereditary groups are separated by caste endogamy, restrictions on commensal relations (exchange of food and water) and physical contact. Despite this separation and exclusiveness, they are interdependent because of the traditional division of labour. The underlying principle of this arrangement is based on the opposition of the pure and impure, a sort of binary opposition.

> **Quick Fact**
>
> **Cultural View**
>
> It emphasises the ideological, religious, and symbolic dimensions of the caste system. The Key aspects of cultural view includes Religious Basis, Customs and Traditions, Language and Behaviour, Cultural Legitimacy etc.

Yogendra Singh makes further elaboration of this arrangement. He talks of universalistic or particularistic categories. The former means that the caste system is regarded as just another manifestation of the universal phenomenon of social stratification while the latter means that the caste system may be viewed as a system of stratification, which is unique to the Indian/Hindu society.

Those who take the **structural view** of caste look at caste at a higher level of abstraction, i.e. 'social structure'. Thus, caste for them is a structural reality. Proponents of this view can be found among the Marxist and functionalist sociologists.

> **Quick Fact**
>
> **Structural View**
>
> The key aspects of structural view includes Hierarchy, Endogamy, Occupational Specialisation, Social Stratification, Hereditary Nature etc. It focuses on the hierarchical and systemic organisation of the caste system.

A.R. Desai, a Marxist sociologist, represents this view among the Indian sociologists. According to the 'structuralists', caste as a social structure is comparable cross-culturally. Yogendra Singh again divides the proponents of this view into two categories: structural universalistic and structural particularistic. For the structuralists, caste system is nothing, but the representation of class relations in caste idiom. The religious sanctions behind caste have been interpreted by the Marxists as simply a legitimising ideology to sustain the existing mode of production. Since the landed castes are mostly upper castes who largely control the means of production and exploit the 'ritually inferior' landless lower castes, the die is cast in favour of its interpretation in terms of class in the Marxian sense of the term. The majority of sociologists studying the Indian society have subscribed to the structural particularistic view of caste. They have treated caste as an institutionalised system of interaction among the hierarchically ranked hereditary groups for marriage, occupation, economic division of labour, enforcement of cultural norms and values by caste panchayats or organisations. Structural analysis of caste views it as a system of institutionalised inequality. Thus, caste may also be understood as the structural basis of inequality.

CASTE MOBILITY

Sorokin, whose pioneering work on social mobility is yet to be surpassed, says that there has scarcely been any society whose strata were absolutely closed or in which vertical mobility in its three forms – economic, political and occupational – was not present. At the same time, there has never existed a society in which vertical social mobility has been absolutely free and the transition from one social stratum to another has had no resistance. Contrary to the popular 'book view', caste as a stratification system provides room for social and occupational mobility.

M.N. Srinivas (1965)[9] exploded the myth of caste system as static. He puts forward a dynamic view of caste and contends that "the caste system is far from a rigid system in which the position of each component is fixed for all times. Movement has always been possible." He further says that the stronger the norms against social mobility, the greater the desire for it. An indication of the widespread desire for mobility comes from an unusual source – the census operations. The Indian census reports of the 19th and early 20th centuries give us abundant idea of this upward mobility.

The caste system discouraged individual mobility from one caste to another during one's lifetime. Thus, mobility manifested itself as the collective splitting off sub-castes or what Hutton (1936)[10] calls the "fissiparous tendencies of Indian castes." The process of mobility becomes more clear if we distinguish models of mobility. Though, there may be two referents: the *dwija* (twice born higher castes) and modern, educated elite. The cultural emulation of caste elite as referent or reference group is more important in the process of caste mobility yet the modern elite is also used as referent. But, in most of the cases both are combined in caste mobility as per the empirical realities.

In his path-breaking study 'Religion and Society among the Coorgs' (1952), M.N. Srinivas explained caste mobility in terms of cultural emulation of the Brahmins by the local lower castes. He then

[9] Srinivas, MN, Religion and Society among the Coorgs of South India, Asia Publishing House, London, 1965
[10] Hutton, JH, Caste in India, Cambridge University Press, New York, 1936

broadened the definition of **Sanskritisation** in 'Social Change in Modern India' (1995)[11] as:

A process by which a low Hindu caste or tribal or other group, changes its customs, ritual, ideology and way of life in the direction of a high and frequently 'twice born' caste. Generally, such changes are followed by a claim to a higher position in the caste hierarchy.

In terms of *varna* referents, the *Kshatriya* model has been the most popular. Surjit Sinha, however, describes it as **Rajputisation** instead of **Kshatriyisation** on the basis of his fieldwork in central India. The popularity of *Kshatriya* model is attested by a large number of petitions by the lower castes before the census officials to change their names and hierarchy and recognise them as *Kshatriya*. The Brahmin model of *Sanskritisation* has been the most difficult because, in most of the cases, the Shudra castes found it difficult to be recognised as Brahmins. William Rowe's (1968) study of the Noniya in Senapur village in eastern Uttar Pradesh shows the success of a middle-level caste in acquiring upward mobility through *Sanskritisation* after achieving economic prosperity. It attests David Mandelbaum's (1970) view that a low caste must accumulate wealth and prosperity before adopting *Sanskritisation* as a means of upward social mobility.

Quick Fact

Sanskritisation

A process described by M.N. Srinivas in which lower castes seek upward mobility by emulating the rituals, customs, and lifestyle of higher castes.

Rajputisation

The historical process through which non-Rajput communities adopted the lifestyle, customs, and social practices of the Rajputs to elevate their social status in the caste hierarchy.

Kshatriyisation

It refers to the socio-cultural process through which non-Kshatriya groups adopted the customs, lifestyle, and status associated with the Kshatriya varna (the warrior class) in the traditional Hindu social hierarchy.

What Do You Think?

To what extent can economic progress and education enable caste mobility in India, and how do societal perceptions and entrenched biases act as barriers to this movement?

Similarly, Pocock (1970) has shown successful upward mobility in the case of *Kunbi*, a traditional middle rung peasant caste of Gujarat to the new and more honourphic status of the *Patidar*. It is generally accepted that untouchability has proved to be such a big barrier that it does not allow any upward mobility. However, F.G. Bailey (1957, 2013) in his study of Bissipara in Odisha has presented a rare example, which shows the success of the untouchables in achieving status elevation through *Sanskritisation*. From liquor distillation, a ritually impure occupation, they moved upward after acquiring land and laying their claim on *Kshatriya* status, which was conceded, though grudgingly, by the local Brahmins and *Kshatriyas*.

In terms of intra-caste mobility, education and occupation have been the most important factors of upward mobility. With the expanding avenues of secularisation of education and occupation, a number of individuals and groups within a caste attain upward mobility. Thus, an elite substratum emerges in every caste. We can witness this phenomenon even among the scheduled castes, other backward castes and tribal communities.

[11] Srinivas, MN, Social Change in Modern India, Orient Longman, Hyderabad, 1995

CHANGES IN THE RITUAL AND ECONOMIC ASPECTS OF CASTE

Traditionally, caste hierarchy has been ritual hierarchy in terms of one's status on the basis of degree of purity or impurity. The secular or material attributes or determinants of status ranking were secondary in nature. These secular attributes were wealth or ownership of land, access to political power, etc. However, certain processes of change which began during the British rule, but acquired momentum after independence have promoted changes in the system of ranking of castes. Urbanisation gave a serious blow to the ritual dimension of caste.

With the manifold increase in secularisation of inter-caste and inter-personal relations, the ritual and social distance between castes narrowed down. People's concern for improving the quality of life promoted levels of consumption. It facilitated the easy entry of secular indicators of prosperity and socio-economic superiority in the caste system. The increased economic development, especially the growth of capitalist mode of agriculture and industrialisation promoted occupational opportunities which were considered 'ritually neutral'. Entry into these new occupations was based on technical skills imparted through modern education. Moreover, new avenues of increasing income and acquiring wealth were introduced.

Thus, these new determinants of status pushed the ritual determinants to the background. In the sphere of inter-caste and interpersonal relations persons belonging to different castes with different ritual statuses came together in modern occupational settings and indulged in closer interpersonal relationship giving big jolt to the ritual aspect of caste. On secular occasions, the non-Brahmin castes occupied more prominent places because of their material endowments. The Brahmins continue to occupy a higher place on such occasions only when they are stronger in material terms. Democratic decentralisation of power right up to the grassroots level has led to increased participation in the political process and besides economic success, access to political power has become another means of status enhancement.

CHANGES IN THE ECONOMIC ASPECT OF CASTE

When we look at the traditional Indian society, we find that the caste system formed the basis of village economy and **jajmani system** was the economic basis of caste system. With the introduction of technological innovations, market economy, backward class and Dalit mobilisation, the jajmani system declined, which was essentially a system of production and exchange of goods and services. Thus, caste as a system broke down in most of the villages in India, though castes survived as social groups with their concomitant caste consciousness. In the urban areas, because of new occupational structures, an 'occupation-free caste structure' emerged. Caste and occupation were delinked because recruitment to the new occupations was based on technical skills which could be acquired through formal, modern education. Look at the skill of ceramics. One need not

Quick Fact

Jajmani System

An economic arrangement in traditional Indian villages where each caste group had specific roles, creating an interdependent system of services.

The members of the lower castes provided services to members of the upper castes in exchange for goods and protection.

belong to a potter's caste to acquire this skill. Jewellery designing can be learned without belonging to goldsmith's caste and so on. But, Lloyd Rudolf (2000) has different ideas. He says that modernity has entered into Indian character and society, but it has done so through assimilation, not replacement while Dipankar Gupta (2000) describes this as 'mistaken modernity', which is only skin deep. Moreover, of late, a new phenomenon may be observed. A number of caste groups have joined hands to protect their 'class interests'. The examples of 'Bharatiya Kisan Union' (BKU) in Uttar Pradesh and *Shetkari Saghtana* in Maharashtra go to prove that the economic functions of caste have undergone transformation, but caste as a unit of social organisation has survived because of its adaptive capability.

What Do You Think?

How does caste influence access to jobs and education in India, and what can be done to create more equal opportunities for everyone?

CASTE SYSTEM AND ITS TRANSFORMATION

Contrary to its textual view and popular perception, caste has never been static. It has been prone to a number of factors of change which have been occurring over the period of time – from the ancient times to the present. The caste system has always undergone adaptive changes. However, during the post-independence period, the pace of change has increased manifold, especially in the ritual and economic aspects of caste. Among the factors of change, right from the British times, the following may be enumerated as the most important:

(i) Industrialisation and Urbanisation;
(ii) Westernisation;
(iii) Social and Religious Reform Movements;
(iv) Dalit and Backward Classes Movement; and
(v) Role of State.

During British rule, the process of industrialisation and urbanisation played a very important role. The process of industrialisation put material and secular indicators and determinants of social status on a high pedestal at the cost of ritual determinants of social status. The process of urbanisation accompanied by secularisation reduced the ritual and physical distance between the higher and the lower castes largely because of the reduced physical segregation between castes and a more secular settlement pattern peculiar to urban centres.

The process of westernisation introduced a new social philosophy and value system oriented towards social equality and increased emphasis on rationalism. It also promoted gender rights and gender justice. The westernised sections of Indian society reinterpreted Hinduism and had a new look at the caste system. They defied the traditional rules of commensality of the caste system and had no inhibitions in taking to new nontraditional occupations. They also did not have any problem of choosing spouse from outside the caste. By and large, westernisation promoted the cultural modernisation of Indian society.

Several religious and social reform movements also played their role. The **Bhakti Movement and Sufi Movement** laid emphasis on oneness of mankind and exposed the idea of inequality as 'man made', rather than 'god made'. Though they could not eliminate the caste system, they definitely facilitated relaxation of caste rigidities. Several social reform movements such as Arya Samaj and Brahmo Samaj movements made a direct attack on the caste system, especially on its ritual aspect of purity and impurity and inequality. The birth of backward castes movements or non-Brahmin movements also gave a direct blow to the philosophy of inequalities and promoted egalitarianism.

Quick Fact

Bhakti and Sufi Movement

Bhakti Movement focussed on devotion and personal connection to a deity, transcending caste and ritualistic practices, while Sufi Movement focused on mysticism, love for God, and spiritual union through meditation and self-purification.

Of all the factors enumerated above, the role of the State was most crucial, especially after independence. When the Constitution of India proclaimed equality, it derecognised caste inequalities and caste superiorities in one stroke. The practice of untouchability, an integral part of caste system, was made a cognisable offence. Democracy and adult franchise were a great step forward towards social justice, equality and empowerment of disadvantaged groups of Indian society. The state-sponsored change, planned, directed and executed by the state, went a long way in attacking the basis of inequality and injustice in the caste system. Uniform legal system and equality before laws was established.

CASTE AND POLITICS

The role of caste in the sphere of politics may be traced back to the British colonial period. In the first half of the 19th century, the British rulers on the one hand encouraged Christian missionaries who, besides spreading the religious message of Christianity, also began projecting it as a reformatory movement and on the other instituted laws against several socially retrograde customs and practices of the Hindu society like sati, female infanticide, human sacrifice, etc. These measures were backed and supported by the reform-minded westernised Indian elite. The implications of several such measures were taken as a direct attack on the caste system, caste norms and Hindu cultural ethos. It gave rise to the tendencies of 'insulation' of caste-minded masses from the external influences. This may be taken as the beginning of the role of caste in the political process of the Indian society.

The introduction of modern means of transport and communication encouraged not only **spatial mobility**, but also **social mobility**. Backed by the new printing technology, caste loyalties and consciousness spread beyond villages, districts and provinces. The establishment of representative educational and legal institutions and new opportunities for achieving power and prestige added new functions to the caste. The Brahmins, Kayasthas and Vaishyas immediately grabbed these opportunities because only they were in a position to take full advantage of the new socio-political system. This background helped

Quick Fact

Spatial and Social Mobility

Spatial mobility refers to the physical movement of individuals or groups across geographical locations, while social mobility refers to the movement of individuals or groups within a social hierarchy or class system.

them to emerge as leaders of the nationalist movement too. That is why we find that the leadership of the nationalist movement and of the Indian National Congress in virtually the entire Indian sub-continent was in the hands of men from the elite Hindu castes. Same was the case with the Muslim caste groups where the Saiyyeds, Shaikhs and Pathans monopolised education and politics.

Paul Brass in his major work, 'The Politics of India since Independence' (1990), makes the comment that among both the elite and middle status castes, a process of caste succession had begun before independence and was intensified after it with the adoption of adult franchise by which in election after election, new leaders from previously unrepresented or underrepresented castes began to emerge and the castes began themselves to be mobilised. The intermediate castes acquired increased voting power through **adult suffrage** and increased economic power through *zamindari* abolition. Intermediate castes with economic resources sought not only political power, but also educational benefits and urban jobs for their children. As they acquired such opportunities, they came increasingly into conflict with persons from upper caste groups represented in far greater proportion and often absolute numbers in educational and political institutions.

Quick Fact

Adult Suffrage

It is the right of all adult citizens to vote in elections, regardless of caste, gender, religion, or economic status.

The Brahmins were the elite in educational and political spheres because of their elite status in the caste system. The earliest social movements were mobilised by the non-Brahmin castes against this virtual monopoly. The mid-19th century witnessed the earliest anti-Brahmin movement in Maharashtra. By the turn of the 20th century, such movements surfaced most vocally and strongly in the south, especially in the regions coming under the present states of Tamil Nadu, Kerala and Karnataka. Thus, the non-Brahmin movement in South India could be seen as the response of the downtrodden lower castes to the challenge of higher caste hegemony. The western liberal rationalist ideas provided a fertile ground for the new liberating ideology. Jyotiba Phule of Pune first urged non-Brahmins not to engage Brahmin priests in rituals. The cause of non-Brahmins was also taken up by Chhatrapati Shahuji of Kolhapur. Soon, a non-Brahmin movement came into existence in the former state of Madras in the first quarter of the 20th century in the form of the Dravidian movement. The Justice Party was founded in 1916 led by Periyar Ramaswami Naicker, the Self-Respect Movement was founded in 1925 and the Dravidar Kazhagam (Dravidian federation) was founded in 1944. It demanded a separate Dravidian state to be run on casteless and egalitarian lines. Many Dravidar Kazhagam members and supporters were atheists like the members of the Justice Party. They denounced and impugned several socially regressive and retrograde Hindu concepts.

In the regions, now under Andhra Pradesh-Telangana, the Reddys and the Khammas emerged as dominant castes, edging out the Brahmins from the seats of power. The state of Karnataka saw the emergence of Vokkaliga and Lingayat as the new dominant castes. The situation in the north was different from the south. As most of the historians and sociologists believe there were hardly any 'pure' *Kshatriyas* or Vaishyas in Madras state and hence there was a head on collision between the Brahmin and the Shudra castes. The situation was different in the north because of the presence of a number of castes in between the Brahmins and the Shudra *jatis* who acted as a sort of 'buffer zone' in the ritual-political hierarchy. Moreover, there always has been a tendency of upward mobility among the middle level and lower castes towards the higher castes through the process of *Sanskritisation*. Perhaps, that is why, the backward class mobilisation took roots in North India at a much later stage, i.e. from 1960s onwards.

India has been an effective democracy since independence. In his recently published work 'Interrogating Caste' (2000)[12], Dipankar Gupta rightly points out that

It is commonplace in the analysis of caste politics to give in to the presumption of numbers. Thus, it is often argued that political outcomes can be determined to a fair degree by the caste composition of electoral constituencies.

Thus, the locus of power and influence has shifted from the ritually higher (but numerically lesser) castes to the numerically large, politically mobilised middle rung and backward castes. In most regions of India, the middle and lower level castes now enjoy empirical strength. The Nairs and Izhavas in Kerala, Vanniyars in Tamil Nadu, Vokkaligas and Lingayats in Karnataka, Reddys and Khammas in Andhra Pradesh, Patidars and *Kshatriyas* in Gujarat, Jats in Haryana and Rajasthan, Yadavas and Kurmis in Bihar and Uttar Pradesh and the Chamars in the whole of North India, especially Uttar Pradesh, are examples of this shift in political power.

In his path-breaking study 'Caste and Politics in India' (1969), Rajni Kothari has made a brilliant analysis of the relationship between caste and politics. Describing politics in India as an enterprise, he dubs the politicians as entrepreneurs. Like any intelligent and skillful entrepreneur, they know their resources and how to utilise them effectively as well. They know that the vast multitude of Indian masses live along their respective castes, have primordial caste loyalties and a strong caste consciousness and hence can be easily mobilised along caste lines. This intimate interaction between caste and politics has changed the face of both. He describes it as 'politicisation of caste'. However, for the traditionally deprived and underprivileged castes, this is a case of democratic assertion for their due rights. Thus, it gives rise to a serious debate on whether caste appeal amounts to casteism?

Rajni Kothari has specified **three typical stages in the relationship between caste and politics in a region**.

Stage 1: This involves politicisation of a powerful elite caste, usually one which responded earliest to the opportunity for western education. In Maharashtra and Tamil Nadu, this was the Brahmins; in Bihar, it was the Kayasthas. With some political success on the part of the entrenched caste, the members of other high castes in the area would respond with resentment, feelings of relative deprivation and possibly antagonism. These castes then challenged the entrenched caste as what Kothari calls an ascendant caste. In three examples given in Kothari's work, the ascendant caste is one of the respectable cultivators who had been slower than the entrenched caste in accepting western education. In Rajasthan, the Rajputs were the entrenched and the Jat cultivators the ascendant caste. In Tamil Nadu, the Brahmins were the entrenched and Shudra non-Brahmins were ascendant and in Maharashtra the Brahmins were the entrenched and the Marathas were the ascendant.

[12] Gupta, Dipankar, Interrogating Caste, Penguin India, Delhi, 2000

Stage 2: Factionalism and fragmentation take place within the competing castes and multicast and multifunctional alignments develop. Lower castes are often brought in to support high caste leaders and to strengthen a faction.

Stage 3: Caste identity tends to languish with the progress in education, urbanisation and the development of an orientation towards individual achievement and modern status symbols. Individuals participate in networks which include persons of several loyalties overlaid by a more sophisticated system of social and political participation with cross-cutting allegiances. Institutions are distinctly different. The present political realities suggest that the Indian society is not fixed in either Stage 2 or Stage 3. It is something beyond Stage 2 with the traditionally deprived moving towards domination of society at several levels.

For the other scholars of caste, the role of caste associations is also an important factor. A voluntary organisation, a caste organisation consists of members of a single caste. It plays an important role of a political instrument. Caste associations link members of a caste within a region and influence the political process, especially electoral politics, significantly. Along with caste associations, the working of democracy at the grassroots level, that is village level, democracy also shows the significant role of caste.

At the national level, Varna mobilisation, that is mobilisation of all *jatis* of a particular varna, is a new phenomenon. For instance, Kanyakubj Sabha, a caste organisation of Kanyakubj Brahmins, has been an old phenomenon, but the organisation of the Brahmins in the form of an All India Brahmin Mahasabha is of recent origin. Same is the case of the *Kshatriya* Mahasabha. Moreover, the pan Indian mobilisation of a *jati* like All India Kurmi Mahasabha is also a phenomenon of recent origin. Such attempts seem to be a part of political mobilisation of castes on an all-India basis to be used as an effective pressure group at the all-India level. The political alignments of different castes including the traditionally opposed caste groups have also emerged as a significant part of the contemporary political scenario.

DEMOCRATIC ASSERTION OF DALITS AND DALIT POLITICS

The democratic, but militant self-assertion of the Dalits today is a socio-political reality of the Indian society. This is a new revolution taking place in Indian society. The caste-ridden Indian society in its inequalities, hierarchies and normative deprivations is transforming itself. The traditionally disadvantaged groups are now mobilising themselves and are becoming articulate through the democratic assertion of their rights. This would certainly result in diffusion of power and more democratisation of Indian society.

Though there is a long history of struggle against social inequalities right from the days of Buddha to Ambedkar, the democratic framework has given the underprivileged and disadvantaged groups better and more effective opportunities for elimination of these inequalities. The 19th-century Dalit and backward classes movement may be looked at as a turning point in this struggle. The Self-Respect Movement in Tamil Nadu led by Periyar Ramaswami Naicker attacked the Vedic scriptures, the caste system, Brahminical social order and the very concept of God. Likewise, B.R. Ambedkar relentlessly fought against the caste system and when he realised that it was a hopeless situation, he rejected Hinduism and adopted Buddhism as an emancipatory movement for the Dalits. Ambedkar tried to evolve a new identity for the Dalits. As Gail Omvedt (1995)[13] comments, "The conversion to Buddhism was seen by Ambedkar as a social rebirth, a gaining of a new identity, a way in which the Dalits were leading, not simply joining, a movement for the re-creation of India." The Phule–Naicker–Ambedkar tradition is not dead. The increasing awakening of the Dalits and the backward castes for the democratic assertion of their rights provides ample testimony to this fact.

In the process of democratic assertion, politics in India has also become 'caste ridden'. Thus, the growing 'casteism' in India has become a debatable issue. Is caste appeal 'casteism' or a part of democratic assertion of disadvantaged groups? The growing role of caste in politics may not be to the liking of most of the modernists, but as Rajni Kothari (1995)[14] argues,

"Politics is a competitive enterprise; its purpose is the acquisition of power for the realisation of certain goals and its process is one of identifying and manipulating existing and emerging allegiances in order to mobilise and consolidate positions…."

This political assertion is giving a new meaning to the progressive agenda of social transformation.

The subaltern assertion, it seems, is powerful enough to enable Hinduism to look at itself and it's evils. Because Hinduism, as it exists, cannot be imagined without caste hierarchies/inequalities, hence the growing attack on Hinduism by the new politics is perhaps more sharper and relevant than what one sees in reformist Hinduism. (Avijit Pathak, 1998)[15]

What Do You Think?

How have grassroots movements and leaders within the Dalit community transformed the discourse on social justice and caste-based inequality in India, and what role should state policy and civil society play in furthering their objectives?

If we take a look at Dalit politics, we find that prior to 1942 the Dalits had no political party of their own. It was partly because Gandhi and the Congress did not like the idea of Dalits having an independent political party or identity of their own. Therefore, the founding of the 'All India Scheduled Castes Federation' in 1942 by B.R. Ambedkar was the first such attempt. The major objective of this organisation was the "attainment by the scheduled castes of a status as a distinct and separate element in the national life and India and to obtain for them their political, economic and social rights to which they are entitled by reason of their needs, their numbers and their importance." In 1956, Ambedkar decided to disband this party because its membership was restricted to Scheduled Castes. In its place he founded another party named as the Republican Party of India (RPI). This party took shape after his death in 1957 with the aim to be the defender of the interests of the Dalit classes, the *Adivasis* or tribal peoples, the backward classes, the peasants and landless labourers. For several years, the bulk of its supporters came from his own caste, the Mahars of Maharashtra. "The

[13] Omvedt, Gail, Dalit Visions: The anti-Caste Movement, Sangam Books Ltd, Delhi, 1995
[14] Kothari, Rajni, Caste in Indian Politics, Orient Black Swan, Hyderabad, 1995
[15] Pathak, Avijit, Indian Modernity: Contradictions, Paradoxes, and Possibilities, Gyan Publication House, Delhi, 1998

chequred electoral history of the Republican Party of India illustrates the liabilities, contradictions and potentialities of Scheduled Caste politics" (Michael Mahar, 1998)[16]. In the 1962 elections, the RPI contested 68 parliamentary seats and won 3, all in U.P. They contested 301 assembly seats and won 11, 3 in Maharashtra and 8 in U.P. These two states represent two quite different patterns of electoral efforts, one of which proved a failure, the other a harbinger of success.

The electoral history of the RPI illustrates the hard facts of political life that have to be faced by any group of Scheduled Castes who seek power under their own leadership. They must obtain a substantial number of caste Hindu votes to win, more stable inter-caste alliances based on common class interests and winning the confidence of similar caste groups among Muslims. The fact that non-scheduled caste voters play an important role in even the reserved constituencies also need to be kept in mind. By 1970s, the RPI became marginalised and had a token presence in two to three states only.

If we take another look at *Shudra* politics, especially in North India, we find that the socialist movement led by Ram Manohar Lohia was the precursor and the notable factor behind the victory of non-Congressism was largely the increased awakening and aspirations of the *Shudra* masses. The state assembly election of 1993 in Uttar Pradesh demonstrated a new model of *Shudra* solidarity. It was popularly named as *Pichra–Dalit Ekta* (backward–Dalit unity) or *Shudra–Atishudra Ekta*. The social base of the political success of C. N. Annadurai of the D.M.K. was the same. It could not work in future largely because of the class interests of these two segments of population and clash of personalities between Mulayam Singh Yadav and Kanshi Ram. Moreover, they could also not achieve a firm ideological footing.

The emergence of the Bahujan Samaj Party (BSP) a Dalit-based party, is one of the most significant developments in the political and social landscape of Uttar Pradesh. It was the result of growing awareness among Dalits that the traditional Hindu social order with its caste-based hierarchy cannot ensure social justice for them. The BSP had its origins in a lower middle class trade union organisation of the government employees, the BAMSEF formed in 1976 by Kanshi Ram, who had briefly joined the RPI in the late 1960, but left it as he felt it was a Congress stooge. It was only later that its base broadened with the formation of the DS-4, both of which came together to form the Bahujan Samaj Party in 1984.

The BSP claims that its ideology and strategies of mobiliosation are based upon the writings and speeches of Ambedkar, but actually draws heavily from those of Kanshi Ram and to a lesser extent Mayawati. (Sudha Pai, 1998)[17]

The ideology of the BSP is similar to that of the anti-Brahmin movements of South India. However, a fundamental difference is that its anti-Brahminism is more political than cultural.

The BSP leadership is today faced with a difficult decision: Is it a movement with an agenda for radical social change or a political party driven solely by the compulsion of achieving power? "As a result, it has reached a plateau from where further growth, as either of the two, seems difficult" (Sudha Pai, ibid). The Party's decision to form an alliance with the Congress in the 1996 assembly

[16] Mahar, Michael: Untouchables in Contemporary India, Rawat Publications, Jaipur, 1998
[17] Pai, Sudha, 'Dalit Assertion and the Unfinished Democratic Revolution', Sage Publication, New Delhi, 2002

elections and two coalition governments with the BJP has invited severe criticism. Due to those developments, the BSP can no longer be described as an 'exclusive Dalit party' because this shows its readiness to compromise Dalit interests for political compulsions.

Not withstanding the efforts of Ambedkar and others, the Dalit movement has so far primarily remained caste based. As a result, it has so far not succeeded in uniting all deprived social groups under the identity of Dalits.[18]

One of the major factors that determine the ultimate success or failure of a movement is the nature and dynamics of its leadership. The leadership of RPI, Dalit Panthers, BAMSEF, and BSP are the glaring examples.

His study includes the concept of Dalit leadership, nature and dynamics of Dalit leadership, political identity of the Dalit leadership and the cause of dearth of more effective and articulated Dalit leadership among Dalits including their womenfolk. But, one thing which we cannot afford to forget is had the undoing of the caste structure been possible merely through objective electoral politics, it would not have been as daunting as it is.

BACKWARD POLITICS, CASTE RESERVATIONS AND 'MANDALISATION'

As already stated, the provisions for compensatory benefits for the Scheduled Castes and the Scheduled Tribes were kept mandatory, those for the Other Backward Classes (OBCs) were left to the discretion and, of course, the convenience of the Governments, Central and State. H.S. Verma in his unpublished paper, *The OBC identity and treatment of the OBCs by the Mainstream Ruling Political Parties in India (2003)*, stretches the argument further by commenting that

> The second major trick[19] played was leaving the identification and scheduling of the OBC undefined in the Constitution. Further the states which had a long historical tradition of affirmative action for the OBCs played another trick with the OBCs: They came out with very long lists of the OBCs and thus brought almost three fourths of their population under this category.

When we look at the history of democratisation, we discover that almost all societies which have attained democratisation have done so only by defeating the landowning classes. But, unfortunately, intentionally or unintentionally, the Mandal Commission recommendations strengthened the landowning backward castes. Perhaps, the commission had some realisation of its consequence when it says that, "it is no doubt true that the major benefits of reservation and other welfare measures for OBCs will he cornered by the more advanced sections of the backward communities." All reformist remedies have to contend with a slow recovery along the hierarchical gradient: there are no quantum jumps in social reform. Moreover, human nature being what it is, a new class ultimately does emerge even in classless societies – an honest acknowledgement. Moreover, the chief merit of reservation is not that it will introduce egalitarianism amongst OBCs when the rest of the Indian society is seized by all sorts of inequalities. But, reservation will certainly erode the hold of higher castes on services.

---

[18] Kumar,Vivek, Dalit Leadership in India, Kalpaz Publication, New Delhi, 2002

[19] Verma, HS, The OBCs and the Ruling Classes in India, Jaipur: Rawat Publications, 2004

But, Chandrabhan Prasad, in his critique of the 'Mandal Project', says that the "entire document was prepared in a fraudulent manner in which, the neo-Kulak block within the broader OBC category sought to reverse the democratisation process." Moreover L.K. Naik, the only Dalit representative in the five-member Mandal Commission refused to sign the report and instead submitted his vote of dissent. While upholding the 27% quota for OBCs, a constitutionally legitimate claim, he argues to split OBC into two – depressed backward classes and intermediate backward classes – and then to divide the 27% quota into both. Naik's stand was dismissed by the majority of the members.

If we look at South India, especially Karnataka and Tamil Nadu, we find that they had already become Mandalised before the term was even coined. In a way Mandalisation is also a result of, 'bourgeoisation'. Upward climbing backward castes also contributed to the expansion of middle class in South India as well as some other parts of the country.

The intended role of the landed OBC elite in future village India is an eye-opener. In pre-independent India, the upper castes had monopoly over the productive assets. This monopoly was attacked through a series of state-sponsored measures such as zamindari abolition and rural development programmes. In the new scheme of redistribution of land and other productive assets, the major beneficiaries were not the Dalits, but the OBCs.

The Green Revolution of 1960s onward further strengthened the landed OBCs who, through *Sanskritisation*, also achieved upward mobility in status hierarchy and emerged as dominant castes in several parts of the country. In contrast, the upper castes, both Hindu and Muslim, slowly, but steadily started migrating to urban areas to take advantage of the more lucrative secondary sector with an added taste for urban life. As demographic projections suggest, if this trend continues, by 2025, village India and its agrarian society would almost become devoid of higher castes and in the absence of any radical land reform measures, as in the past, the entire productive agrarian assets and institutions may be captured by the landed elite of the OBCs, described as neo-Kulak by many scholars. In the changed land–labour equations, the Dalits and 'more backward castes' (from among the OBCs) would be easily prone to ruthless exploitation by this OBC elite. This is an alarming scenario. This new role of the landed, dominant OBC elite may be observed even today (a case of anticipatory socialisation) in some regions where the immediate oppressors of the Dalits are no more the Brahmins or *Kshatriyas*, but this new ruling elite. The 'most backward castes' are only next to Dalits in terms of **pauperisation** and marginalisation.

Quick Fact

Pauperisation

It refers to the process by which individuals or groups become impoverished or fall into extreme poverty.

On the issue of 'Mandalised' politics, social scientists and other intellectuals are sharply divided. Those "on the political left tend to accord greater priority to equality as policy and support the expansion of reservations through implementing the Mandal Commission[20], whereas those on the right favour equality as a right and oppose any extension." The issue has been so much emotionally charged that even a person of M.N. Srinivas's stature could not escape the label of 'higher caste partisanship'.

[20] Fuller, Christopher, The Everyday State and Society in Modern India, Hurst, 2001

▸▸ Backward Segments/Weaker Sections of Indian Population: Protective and Compensatory Discrimination, Social Justice, Equal Opportunity and Special Opportunities

Traditional Indian society was characterised by the most extreme and the most pervasive forms of inequality and their marks are readily visible in contemporary India. At the same time, we now have a constitution that has the most comprehensive guarantees of equality.

The ideology of hierarchy justifies the claims of superiority and rationalises resignation to inferior status. Thus, the graded inequalities of castes provided differential access to life chances.

The social hierarchy of the Indian society operating through centuries and millennia imposed a number of socio-economic disabilities on the castes (*jatis*) belonging to the *shudra* Varna. The result of these cumulative inequalities and disabilities was the social, educational and economic backwardness of today's scheduled castes and other backward classes. The tribal communities who remained, by and large, outside the caste system remained backward largely because of their comparative geographic isolation. Thus, their problems of backwardness are mainly related to technological and economic backwardness rather than social backwardness.

Contrary to popular perception (even among the educated sections of the society), the Constitution uses the term 'Backward classes' to include not only backward castes, but also the constitutional categories of Scheduled Castes (untouchables) and Scheduled Tribes.

The core compensatory provisions for them are the following:

(i) Reservation of seats, in proportion to their numbers, for Scheduled Castes and Scheduled Tribes, in the Lok Sabha (Article 330) and the legislative assembly of every state (Article 332).

(ii) Consideration of the claims of the members of Scheduled Castes and Scheduled Tribes, consistent with the maintenance of efficiency of administration, in the making of appointment to services and posts, in connection with the affairs of the union or of a state (Article 335).

(iii) Making any special provision for the advancement of any socially and educationally backward classes of citizens or the Scheduled Castes and Scheduled Tribes (Article 15-4).

(iv) Making reservation of appointments or posts in favour of any backward class of citizens which, in the opinion of the State, is not adequately represented in the services of the state (Article 16-4).

The Backward Classes being a residual category any measures for their welfare has been state based. The heterogeneity of this class of people and its large size is also responsible for the problem of its identity. Moreover, as Marc Galanter in his landmark work 'Competing Equalities: Law and the Backward Classes in India' (1991)[21] comments,

"The efforts to secure equality by means of preferential treatment must be seen in its constitutional context. The provisions for compensatory preference appear as exception within a framework of enforceable fundamental rights"

[21] Gallanter, Marc, Competing Equalities: Law and the Backward Classes in India, University of California Press, 1984

But, the attack on discrimination, private and public, is only one facet of the constitutional scheme to secure equality. The Constitution also directs the government employment and legislative representation, the constitution declares as a 'Directive Principle of State Policy':

The State shall promote with special care the educational and, economic interests of the weaker sections of the people and in particular of the Scheduled Castes and the Scheduled Tribes and protect them from social injustice and all forms of exploitation. (Article 46)

The issue of social justice versus equality of opportunity is beset with a number of problems to be sorted out. Social justice may be defined as the right of the weaker – the aged, destitute, poor women, children and other underprivileged persons. The state is expected to protect these sections against ruthless competition of life and help them in such a manner as they may enjoy this equal opportunity with the more advanced and stronger sections.

Equality and distributive justice are universal concerns in the modern world and it has been said that these concerns were activated among Indians by their exposure to the world outside, particularly the western world.

The policy of protective discrimination forms the basis for social development. Marc Galanter (ibid)[22] rightly comments that,

Reservation constitutes protective discrimination in favour of backward classes for mitigating inequalities. Thus, proclamation of equality would be devoid of justice without protective and compensatory discrimination.

CASTE AND NON-HINDUS

Though caste is a predominantly Hindu phenomenon, non-Hindu communities in India have also been found to possess certain specific features of the caste system of the Hindus. The majority of sociologists look at caste as a unique feature of Hindu society, but a number of sociologists and social anthropologists are of the view that caste-like groups do exist in non-Hindu societies too. Not only this, they see caste-like features in Pakistan, Sri Lanka, Bangladesh, Bhutan and some of the Southeast Asian societies, which at one time or the other came into contact with centres of Indian civilisation. As a result of culture contact and the resultant process of Hinduisation, they have also come to acquire caste-like features, if not the ideology of caste, as sanctioned in Hindu scriptures.

Studies on the impact of the caste system on non-Hindus reveal the extent to which their life patterns have been influenced by the social organisation of the Hindus. A look at the Muslim, Sikh and Christian societies (especially Muslims and Sikhs) finds that the egalitarian ideologies of Islam, Sikhism and Christianity made social adaptation with the social stratification of the Hindu society. It reminds one of a perceptible comment made by J.H. Hutton (1936)[23] who says that "when Islam and Christianity came to India caste was in the air and even these egalitarian ideologies could not escape the infection of caste." It is also true that of all the non-Hindu societies, the impact of caste on Muslims is visible most strongly.

---

[22] Gallanter, Marc, Competing Equalities: Law and the Backward Classes in India, University of California Press, 1984

[23] Hutton, JH: Caste in India, Cambridge University Press, New York, 1936

CASTE AMONG THE MUSLIMS

The question whether the concept of caste can be applied to the system of social stratification of a community professing a faith other than Hinduism has often been posed. It is true that the egalitarian social order of Islam stands in sharp contrast with the ideology of caste, yet the Indian Islam and 'Hindu caste system' have been able to achieve a substantial compatibility. Moreover, the majority of Indian Muslim population comes from the lower Hindu castes that have been coming into Islam to escape from social persecution and the oppressive socio-economic disabilities perpetrated by the caste system. However, the search for equality proved a mirage for them. There were improvements in their social conditions, yet the goals of social equality remained elusive. Significantly, in most of the cases, people embracing Islam gave up their religion, but not the caste that was brought forward even to the new socio-religious milieu. Thus, it would be apt to say that while Islam may not be having caste system, Indian Muslims do have. Hence, the interface between ideology and social structure in the context of caste may be full of academic issues requiring discussion. Within the larger framework of the Hindu caste system there are regional variations of caste-like groupings among Muslims.

Ghaus Ansari (1960), in his pioneering study on caste and social stratification among north Indian Muslims, places Muslim castes into three categories:

(i) *Ashraf*;
(ii) *Ajlaf*; and
(iii) *Arzal*.

Ashraf, literally meaning noble or superior, includes the Muslim nobility that claims to be the descendants of early Muslim immigrants, Saiyyad, Shaikh, Mughal or Pathan and may also include descendants of higher Hindu castes such as Rajputs. Even in this category, the Saiyyad occupies the highest rung in the status hierarchy. In the category of *Ajlaf* (mean or commoner) clean occupational castes are included such as *Julaha* (weaver), *Darzi* (tailor), *Qassab* (meat seller), *Hajjam* (barber), *Kunjra* (green grocer or vegetable vendor), *Mirasi* (bards, singers and musicians), *Manihar* (bangle maker/seller), *Dhunia* (cotton carder), *Gaddi* (grazier, milkmen), etc. While in the third category of *Arzal* (literally the meanest) the unclean or ritually polluting castes such as *Bhangi* or *Mehter* or *Halalkhor* (sweepers and scavengers) are included.

By and large, all these castes or caste-like groupings occupy specific places in the caste hierarchy with its own norms and patterns of behaviour. These are largely endogamous groups and all the relatively lower castes aspire for upward mobility by emulating the lifestyle of the higher ones. It presents a strange synthesis of Islamisation, Hinduisation and modernisation. As a substitute for *Sanskritisation*, this process may be described as *Ashrafisation*.

CASTE AMONG THE SIKHS

The Sikhs or the followers of Sikhism emerged in the 16th century. It is popularly considered a reformed sector of Hinduism and a protest movement against the prevailing orthodoxy of Hinduism, especially in the spheres of ritualism, idolatry and casteism. Deeply influenced by Islam, it adopted an egalitarian ideology. Thus, in principle, Sikhism like Islam does not recognise caste system, yet like Islam, the Sikh society too has castes and caste system.

The Sikhs are broadly distributed into upper and lower caste groups and inter-caste marriage is strongly frowned upon. Like the Hindus, in matters such as exchange of food and water and social intercourse, the Sikhs of the upper caste groups can be distinguished from those of the lower caste groups. The ritual dimension of caste is, therefore, considerably on the hierarchical dimension of the system. Broadly speaking, Sikhs are distributed among four endogamous groups which are hereditary occupational groups and they are placed in a hierarchical order. These four endogamous groups are:

- **(i)** *Jats* who are predominantly agriculturists occupy the highest position in status hierarchy.
- **(ii)** Trading castes come next.
- **(iii)** *Ram Garhias* who are artisans and clean occupation castes occupy a further lower rung.
- **(iv)** *Mazhabi* are the converts from the Hindu untouchable castes.

They practice endogamy, but hardly place any restrictions on commensality except in the case of the Mazhabis. The Mazhabis, in most of the cases, are Sikh Scheduled Castes and like other Dalit sections of the Indian society, have developed Dalit consciousness. The violence (June 2003) in village Talhan, Jalandhar which attracted national attention was the eruption of the simmering discontent among the Dalits of Punjab. When violence broke out in Talhan, politicians and the media woke up to what sociologists had been warning for long. Talhan's Dalits, 70% of the village population, wanted a stake in the management of the local gurudwara and it resulted in the Dalit–Jat Sikh clash which showed how religious institutions had defeated Sikhism's central tenet of a casteless society. A very significant fact to be understood is that caste in Punjab can perhaps be understood in the framework of 'agrarianism' rather than through the more popular notion of Brahminism. The Punjab Alienation of Land Act, 1901 clubbed the Dalits, including both Sikhs and Hindus, with non-agriculturist castes legally denying them access to land ownership. While the Act was scrapped after partition, its impact is still visible. The situation is now explosive in a state where the Jats have all the power and where the scheduled castes account for over 30% of the population – the highest ratio in the country. Thus, we find that casteism has claimed even Sikhism.

CASTE AMONG THE CHRISTIANS

Christians are the second largest community of non-Hindus after Muslims. The overwhelming majority of the Christian population in India comes from the lower Hindu castes, especially from the untouchable castes. Studies from Kerala and Tamil Nadu, states with substantial Christian population, show the element of caste in the local Christian society. While the converts from higher castes have been largely integrated in the main group of Syrian Christians, social distinctions between Palayas, converts from untouchable groups and Syrian Christians have been maintained. It has also been observed that Bengali Christians continue to use the surnames showing their pre-conversion castes about which they are very particular in social intercourse and marriage. Moreover, it has also been observed that in several churches in South India, the lower caste converts are segregated and given backbenches. Thus, even the egalitarian Christian ideology could not break the barriers of caste and caste consciousness.

Questions and Indicative Answers

1. Defining caste, give its main features.

- After analysing a couple of definitions, its main features are to be discussed;
- Membership determined by birth, thus it is a closed group;
- Ascribed status;
- Endogamy, rules of commensality, fixed occupations; and
- Lowly status, untouchability and other disabilities of lower castes.

2. Explain caste mobility.

- Contrary to the textual view, there has always been some scope of mobility in the caste system.
- Describe *Sanskritisation* as the best way to explain mobility in caste system.

3. Discuss transformation or changes in the caste system.

- Caste system has shown immense adaptability.
- Briefly explain the role of industrialisation and urbanisation, social and religious movements, Dalit and backward classes movement and the role of a state.

4. Discuss the role of caste in politics.

- Emergence of caste-based organisations and movements;
- Mobilisation along caste lines; and
- Rajni Kothari's description of 'politicisation of caste'.

5. Discuss the presence of caste or caste-like groups among non-Hindus.

- Though caste is predominantly a Hindu phenomenon and institution, it has strongly influenced non-Hindu communities too.
- The majority of the Muslim population comes from lower castes of the Hindus as they walked out of the oppressive and exploitative nature of the caste system. They changed their religion, but not caste and the occupation and that is why the Muslim population comes closest to have adopted the Hindu caste system.

6. What do you mean by untouchability? Discuss its bases.

- Describe the notion of ritual purity/impurity.
- Discuss the socio-economic disabilities of the untouchable castes.

Previous Years' Questions

1. What do you understand by dynamics of caste mobility? How did the concept of Sanskritization contribute to its functionality? **(UPSC CSE Mains Anthropology, Paper II, 2015)**
2. Louis Dumont's perspective on caste system **(UPSC CSE Mains Sociology, Paper II, 2015)**
3. Is caste system changing, weakening or disintegration in India? **(UPSC CSE Mains Sociology, Paper II, 2015)**
4. How far Srinivas's Sanskritization is modernizing force or traditionalizing force in understanding the changes in caste system? **(UPSC CSE Mains Sociology, Paper II, 2015)**
5. Different forms of Dalit assertion. **(UPSC CSE Mains Sociology, Paper II, 2016)**
6. Relevance of caste in contemporary Indian Politics. **(UPSC CSE Mains Anthropology, Paper II, 2016)**
7. Caste System is assuming new identities and associational forms. Hence, caste system can't be eradicated in India. Comment. **(GS Mains Paper I, 2018)**
8. Elaborate various forms of Dalit assertions in contemporary India **(UPSC CSE Mains Sociology, Paper II, 2018)**
9. Write a note on Ghurye's conception of caste in India. **(UPSC CSE Mains Sociology, Paper II, 2019)**
10. What is caste politics? Substantiate your answer with examples of how identities are defined by caste dynamics? **(UPSC CSE Mains Sociology, Paper II, 2019)**
11. Discuss the characteristics of caste system in India. **(UPSC CSE Mains Anthropology, Paper II, 2020)**
12. Write a short note on: Concept of Sanskritization **(UPSC CSE Mains Anthropology, Paper II, 2020)**
13. Caste system studies in India have been dominated by the 'book view' initially. How did the entry of 'field view' bring about a balance in the study of Indian caste system? Discuss. **(UPSC CSE Mains Sociology, Paper II, 2021)**
14. Caste like formations are present in non-Hindu religious communities as well. Discuss with examples. **(UPSC CSE Mains Sociology, Paper II, 2021)**
15. What are various forms of untouchability in India? Critically Examine. **(UPSC CSE Mains Sociology, Paper II, 2021)**
16. Explain the different forms of untouchability in India. **(UPSC CSE Mains Sociology, Paper II, 2022)**
17. Elaborate on the changing nature of caste system with suitable illustrations. **(UPSC CSE Mains Sociology, Paper II, 2022)**
18. Sanskritization is a culture bound concept. Critically comment to assess the strength and limitation of this concept. **(UPSC CSE Mains Anthropology, Paper II, 2023)**

19. Contextualize Louis Dumont's concept of 'binary opposition' with reference to caste in India.

(UPSC CSE Mains Sociology, Paper II, 2023)

20. Critically examine the concept of Sanskritization with suitable illustrations.

(UPSC CSE Mains Sociology, Paper II, 2023)

Focus Areas for the Examination

1. Untouchability
2. Caste Mobility and Sanskritization
3. Dominant Caste
4. Dumont's and Srinivas's view of Caste system
5. Caste among Non-Hindus

CHAPTER 6

Scheduled Castes and Other Backward Classes

Chapter Outline

1. Recognising the socio-historical reasons behind the creation of Scheduled Castes (SCs) and Other Backward Classes (OBCs)
2. Understanding the constitutional provisions such as Articles 15, 16, 17, 46, and others designed to uplift marginalised groups
3. Conceptual understanding of untouchability and ritual purity/pollution, socio-economic issues like landlessness, lack of education, forced labour, and chronic indebtedness
4. Insight into Governmental Measures like the Mandal Commission, Backward Classes Commission, and their recommendations for reservations and reforms
5. Exploring legislation such as the Protection of Civil Rights Act, 1955, and the Scheduled Castes and Scheduled Tribes (Prevention of Atrocities) Act, 1989
6. Analysing Constitutional Safeguards and Reservations in education, employment, and politics for SCs and OBCs
7. Understanding the concept of 'creamy layer' and its role in ensuring equitable access to benefits among OBCs
8. Comparing the nuances of the challenges faced by SCs and OBCs to understand how different communities are influenced by different religions and beliefs
9. Examining the effectiveness of land reforms, educational initiatives, and vocational training programs in uplifting these groups
10. Reflecting on ongoing issues such as discrimination, inadequate implementation of policies, and the persistence of atrocities

Both Scheduled Castes (SCs) and Other Backward Classes (OBCs) are constitutionally created categories and rooted in, and a by-product of, the caste system. If somebody wishes to situate these categories in the fourfold Varna system, one may conclude that in the Varna hierarchy, after *Brahmin*, *Kshatriya* and *Vaishya* comes the *Shudra* Varna which may be divided into two subcategories. The upper segment of the *Shudra* Varna consists of a multicity of artisans or clean occupation castes which may be considered as OBCs. The lower segment consists mainly of the victims of untouchability or untouchable castes, now may be described as Scheduled Castes.

SCHEDULED CASTES

Scheduled Castes are those castes which are scheduled under Article 341 of the Constitution. During the British times, similar caste groups were clubbed under 'Depressed Classes'. The term *Harijan* (children of Hari, God) was popularised by Mahatma Gandhi. However, in academic and political discourses, the term *Dalit* (oppressed) is more popular. Thus, the term scheduled caste is constitutionally and administratively created and not socially created.

Population and Distribution

The scheduled caste population constitutes around 18% of the total population of India. This population is divided into around 1000 castes distributed all over India with a number of names being synonymous. Some of these scheduled castes number several million members each. Some of the large scheduled castes are the Chamar (constituting about one-fourth of the total population of the scheduled castes), Bhangi, Adi-Dravida, Pasi, Madiga, Dusadh, Mali, Parayan, Koli/Kori, Mahar, Adi-Karnataka, Namasudra, etc. Each state has its own list of scheduled castes.

Following is the tabular description showing the position of the prominent states:

S.No.	State	Number of Scheduled Castes
1	Karnataka	95
2	Odisha	88
3	Rajasthan	76
4	Tamil Nadu	74
5	Madhya Pradesh	60
6	Maharashtra	60
7	Uttar Pradesh	60
8	West Bengal	60
9	Andhra Pradesh	60

If one goes through the demography of the scheduled caste population, one comes across some important and interesting facts. For example, almost half of the total number of scheduled caste population inhabits five states of the Hindi-speaking belt, namely Uttar Pradesh (23.5 million), Bihar (10 million), Madhya Pradesh (7.3 million), Rajasthan (5.8 million) and Haryana (2.5 million). Among the southern states, the population is concentrated mainly in Tamil Nadu (8.8 million) and Andhra Pradesh (7.9 million) and in the east in West Bengal (12 million). Interestingly, the highest ratio of the scheduled caste population in the total population is in Punjab (30%), closely followed by Himachal Pradesh (25%), West Bengal (22%), Uttar Pradesh (21%) and Haryana (19%). The bulk of the scheduled caste population (84%) live in rural areas as agricultural workers, share croppers and marginal farmers.

What Do You Think?

Imagine a talented student from a Scheduled Caste or Other Backward Class background, who excels academically but struggles to secure a job due to subtle biases during interviews. What steps can society, employers, and policymakers take to ensure such individuals are given equal opportunities to succeed?

▶▶ Socio-Economic Problems and Disabilities

Since the very creation of the scheduled castes is the product of highly discriminatory and sometimes inhuman nature of the functioning of the caste system, one cannot understand the problems being faced by the scheduled castes and suggest the remedial measures required without having a sound understanding of the caste system. The idea of ritual purity/pollution, manifested through untouchability, is the cornerstone of the highly discriminating nature of the caste system. An entire segment of the population was assigned 'unclean' occupations like scavenging, flaying, tanning, etc. and converted into untouchables. To be untouchable did not mean only that his physical touch was to be shunned or avoided due to ritual reasons, it was to enter a fatal and futile universe totally impervious to hope and total denial of education. One problem led to the other and one social disability created another. For example, if a section of the society is barred from entering a sacred place like temple and in the traditional set-up if formal education is imparted within the temple/*math* premises, this section of society shall definitely be deprived of education supplemented by the force of custom. If a section of the society is forbidden to own land by force of custom, it will be without any economic backbone. Moreover, in an **agrarian society** where all powers emanate from the ownership of land, landlessness forms a vicious cycle of deprivation. If a section of society is prohibited from touching/owning gold, it cannot ward off an economic crisis by mortgaging or disposing off a gold ornament; it will be clearly vulnerable to all sorts of exploitation. To top it all, because of reasons of ritual pollution, it may not be getting the services of a washerman, barber, priest, etc.

Quick Fact

Agrarian Society

It is a community, where the economy is based on producing and maintaining crops and farmland.

Among the main socio-economic disabilities, the bulk of the scheduled caste population has been suffering from (i) lack of freedom to choose occupation; (ii) landlessness; (iii) forced labour; (iv) lack of access to education; (v) segregated housing; and (vi) lack of freedom to exercise political rights. Obviously, the mother of all these is the enforced notion of ritual purity/ritual pollution, the resultant obnoxious practice of untouchability and the perpetuation of all these by a highly discriminatory social system. The main socio-economic problems afflicting the bulk of the scheduled caste populations are:

(i) chronic indebtedness, landlessness/land alienation, lack of other productive assets such as cattle, etc.;
(ii) lack of education;
(iii) forced labour, bonded labour and prostitution;
(iv) lack of 'minimum wages'; and
(v) child labour, etc.

Because of the traditional landlessness, chronic indebtedness has been a concomitant problem with the scheduled castes. Many of those who got some land after independence as a result of *Zamindari* abolition and the ensuing land reforms had to part with the land as a result of land alienation. Whether landless or marginal farmers, the lot of an average scheduled caste person in the rural areas has been pitiable because his existence is characterised by all sorts of deprivations and exploitation. Education takes a back seat in such a scenario. Obviously, when children play an important role in the family economy, sending them to school means depriving oneself of their contribution.

In such a situation, opening schools and providing free education may not bear any fruit because of lack of takers of such amenities. Wherever feudal tendencies persist and agricultural workers are not organised (as in the case throughout the country), forced labour *(begaar)* or very low wages has been a normal phenomenon. Because of a number of factors, the *Jajmani* system, even in rural areas, has been crumbling during the last four decades. It has made important bearing on inter-caste relations and caste equations in rural India.

The adoption of laws meant to protect the rights of the scheduled castes, the realisation of socio-economic measures in their interests and the atmosphere of support to the just and lawful demands of the scheduled castes that was created as a result of the work done by some government bodies, democratic and left organisations and the progressive press has led to further activisation of both socio-economic and political life of the scheduled castes.

▶▶ Constitutional Safeguards

When our founding fathers sat down to frame the Constitution for free India, they took care to see that the protection and safeguards for the Scheduled Castes, especially or by way of general rights of citizens, was totally ensured with the object of promotion of their educational and economic interests and of removing their social disabilities. The important articles in the constitution which are intended to protect and promote the interests of the scheduled castes are as follows:

1. Article 15(4) says that nothing in this Article or in clause (2) of Article 29 shall prevent the state from making any special provision for the advancement of any Socially and Educationally Backward Classes (SEBCs) of citizens or for the scheduled castes and scheduled tribes.

What Do You Think?

1. How should constitutional safeguards balance individual rights with collective societal needs (e.g., public health, national security)?
2. Can constitutional safeguards address global issues such as climate change, migration, and pandemics that transcend national boundaries?

2. Article 16(4) states that nothing in this Article shall prevent the state from making any provision for the reservation of appointment or posts in favour of any backward class of citizens which, in the opinion of the state, is not adequately represented in the services under the state.
3. Abolition of untouchability and forbidding of its practice, in any form, is the basis of Article 17 of the Constitution. (It is being dealt with separately in this chapter because of its implications of far-reaching importance).
4. Article 25b deals with throwing open, by law, of Hindu religious institutions of public character to all classes and sections of Hindus.
5. Article 15(2) deals with removal of any disability, liability, restriction or condition with regard to access to shops, public restaurants, hotels and places of public entertainment or use of wells, tanks, bathing *ghats*, roads and places of public resort maintained wholly or partially out of state funds or dedicated to the use of general public.

6. Forbidding or any denial of admission to educational institutions maintained by the state or receiving grant out of state funds – Article 29(2).
7. Article 46 states that the state shall promote with special care the educational and economic interests of the weaker sections of the people and in particular, of the scheduled castes and scheduled tribes and shall protect them from social injustice and all forms of exploitation.
8. Under Articles 330 and 332, seats are reserved in Parliament and state legislative assemblies for the scheduled castes except in the tribal areas of Assam, Nagaland, Meghalaya, Arunachal Pradesh and Mizoram.
9. Under Article 338, a special officer (designated as Commissioner for Scheduled Castes and Scheduled Tribes) is to be appointed to investigate all matters, relating to safeguards provided under the constitution and report to the President upon the working of those safeguards. With the 65th amendment of the Constitution Article 338 stands amended and from 1992 the special officer's post has been substituted by the National Commission for Scheduled Castes and Scheduled Tribes.
10. Article 341 empowers the President to declare a caste, race or tribe as Scheduled Caste.

▶▶ Legislation Against Untouchability and Protection of Civil Rights

For enlarging the scope and making the penal provisions more stringent, the Untouchability (offences) Act, 1955 had been comprehensively amended by the Untouchability (offences) Amendment and Miscellaneous Provision Act, 1976, which came into force from 19 November 1976. With this amendment, the Principal Act has been renamed as **Protection of Civil Rights Act, 1955**. The Act provides for penalties for preventing any person on the grounds of untouchability from enjoying the rights accruing on account of abolition of untouchability. Enhanced penalties/punishments have been provided for subsequent offences.

Under the provision of Section 8 of the Representation of Peoples Act, 1951, a person who is convicted of an offence under the Act is disqualified from contesting elections to Parliament and State Legislatures for a period of 6 years commencing from the date of such conviction.

The PCR Act, 1955, is administered by the State Government. Under the provision of Section 15A (4) of the Act, the Government also places every year, before each House of Parliament, an annual report on the working of the provisions of Section 15A of the Act.

▶▶ Measures to Check Atrocities Against Scheduled Castes

With a view to effectively deal with crimes against Scheduled Castes and Scheduled Tribes and to tone up administrative machinery to tackle this vital issue, comprehensive guidelines containing precautionary, preventive, punitive and rehabilitative measures exist, which States/UTs have to follow. Still these communities continue to be vulnerable and atrocities are committed against them in one form or the other. In order that Scheduled Castes and Scheduled Tribes are fully protected from atrocities, the Government of India enacted the Scheduled Castes and the Scheduled Tribes (Prevention of Atrocities) Act, 1989. The Act came into force from 30 January 1990. It specified the offences which are considered as 'atrocities' and provides for different punishments for commission of the same. The Act also envisages preventive measures and states have to evolve schemes, among other things, for economic and social rehabilitation of such victims.

OTHER BACKWARD CLASSES

The Constitution of India recognises three categories of backward segments of Indian society, i.e. SC, ST and OBCs. The categorisation of the first two has been fairly clear from the beginning. The third segment, that is, the OBCs, carried lots of ambiguity. But, it was generally assumed that this category of OBCs was meant to include the whole of middle bands of castes and communities situated above the Scheduled Castes and lower than the Brahmins, *Kshatriya* and Vaishya castes. In simpler and popular terms, all such castes that are considered lower in the caste hierarchy, but are not considered 'untouchable' may be included under the OBCs. These are mostly 'clean' occupational castes such as weaver, barber, goldsmith, blacksmith, etc. Traditionally, they did not exercise control over sources of power – political, social and economic. The Scheduled Castes and Scheduled Tribes are clearly listed in the constitution. The non-*dwija*, non-scheduled castes not listed in the constitutional order are the OBCs. They comprise a little over 3700 castes in all.

The framers of the constitution, instead of using the term 'Castes', applied the term 'Classes' for this segment of backward population. There may be several reasons for this. First, they followed the old historical process (whereby the term 'depressed classes' was used even for the untouchable castes, now scheduled castes). Secondly, the word 'Caste' sounded obscurantist and outdated and the torchbearers of modern India wanted to banish this word from the new and modern India. And thirdly, the usage might have created problems vis-à-vis the placement of the non-Hindu counterparts of other communities which, despite embracing the **egalitarian ideology** of Islam, Christianity and Sikhism, had also developed caste-like stratification under the social impact of the Hindu society.

Quick Fact

Egalitarian Ideology

Egalitarian ideology is a philosophical perspective that emphasizes equality and equal treatment across gender, religion, and social-economic status

The non-*dwija* intermediate castes or lower castes other than scheduled castes have also been victims of the caste system. Most of these have been small peasants or artisans. They also come under the category of disadvantaged groups suffering in poverty. For the peasant segment of OBCs, agriculture is the chief means of economy. But, they have little land except for castes like Yadavas and Kurmis in parts of Uttar Pradesh and Bihar and such other castes in different parts of the country. Quite a substantial number of OBCs in different parts of the country have no land at all. The second category of OBCs includes mainly artisans and their plight is really miserable. Because of growing industrialisation, their traditional skills and crafts are in ruined state. The socio-economic condition of weavers, potters, carpenters, fishermen/boatmen, blacksmiths, vegetable vendors, butchers and a host of other castes in village India is there for all to see. Educational deprivation has worsened the situation further. The organised industrial sector enjoys subsidised credit, infrastructural support and other advantages at the cost of the taxpayer; the handicrafts and artisans hardly get all these benefits. The net result of this state of affairs is that they are always trapped in the vicious cycle of poverty and deprivation. As a number of surveys and studies in different parts of the country indicate, OBCs have little access to employment and education, enjoy low rates of literacy and are trapped in indebtedness. The high incidence of indebtedness is attributed to illiteracy, poverty, social customs, etc.

In order to help the OBCs come up in socio-economic development, the first Backward Classes Commission was set up by a Presidential Order under Article 340 of the Constitution of India on 29 January 1953 under the chairmanship of Kakasaheb Kalelkar. It submitted its report on 30 March 1955. After sorting out the facts, the commission formulated the following criteria for identifying SEBCs:

(i) low social position in the traditional caste hierarchy of Hindu society;
(ii) lack of general educational advancement among the major sections of a caste or community;
(iii) inadequate or no representation in Government services; and
(iv) inadequate representation in the field of trade, commerce and industry.

The commission could not present a unanimous report. The majority of members including the chairman were opposed to the view of linking caste with backwardness. They were also opposed to the reservation of posts on the basis of caste. While rejecting the main recommendations of this commission, the central government ultimately took a decision that no all-India list of backward classes should be drawn up, nor any reservation made in the central government service for any group of backward classes other than scheduled castes and scheduled tribes. However, the central government informed the state governments that they were free to draw their respective lists of backward classes on the basis of criteria worked out by them and take whatever further action they deemed necessary in the matter. Consequently, a number of state governments set up their own commissions or committees for defining criteria for backwardness and recommending measures for its removal. So far, 18 states and union territories have set up commissions and have notified lists of OBCs for the grant of various educational, employment and other benefits. These are Andhra Pradesh, Bihar, Gujarat, Jammu & Kashmir, Karnataka, Kerala, Maharashtra, Punjab, Uttar Pradesh, Tamil Nadu, Assam, Delhi, Haryana, Himachal Pradesh, Meghalaya, Odisha, Puducherry and Rajasthan.

The new commission, the Second Backward Classes Commission, is popularly called the Mandal Commission. Its chairman B.P. Mandal was appointed by a Presidential order under Article 340 of the Indian Constitution on 20 December 1978. It was required:

(i) to determine the criteria for identifying the SEBCs;
(ii) to recommend steps to be taken for the advancement of the SEBCs of citizens so identified;
(iii) to examine the desirability or otherwise of making provision for reservation in appointments or posts in favour of such backward classes of citizens which are not adequately represented in public services and posts in connection with the affairs of the Union or of any State; and
(iv) to present to the President a report setting out the facts as found by them and making such recommendations as they think proper.

The commission was required to submit its report by 31 December 1980. In view of the enormity of its task and paucity of time at its disposal, the commission worked with speed. To begin with, it conducted a countrywide socio-educational survey, covering 405 districts, with the help of the Bureau of Economics and Statistics of various states. The data gathered from the survey were computerised and 31 primary tables were generated from these data in respect of each State and Union Territory. Then, on the basis of these tables, 11 indicators or criteria for social and educational backwardness were derived under three heads – social, educational and economic. These are as follows:

▶▶ A. Social

(i) Castes/classes considered as socially backward by others;
(ii) Castes/classes which mainly depend on manual labour for their livelihood;
(iii) Castes/classes where at least 25% females and 10% males above the state average get married at an age below 17 years in rural areas and at least 10% females and 5% males do so in urban areas; and
(iv) Castes/classes where participation of females in work is at least 25% above the state average.

▶▶ B. Educational

(i) Castes/classes where the number of children in the age group of 5–15 years who never attended school is at least 25% above the state average;
(ii) Castes/classes where the rate of student drop-out in the age group of 5–15 years is at least 25% above the state average; and
(iii) Castes/classes amongst which the proportion of matriculates is at least 25% below the state average.

▶▶ C. Economic

(i) Castes/classes where the average value of family assets is at least 25% below the state average;
(ii) Castes/classes where the number of families living in *kuccha* houses is at least 25% above the state average;
(iii) Castes/classes where the source of drinking water is beyond half a kilometre for more than 50% of the households; and
(iv) Castes/classes where the number of households having taken consumption loan is at least 25% above the state average.

Thus, the Commission identified 3743 castes as backward. After this, the commission computed the strength of the OBCs which was little over 52% of the total population of the country.

A Research Planning Team was also constituted to help the commission in the identification of the deserving backward castes. This team, consisting of some top sociologists and anthropologists of the country, in order to gauge social–educational backwardness of the castes in the present times, suggested a number of ways and means and used existing studies/literature. It also emphasised upon the importance of trends of upward mobility of a number of traditionally backward castes before reaching any firm conclusions. The team further suggested that while designing empirical studies, the extent of prevalence of the following variables may be taken into account:

(a) socio-ritual services extended by other ethnic groups;
(b) 'low' status of occupations of the category concerned;

(c) 'low' self-evaluation compared to other ethnic groups in the region (Gram Panchayat/Block Taluqa);
(d) literacy rates in relation to other neighbouring groups in Gram Panchayat/Block Taluqa;
(e) occupations requiring investment of child labour (up to 15 years);
(f) economic levels of castes and communities; and
(g) representation in public or private sector services or in profession.

When the Mandal Commission submitted its report containing a number of recommendations of far-reaching importance, some of these social scientists disowned the findings and recommendations on the ground that the criteria, modus operandi and variables suggested by them were not employed by the commission while finalising the findings and recommendations.

Undertaking this massive exercise, the Commission came out with a number of recommendations, of which some were found most important for upliftment of the socio-economic conditions of the OBCs:

(i) The OBCs are not properly represented in public services and hence they should be accommodated through reservations.

(ii) There is a legal obligation to keep the reservations, under Articles 15(4) and 16(4) of the constitution, below 50% so the reservation should be 27%.

(iii) Special educational facilities designed at upgrading the cultural environment of the OBC students should be created in a phased manner in selected areas containing high concentrations of OBCs.

(iv) Special emphasis should be placed on vocational training of students belonging to the OBCs. Separate coaching facilities should be provided in technical and professional institutions to enable them to catch up with students from open quota.

(v) Special programmes for upgrading the skills of village artisans should be prepared and subsidised loans from financial institutions granted to them for setting up small-scale industries.

(vi) To promote the participation of OBCs in the industrial and business life of the country, all state governments should create a separate network of financial and technical institutions.

(vii) Under the existing scheme of production relations, backward classes comprising mainly small landholders, tenants, agricultural labour, village artisans, etc. are heavily dependent on the rich peasantry for their sustenance. In view of this, OBCs continue to remain in mental and material bondage of the dominant castes and classes. Unless these production relations are radically altered through structural changes and progressive land reforms implemented rigorously all over the country, OBCs will never become truly independent. In view of this, highest priority should be given to radical land reforms by all the states.

Through the Memorandum of Action, vide its circular issued on 13 August 1990, the Government of India accepted the recommendations of the Mandal Commission. This was followed by violent and sustained movements by different sections of the Indian society against the acceptance of the Mandal Commission Report by the Government of India. Writs were filed in different courts and after prolonged hearings the Supreme Court of India decided in favour of the recommendations and held these constitutionally valid excluding the so-called 'creamy layer' of the SEBCs. In pursuance of the Supreme Court verdict, an expert committee under the chairmanship of Justice R.N. Prasad, former judge, Patna High Court was set up for specifying the criteria for identification of Socially Advanced Persons among the SEBCs. This expert committee submitted its report on 10 March 1993. The Government of India accepted the criteria formulated by this expert committee and announced a reservation of 27% of the vacancies in Civil Posts and Services in the Government of India for SEBCs subject to the exclusion of the socially advanced persons/sections known as the 'creamy layer'. Thus, reservation was applied to all vacancies for which recruitment commenced from 8 September 1993.

▶▶ Creamy Layer

The rule of exclusion of 'creamy layer' is applicable to the son(s) and daughter(s) of:

- persons holding constitutional positions;
- parents either of whom is a Class 1 Officer;
- parents both of whom are Class 2 Officers;
- parents either or both of whom is or are in the rank of colonel and above in the Army or hold equivalent positions in the navy, air force and the paramilitary forces;
- families owning irrigated land which is equal to or more than 85% of the ceiling in terms of irrigated area as laid down by the State Land Ceiling Laws; and
- persons having gross annual income of ₹1 lakh or above or possessing wealth above the exemption limit as prescribed in the Wealth Tax Act for a period of three consecutive years (this limit is revised from time to time on the basis of mainly inflation and rising cost of living).

Income from salaries and agricultural land shall not be clubbed. The benefit of reservation is extended, in the first phase, to the castes and communities which are common to the lists of the Mandal Commission Report as well as the State Government's lists.

▶▶ OBCs among Non-Hindu Communities

Since the caste system with all its concomitants has been replicated by Muslims, Sikhs, Christians and Buddhists, their backward sections have also been included in the list of OBCs in Mandal Commission. After giving a good deal of thought to the obvious problems of categorisation, the commission has evolved the following and ready criteria for identifying non-Hindu OBCs:

(i) all untouchables converted to any non-Hindu religion;

(ii) such occupational communities which are known by the name of their traditional hereditary occupation and whose Hindu counterparts have been included in the list of Hindu OBCs.

Example: Dhobi (washerman), Teli (oil seed tillers), Dheemal, Nai (barber), Gujar, Kumhar (potter), Lohar (blacksmith), Darzi (tailor), Badhai (carpenter), etc.

What Do You Think?

India, being one of the most populous country, faces intense competition for government jobs, further complicated due to the existing quota system. Is/Isn't it better to discontinue the reservation benefits once one generation of the family utilises the same?

Questions and Indicative Answers

1. Why certain castes have been put under the category of scheduled caste?

- Because of the discriminatory and oppressive nature of the caste system, a number of castes were transformed into untouchables.
- Untouchability and sometime unseeability too created certain socio-economic disabilities for such people.
- Because of these restrictions and disabilities, the whole segment of people lagged behind in every respect and hence the founding fathers of the constitution made a provision under Article 341 to protect and promote such people.

2. What are the socio-economic problems and disabilities the Scheduled Castes have been suffering from?

- Mother of all disabilities is untouchability;
- Lack of freedom to choose occupation;
- Landlessness under the force of custom. In agrarian Indian society, all types of power emanate from land ownership and to be landless under these conditions means powerlessness;
- Forced labour without any renumuneration;
- Lack of productive assets such as land, cattle, etc. led to chronic indebtedness and debt bondage; and
- Lack of education because children have to work and contribute to family economy.

3. Who are the OBCs? Trace the constitutional and administrative history of OBCs.

- Constitution recognises three categories of backward segments of Indian population – SC, ST and OBCs. The first two are clearly identified, but there was ambiguity with regard to the third.
- Kalelkar Commission was appointed in 1953 under Article 340 to identify these categories of people and make recommendations accordingly.
- Low social position in the traditional caste hierarchy of Indian society, but not untouchables was the crux of indicator for identifying OBCs.
- There was no unanimity over the proposed remedial measures.

- Later the states were told to constitute state-level backward classes commissions and do the needful.
- The second national backward classes commission popularly known as Mandal Commission, was appointed by a presidential order under Article 340 in 1978. It submitted its report in 1980 and when it was accepted, for the first time reservation was decided for OBCs in central services.
- The recommendations of the Mandal Commission were challenged in the Supreme Court for its constitutional validity. It was upheld by the Supreme Court with the rider of excluding the 'creamy layer' of the OBCs.

4. Do some non-Hindu communities also come under OBCs? If yes, what are the criteria for their inclusion under this category?

- The non-Hindu communities too have adopted caste-like social system and thus have socially backward segments among them.
- It would have been unjust not to have included them under OBC category, so that they too could enjoy the benefits given to Hindu OBCs.
- Thus, castes or caste-like groups from among Muslims, Sikhs, Christians and Buddhists were included.
- The criteria for identifying non-Hindu OBCs are:
  1. All untouchable groups who converted to non-Hindu religions.
  2. Such occupational communities, which are known by the name of their traditional hereditary occupation and whose Hindu counterparts are included in the list of Hindu OBC list – such as Teli (oil seed tillers), Nai (barbers), Kumhar (potters), Lohar (blacksmiths), Qasai/Chikwa (butchers), Darzi (tailors), Julaha (weavers), Badhai (carpenters), etc.

Previous Years' Questions

1. Examine the factors responsible for the exploitation of scheduled castes in India.

(UPSC CSE Mains Anthropology, Paper II, 2016)

2. Critically discuss the constitutional safeguards for scheduled castes.

(UPSC CSE Mains Anthropology, Paper II, 2017)

3. Write a short note on: Other Backward Classes

(UPSC CSE Mains Anthropology, Paper II, 2017)

4. How are other backward classes identified? Enumerating the important features, elucidate the recent changes in their social and economic life.

(UPSC CSE Mains Anthropology, Paper II, 2023)

Focus Areas for the Examination

1. Socio-economic Disabilities of Scheduled Castes
2. Constitutional Provisions for SCs and STs
3. Creamy Layer
4. Legislation against Untouchability and protection of civil rights

CHAPTER 7

Scheduled Tribes

Chapter Outline

1. Understanding the concept of tribe and the various criteria used to identify tribal communities
2. The socio-cultural and economic characteristics of Scheduled Tribes in India
3. Recognising the historical and colonial influences on the categorisation and treatment of tribal groups
4. Identifying key legislative acts and policies affecting Scheduled Tribes, including the Indian Forest Act and the Forest Rights Act
5. Exploring the geographic distribution and classification of tribes across different regions of India
6. Analysing the impact of socio-economic changes on tribal livelihoods, including the shift from traditional practices to modern occupations
7. Examining the role of acculturation, assimilation, and integration in the evolution of tribal communities
8. Understanding the significance of forest policies in shaping the relationship between tribal communities and natural resources
9. Problems faced by Scheduled Tribes, such as land alienation, displacement, and lack of access to basic amenities
10. Tribal movements, their causes, and their impact on social and political dynamics in India

What is a tribe? What exactly are the criteria for considering a human group a tribe? What are the indices of tribal life?

Interestingly, but sadly, anthropologists, sociologists, social workers, administrators and such people who have been involved with tribes and their problems either on a theoretical plane or on practical grounds are still not on the same wavelength regarding the concept and definition of their subject matter, but that does not mean that we are in the dark and groping for understanding. The term 'tribe' is a British colonial construct and the popular term has been *Adivasi* (oldest inhabitants). Among multiple definitions, in the Indian context, the following definition is most acceptable:

> A tribe is a social group with territorial affiliation, endogamous, with no specialization of functions, ruled by the tribal officers, united in language or dialect, recognising social distance with other tribes or castes.
>
> —D.N. Majumdar[1]

[1] D N Majumdar & T N Madan, An Introduction To Social Anthropology, Asia Publishing House, Bombay, 1961

T.B. Naik goes on to present viable indicators for a tribe which are as follows:

1. A tribe to be a 'tribe' should have the least functional interdependence within the community (the Hindu caste system is an example of high interdependence).
2. It should be economically backward which means:
   - (i) the full import of monetary economics should not be understood by its members;
   - (ii) primitive means of exploiting natural resources should be used;
   - (iii) the tribe's economy should be at an underdeveloped stage; and
   - (iv) it should have multifarious economic pursuits.
3. There should be a comparative geographic isolation of its people from others.
4. Culturally, members of a tribe should have a common dialect, which may be subject to regional variations.
5. A tribe should be politically organised and its community Panchayat should be an influential institution.
6. A tribe's members should have the least desire to change. They should have a sort of psychological conservatism making them stick to their old customs.
7. A tribe should have customary laws and its members might have to suffer in a law court because of these laws.

It would be more realistic to consider 'Tribe' as a stage in the techno-economic evolution and their affinities with the centres of modern civilisation. Those who go beyond this stage cease to be 'Tribe' though they may be maintaining some of their socio-cultural characteristics and continue to enjoy Scheduled Tribe (ST) status.

Under the Indian Constitution any tribal group which is scheduled under Article 342 by the President of India becomes an ST. Presently there are more than 400 STs and several others are waiting/demanding to be scheduled.

Arthur Wilke, *et al* (1979) puts the problem in proper perspective by stating that for years ambiguity has stalked India's official portrait of tribal people. From 1917 through the 1931 Census, for instance, the nomenclature referring to tribes under-went successive modifications, involving primarily changes in descriptive adjectives such as 'aboriginal' or 'depressed classes'. By the 1941 Census, these qualifying adjectives were dropped, a practice continued after independence with the adoption of the notion of scheduled tribes or as they are commonly called, *Adivasi*. Such standardisation did not, however, remove all ambiguity.

No Doubt with the passage of time, the differences on the concept and definition of a tribe have certainly narrowed down to an appreciable extent, but a theoretical discussion seems imperative to understand this problem in its proper perspective.

Most of the above mentioned definitions present a static definition of tribe. B.K. Roy Burman (1994) presents a refreshingly new idea of defining and identifying 'tribe'. He is of the view that a tribe should be understood in in terms of a stage in the techno-economic-cultural evolution and relationship of man with nature. Once a group of people goes beyond this stage, it ceases to be a 'tribe' though it may continue to retain its ethnic or 'tribal' identity. Even this approach may be debatable because those who wish to identify or define tribe in these terms may be accused of imposing their model of techno-economic development.

Interestingly there has been no unanimity among the scholars-anthropologists, sociologists, social workers or administrators in achieving a universally acceptable definition of Tribe yet it is also true that with the passage of time differences on the concept and definition of 'tribe' has narrowed down. In various types of literature usage of terms such as *Adivasi, Adimjati, Aboriginal groups, Natives, Girijan, Primitive, Indigenous* in various types of literature point towards the same people. In this discussion *Adivasi* and Scheduled Tribe (ST) shall be used interchangeably.

In the constitution of India no criteria have been spelt out for the specification of a community as 'Scheduled Tribe'. However, taking into account the definitions in the 1931 Census and the Report of the First Backward Classes Commission (Kalelkar Commission, 1955), the Advisory Committee on the Revision of SC/ST Lists (Lokur Committee) 1965, and the Joint Committee of Parliament on the SCs and STs Orders (Amendment) Bill, 1967, (Chanda Committee) 1969, the following criteria are followed for specification of a community as a Scheduled Tribe:

- Indications of primitive traits
- Distinctive culture
- Geographical isolation
- Shyness of contact with the community at large
- Backwardness

The Commission has further elaborated these characteristic features for scrutinising the claim of any community applying for ST status.

Commenting on the scholarship on the STs in India Nandini Sundar (2016) writes that "it must be seen against the background of two separate contexts: changing political and administrative concerns in India; as well as changing trends in scholarship internationally". Further, most of the scholars are of the view that 'tribe' is a colonial construct. The concept of tribe has been a colonial legacy as most of the literature on tribal studies was a product of the scholars having colonial outlook. Commenting on this issue Meena Radhakrishnan (2016) says that "while use of the word 'tribe' may denote deep imperial prejudice, 'adivasi' (literally *adi* 'earliest' plus *vasi* 'inhabitants') has come to embody protest and assertion." Most of the scholars agree that conceptualization of 'tribe' in the Indian context is a complex issue largely because of its affinity and overlapping with caste and peasantry and hence defining tribe is even more complex. Andre Beitelle (1995) is of the view that the construction of the category of tribe in independent India is more a political than a social fact. Considering *adivasi* as a better and more meaningful word Xaxa (1999) argues that the problems inherent in the use of the term 'tribe' can be addressed to some extent by the term indigenous (or adivasi). However, he also points out to the problems inherent in this term.

SOME BASIC FACTS TO REMEMBER

- The STs constitute about 8% of the total population of India, second only to Africa in terms of absolute number.
- They are distributed all over India and recognised as such in most of the states and union territories.
- STs are in majority in four states, viz. Meghalaya, Mizoram, Nagaland and Arunachal Pradesh and in two union territories, Lakshadweep and Dadra & Nagar Haveli.
- More than 50% of their population inhabit the central zone consisting of Madhya Pradesh-Chhattisgarh, Bihar-Jharkhand and parts of Maharashtra and Gujarat.
- Some of the large tribes are Bhil and Gond (7.9 million each), Santhal, Munda, Oraon, etc., all inhabiting the central zone. On the contrary, the smallest tribes are those living in Andaman & Nicobar Islands, the Great Andamanese being the smallest consisting of merely 32 souls.
- The Government of India has put 75 tribes under the category of Vulnerable Tribal Groups (earlier known as Primitive Tribal Groups) who are relatively small tribes living at the food gathering-hunting stage of technological evolution for special treatment.
- More than 80% of the tribal population earns its livelihood in the agricultural sector either as peasants or as agricultural labour while among the remaining some are pastoralists (cattle herders), some earn through industrial labour, etc.
- Tribal India exhibits a great cultural heterogeneity speaking different languages/dialects and professing different religious beliefs – a small number has embraced Christianity (mainly from the north-eastern region), in very small numbers Islam and Buddhism while the overwhelming majority have their own religious systems, but passing through various stages of Hinduisation as a result of cultural contact.
- Most of the tribal areas are rich in natural resources – forests, minerals, water, but the inhabitants are steeped in poverty.
- More than 90% of their population is now covered by radio and more than 60% by TV.
- Literacy has also been rising fast among the STs and as per the 2011 census, 59% of the ST population has achieved literacy and children in increasing numbers are going to schools.
- Like other disadvantaged sections, an elite segment has emerged among the STs too consisting of doctors, engineers, bureaucrats/administrators, political leaders, etc.

GEOGRAPHICAL SPREAD AND CLASSIFICATION

Looking at the physical map of India and the distribution of tribal population, we find that both geography as well as tribal demography permit a regional grouping and a zonal classification. B.S. Guha has classified Indian tribes into three zones:

(i) The north and north-eastern zone;
(ii) The central or the middle zone; and
(iii) The southern zone.

▶▶ (i) The North and North-Eastern Zone

The northern and north-eastern zone consists of the sub-Himalayan region and the mountain valleys of the eastern frontiers of India. The tribal people of Assam, Manipur and Tripura may be included in the eastern part of this geographical zone while in the northern part are included the tribal communities of eastern Kashmir, eastern Punjab, Himachal Pradesh and northern Uttar Pradesh.

Some of the important tribes living between Assam and Tibet are **Aka, Dafla, Miri, Gurung** and the **Apatani** on the west of the Subansiri River. The **Mishmi** tribes live in the high ranges between the Debong and Lohit rivers. Further east is found the **Khamti** and the **Singpho** and beyond them are the different Naga tribes. South of the Naga Hills running through the states of Manipur, Tripura and the Chittagong hill tracts live the **Kuki,** the **Lushai,** the **Khasi** and the **Garo** (now the inhabitants of the Meghalaya state). In the sub-Himalayan region of Sikkim and the northern portions of Darjeeling, there are a number of tribes, **Lepcha** being the best known of them. The Himalayan region of Uttar Pradesh (now in Uttarakhand) also contains some important tribes **like Tharu, Bhoksa, Jounsari (Khasa), Bhotia, Raji,** etc.

The entire geographical zone, though quite large in area, does not contain dense population. As a result of geographical similarities, most of the tribes of this zone are engaged in either terrace cultivation or Jhum (shifting) cultivation and are steeped in poverty and economic backwardness.

▶▶ (ii) The Central or the Middle Zone

This zone consists of plateaus and mountainous belt between the Indo-Gangetic plain to the north and roughly the Krishna River to the south and this is separated from the north-eastern zone by the gap between the Garo hills and the Rajmahal hills. In this zone, we have another mass of tribal peoples in Madhya Pradesh-Chattisgarh with extensions in Uttar Pradesh, Madhya Bharat, Southern Rajasthan, Northern Maharashtra, Bihar-Jharkhand and Odisha. Northern Rajasthan, Southern Maharashtra and Bastar form the peripheral areas of the zone. The important tribes inhabiting this zone are the **Savara, Gadaba** and **Borido** of the Ganjam district; the **Juang, Kharia, Khond, Bhumij** and the **Bhiya** of the Odisha hills. In the plateau of Chotanagpur live **Munda, Santhal, Oraon, Ho** and **Birhor**. Further west along Vindhya ranges live the **Katkari, Kol** and the **Bhil**; the Gond forms the largest group and occupy what is known as the 'Gondwana land'. On both sides of the Satpuras and around the Maikal hills are found similar tribes like **Koraku, Agaria, Pardhan** and **Baiga**. In the hills of Bastar live some of the most colourful of these tribes like **Muria, the Hill Muriya** of the Abhujmar hills and **Bison-horn Maria** of the Indravati valley. Most of the tribes of this zone used to practice shifting cultivation as means of their livelihood, but the **Oraon, Santhal, Munda and Gond** have learnt plough cultivation as a result of their cultural contact with neighbouring rural populations.

▶▶ (iii) The Southern Zone

This zone consists of that part of southern India which falls south of the river Krishna stretching from Wynad to Cape Cameron, Andhra Pradesh, Karnataka, Coorg, Travancore, Cochin, Tamil Nadu, etc. Beginning from the north-east of this zone, the **Chenchu** occupy the area of the Nallamala Hills across the Krishna and into the erstwhile Hyderabad state. Along the Western Ghats from the **Loraga** of South Kanara, the **Yeruva** and the **Toda** live on the lower slopes of Coorg hills while the

Irula, Paniyan and the **Kurumba** inhabit Wynaad area. The most primitive of Indian aboriginals such as **Kadar, Kanikkar, Malvadan, Malakuravan,** etc. inhabit the dense forests along the ranges of Cochin and Travancore. They are also included among some of the most economically backward communities of the world. Except **Toda, Badaga** and **Kota** who live in Nilgiri Hills, most of the tribal groups of this zone depend upon hunting and fishing for food gathering.

Although Guha did not include the inhabitants of Andaman and Nicobar Islands in any of these zones and had skipped their description, these tribal people may be said to constitute a fourth zone. The main tribes living in this zone are the Jarwa, Onge, North Sentinelese, Andamanese, Shompen and Nicobari. Though separated from the main body of India's primitive tribes, they are ethnically close to the South Indian tribes.

TRIBAL ECONOMY

The classical classification of Adam Smith and the more recent classifications of Thurnwald and Herskovits have been applied throughout the world in classifying tribes on the basis of their economic life. The scheme presented by Thurnwald is taken as most acceptable in the Indian context and is as follows:

1. **Homogeneous communities of men as hunters and trappers, women as collectors** – the Kadar, the Chenchu, the Kharia and the Korwa are some of the Indian tribes falling into this category.
2. **Homogeneous communities of hunters, trappers and agriculturists** – the Kamar, the Baiga and the Birhor are examples of this type from tribal India.
3. **Graded society of hunters, trappers, agriculturists and artisans** – most of the Indian tribes fall under this category. The Chero and the Agaria, among so many others, are famous artisans.
4. **The herdsmen** – the Toda and some sections of the great Bhil tribe furnish classic examples in India.
5. **Homogeneous hunters and herdsmen** – this category is not represented among Indian tribes. The Todas do not hunt, nor do they catch fish or birds.
6. **Ethnically stratified cattle breeders and traders** – the Bhotias of the sub-Himalayan region of Uttar Pradesh (now under Uttarakhand) breed yaks and are itinerant traders.
7. **Socially graded herdsmen with hunting, agricultural and artisan population.**

Majumdar opines that such a classification, though useful, does not help much because the purpose herein, in attempting a classification, is mainly to indicate the nature of economic difficulties experienced by the tribal communities.

Taking mainly technological achievements into consideration, a more lucid and clear-cut classification on the basis of the conditions of economic life may be attempted as follows:

1. Tribes hunting in forests;
2. Tribes engaged in hilly cultivation (shifting or slash-and-burn cultivation);
3. Tribes engaged in cultivation on levelled (plain) land;

4. Simple artisan tribes;
5. Pastoral tribes;
6. Tribes living as folk artists;
7. Agricultural and non-agricultural labour-oriented tribes; and
8. Tribes engaged in service and trade.

Those tribes who live by hunting in forests earn their livelihood through collection of edible roots and fruits, hunting and fishing. This class of tribes is found mostly in southern India. The **Chenchu** and **Chandi** of Telangana-Andhra Pradesh; **Kadar, Malapatram** and **Kurumba** from Kerala; **Paliyan** of Tamil Nadu; and **Onge, Jarwa, Sentinelese** and **Nicobarese** of Andaman and Nicobar Islands are some of the important tribes living in southern zone. The **Raji** of Uttarakhand-Uttar Pradesh; **Hill Garo** of Meghalaya; **Birhor, Korwa** and **Hill Kharia** of Chotanagpur; and **Juang** of Odisha are also some of the notable examples of this class. Although some groups of these tribes are slowly learning cultivation, their cultural ethos are still basically of a hunting-gathering type.

A vast chunk of Indian tribes has been engaged in shifting cultivation on hilly or mountainous tracts of north-eastern and central India. This mode of cultivation is different from the conventional settled cultivation. Under this system, bushes and trees are slashed and burnt. Thereafter seeds are scattered on the ashes and the rest is left to nature. Most of them have now moved to terrace cultivation. Almost all the tribes of Assam, Meghalaya, Arunachal Pradesh, Mizoram, Manipur and Tripura used to produce their crops through this mode of cultivation. Some tribes of Odisha such as **Gond** and **Baiga** of Madhya Pradesh-Chhattisgarh are also engaged in this mode of cultivation.

Due to intimate contacts with the 'civilised' groups, most of the Indian tribes have taken to settled agriculture on plain land as means of their livelihood. Their technique and mode of cultivation are the same as those of other peasant groups and they also use bullocks, plough and other common implements of agriculture, but most of their land is unirrigated and hence, they are often seen to be victims of vagaries of nature. Beside their total dependence on rain, they have to be content with low and meagre yield because of the absence of other agricultural inputs like fertilizers, high-yielding varieties of food grains, pesticides, etc. Among the numerically big tribes, **Oraon, Munda, Ho** and **Santhals** are successful cultivators.

Some of the Indian tribes earn their livelihood through cottage industries. They are engaged in basket and mat making, weaving, blacksmithing, etc. and supplement the needs of their neighbouring tribal and non-tribal societies. The **Gujjar** of Kashmir and **Kinnauri** of Himachal Pradesh work on wood. **Asur** of Bihar and **Agaria** of Madhya Pradesh are proficient in iron smelting; the **Kolam** of Maharashtra are traditional mat weavers and the **Irula** of Tamil Nadu make beautiful mats and baskets on bamboo.

Totally pastoral tribes are few in number, but **Toda** of Nilgiri Hills, **Gaddi and Bakriwal** of Himachal Pradesh and Kashmir, **Nageshia** of Madhya Pradesh, **Maldhan** of Gujarat and some other tribes of northern and southern India are notable examples of this class of tribes. It is also worth mentioning that not all the pastoral tribes trade in milk. Some of them rear cattle like sheep and goat for selling them in the market.

Another category of tribes earns their livelihood by performing dances, acrobatics, snake charming, etc. and hence they may be termed as 'folk artists'. The **Nut and Sapera** of Uttar Pradesh are good examples of this category. The **Munduppttu** of Odisha are expert acrobats, the **Kota** of Tamil Nadu are snake charmers, some groups of Gonds of Madhya Pradesh are tattooers and dancers and some other tribes of eastern India and southern India may also be put in this category.

Among the tribes engaged in agricultural labour are those which are traditionally agriculturists, but due to their landlessness they work as agricultural labour on others' land. According to a conservative estimate, about one-fifth of the total tribal population is engaged in agriculture as wage earners. Non-agricultural tribal labour force includes those tribals who are working in local factories and mines of Bihar-Jharkhand, Odisha and West Bengal and tea plantations of Assam and neighbouring areas.

A comparatively small number of tribal people are engaged in government and semi-government jobs as a result of the application of Constitutional provisions. Among such tribes are those of Meghalaya, Mizoram and Nagaland on the north-eastern fringe of the country, mainly **Christian tribals** of Chotanagpur and **Meena** of Rajasthan.

CULTURE CONTACT

Indian tribes may also be classified according to their cultural distance from the rural–urban groups. Majumdar opines that this comparative approach is the most useful in evolving a plan of rehabilitation because it focuses our attention on those problems of tribal India which are the outcome of haphazard contact with, or the isolation of, these tribes from the rural–urban groups.

According to him, the tribal cultures fall into three groups:

(i) those who are culturally most distant from the rural–urban groups; that is, more or less out of contact;
(ii) those who are under the influence of the culture of rural–urban groups and have developed discomforts and problems consequently; and
(iii) those who, though in contact with rural–urban groups, have not suffered thereof or have turned the corner and do not suffer any more, though they may have in the past, because they have now got acculturated into rural or urban culture.

Majumdar disagrees with Elwin that every contact with civilised world brings misery to the tribals. He takes the stand that our goal should be to take ahead all these three types of tribal communities and establish, under planned conditions, healthy and creative contacts between them and the rural–urban groups.

RELIGION

The major religions of India have invariably influenced various tribal religions and pantheons and only those tribal communities still maintain their native religious beliefs with purity who are leading an almost isolated social existence in dense forests. On the basis of the latest census data, the tribes may be classified into followers of following religions:

(i) Hinduism
(ii) Christianity

(iii) Buddhism
(iv) Islam
(v) Jainism
(vi) Other religions

Among the above-mentioned religions, the influence of Hinduism on the tribes is tremendous and almost 80% tribal people follow popular Hinduism in one form or the other, in varying degrees. Those who have embraced Christianity are also quite considerable in number and about 6% are under the 'shadow of the cross', but those following Buddhism, Islam or Jainism are negligible in number. One important point to be kept in mind in this context is that even those tribes who have embraced any of the above-mentioned major religions have not necessarily shed their local tribal beliefs and rituals and many of them are found to be practicing their traditional faith along with their acquired faith.

When we view this situation in the geographical perspective, we see that barring the tribes inhabiting the islands falling under the Bay of Bengal and the Arabian Sea, most of the tribes of South India along with the tribes of western India and central India are more or less Hinduised in faith. Christianity has made tremendous headway among most of the tribals of north-eastern India and more than 90% of the population of Nagaland and Mizoram follows Christianity. In central India, segments of some major tribes of Chotanagpur also follow Christianity and notable among these are Oraon, Munda and Ho. The tribes following Islam are mostly scattered in Lakshadweep, Himachal Pradesh, West Bengal, Maharashtra and Jammu and Kashmir. Among such tribes, about 98% of the total tribal population of Lakshadweep are followers of Islam. Buddhism among Indian tribes is represented mainly by some tribal groups of Arunachal Pradesh. The impact of Buddhism, however, is visible in some other Himalayan and Maharashtrian tribes also.

TRIBAL POLICIES AND APPROACHES

For thousands of years, primitive tribes persisted in forests and hills without having more than casual contacts with the populations of the open plains and the centres of civilisation.

> Now and then, a military campaign extending for a short spell into the vastness of tribal country would bring the inhabitants temporarily to the notice of princes and chroniclers, but for long periods there was frictionless co-existence between the tribal folks and Hindu caste society in the truest sense. (Haimendorf, 1960)[2]

But, the physical isolation of the **aboriginal tribes** drew to an end when the modern means of communication like railways and roads were introduced in the 19th and early 20th century coupled with the sudden growth of India's population. This caused land-hungry peasants of the plains to invade the sparsely populated tribal regions of middle and South India. Moreover, the extension of law and order to areas which in earlier days had been virtually unadministered

Quick Fact

Aboriginal Tribes

They refer to the indigenous people native to a particular region, who have distinct cultural, linguistic, and social practices rooted in ancient traditions.

[2] Haimendorf, Christoph von-Furer, The Konyak Nagas, New York, Holt, Rinehart & Wilson, 1969

enabled traders, moneylenders and a host of administrators, social workers, etc. to establish themselves in their villages.

The onslaught of moneylenders and traders from the plains played havoc with the tribals who, as many examples show, lost their economic independence and lot of land within a span of 20–30 years of their contact with the cunning and professional people of the plains. The plight of the poor and vulnerable Indian tribals has been surfacing from time to time for about hundred years or so. But, after independence they have been considered a 'problem' for the government and their more advanced fellow citizens. The administrators, anthropologists, Christian missionaries and social workers have viewed this 'problem' from different angles with different perspectives. As a matter of convenience, these views and policies/approaches may be divided into three categories. The discussion that follows this categorisation rotates round the three views:

(i) No change/Isolationism;
(ii) Assimilationism; and
(iii) Integrationism.

Many of the so-called aboriginal peoples or tribals have been pronounced by all those who came into close contact with them as rather simple, truthfully honest, usually jovial, colourful and happy-go-lucky. They had their own peculiar social organisation and some of them had retained it till their contact with the British.

Let us take a brief view of their social and economic organisation and the resultant problems:

1. Most of these tribes had been practicing a crude type of cultivation called 'shifting cultivation' known by respective vernacular names. It required little labour, care and vital inputs. Under this scheme of cultivation, trees and shrubs are axed before the start of the monsoon, fired and allowed to burn down into ashes. Now the desired seed is thrown and nature is left to take care of the yield. To supplement their dietary requirement, they collect all kinds of edible roots and fruits and hunt their favourable animals.
2. Further, most of the tribal people are habituated to drink, formerly to their home-brewed liquor of rice, mahua flower and other varieties and later to all kinds of distilled liquor. As a group, Jounsari, Bhil, Gond and numerous other tribes drink and even their children drink liberally. This is due to their local environmental and ecological conditions. Liquor has also been a part of their ritual and religious practices.
3. Contacts with Christian missionaries, especially in Bihar-Jharkhand and north-eastern regions, played havoc with their spiritual world. The faith in their old gods was shaken and everything tribal was called blasphemous.
4. Different tribes have different customs in regard to marriage and inheritance. The tribal customs were not properly understood and they were punished by the regular courts. It hurt the tribal sentiments.
5. Tribal people have been, naturally, illiterate. When various schemes were taken up for their educational upliftment, very little care was taken to impart primary education in their respective mother-tongues even in case of informal education.

Among the main causes enumerated by DN Majumdar, excise laws, replacement of tribal officers by the outsiders, curb on shifting cultivation and marriage by capture, unsuitable education, missionary activities and new diseases played havoc with their lives.

A.V. Thakkar, popularly known as 'Thakkar Bapa', one of the most vociferous champions of tribal cause, has analysed the situation from the viewpoint of a social worker. According to him, the problems of the aborigines may be divided into

1. poverty;
2. illiteracy;
3. ill health;
4. inaccessibility of the areas inhabited by tribals;
5. defects in administration; and
6. lack of leadership.

After viewing an anthropologist's and a social worker's reactions, let us take up Hutton's view – a defender of British policy of tribal affairs. According to Hutton, most cruel tribal customs were put down and warfare was stopped. Modem medicine was applied and infant mortality curtailed. The arts of reading and writing were introduced and easier intercourse and communication placed at their disposal through roads and post offices. However, the ills to which primitives were exposed to came from two slightly different aspects of British rule.

1. Introduction of an administrative system which failed to take into account any special needs.
2. Deliberate measures intended to ameliorate the condition of these tribes.

Three major evils proceeded from these sources:

1. loss of land and supplanting of the tribal village headman by foreigners, *particularly* by the Hindus from the plains, whether cultivators, moneylenders, traders, or mere land grabbers;
2. loss of means of subsistence and other evils;
3. disintegration of tribal solidarity.

After analysing the plight of the tribal people let us go back to the three major approaches/policies to assess their impact.

Protagonists of the first approach (Isolationism) hold the view that all the alien links, responsible for the unregulated and unrestricted contacts with the modern world and the resultant miserable condition of the tribes, should be snapped and the primitive people should be allowed and encouraged to flourish in their own environment.

This approach also includes what is now widely known as 'National Park Theory' credited to Verrier Elwin. Elwin suggested that the best way to protect tribal culture and their economic interests was to insulate them from all outside influences and their exploiters. Moreover, no missionary of any religion were to be allowed to breakup the tribal life.

This approach has been severely criticised on the ground that in the name of protecting the culture of the tribals, they cannot be kept aloof from the rest of India. They are not domestic cattle or zoo exhibits, but equal citizens of free India and thus they should be allowed to contribute towards the advancement of their country and enjoy the resultant fruits of development. Elwin claimed that he was misunderstood and with the passage of time, he distanced himself from this policy.

The second approach (Assimilationism) had got considerable acceptance when lobbied by social workers. The protagonists of assimilation advance the view that tribes should be assimilated with their neighbouring non-tribal cultures. The policy of total assimilation has also not been in conformity with the trend of Indian history. Despite thousands of years of cultural contacts and intercultural exchanges, the Indian society could not become totally homogeneous. Though some cultural characteristics did take shape that are truly 'national' in character as the by-product of historical development of Indian society, it cannot be denied that Indian society has been formed with Santhal, Gond, Oriya, Telugu, Kashmiri and numerous other cultural currents. Under such conditions, the policy of total assimilation of tribal culture as the solution of their problems is unfair and futile. Even the thought of forced assimilation or putting it as *fate accompli* smacks of '**cultural authoritarianism**'.

Quick Fact

Cultural Authoritarianism

It refers to the imposition of strict control over cultural norms, values, and behaviours by authorities – whether political, social, or institutional.

Nehru has been very outspoken in condemning the imposition of the Hindu way of living on tribal populations reared in another tradition. Due to his deep sympathy for the tribal people and keen appreciation of their problems, the approach of the state towards the tribal people is based on the theme of 'integration'.

The approach of 'integration' of the tribal population with the rest of the Indian population on the basis of equality and mutual respect is propagated by anthropologists too. The principle of 'cultural autonomy' has been an article of faith with the anthropologists. Integration should be differentiated from forced assimilation. We have got so many linguistic and religious groups who are being integrated to form one Indian nation without anybody making a demand, that they should be forced to give up their cultural identity and identify themselves with the majority community. Perhaps, there will be more meaningful and durable 'integration' when every minority group feels secured; when, in this pluralistic society that India is, people can exist as Hindus, Muslims, Christians, Sikhs, etc. one can exist here as Tamil, Odiya, Gujarati, Bengali, Punjabi, etc. then why not a person can exist here with respect and dignity as a Santhal, a Gond, a Tharu, a Meena and a Yenadi, a Khasi, Naga or Mizo? Integration can never be achieved under the shadow of threat and no plural society can afford to keep disgruntled, distressed, restless and frustrated minorities in its fold and still aspire for the harmonious development of the country. To ensure integration in this way, the non-tribals need education as much as the tribal people.

JAWAHARLAL NEHRU'S FIVE-POINT CHARTER (PANCHSHEEL) FOR THE TRIBAL PEOPLE

1. Tribal people should develop along the lines of their own genius and the imposition of alien values should be avoided.
2. Tribal rights in land and forest should be respected.
3. Teams of tribals should be trained in the work of administration and development.
4. Tribal areas should not be over administered or overwhelmed with a multiplicity of schemes.
5. Results should be judged not by statistics or the amount of money spent, but by the human character that is evolved.

What Do You Think?

How relevant are Jawaharlal Nehru's Five Principles (Panchsheel) for tribal policy in addressing the challenges faced by tribal communities today, and how can they be adapted to meet contemporary needs?

COLONIAL POLICIES AND SOCIAL CHANGE AMONG THE TRIBES

Tribal societies like other societies have also been undergoing change. However, the fact remains that powerful forces of change were released for the first time only during the colonial period and that is why colonial transformation of the tribal society forms an important area of study and investigation in the Indian subcontinent. The most apparent aspect in any such study is the fact that with the extension of authority of the state to the forest regions largely inhabited by the tribal populations, a number of minor and major tribal uprisings occurred.

Before taking up the emerging dimensions of tribal transformation that began more or less with the advent of colonial rule, it would not be out of place to take a brief look at some features of the precolonial situation. In any such analysis we should, first of all, give up the popular notion that before the advent of the British Colonial rule the tribal communities were leading the existence of total isolation – geographical and cultural – from the centres of Indian civilisation. The presence of **ant mahamatya** during the Mauryan period, whose reference is found on the rock edicts of Asoka, bears testimony to the fact that the polity of even such an ancient period had contacts with the communities living in hills and forests (*Girijan, Vanvasi*). There was a definite orientation of the Adivasis towards the larger Hindu population though the tribals were not 'Hindus' following their customs and traditions including their animistic beliefs. A number of anthropologists brought out classification of tribal communities

Quick Fact

Ant Mahamatya

It refers to an high rank official in the Mauryan Empire, who was responsible for looking after a specific group of people.

focussing on cultural process. This exercise was largely in terms of the orientation of the tribal communities towards the Hindu society. B.K. Roy Burman (1970)[3] classified the tribes as follows:

(a) Tribes incorporated in the Hindu social order;
(b) Tribes positively oriented towards the Hindu social order;
(c) Tribes negatively oriented towards the Hindu social order; and
(d) Tribes indifferent towards the Hindu social order.

Amplifying his position, Roy Burman observed that tribes like the **Bhil, Bhumij,** etc. may be considered to be incorporated in the Hindu social order. They had accepted the ethos of the caste structure and now can hardly be differentiated from the neighbouring Hindu peasantry. The tribes like the Santhal, the Oraon, the Munda, the Gond etc. may be considered to be positively oriented towards the Hindu social order. Though the bulk of their population were not in caste frame and they are still not, to a considerable extent they have adopted the symbols, ethos and the worldview of their Hindu neighbours. Tribal communities like the Mizo and the Naga can be considered to be negatively oriented towards the Hindu social order. They definitely rejected caste as a frame for social organisation. Most of the tribal communities in Arunachal can be considered to be indifferent to Hindu social order. They were and still are hardly aware of the tenets of Hinduism. Many of them traditionally eat beef and their moral constraints and systems of pollution and purity do not appear to bear any significant degree of resemblance to those of the Hindus. Yet, as Roy Burman (1994) himself acknowledges, positive and negative orientation towards dominant cultural influences is not a rigidly fixed pattern for all times to come. The situation has definitely changed in varying degrees. In later years, Roy Burman has disassociated himself with this approach, but as a referent to the precolonial or colonial set-up, this can still be used to understand the socio-cultural situation vis-à-vis tribal communities.

In order to understand the colonial and post-colonial situation, vis-à-vis social-cultural change, the classifications of L.P. Vidyarthi (1977) and S.C. Dube (1977) may also be referred to which talked about different levels and stages of **acculturation** vis-à-vis the larger Hindu society, more precisely Hindu peasantry in different regions of the country.

Quick Fact

Acculturation

The process of cultural change and adaptation resulting from contact between different cultural groups, especially in the context of tribal communities integrating with mainstream society.

Commenting on the precolonial situation, K.S. Singh in his essay on *Colonial Transformation of the Tribal Society in Middle India* agrees with the view that most of the ethnographers described the precolonial situation as static. Through his case study of the tribal communities of Middle India, K.S. Singh relies on historical evidence and says that three major trends were visible during the precolonial period. His analysis is largely oriented towards politico-economic dimensions. Citing three major trends, he says that the first was colonisation and establishment of settlements *(bhums)* by peasant castes, who were encouraged by the Mughal rulers and zamindars to reclaim lands and offered various incentives for this purpose or by other categories of immigrants. Trade and strategic routes passing

[3] Roy Burman, B K, Tribes in Perspectives, Mittal Publication, Delhi, 1970

through the jungle regions acquired a new significance. Jharkhand and Gondwana emerged as historical regions in the medieval period. Secondly, many tribes, such as Bhils, Mina, Kols and Gond, were recognised as dominant communities by the Mughal empire. Thirdly, we witness the rise of state either out of the tribal matrix as in the case of the Gond and Chero or as a result of imposition on the tribal system of the authority of the Rajputs and other castes, which established their power in the highlands of Odisha, Central India, Gujarat and Rajasthan. A crucial precondition of the formation of state in middle India was the extension of cultivation through the reclamation of land and the introduction of a new agricultural technology by the peasantry from plains. The Gond, Nagabansi and Chero chiefs encouraged the settlement of non-tribal peasant communities such as Kurmi, Keori and Kunbi, who with their superior agricultural technology alone could generate the agricultural surpluses that the new states required. A new mode of production thus emerged. A consequence of the imposition of the feudal super structure on the tribal society was its breakdown and fragmentation into distinct social strata, based on corresponding distribution of power and economic interests in land and defined in terms of ritual status. The new states acted as the agents of **Sanskritisation**, but they also strengthened the sense of tribal identity. State formation stimulated commercial activities, developed trade routes and promoted small-scale urbanism. A variety of castes ranging from the Brahmins, who were tempted by generous grants of land, to the artisan communities flocked to the new fort cities. All in all, a complex social-economic system had emerged in certain parts of tribal middle India even before the colonial system was established there.

Quick Fact

Sanskritisation

A social process where lower social strata or tribal groups adopt the customs, rituals, and practices of higher castes to elevate their social status.

Thus, with the establishment of the colonial rule, the relative (geographical/cultural) isolation of most of the tribal societies in India came to an end. Radical changes in tribal situation occurred. The British colonial rule created new problems by replacing the old social organisation, agrarian system and socio-economic values with the new ones the tribals were not familiar with. Old forms of social controls and agencies of social change were revised. New forms of commercialisation began – not only land became property, but significantly private property. A new rule of law was established. The colonial rule

> initiated commercialisation of production, consumerism and money/cash economy to precisely serve their exploitative interest. The State power played a decisive role in determining the future of the people and during the British period it experienced a basic transformation. As a result, the self-contained subsistence economy based on agriculture and forest produce was weakened and destroyed. (S.R. Sharma, 1999)[4]

The customary law of tribal communities was replaced by the new law of the centralised state power during the British rule and this continued even after that. The new law operated through its administrative and judicial organs and helped the process of Hinduisation to some extent. This process progressed in proportion to the urbanisation and transformation into capitalist economic development.

[4] Sharma, S R, Mughal Empire in India, Atlantic Publishers, New Delhi, 1999

The most striking feature of this period was the breakdown of the communal mode of production and the emergence of private right in land. A further stage in the development of the peasant system was the penetration of tribal economy by market. The colonial system created a demand for money in largely non-money economies to pay land revenue and other levies, to defray expenditure of various kinds and to buy necessities.

> The traditional form of barter exchange died away. There was some evidence that sections of the tribes took to commodity production on at a limited scale. (K.S. Singh, ibid)[5]

Even the most primitive economies came gradually within the operation of the market system. With the market came the middleman, merchants and moneylenders. Here the concept of *diku* (the aliens, outsiders) becomes crucial to the understanding of agrarian relations. A *diku* was the creature of the colonial system who performed a variety of functions as a middleman in administrative matters, as a moneylender, as a trader who controlled production of food grain through the system of advance credit and as a land grabber.

During this period, **peasantisation and depeasantisation** operated simultaneously. Several tribal communities who were not peasants were coming into the fold of peasantry while a number of tribal people after losing their land were entering into a different economic system. Substantial sections of tribes from middle India such as Santhals, Oraon and Munda had to migrate to the tea plantations of Assam and the adjoining areas while others became industrial labour, share-croppers, etc.

> **Quick Fact**
>
> **Peasantisation and Depeasantisation**
>
> In tribal context, Peasantisation is a process through which a tribe when comes into contact with (Hindu) peasantry, learns the art of cultivation and becomes peasant.
>
> After losing land, it enters into the process of depeasanisation.

Inter-tribal markets had been traditionally an institution of socio-cultural importance. These were not the places only for economic transactions. It also served as an agency of culture change. With the entry of new market forces and creation of demand for commodities triggered by the outsiders, the traditional tribal markets either declined or were transformed into places of formal economic exchanges and activities. Profit-making had never been the dominant value in tribal economy; redistribution and cooperation were the bases of the traditional tribal economy. All these values were eroded. Now the tribal society was moving closer and closer to the peasant/caste stratified system. This strengthened the role of *Sanskritisation*. Several tribes of middle India unitedly moved towards the Varna system and laid their claim over *Kshatriya* status mainly because the *Kshatriya* model of *Sanskritisation* or *Kshatriyaisation* was the easiest and most popular process. The Santhals and the Gonds are the most obvious examples of this process.

The role of Christianity as an agent of change also deserves some discussion, mainly in the north-east regions as well as stray pockets of Madhya Pradesh-Chhattisgarh, Bihar-Jharkhand and West Bengal. Since Christianity was perhaps the earliest agency of welfare in a number of tribal areas, it took a back seat as an ideology. The modernising role of Christian missions is also an important

[5] Singh, K S, Tribal Movements in India, Manohar Publishers, New Delhi, 2000

feature of social change in those tribal areas where it had a deep impact. But, unfortunately there always existed a close link between Christianity and colonialism.

> Missionaries enjoying the patronage of colonial administration tried to legitimize and rationalize the British rule and thus tried to create new channel of support among the backward and disadvantaged sections of Indian population.

In the north-eastern region and middle India, they mainly worked on the tribes and elsewhere on non-tribal communities, mainly the lower social strata of Hindus and Muslims. Under the impact of Christianity, a number of values and institutions of the affected tribal communities wilted. The fate of 'youth dormitories', a very popular institution of tribes declined. Obviously, the missionaries wanted the churches only to be the places of congregation. At the same time it is also true to an extent that Christianity gave a new sense of self-respect to the tribal peasants and sought to create a separate identity for them.

In any analysis of social change among tribal communities during the colonial period, the role of tribal movements cannot be ignored. Many tribes reacted to the changes brought about by the colonial administration in a variety of ways. Because of their prolonged relative isolation, the tribal communities had developed their own social structure and mechanism of social control and they were quite sensitive to them. Perhaps that is why they reacted to these changes more strongly and often violently than other populations. We have got a chronicled description of tribal movements and revolts – minor and major – and studies of unrest and disturbances. Most of the tribal movements could be covered under the headings of Anti-Colonial, Anti-Diku and Pro-Ethnic. Analysing the nature and consequences of these tribal movements in Middle India, K.S. Singh (ibid) writes that "the first phase (1795–1860)[6] coincided with the rise, expansion and establishment of the British empire. It saw the rise of what we may call the 'primary resistance movements." It was led by traditional chiefs and their subordinates who had been dispossessed of their property and thrown out of their occupations by the new system. The Chuar rebellion (1795–1800), the uprisings of Chero and disturbances in Chotanagpur in 1820, the Kol and Bhumij insurrections, the resistance offered by Gond zamindars in 1819 and 1842 and the Khond resistance of the mid-1830s are some of the examples of this phase. The Santhal insurrection (1855–1859) was both a resistance and agrarian cum revivalistic movement. All these movements sharpened the tribal ethnicity and gave them a new identity. The second phase (1860–1920) coincided with the intensive phase or colonialism, which saw a much deeper penetration of tribal and peasant economies by merchant capital, higher incidence of rent, etc. All gains registered during the first phase of the movements were washed away. Not only those who were expelled came back, but many more also came, intensifying the exploitation of tribes. Unlike the peasants, the tribal movements developed a religious and political overtone. The failure of the first phase of movements had made the tribals look inward. They sought to restructure the entire social system. This was the beginning of revitalisation movements. The Munda-Oraon Sardar Movement (1869–1895) led by Birsa Munda, the Tana Bhagat Movement (1895–1901) and the Bhil's movement led by Govind Giri may be cited as examples of this phase, which were largely socio-cultural in nature. It involved participation

[6] Singh, K S, Tribal Movements in India, Manohar Publishers, New Delhi, 2000

of the tribes in the national and agrarian movements and emergence of a separatist movement in Chotanagpur. It also reflected a deep yearning and craving for the roots and a sense of pride in tribal cultures. The followers of Mahatma Gandhi sprung up among the Bhils, Gonds, Hos, Oraon, Mundas and Santhals. It also coincided with the politicisation of the tribes bringing them into the mainstream of national politics and political processes (for details see the chapter on Tribal Movements). The tribal movements of the colonial period had a deep imprint on the struggle of the tribal people in the post-independence period.

Peter Gardner (1978) in his review of social-cultural change among the tribal peoples of India has selected five tribes, namely the Garos of Assam, now of Meghalaya (studied by Burlington, 1963), Bhumij of Bengal (Sinha, 1957, 1959, 1962, 1965), Konds of Odisha (Bailey, 1960), Kotas from the Nilgiri Hills (Mandelbaum, 1954, 1955, 1960) and Paliyans from the southern extremity of Tamil Nadu (Gardner, 1966, 1969, 1972). Talking about the Garos, he says that "basically there are two broad phases to the recent history of the Garos as Burlington recreates it. First, there was a protracted period during which endemic head hunting in the hills and other war-like behaviour kept outsiders at arm's length". It did not prevent active market links between the Garos and plainsmen in market towns at the foothills, but it did prevent even the most concerted efforts of zamindars from bringing any, but the edge of the plateau under their authority. Burlington describes the border as being in constant turmoil. Phase 2 began abruptly. In 1867, the British moved troops onto the plateau, 9 years later, by a symbolic gesture in which they destroyed two hundred skulls. As for the other areas of society and culture they adopted change on their own terms. Except some changes in the life of the converted Christian Garos, they remained largely unaffected. Moreover, one way or the other, Garos did not comply with whatever pressure there might have been from their Hindu neighbours to give up widow remarriage, slaughtering and eating of beef or casual handling of cooked food. They chose to judge behavioural propriety in their own terms.

In many superficial ways, the Konds of Kondmals, in northern **Odisha**, live in circumstances startlingly like those of the Garos. The East India Company, repelled morally by the practice of Kond human sacrifice, waged a 20-year war in the mid-19th century to bring the whole Kond area under its jurisdiction. Protective policies enunciated in 1855 amounted to little at first. Between 1875 and 1924, a great deal was done by way of road building and vocational education. And in 1897, Konds were offered special compensatory rights and privileges under laws to ensure them justice in the face of Oriya exploitation. They were protected, for example, from loss of their land (Bailey, 1960). Bailey sums the situation up in terms of two trends, the results of different administrative policies: (a) assimilation through opening up of the area and (b) protection from exploitation through education, laws, reserved jobs and general 'uplift'. The area did open up, exploitation was not severe, but educational advances in retrospect have to be viewed as modest. Other outcomes of change during the period include improvement of the medical situation, articulation with the world of caste, establishment of regular dominance–submission relationships with other peoples and retention with changed functions of territorial clans and lineages.

The Bhumij of Barabhum, in the eastern foothills of the Chotanagpur Plateau, have been associated with the Barabhum kingdom since the 13th to 16th centuries (Surajit Sinha, 1962). A century ago there were fewer non-Bhumij in the area and the land was more forested. While they are known to have been speakers of a Munda language in the past, by the early 19th century the Bhumij were reported to be speaking Bengali, the language of the great agricultural plain around them and by the 1880s they were said to speak only Bengali. A century ago, there were no weekly markets in the area, only itinerant traders. With the general opening up of the area to Hindu immigrants, gradual Hinduisation of the Bhumij began from the apex of their society downward. They claimed a true Rajput-*Kshatriya* ancestry. New festivals of major Hindu deities and the much admired behavioural model of the Rajput-*Kshatriya* were the obvious features of this transformation. The link with an interfering external British administration was to stay and Hinduisation was to continue.

The Kota have been studied several times by David Mandelbaum who has published a steady stream of articles on their changing relationship with the outside world. As he reconstructs the past, Mandelbaum gives some credence to a folk-historical idea that, once, the Kotas who are artisans, the Todas who herd buffaloes and the Kurumbas who are food collectors were the sole occupants of the Nilgiri plateau. Then, centuries ago, Badaga cultivators arrived from Mysore as refugees of war. The four peoples worked out a small social system of their own with caste-like economic and ritual interdependence and with a distinct hierarchy in terms of both power and considerations of purity. The new era began with a peaceful influx of Britishers and plainsmen having special interests in the plateau. When the British arrived to establish hill stations in the early 19th century, traders were already visiting the area and labourers were infiltrating from the plains. There was some missionary and government education of Kotas. The Kotas gradually became sophisticated. A reformist faction of the Kotas undertook to Sanskritise their behaviour, especially that which other Nilgiri tribes took to be demeaning. Mandelbaum contends that these changes have been slow and self-determined.

The **Paliyans** are, largely, food-collecting people of southernmost India who have been known for centuries as shy honey-collectors. They live in bands scattered along the east slope of the ranges dividing southern Tamil Nadu from Kerala. For many centuries, Paliyans have maintained sporadic, tangential contact with the Tamil plainsmen around them. In its most circumspect form, this contact has been silent barter of forest produce for commodities such as metal implements, cloth and condiments. Forest contractors, however, pursued Paliyans into their inhospitable dry thorny forest to arrange for special kinds of labour such as the extraction of soap, nuts, hemp and elkhorn. Paliyans had to enter into contract labour under threats, even at gun point and some bands, after experiencing episodes of such bullying, retreated into an almost fully nomadic existence. Thus, the variation between contact and isolation is best seen as cyclical. The second phase of Paliyan contact with outsiders could be thought of in quantitative rather than qualitative terms. Mandelbaum attributed this to (a) increased exploitation of forest produce, (b) development of plantations in the lower valleys which Paliyans have long inhabited, (c) entry of benevolent development officers, malaria eradication crew, etc. and (d) the lure of material advantages (Peter Gardner, 1972). But, a qualitative change did take place when Paliyans settled down.

The colonial administration was, by and large, a law and order–oriented administration. It certainly acted as a catalytic agent, but the pace of social change increased manifold in the post-independence period.

PROBLEMS

Most of their problems may be traced back to the advent of British rule in India when the effective authority of the state was extended to forests, hills and other difficult-to-access areas for colonial, administrative, economic and political reasons. Strict and draconian forest laws and policies were framed and implemented and the forest-dependent people were exposed to all types of exploitation by the outside people such as officials, traders, moneylenders and liquor and forest contractors. When the harassment, exploitation and deprivation crossed all limits, tribal people revolted. If we look at the chronology of revolts and uprisings, we find more than 150 minor and major revolts, the most prominent of which was the Santhal Revolt (1855–1859).

Post-independence, even after the promulgation of the constitution carrying important safeguards and developmental provisions, the exploitation continued unabated. Now the entire tribal areas are simmering with discontent, unrest and violence in varying degrees. The latest and the most serious problem is their displacement and lack of rehabilitation. It is now like a national problem (discussed in this book under the chapter 'Some Current Social Issues/Problems'). The following are some of the serious problems they have been suffering from:

- (Chronic) Indebtedness;
- Land alienation;
- Lack of healthcare, education and access to safe drinking water;
- Forest-related problems; and
- Displacement.

FOREST, TRIBAL PEOPLE AND FOREST POLICIES

The tribal people everywhere have lived in intimate relationship with forests and their entire existence has been linked with forests due to historical factors. Forests have been sustaining their inhabitants. In fact, there existed a '**symbiotic relationship**' between the tribals and the forests. Forests have been their abode and source of livelihood. Thus, it has been a unanimously-held view that forest economy is tribal economy and vice versa.

> **Quick Fact**
>
> **Symbiotic Relationship**
>
> A symbiotic relationship is a long-term interaction between two or more species that can benefit one or more of the organisms involved.

Not only their economic life, but the religious and religio-magical beliefs of the tribal people have also been centred around the forests. Many a flora and fauna have been their objects of worship (Totems). Thus, the tribal people were able to achieve such a harmony that has always been a matter of envy for the non-tribals.

In the mid-19th century, the importance of relationship between wildlife and botanical wealth and soil, moisture, rainfall and general environment was realised and it was decided to extend the authority of the state to the hitherto neglected parts of the territory. Following gradual extension of state authority, the 'lords' and 'masters' of forests were continually put under pressure and inconvenience. Following is the chronicled narration of evolution of forest policy along with various measures taken by the state to manage the forests.

▶▶ The First Forest Act, 1865

This Act was the first attempt in the direction of regulation of collection of forest produce by forest dwellers. In the process, the socially regulated practices of the local people were restrained by law.

▶▶ The Forest Act, 1878

This was the second step in the direction of further extension of state authority over forests. The control over forests was further tightened by prohibiting certain acts such as trespassing or pasturing of cattle and declaring certain activities as forest offences. Imprisonment and fines were also prescribed for these offences.

▶▶ The First Forest Policy, 1894

The First Forest Policy envisaged, for the first time, the regulation of rights and restriction of privileges of the users in the forests. These regulations and restrictions were justified only when the advantages to be gained by the general public were great and the cardinal principles observed, i.e. the rights and the privileges of individuals must be limited in the larger public interests. It is to be noted here that it was only in 1894 that forest officials seriously appeared on the scene and claimed the authority to limit and regulate the traditional tribal rights over forests.

▶▶ The Indian Forest Act, 1927

In continuation of the measures already taken, this act was an attempt to regulate further people's rights over forest land and forest produce. Through this Act, elaborate provisions were made in the direction of further extension of state authority and control over the forests. Forest offences were defined as offences punishable under the Act. This Act created an extremely powerful and adequately protected executive consisting of Forest Officers of Indian Forest Service, State Forest Service, Rangers, Foresters and Forest Guards. This Act gave the powers to the executive to make rules which were not necessarily permanent in nature. These officers enjoyed legal powers. For example, Section 64 of the Indian Forest Act states that any Forest Officer without a warrant could arrest any person against whom a 'reasonable' suspicion exists of his motive to pilferage forest or forest wealth and his act was punishable with imprisonment for one month or upwards. Section 68 deals with the power to compound the offences while Section 70 deals with the power to seize and impound the cattle of the offender under Cattle Trespass Act, 1871.

Such provisions, as stated above, made even some of the lower level officials of forest department like Rangers and Forest Guards very strong. Since it is these officials who regularly come in contact with the forest dwellers, they used their power arbitrarily and played havoc with the lives of the tribal people. The story of their interaction with the tribals is replete with instances in which these officials claimed indemnity for acts done in good faith according to Section 74 and got away. It further states that no suit shall be filed against a public servant for acts done in good faith and that all forest officials are deemed public servants. In 1935, forest was transferred to the state list according to the Government of India Act, 1935.

The National Forest Policy, 1952

When post-independence India formulated its first National Forest Policy in 1952, it belied all hopes of a just and generous treatment of the tribal people. It followed, by and large, the lines of the British administration where the tribals had virtually no statutory right, but enjoyed only certain concessions/privileges such as the right to take water for agricultural purposes, digging of wells and canals for agricultural purposes, free grazing in open forests, removal of timber, bamboos, reeds, canes, etc. for construction and repair of houses and for agricultural implements, collection of dead wood for domestic use as fuel, collection of grass for cattle and for thatching their huts, fishing and hunting excluding the protected fauna and cultivation of forest land.

The President of India, under Article 339 of the Constitution of India, appointed a commission in 1960 under the chairmanship of the late U.N. Dhebar, popularly known as **Dhebar Commission**. In its comprehensive analysis, it also studied the forest policy vis-à-vis tribals. The Commission noted that the tribals who had hitherto treated himself as the lord of the forest were made subservient to the forest department. The traditional rights of the tribals were no longer recognised as rights. "In 1894 they became rights and privileges and in 1952[7] they became rights and concessions. Now they are being considered as concessions only."

NATIONAL FOREST POLICY, 1988 AND THE TRIBAL RIGHTS

It was a major departure from the past ensuring forest management with the active participation of forest-dwelling communities who are the important stakeholders.

It states that the principal aim of the forest policy must be to ensure environmental stability and the maintenance of ecological balance including atmospheric equilibrium, which are vital to the sustenance of all life forms – human, animal and plant. The derivation of the economic benefit must be subordinated to the principal aim.

One of the striking features of the new forest policy is its referent to the relationship of the tribal communities with the forests. It states that having regard to the symbiotic relationship between the tribal people and the forests, a primary task of all the agencies responsible for forest management, including forest corporations, should be to associate the tribal closely in the protection, regeneration and development of forests as well as to provide gainful employment to the people living in and around the forest. While safeguarding the customary rights and interests of such people, the forestry programmes should pay special attention to the following:

1. To reduce illegal cutting and exploitation of the forest, contractors should be replaced by forest corporations, labour cooperatives and tribal cooperatives.
2. Special attention should be paid to the protection, regeneration and optimum collection of the minor forest produce along with institutional arrangements for its marketing.

[7] Dhebar Commission Report, Parliament Digital Library, 1961

3. Family-oriented schemes for improving the status of the tribal beneficiaries.
4. Integrated area development programmes to meet the needs of the tribal economy in and around the forest areas.

The above-mentioned provisions are some of the important provisions of the new forest policy with regard to the tribals.

Regarding the rights and concessions enjoyed by the tribal people, the new forest policy categorically stated that the rights and concessions enjoyed by them should be fully protected. Their domestic requirements of fuel, wood, fodder, minor forest produce and construction of timber should be allowed to be fulfilled through forest produce. This is the most welcome feature since it emphasises the needs of the forest dwellers for the first time since the forest administration began in India.

THE SCHEDULED TRIBES AND OTHER TRADITIONAL FOREST DWELLERS (RECOGNITION OF FOREST RIGHTS) ACT, 2006

Popularly known as Forest Rights Act, this is a major victory gained by the tribal communities after long struggles. If implemented honestly and sincerely, it will be a big relief to the tribal people and a leap forward for the conservation of forests.

Millions of people live in and near India's forest lands, but have no legal right to their homes, lands or livelihoods. A few government officials have all power over forests and forest dwellers. The result? Both forests and people die. This Act recognises forest dwellers' rights and makes conservation more accountable.

WHY IS THIS LAW NECESSARY?

What are called 'forests' in Indian law often have nothing to do with actual forests. Under the Indian Forest Act, areas were often declared to be 'government forests' without recording who lived in these areas, what land they were using, what uses they made of the forest and so on. 82% of Madhya Pradesh forest blocks and 40% of **Odisha's** reserved forests were never surveyed; similarly 60% of India's national parks have till today (sometimes after 25 years as in Sariska) not completed their process of enquiry and settlement of rights. As the Tiger Task Force of the Government of India put it, "in the name of conservation, what has been carried out is a completely illegal and unconstitutional land acquisition programme."[8]

WHAT ARE THE LIVING CONDITIONS AND ENVIRONMENTAL CIRCUMSTANCES IN FOREST AREAS?

Millions of people are subject to harassment, evictions, etc. on the pretext of being encroachers in their own homes. Torture, bonded labour, extortion of money and sexual assault are all extremely common. In the latest national eviction drive from 2002 onwards, more than 3,00,000 families were driven into destitution and starvation. In Madhya Pradesh alone, more than 125 villages have been burned to the ground.

[8] Tiger Task Force initiated by Govt. of India, Ministry of Forest and Environment, 1973

The situation was so bad that the then Commissioner for Scheduled Castes and Scheduled Tribes, in his 29th Report, said that "The criminalisation of the entire communities in the tribal areas is the darkest blot on the liberal tradition of our country."[9]

WHY WERE PEOPLE'S RIGHTS NOT RESPECTED WHEN THESE FORESTS WERE DECLARED?

The Indian Forest Act, 1927, India's main forest law, had nothing to do with conservation. It was created to serve the British need for timber. It sought to override customary rights and forest management systems by declaring forests state property and exploiting their timber. The law says that, at the time a 'forest' is declared, a single official (the Forest Settlement Officer) is to enquire into and 'settle' the land and forest rights people had in that area. These all powerful officials unsurprisingly either did nothing or recorded only the rights of powerful communities.

The same model was subsequently built into the Wild Life Protection Act, passed in 1972, with similar consequences.

ARE THESE LAWS THE BEST WAY TO PROTECT OUR FORESTS?

The very purpose of the Forest Acts was to convert forests into the property of a colonial department; and when you convert an ecosystem into someone's property, there will always be stronger claims to that property than conservation. To destroy a forest today requires nothing more than either a bribe to the local forest officer or an application to a committee in Delhi. The results include:

- The loss of more than 90% of India's grasslands to commercial Forest Department plantations;
- The destruction of five lakh hectares of forest in the past 5 years alone for mines, dams and industrial projects;
- The clearing of millions of hectares of forest for monoculture plantations by the Forest Department; and
- Recent proposals to privatise 'degraded' forest lands for private companies' timber plantations.

Moreover, the forest laws destroyed all the community management and regulation systems that had existed before, forcing people to choose between either abandoning the forest entirely or living as 'criminals' within or near it. At present, it is a criminal offence for you or me to plant a tree in a reserved forest; but it is legal for the Department to fell the entire forest so long as it has Central Government permission.

WHAT DOES THE FOREST RIGHTS ACT DO?

The Act basically does two things:

1. Grants legal recognition to the rights of traditional forest-dwelling communities, partially correcting the injustice caused by the forest laws.

[9] 29th Report of Commissioner of SC and ST, 1987–89, Govt. of India

2. Makes a beginning towards giving communities and the public a voice in forest and wildlife conservation.

WHO IS A FOREST DWELLER UNDER THIS LAW AND WHO GETS THE RIGHTS?

There are two stages to be eligible under this Act. First, everyone has to satisfy two conditions:

1. Primarily residing in forests or forest lands; and
2. Depends on forests and forest land for a livelihood (namely 'bona fide livelihood needs').

▸▸ Second, You Have to Prove

- That the above conditions have been true for 75 years, in which case you are an *Other Traditional Forest Dweller* [s.2(o)];

OR

- That you are a member of a Scheduled Tribe [s. 2(c)]; and
- That you are residing in the area where they are Scheduled [s. 4(1)].

In the latter case you are a Forest Dwelling Scheduled Tribe.

WHAT KIND OF RIGHTS DO FOREST DWELLERS GET UNDER THIS ACT?

The law recognises three types of rights:

▸▸ Land Rights

No one gets rights to any land that they have not been cultivating prior to 13 December 2005 [see Section 4(3)] and that they are not cultivating right now. Those who are cultivating land, but do not have documents can claim up to 4 hectares, as long as they are cultivating the land themselves for a livelihood [Sections 3(1) (a) and 4(6)]. Those who have a *patta* or a government lease, but whose land has been illegally taken by the Forest Department or whose land is the subject of a dispute between Forest and Revenue Departments can claim those lands [see Sections 3(1)(f) and (g)].

There is no question of granting 4 hectares of land to every family. If I am cultivating half a hectare on 13 December 2005, I receive title to that half a hectare alone; and if I am cultivating nothing, I receive nothing. If I am cultivating more than 4 hectares without documents or a dispute, I receive title to only 4 hectares.

The land cannot be sold or transferred to anyone except by inheritance [see Section 4(4)].

Use Rights – The law secondly provides for rights to use and/or collect the following:

(a) Minor forest produce things like tendu patta, herbs, medicinal plants, etc. that has been traditionally collected [see Section 30 (c)]. This does not include timber;

(b) Grazing grounds and water bodies (Section 3); and

(c) Traditional areas of use by nomadic or pastoralist communities, i.e. communities that move with their herds, as opposed to practicing settled agriculture.

▸▸ Right to Protect and Conserve

Though the forest is supposed to belong to all of us, till date no one except the Forest Department had a right to protect it. If the Forest Department should decide to destroy it or to hand it over to someone who would, stopping them was a criminal offence.

For the first time, this law also gives the community the right to protect and manage the forest. Section 3(1)(i) provides a right and a power to conserve community forest resources, while Section 5 gives the community a general power to protect wildlife, forests, etc. This is vital for the thousands of village communities who are protecting their forests and wildlife against threats from forest mafias, industries and land grabbers, most of whom operate in connivance with the Forest Department.

HOW ARE THE RIGHTS RECOGNISED?

Section 6 of the Act provides a transparent three-step procedure for deciding on who gets rights. First, the gram sabha (full village assembly not the gram panchayat) makes a recommendation – i.e. who has been cultivating land for how long, which minor forest produce is collected, etc. The gram sabha plays this role because it is a public body where all people participate and hence is fully democratic and transparent. The gram sabha's recommendation goes through two stages of screening committees at the taluka and district levels. The district level committee makes the final decision [see Section 6(6)]. The Committees have six members – three government officers and three elected persons. At both the taluka and the district levels, any person who believes a claim is false can appeal to the Committees and if they prove their case the right is denied [Sections 6(2) and 6(4)]. Finally, land recognised under this Act cannot be sold or transferred.

HISTORY OF TRIBAL ADMINISTRATION

The so-called aborigines had been, even much before independence, a subject of research. They have been painted in different colours by different people. Hence, the general masses in India have been holding and perpetuating somewhat confusing and amazing and sometimes fantastic myths about this section of the society. Their image of primitive, simple, cheerful and colourful people having exotic dances and music, Ghotul, Rorung and Dhumkuria is based on several myths. Behind these myths lies a bitter reality – heart-breaking poverty, ignorance, disease and exploitation. It is heartening to note that a number of honest scholars and researchers refused to be swayed by mere romanticism and have scrupulously portrayed the ugly reality as it is.

BEFORE 1947

The British administrators of pre-independence India were probably the first people who tried to grapple seriously with the problem of administering the tribal areas and they had a vested interest in cultivating and perpetuating the above-mentioned myths about the tribal people of

India. They did everything to ensure that the so-called aborigines, the Scheduled Tribes, remain isolated from the rest of the Indian masses, because the British imperialists had realised the potentiality of Indian tribes as an explosive force in any national movement. The tribals were isolated and their places of habitation were declared as prohibited area. Thus, the alien rulers and Christian missionaries were the only people who had access to the tribal areas in the initial stages.

The first serious attempt made by the British rulers in India, to deal with the local tribes, was in connection with the Paharias or Malers of the Rajmahal Hills. The implicit intention behind this beginning was to deal with 'turbulent' tribes only. Leaders of these tribes were granted *Sanad* and they were assigned the responsibility of reporting all outbreaks. Ghurye (1963) writes that those leaders living near the lines of communication were to be paid a fixed sum to protect the mail runners. The payment is described by the competent authorities as 'a bribe pure and simple as in Musalman days'. At the foot of the hills, lands were granted to retired or disabled soldiers and thus a ring fence of military minded people was created round the marauding Paharias. Slowly working through the corps that were raised, a court was appointed from among the officers of the corps for the purpose of justice. Encouraged by its utility, the government was approached to withdraw the Rajmahal Hill tract from the jurisdiction of the ordinary courts. Thus, in 1782, this tribal tract was withdrawn from the jurisdiction of the ordinary courts and the hereditary leaders of the tribe were called into a sessions court, which was to meet twice a year and try all offences. The council came to be known as Hill Assembly and it had the power to inflict or rescind even capital punishment.

Having achieved the objective of internal justice and peace through the creation of the Hill Assembly, Cleveland, the clever administrator, tried to solve another important problem, the problem of encroachments by the hated 'foreigners'. The lands held by the Paharias were "formed into government estate, held by them direct from Government and free from rent. These measures induced those Pahariya Chiefs, who had still held out, to join in and accept the rule of the British, which for all practical purposes was their own rule." (Ghurye, 1963).[10] In this way, the turbulent and problematic Paharias or Malers were pacified and the rules were made law as Regulation I of 1796. With the passage of time, the prestige of Hill Assembly dwindled and Regulation I of 1796 was repealed by Regulation I of 1827.

At this stage, some other tribal groups, groaning under the yoke of exploitation, rebelled. In this context, such uprisings as Ho mutiny of Singbhum in 1831, Khond uprising of 1846 and famous Santhal rebellion of 1855 are worth mentioning. The British Indian Government was also forced to send punitive expeditions to Assam, Nagaland and Jaintia Hills between 1850 and 1890 and repeatedly to the Lushai Hills, Naga Hills and to the Abor during the last decade of the 19th century and the first decade of the 20th century.

The underlying causes of these uprisings and disturbances were almost always the same: the deep resentment and dissatisfaction created as a result of exploitation by their technologically and culturally more advanced neighbours.

[10] Ghurye, G S, The Scheduled Tribes, Popular Prakashan, Bombay, 1963

At this stage the idea that 'distinct and special arrangements were necessary for isolated tribal regions gained acceptance. The findings of anthropological researches seemed to support it' (Report of the Scheduled Areas and Scheduled Tribes Commission, Vol. I, 1960–1961). The British Government finally decided on a policy of segregating the tribes into special areas where their lives and interests could, supposedly, be adequately protected. Keeping this purpose in mind, an Act was passed in 1874 to specify tribal areas into 'Scheduled Districts'. These areas were reconstituted under Section 52A of the Government of India Act of 1919. This Act provided for the appointment of officers to administer civil and criminal justice, to superintend the settlement and collection of public revenues and all matters relating to rent and otherwise to conduct the administration within the Scheduled Districts. It also provided for the extension, by notification, to the Scheduled Districts, laws in force in any part of British India, with such special restrictions and modifications as were deemed fit. Thus, wide powers of legislation by simple executive order were vested in the Executive. With the freedom movement gaining momentum, there was increasing anxiety on the part of the British administration to isolate the tribes from the national mainstream. The Indian Statutory Commission (Simon Commission) suggested that on financial and constitutional grounds the responsibility for the tribal tracts should be entrusted to the centre. In the subsequent years and up to 1947, numerous acts and regulations were promulgated and various reforms introduced. Thus, in 1935, more stringent provisions for a special treatment of the tribal areas were incorporated by converting them into 'Totally and Partially Excluded Areas'.

AFTER 1947

With the dawn of independence, the nation witnessed a considerable awakening about the welfare of the tribal people. This was reflected in various provisions of the Constitution of independent India adopted by the Constituent Assembly on 26 January 1950. It visualised a policy of progressive assimilation of the tribal people in the 'national mainstream'. In order to promote the integration of the tribal people with the rest of their Indian brethren, the Constitution provided special safeguards for the tribal communities for a period of 10 years. This period continues to be extended till now.

A tribal welfare department was instituted in 1951 for the protection and advancement of the Scheduled Tribes and with the help of various provisions of the Constitution, a new line of administration was chalked out. Article 244 of the Constitution provides for the administration of 'Scheduled Areas' in accordance with the Fifth Schedule and (in Assam) 'Tribal Areas' under the Sixth Schedule.

The Schedule Areas, thus defined, are administered as part of the states in which they are situated, but the Governor is given powers: (a) to modify Central and State laws in their application to them; (b) to frame regulations for their peace and good government and in particular for the protection of rights of tribals in land, the allotment of wasteland and their protection from moneylenders. In the framing of the regulations, the Governor is required to consult the Tribes Advisory Council in the state. The governor is further required to submit to the President of India an annual report or a report at such intervals as may be required by the Union Government. Thus, in the Constitution, ample provisions exist to protect the rights of the Scheduled Tribes in land, to protect them against exploitation by moneylenders and to preserve their social and cultural life.

The Scheduled Areas have been constituted with two clear objectives. One is to assist the tribals in enjoying their existing rights and the second is to develop the Scheduled Areas and promote the economic, educational and social progress of Scheduled Tribes.

The Fifth Schedule visualises a division of responsibility between the state governments and the Union Government in the matter of administration of the Scheduled Areas. The State Government is directed to screen legislation unsuitable for extension to the tribal areas and to frame regulations for peace and good government. It is also the responsibility of the state government to implement special schemes of tribal welfare and general development of the Scheduled Tribes inhabiting within its boundaries. The Union Government takes the responsibility of providing guidance to the state government regarding administration of the Scheduled Areas and also to make available additional funds required to raise the administrative capability and standard of living of the tribal people. The Union Government also enjoys power to give directions to the state governments regarding the implementation of any particular scheme, laying down priorities in their implementation and in regard to the general administration of the tribal areas.

The Union Government's responsibility for the administration of the Scheduled Areas is not limited only to the provisions of funds for their development, but extends to guiding the state governments and giving directions to them. This crucial role is provided for in Article 339(2) and Para 3 of the Fifth Schedule of the Constitution. It augers well for the tribal communities that the Union Government has relied upon persuasion and the good sense of the state government to adopt a uniform policy for the development of Scheduled Areas and rarely the situation demands a directive to the state governments. It is better if the unfortunate tribals are not dragged in unnecessary bickering and tug of war between crucial administrative agencies. Further, periodical conferences are held with the Planning Commission and the Ministry of Home Affairs to review the progress in regard to the programmes and to consider difficulties in their implementation.

CONSTITUTIONAL PROVISIONS FOR THE STs

The term 'tribe' is nowhere clearly defined in the Constitution and in fact there is no perfect or foolproof definition anywhere. To the ordinary/layperson, the word suggests simple folk living in hills and forests with their 'exotic' customs and practices; to people who are a little 'better' informed, it signifies 'colourful' folks known for their dance, songs and folk medicine; to an administrator, it means a group of citizens who are the special responsibility of the President of India; to an anthropologist or sociologist, it indicates a special field for the study of a social phenomenon. In their own way, all these impressions are correct.

The Constitution has defined 'tribe' to the extent that the STs are "the tribes or the tribal communities or parts of or groups within tribe or tribal communities" which the President may specify by public notification, through Article 342. This ambiguity sometimes leads to confusion in classifying and identifying a tribal population for declaring it an ST, but it should not be regarded as a hindrance in implementing tribal welfare programmes.

With the dawn of independence and adoption of the Constitution of free India, the responsibility for their welfare and development was placed on the popular government through the President and Governors. In pursuance of the Directive Principles, special articles have been provided for the welfare of the Scheduled Castes and the STs. Most of these are common to both these categories while a few of these are exclusively meant for either of these. These constitutional provisions may be divided into two groups underlying the following themes:

1. Protection
2. Development

The protective provisions, essential for their development, are meant to provide them protection from social and economic exploitation and injustice. The provisions relating to the development of the STs are meant for providing them positive steps for their socio-economic development. The following is the summarised narration of these constitutional provisions.

PROTECTIVE PROVISIONS

Article 15(4): Promotion of social, economic and educational interests.

Though Article 15 prohibits any discrimination on grounds of religion, race, caste, sex or place of birth, clause (4) of this Article provides an exception to this. It empowers the state to make any special provision for the advancement of socially and educationally backward classes of the citizens or for the SCs and STs. This provision is in accordance with the policy envisaged in Article 46 that the state should promote with special care educational and economic interests of the weaker sections of the people and protect them from social injustice. This clause has been especially incorporated to prevent any special provision made by a state for the advancement of socially or educationally backward classes of citizens from being challenged in the law courts on the ground of it being discriminatory.

Article 16(4): Reservation in Posts and Services and

Article 19(5): Safeguard of Tribal Interest in Property

While the right of free movement and residence throughout the territory of India and of acquisition and disposition of property are guaranteed to every citizen, special restrictions may be imposed by the state for the protection of the interests of members of the STs under Article 19(5). Since they are vulnerable to all sorts of deception and exploitation, there are various provisions disabling them from alienating even their own property except under special conditions. In their own interest, laws may be made restricting the right of the ordinary citizen to move freely or settle in particular areas or acquire property there. This restriction is effective in some tribal areas of some states.

Article 23: Prohibition of Traffic in Human Beings, Forced Labour, etc.

It prohibits traffic in human being, *begaar* or forced labour and other similar forms of forced labour. This is a very important provision because the STs being much vulnerable to economic exploitation may be made bonded. In fact, a substantial number of tribal population in the country has been leading a miserable life in bondage.

Article 29: Cultural and Educational Rights

Article 29(2): It is controlled by the Clause 4 of Article 15, incorporated in the Constitution by the First Amendment Act, 1951. This has brought Articles 15 and 29 in line with Articles 16(4), 46 and 340 and made it constitutional for the state to reserve seats for the backward classes of citizens in public educational institutions. According to Article 29, a cultural or linguistic minority has a right to conserve its language or culture. This article provides protection to ST communities to preserve their languages, dialects and cultures. The state would not, by law, enforce upon it any other culture or language.

Article 46: Promotion of Educational and Economic Interests of Scheduled Castes, Scheduled Tribes and Other Weaker Sections

Article 164: Minister in charge of Tribal Welfare in the States of Bihar, Odisha and Madhya Pradesh

This Article provides for a Minister in charge of tribal welfare in the states of Bihar, Odisha and Madhya Pradesh. These states have substantial tribal populations and special provision of a Minister looking after tribal welfare is an evidence of the concern of the framers of the Constitution for safeguarding the interests of STs.

Articles 330, 332 and 334: Provide reservation in the Lok Sabha and the Vidhan Sabha

Article 335: Limits of Reservation

Article 338: Appointment of Special Officer

There shall be a special officer for the Scheduled Castes and STs to be appointed by the President. It shall be the duty of the Special Officer to investigate all matters relating to the safeguards provided for the Scheduled Castes and STs under the Constitution. He shall report to the President upon the working of these safeguards at such intervals as the President may direct. The President shall call all such reports to be laid before each house of Parliament. Such an officer was designated as Commissioner for Scheduled Castes and STs.

By virtue of Constitution (Sixty-Fifth Amendment) Act, 1990, the post of 'Special Officer' has been substituted by the *National Commission for Scheduled Castes and Scheduled Tribes.* The Commission shall consist of a chairperson, vice-chairperson and five other members to be appointed by the President. The Commission shall have the power to regulate its own procedure. Later this commission was bifurcated into two independent commissions – National Commission for Scheduled Tribes and National Commission for Scheduled Castes.

ARTICLE 339(1) APPOINTMENT OF A COMMISSION

The President may, at any time and shall, at the expiration of 10 years from the commencement of the Constitution, by order appoint a commission to report on the administration of Scheduled Areas and the welfare of the STs in the States. Only one such commission, namely Scheduled Areas and Scheduled Tribes Commission, was appointed on 28 April 1960 and it submitted its report in October 1961. It was headed by late Shri U.N. Dhebar and it is popularly known as the Dhebar Commission. The second such commission was appointed in 2002 under the chairmanship of Dilip Singh Bhuria, popularly known as the Bhuria Commission, which submitted its report in 2004.

PROVISIONS MEANT FOR ECONOMIC DEVELOPMENT

Articles 275 and 339

Provisions relating to economic development of STs are mainly contained in Articles 275 and 339. Article 275 of the Constitution provides for assistance to the states for the implementation of the provisions of the Constitution. Article 339 lays down that the 'executive power of the Union government extends to the giving of directions to a state as to the drawing up and execution of schemes specified in the direction to be essential for the welfare of the Scheduled Tribes in the state.'

▶▶ Fifth and Sixth Schedule

Articles 244 and 244(A) under Part-X of the Constitution provide for administration of Scheduled Areas and Tribal Areas. Under the Constitution, the terms Scheduled Areas and Tribal Areas have definite connotations. The Scheduled Areas are governed by the provisions contained in the Fifth Schedule and the areas thùs covered may also be called the *Fifth Scheduled Areas.* The Tribal Areas are governed by the provisions of the Sixth Schedule.

▶▶ Fifth Schedule

The Scheduled Areas and their administration fall under the Fifth Schedule. Here, it means such areas as the President may, by order, declare to be Scheduled Areas. The Parliament is empowered to make any amendment in the Schedule and it shall not be deemed to be an amendment of the Constitution for the purpose of Article 368.

The history of the Scheduled Areas may be traced back to the 'Scheduled District Act, 1874' which provided for the appointment of special officers to administer civil and criminal justice, to superintend the settlement and collection of public revenue and matters relating to rent and otherwise, to conduct the administration within the Scheduled Districts. Passing through 'Government of India Act, 1919' and 'Government of India Act, 1935' (Excluded and Partially Excluded Areas Act), it is under the present Constitution known as the Fifth Schedule.

The Scheduled Areas have been constituted with the clear objectives to

(a) assist the tribal people in enjoying their existing rights without any hindrance by others and
(b) develop the Scheduled Areas and protect and promote the interest of the STs.

Under the Presidential order certain tribal areas have been declared as Scheduled Areas in the states of Andhra Pradesh, Bihar, Gujarat, Madhya Pradesh, Maharashtra, Odisha, Rajasthan and Himachal Pradesh. The main features of the Fifth Schedule are the

(a) Special legislative powers of the Governor;
(b) Governor's Report to the President; and
(c) Constitution of a *Tribes Advisory Council.*

▶▶ Sixth Schedule

The Sixth Schedule applies to Tribal Areas within the states of Assam, Meghalaya, Mizoram and Tripura. Among the main features of the Tribal Areas are

(a) their full autonomy in respect of matters falling within the jurisdiction. In other words these areas may be described as 'states within state';
(b) power of self-management to the tribals through *autonomous district and autonomous regions*; and
(c) autonomy of these areas to such an extent that the writ of the Parliament or the state legislature does not run automatically unless the Act in whole or part is specifically extended to the Tribal Areas by notification of the Governor.

TRIBAL DEVELOPMENT

In pursuance of the constitutional provisions, machinery was created for socio-economic development and educational advancement of the STs. Moreover, protecting them from all forms of exploitation and social injustice was also accepted as the duty of the state. For most of the states having substantial tribal population, tribal development was sought to be achieved through the Tribal Sub-Plan and the Integrated Tribal Development Project. Under these, both types of schemes/programmes – centrally sponsored and state sponsored – have been taken up. For the centrally sponsored schemes, the central government provides 100% funding, does the monitoring, but gets it implemented through the state machinery while the state-sponsored ones are the sole responsibility of states.

What Do You Think?

How can tribal development initiatives balance the preservation of indigenous cultures and traditions with the push for economic integration and modernisation in a rapidly changing world?

Several official and non-official evaluations and appraisals of tribal development programmes done so far admit that the results have been unsatisfactory in terms of investment of money and efforts. This was mainly because of indifferent and corrupt administration, wrong priorities and lack of understanding of the 'felt needs' of the tribal people. The irony is that all the rules and laws favour the tribal people, but they continue to be oppressed and exploited.

Questions and Indicative Answers

1. What is the idea or concept of tribe? Differentiate between tribe and Scheduled Tribe.

- Though there is no universal definition of tribe, in the Indian context the definition given by D. N. Majumdar along with the indicators provided by T. B. Nayak shall suffice.
- Any tribe or part thereof may be scheduled under Article 342 of the constitution, through a constitutional order issued by the president. Thus, a tribe is a sociological category while a scheduled tribe is a constitutionally created category.

2. What are the mains problems being faced by Scheduled Tribes?

- Before the advent of British rule, the tribal communities were living in geographically isolated areas, in conformity with nature and natural resources.
- The British rulers extended the state's authority to forests to serve colonial interest.
- With the introduction of cash economy and exploitative colonial rule the tribal communities were trapped in the vicious cycle of indebtedness, land alienation and forest-related problems.
- After independence, the resource rich tribal areas were opened for exploitation of natural resources. In this process millions of tribal people were displaced and ousted without proper rehabilitation. This was one of the main reasons behind armed resistance of tribal communities.

3. Discuss the constitutional provisions for the Scheduled Tribes.

- As per the text.

Previous Years' Questions

1. Why are the tribals in India referred to as 'the scheduled tribes?' Indicate the major provisions enshrined in the Constitution of India for their upliftment. **(GS Mains Paper I, 2016)**
2. Critically evaluate the term 'tribe' (as used in India) as compared to the term 'indigenous' in some other countries. **(UPSC CSE Mains Anthropology, Paper II, 2017)**
3. Discuss the significance and implementation of 'Recognition of Forest Rights Act 2006'. **(UPSC CSE Mains Anthropology, Paper II, 2018)**
4. What are the constitutional safeguards to protect the interests of the Indian tribes? **(UPSC CSE Mains Anthropology, Paper II, 2019)**
5. Discuss the impact of Forest Rights Act (2006) on the livelihood and culture of the tribal people in India **(UPSC CSE Mains Anthropology, Paper II, 2021)**
6. Write a short note on the following : Scheduled Areas (150 words) **(UPSC CSE Mains Anthropology, Paper II, 2023)**
7. Sanskritization is a culture bound concept. Critically comment to assess the strength and limitations of this concept in developing a theoretical framework to study social change. **(UPSC CSE Mains Anthropology, Paper II, 2023)**
8. Analyse the perspectives of Isolation, Assimilation and integration in understanding the trajectory of Indian tribal development **(UPSC CSE Mains Sociology, Paper II, 2023)**
9. What are the definitional problems involved in identifying tribes in India? **(UPSC CSE Mains Sociology, Paper II, 2024)**

Focus Areas for the Examination

1. Problems Faced by Scheduled Tribes
2. Forest Policy and Tribal communities
3. Constitutional Safeguards for STs

CHAPTER 8

Religion, Religious Communities and Religious Minorities

Chapter Outline

1. Concept of religion and its significance in Indian Society
2. Differentiating between Indic and non-Indic religions
3. Identifying the demographic distribution of different religious groups in India
4. Concept of religious minorities and the socio-economic challenges they face
5. Impact of commercialisation on religious practices
6. Constitutional rights and protections for religious and linguistic minorities in India
7. Findings of the Sachar Committee on the socio-economic status of Muslims

Religion plays a major role in Indian way of life and, perhaps, the most important value in life. Religion is present in all societies of the world in one form or the other. It may be understood as a cultural system of behaviour and practices, worldviews, ethics and social organisation that relate humans to an order of existence. In the entire animal kingdom only humans have religion. Through religion, humans communicate with their own concepts of superhuman and supernatural powers. Religion consists of two components – beliefs and rituals. Rituals are merely manifestations or demonstrations of beliefs and hence several people may be seen who are extremely religious, but do not perform any rituals.

RELIGIONS AND RELIGIOUS COMMUNITIES IN INDIA

All the major religions and their followers may be found as constituents of Indian society. India's religions may be classified into two: Indic religions and non-Indic religions.

Indic religions include those which originated and evolved in India such as Hinduism, Jainism, Buddhism and Sikhism. In the second category come those that were not born in India, but came from outside, accepted by the people and got integrated with the Indian society such as Islam, Christianity, Judaism, Zoroastrianism and Bahaism. According to the 2011 Census, the percentages of different religious groups are as follows:

1. Hindus 80% approx.;
2. Muslims 14% approx.;

3. Christians 3% approx.;
4. Sikhs 2% approx.;
5. Buddhists 0.70%;
6. Jains 0.37%; and
7. Others and with no religious affiliation 1%.

Data are not available for Jews and Zoroasters (Parsees), but it is estimated that the Parsees should be around 0.6 lakh and Jews just a handful. While the Parsees have been depopulating largely because of inbreeding and migration, Jews were always there in small number and have been migrating to the United States, Canada and Israel. Thus, the Indian Muslims are the largest religious minority in Indian society. In fact, they are the third largest Muslim population in the world after Indonesia and Pakistan. Because of religious persecution in the Arab world, the minority Shia Muslims have been coming and settling down in India and thus the Indian Shias are the third largest Shia population of the world after Iran and Iraq.

Another minority sect in Islam, the Ahmedi or Qadiani, is also living here in harmony. The cradle of Ahmedi faith is also located here, in a town called Qadian in Gurdaspur, Punjab. Indian Islam has been a citadel of Sufism and shrines of some of the great Sufi saints such as Khwaja Moinuddin Chishti and Nizamuddin are located in India at Ajmer and Delhi respectively. The Sufi saints represent the best in **syncretic culture** and practices and their shrines are the centres of devotion for millions of Hindus too and people of other different faiths. The Christians are also an integral part of Indian society. Most of them live in South India, mostly in Tamil Nadu, Kerala and Goa and the North-Eastern States and the rest are distributed all over the country. In the North-Eastern States, most of the Christians belong to the Scheduled Tribes.

> **Quick Fact**
>
> **Syncretic Culture**
>
> A culture that blends elements from multiple religious or cultural traditions, often seen in regions with diverse religious communities.

Sikhism is the youngest of all Indian religions. Founded in the 16th century by Guru Nanak, its adherents are mostly concentrated in Punjab, Haryana, Chandigarh and Delhi. A very enterprising community, they live in many parts of the world. They have also contributed significantly to the Green Revolution in Punjab, Haryana and **Terai regions** of Uttar Pradesh and Uttarakhand. They are progressive farmers in rural areas and mainly businessmen and traders in cities.

> **Quick Fact**
>
> **Terai Region**
>
> A lowland area located at the foothills of the Himalayas, spanning across parts of India and Nepal, known for its fertile land.

COMMERCIALISATION OF RELIGION

The rapid expansion of markets and market forces has also contributed to the growing commercialisation of Indian society. The market forces are pushing out spirituality from the religion and transforming religion into a saleable commodity. Significantly, religious festivals in different areas are undergoing a change. They used to take place in a localised manner. There were local rituals, local deities and local, austere, peaceful and simple celebrations.

The nature of most of the festivals has changed. Ganesh Chaturthi and Durga Puja are the most glaring examples. Both are now very noisy and market oriented. Moreover, both have become pan Indian largely because of market forces and mass media. This may be called as 'universalised Hinduism'.

The *Navratri* festival in Gujarat, where the *garba* pandals have been transformed into high-tech, pop, commercial centres in which entry fee escalated to hundreds and thousands of rupees may be seen as the most obvious example of this phenomenon. Moharrum, a solemn and simple festival of mourning, is also being transformed into a commercialised occasion with the entry of high-tech electronic devices. Similar is the case with Christian and Sikh festivals.

What Do You Think?

How does the commercialisation of religion impact its spiritual essence and societal role, and where should the line be drawn between faith-based practices and profit-driven ventures?

RELIGIOUS AND LINGUISTIC MINORITIES

India is widely known as a 'nation of pluralism/multiculturalism'. People speaking hundreds of languages and dialects and followers of all major religions of the world inhabit this land of amazing cultural pluralism. However, there appears to be substantial differentials in the socio-economic and demographic profiles of major religious communities in India, mainly emerging from socio-cultural and historical reasons. The status of linguistic communities is also largely related to these factors.

The Constitution of India uses the term 'minority', but does not define it. In order to have some understanding of the term 'minority', one refers to the works and interpretations of social scientists and to judicial decisions. The term 'minority' is a compound of the Latin word '*minor*' and the suffix 'ity' meaning inter alia 'the smaller in number of the two aggregates that together constitute a whole.' The Webster dictionary defines it as 'a group characterised by a sense of separate identity and awareness of status apart from a usually larger group of which it forms or is held to form a part.' The Oxford English Dictionary defines minority as 'the condition or fact of being smaller, inferior or subordinate or as a number which is less than half of the whole number. The meanings and definitions just referred to contain a common criterion, namely, the statistical criterion.' Apart from the statistical criterion mentioned above, the term 'minority' may also be defined on the basis of certain characteristics which are commonly possessed by the members constituting it. In this sense, the term signifies such groups of people as are united by certain common features and feel they belong to one common unit. Such groups may be held together by ties of common descent, physical characteristics, traditions, customs, language or religious faith, or a combination of these. In any case, therefore, there is a sense of akinness, a sense of community or unity prevalent in the group or groups that distinguish them from the majority of the inhabitants of the area where such minorities function. It is this sense of akinness within the group coupled with the consciousness of a difference with the majority which may serve as the basis of various political or other claims. There may also be cases when differential treatment alone is the pointer that may determine the minority status. Such differential treatment may be shown by another group or other groups of people towards this group or it may be self-imposed by the 'minority' group itself.

Sumanta Banerjee (1999)[1] adding a very important dimension to the meaning and interpretation of minority says that "in the context of human rights today, the term 'minority' is no longer a numerical concept, but has come to signify a non-dominant and disadvantaged group in a state or society, be it ethnic, religious or linguistic. The Muslims for instance are a disadvantaged minority group in India." Thus, the place of a group of people in the power structure of the society and the state becomes very crucial in identifying it as a 'minority'.

Though the Constitution of India does not define 'minority', it recognises two types of minorities, based on religion and language. That is how and why we talk about religious and linguistic minorities. The Constitution uses the term 'minority/minorities' only in four articles, namely Articles 29, 30, 350-A and 350-B:

- **Article 29** (1) Any section of citizens residing in the territory of India or any part thereof having a distinct language, script or culture of its own have right to conserve the same.
  (2) No citizen shall be denied admission into any educational institution maintained by the state or receiving aid out of state funds on grounds of religion, race, caste, language or any of them.
- **Article 30** (1) All minorities, whether based on religion or language, shall have the right to establish and administer educational institutions of their choice.
  (2) The state shall not, in granting aid to educational institutions, discriminate against any educational institution on the ground that it is under the management of minority, whether based on religion or language.
- **Article 350 (A)** It shall be the endeavour of every state and of every local authority within the state to provide adequate facilities for instruction in the mother tongue at the primary state of education to children belonging to Linguistic Minority groups; and the President may issue such directions to any state as he considers necessary or proper for securing the provision of such facilities.
- **Article 350 (B)** (1) There shall be a special officer for linguistic minorities to be appointed by the President.
  (2) It shall be the duty of the special officer to investigate all matters relating to the safeguards provided for linguistic minorities under this Constitution and report to the President upon those matters at such interval as the President may direct and the President shall cause all such reports to be laid before each House of Parliament and send to the governments of the state concerned.

Thus, in the absence of any formal or definite definition, we largely go by the judicial pronouncements given from time to time. But, one thing is absolutely clear and that is the fact that all the internationally recognised normative principles are enshrined in the Constitution of India. On a practical plane, the word 'minority' in India is most often used in the context of religious communities – Muslims, Christians, Sikhs, Parsees (Zoroastrians) and Jews. This category also includes Buddhists and Jains which means that all non-Hindu communities come under the category of

[1] Banerjee, Sumanta, Homes in Emptiness, New Delhi: Srishti Publishers & Distributors, 1999

minorities. Following are the profiles and important facts and figures about the social, economic and political status of the religious minorities.

MUSLIMS

Muslims in India are the largest and the most important religious minority of the country. Though a minority in its numerical strength, it is so big as to make it the second or third biggest Muslim population in the world, after Indonesia and Pakistan. Muslims constitute about 14% of the total population of India and form an important segment in the social fabric of the country. They are distributed all over the country and live in every region, state and Union Territory in varying numbers.

Muslims are in majority in Jammu and Kashmir and Lakshadweep and constitute a significant minority in several other states:

1. They are more than 20% of the total population of Assam, Kerala and West Bengal.
2. They are 10–20% in Uttar Pradesh, Bihar-Jharkhand and Karnataka.
3. They are 5–10% in Telangana-Andhra Pradesh, Madhya Pradesh, Haryana, Rajasthan and Gujarat.
4. In terms of absolute number, they are most numerous in Uttar Pradesh and Bihar.
5. In the remaining states they constitute 1–5% of the total population.
6. In states like Sikkim, Mizoram, Meghalaya and Nagaland, they are less than 1%.
7. Significantly, states with a higher percentage of Muslims do not account for larger Muslim population.

A significant fact about Muslim demography is their higher urban population. About 35% or more of Muslims live in urban areas and it has significant bearing on their economic profile and access to healthcare and educational facilities.

ECONOMIC SCENE

All the available studies, surveys and reports reveal that Muslims are educationally and economically backward community. A sizeable majority of Muslims live in **abject poverty**. The percentage of Muslim population below the poverty line stands around 40 – higher than the national average. In rural areas, they are mostly landless and lack access to employment opportunities and other wage employment avenues. The majority (53%) of Muslims are self-employed and earn their livelihood through petty business, small-scale enterprises and low-paid jobs. In the rural areas their overwhelming majority is agricultural labourers and artisans, while in the urban areas they earn income from artisan and industrial works. As compared to other religious communities, the participation of women in their workforce is much lower. They contribute to the family economy largely through jobs performed within the four walls of the house, especially in the urban areas where they are involved in such works as *Bidi* making, *Chikan* embroidery work in and around Lucknow and similar other occupations.

> **Quick Fact**
>
> **Abject Poverty**
>
> The most severe form of poverty, where people live in conditions of extreme deprivation.

It is unanimously accepted that, through the ages, Muslims have been excellent artisans involved in different types of handicrafts and this has proved to be their undoing. In the face of the challenges of mechanisation and industrialisation, emergence of new market forces and lack of access to institutional finance, they have been reduced to mere wage labour and cease to be the owners of these units in most of the cases. The following table may give the reader some idea of this problem:

Industry	Region
Bangles, glassware	Ferozabad (U.P.)
Wool, woodwork	Saharanpur (U.P.)
Carpets	Bhadohi, Mirzapur (U.P.)
Brasspots	Moradabad (U.P.)
Lungis	Chennai (T.N.)
Woollen shawls, carpets	Kashmir
Handloom	Madras (T.N.), Bhiwandi (Maharashtra), Mau (U.P.)
Chikan embroidery	Lucknow (U.P.)
Locks	Aligarh (U.P.)
Shoes	Kanpur (U.P.)
Leather	Kolkata, Chennai, Kanpur
Scissors	Meerut (U.P.)
Silk	Ramanagara (Karnataka)

Survey reports reveal that only in some of these industries they dominate while in others most of them are wage earners.

EDUCATION

As stated earlier, Muslims are below the national average in literacy and education. Some attribute it to their economic backwardness, some are of the view that it is on account of their religion. There is a popular perception that Islam prohibits secular education and encourages only religious education and that's why there are so many *madrasas* and few schools and colleges maintained by them. If the religion is any hindrance to secular education, then why even a theoretic country like Iran ruled by religious priests put so much emphasis on the teaching of science and technology or Indonesia with the largest Muslim population of the world invest so much on secular education? Moreover, only a small percentage of children go to madrasas.

The partition of the country in 1947 had an important bearing on the educational status of Muslims. The modern, educated middle- and upper-class Muslims left for Pakistan, especially from the north and western India and among those left behind were a large number of poor and illiterate masses. Apart from a small middle-class community of Muslims, those left behind were artisans, small traders, coolies, rickshaw pullers, tongawallas and lumpen elements in urban areas and small peasants, landless labour and others in rural areas. With such backward economic status, there was hardly any incentive for modern secular education. There are some other factors that have contributed to the educational backwardness. Firstly, most of the Muslims in urban areas are artisans and others like dyers, weavers and bangle makers. They consider it beyond their means to send their children to school and also a sheer waste of time as their children supplement the parental or family work. However, they can be sent to a madrasa either in the early morning or late evening. Moreover, Muslim's low economic status and the parental perception that their children will not get jobs anyway on account of prejudices and discrimination (though this may not always be correct) also discourage them from sending their children to schools or colleges. The lack of higher aspirations and opportunities for upward mobility are also discouraging factors. On account of low economic status of their parents, the rate of dropout is also high among them. Beyond the primary level, it exceeds 60% and therefore graduates hardly account for 2% though their population is more than 14%.

The much maligned and condemned madrasas have played an important role in Muslim education, especially promoting literacy among Muslims. Though Islamic theology, logic, philosophy and history have been the traditional areas of knowledge in madrasas, education, modern and secular areas of knowledge are now being added to them. The existing **maktabs** and *madrasas* need to be revamped so as to provide scope for the introduction of modern education along with religious education. States like Karnataka, Kerala and Telangana–Andhra Pradesh and some madrasas from Uttar Pradesh and Bihar have already introduced the teaching of science, mathematics, geography and computer education in the madrasa curriculum. The Union Government as well as a number of state governments are helping in the modernisation of madrasa education. Part of the reason why maktabs and madrasas flourish is because the state has not done enough to promote modern education in mofussil towns and the rural hinterlands. Hence, children of poor Muslim families flock to religious schools – *madrasa* among the Muslims and *pathshalas* among the Hindus. Of late, some politically vested interests have launched a vicious campaign of misinformation against the madrasas by dubbing them as centres of anti-national activities. One may condemn the madrasas for their orthodox, conservative, dogmatic and outdated syllabi, but the general accusation that they harbour ISI agents and terrorists is highly irresponsible. Education is both a challenge and a solution to most of the problems faced by Indian Muslims.

Quick Fact

Maktab

A maktab is a traditional elementary school for the Muslims, that teaches Islamic studies and basic reading and writing skills. *Maktab* comes from the Arabic word *kataba*, which means 'to write'.

SOCIAL CONDITIONS

Indian Muslims are not a 'cultural community' in the sense that they do not have a common language or adhere to the same lifestyle. They do not occupy a common geographical space. They are not regional communities either.

> They are born, live and die in different parts of India and speak a multiplicity of languages. What is, however, common to them is their religion, which they share with fellow Muslims all over the world. Therefore, to identify religion as the sole basis of their identity is incorrect and illogical.
>
> ... (T.K. Oommen,[2] 1998)

But, the irony is that the religion based socio-cultural specialties are magnified and utilised to mark out the religious minorities.

To many people, they are held responsible for the partition of India. But, three important facts should not be ignored here. First, the allegation that Muslims were responsible for partition may be applicable to urban Muslims of North India, particularly of Uttar Pradesh. Second, a substantial section of the Muslims were vigorous participants in the anti-colonial, freedom movement. Third, at the time of partition, only a small number of Muslims from the territory allocated to India migrated to Pakistan; the vast majority stayed back.

Indian Muslims, like Hindus and others, are steeped in the caste-based social stratification contrary to the ideology of Islam. They, too, have higher and lower caste groups – *Ashraf* is referred to the higher castes such as *Saiyyed* and *Shaikh* and *Ailaf* refers to the lower castes, mostly the occupationally specialised castes and artisan groups such as *julaha* (weaver), *Qasai* or *Chikwa* (butcher), *Raeen* (vegetable vender), *Manihar* (bangle seller), *Badhai* (carpenter), etc. At the same time, there is a strong backward class movement among them marginalising the ashraf castes.

Doctrinal variety, social hierarchy and economic stratification are quite pronounced characteristics of Muslims as well – though they are, perhaps, not as marked, open, obvious and proclaimed as in the case of Hindus. The *Shias*, the *Sunnis* and the *Wahabis* or the *Khojas*, the *Bohras* and the *Aghakhanis* are just a few examples of a large number of differentiations based on religious as well as quasi-religious beliefs and rituals.

The status of women, polygamy, family planning (birth control) and 'uniform civil code vs. personal law' have been issues steeped in subjective prejudices, preconceived notions and speculations. For having a correct understanding of their social status, one must have an objective understanding of these issues in their proper perspectives. When we have a look at the status of women among Muslims, we must honestly acknowledge the fact that the status of women in India as a whole is lower than those in western societies. If the status of Muslim women is sought to be determined only on the basis of one determinant, i.e., easy divorce or triple *talaaq* (divorce), then what about the rampant dowry problem, maltreatment and bride burning among Hindus? The case of several Muslim countries where women are more empowered and enjoy a

Quick Fact

Uniform Civil Code

The Uniform Civil Code (UCC) proposes a single set of laws for all of India, applicable to all religious communities in areas like marriage, divorce, inheritance, and adoption. This code is referenced in Article 44 of the Constitution, which directs the state to work toward implementing a Uniform Civil Code for citizens across India.

This proposal remains a subject of debate and is seen as a way to unify diverse legal practices across communities

[2] Oomen, TK, Citizenship, Nationality and Ethnicity, American Journal of Sociology, 103(5) 1998

higher social status point to the fact that religion has never been a barrier to social mobility among Muslim women. The case of theocratic Iran, Egypt, Indonesia, Turkey, etc. may be cited in support of this argument while looking at the educational backwardness of Indian Muslim women. The traditional, patriarchal society always tried to keep her uneducated or gave her only elementary religious education so that she can perform certain religious duties, nothing more. However, this is more a social than a religious or ideological problem. Our attitudes are determined as much by social factors as by religious or ideological factors. At times societal aspects prevail, overriding religious or ideological aspects. If educational level among them is comparatively lower, the reason is socio-economic rather than religious. It is true that education and socio-economic status are closely related. But, it is also conditioned by the value system prevalent in a given society. The fact remains that what Islam had given her, the male-dominated society took away. But, the situation is fast changing. The winds of modernisation are sweeping Muslims too. Muslim girls are going for modern education, participating in all spheres of life, have a better share than ever in the decision-making process at the family level and quite a few of them have started refusing to be cowed down by religious threats.

Powerful myths are promoted to achieve narrow political ends in India. One glaring example is the prevailing communal propaganda about polygyny and population growth. A rational and objective examination of empirical data is essential to know the truth. Though the religion and the law allow a Muslim to have more than one wife, is it empirically true? As per the 2011 census data, there are 951 females per 1000 males among Indian Muslims, better than Hindus, Sikhs and Jains. Is polygyny possible on a substantial scale? Any demographer worth his salt would immediately rubbish it. When the report of the *National Committee on the Status of Women in India (1971–1974)* came out with the startling revelation presented below, it shocked many a people.

These figures are corroborated by the figures from the Office of the Registrar General and Census Commissioner of India found in *Polygynous Marriages in India – A survey* and *Peoples of India Project* (Anthropological Survey of India).

Incidence of Polygyny in India		
1.	Tribal Communities	15.2%
2.	Buddhists	7.8%
3.	Jains	6.7%
4.	Hindus	5.8%
5.	Muslims	5.7%

What Do You Think?

How do cultural traditions and religious beliefs that permit polygyny align with India's predominantly monogamous legal framework under civil law?

As per the findings of this report, the cultural motivation for plural marriage besides barrenness of wife, absence of son, the custom of marrying a brother's wife, etc. economic gain is also an important motivation for polygamy among communities where women contribute substantially to the family economy. Some artisan groups, both Muslim and Hindu, find it cheaper to have another wife as extra hand than hiring labour. Thus, the incidence of polygyny is directly related to the status and role of women in their respective societies.

As far as population growth is concerned, it is true that the birth rate has always been higher among Muslims. The acceptance of family planning methods and birth rate is dependent upon a large number of factors. The major ones are occupation, income, access to technology, child survival, education and skills, the economic value of children and security in old age (*Report of the Working Group on Population Policy, Planning Commission*). The significance of these and other factors lend credence to the possibility of Muslims having a higher birth rate because they are relatively more disadvantaged in all these areas. But, this is also true that as per the latest 2011 census, the decline of birth rate among them is highest among all the religious communities showing that birth control among them is fast picking up. If the facts are examined without prejudice, the inescapable conclusion is that religion is not the primary determining factor in population. Against this background, one must also note that birth rates in the Malabar region of Kerala, an area with a Muslim population of 40%, are significantly lower than those in Uttar Pradesh with only about 18% Muslim population. Goa, with its large population of Catholics, has one of the lowest birth rates in the country. Then, if religion does not matter much, what accounts for the persistently higher rate of population growth of Indian Muslims besides the factors enumerated above? However, the 2011 census shows that the decline in total fertility rate among the Muslims is highest among all religious communities showing that they, too, have taken to the small family norm in a big way. Thus, it is hoped that in the next or next two decades their birth rate would be at par with others. Moreover, some other factors should also not be ignored. Among the Muslims the world over widow remarriage is popular while among the traditional Hindus, it is not. Muslims are comparatively more educationally backward especially their women folk. Further, we should not ignore the fact that their religion is not the main factor for their higher fertility because a number of Muslim countries, even the theocratic Iran, encourages family planning. It is also failure of the state and hence one should not blame their religion and culture.

What Do You Think?

Is the status of women in India primarily a reflection of the failure of the state and its policies, or is it rooted in the influence of religion and cultural traditions within Indian society?

The debate on **Uniform Civil Code versus Muslim Personal Law** has also been a contentious issue steeped in misconceptions, sociological distortions and preconceived notions. Historically speaking, Islam in India functioned as a political entity rather than as a legal system. The *Shariat* was never really enforced during centuries of Muslim rule. Social, political and economic rather than religious factors were more important. As rightly pointed out by Rafiq Zakaria (1994), the Muslim Personal Law is merely a compilation of some *moulvis* (religious priests/scholars) at the instance of Lord Macaulay; it is based in many respects on the *Futuhaat-i-Alamgiri*, the judicial pronouncements in the reign of the raised Mughal emperor Aurangzeb. It bristles with innovations and is known as 'Muhammadan Law' which itself is a misnomer. It has been considerably modified by the decisions of the Privy Council during the British rule and by some of the legislative measures introduced by the Muslim members of the pre-partition Central Assembly. Moreover, some sections continued to be governed by customary laws. Similarly, usury, which is prohibited by the *Shariat*, was widely practiced by such orthodox practicing Muslims as the Pathans and the Arab immigrants. The theologians connived at these lapses because of worldly compulsions.

If we take a look at the demand often made by the secular sections of the Indian society for reforms in **Muslim Personal Law**, there is hardly any evidence of an attempt to change the whole of it. Muslim Personal Law from the progressive and secular forces does not seem to be contrary to the spirit of Islam. Essentially, whatever controversy there has been arose around the issues of polygamy and divorce. Islam can be shown to allow polygamy within certain restrictions, but it certainly does not enjoin it on everyone. This right has been severely restricted in most of the Muslim countries and there is no reason why polygamy cannot be completely banned, for Muslims and non-Muslims alike, if the Indian Parliament so desires. It will be entirely in the spirit of Islam. As to the matter of divorce, in actual practice Muslim males are at some advantage compared with the females, though the concept of allowing women to get a divorce is in the books from the beginning. There is no reason why uniformity should not be established in this respect by simply requiring a uniform marriage contract and by providing relevant safeguards to protect both the parties from economic hardships.

> **Quick Fact**
>
> **Shariat/Muslim Personal Law/ Islamic Law**
>
> A body of religious law in Islam derived from the Quran and Hadith, governing various aspects of a Muslim's personal and community life. The Muslim Personal Law (Shariat) Application Act of 1937 was enacted by the British colonial government to ensure that Islamic law was applied consistently among Indian Muslims. The law applies to all Indian Muslims, except in the states of Goa and Uttarakhand.
>
> The law does not apply to criminal matters, which are governed by the Indian Penal Code.

It is tragic and dangerous on the part of the present (largely self-acclaimed) leaders of the Muslim community to assert that the national parliament is not competent to make these changes. They fear that if changes are allowed in one area, then more changes will follow in other areas too and the Muslim Personal Law will be replaced by the present Hindu code. This fear is baseless. Even for highly religious Muslims any and every change should not be opposed as long as it does not violate the spirit of their religion. Do not let the male-dominated society take away what Islam gave to women and weaker sections of the society.

What Do You Think?

Can the minority rights be different from human rights?

POLITICAL STATUS

Indian Muslims enjoy all the civil and political rights enshrined in the Constitution for all the citizens of India. They are an integral part of the socio-political fabric of Indian society. Their electoral behaviour has been a matter of great interest for political scientists. It is heartening to see that, by and large, Muslims have preferred non-communal, political parties and except Kerala (where the Muslim League has a different structure and character), they have never supported, after independence, any communal Muslim political party even in Muslim-dominated constituencies. The Muslims, along with other religious communities, have been participating actively in the democratic political process. However, serious communal riots, especially after the 1960s, have instilled a sense of insecurity among the Muslims and tend to push them into their narrow communal shell. The serious violence in Gujarat during February–May 2002 supposedly in retaliation to the Godhra train burning incident has shaken not only the Indian Muslims, but all the concerned Indian citizens. This must be a thing of the past and Indian polity should never allow any similar episode, otherwise the authority of the state shall lose its legitimacy.

In his outstanding work of formidable scholarship *Ethnic Violence and Civic Life: Hindus and Muslims in India* (2002), Ashutosh Vashney writes that In Hindu-Muslim relations in India the state tends to act in a politically strategic, not a legally correct manner. The state in Gujarat acted in primarily strategic, not a legally correct manner.

Political integration does not mean political subordination. It means closer unity for political purposes in a heterogeneous country and multicultural society like India. Healthy regionalism, autonomy of cultures, free development of languages, liberties of social organisation are the very lifeblood of a federal democratic polity. The majority – communal and political – more than the minorities ought to remember this. Rasheeduddin Khan (1987) says that taking advantage of constitutional possibilities and the establishment of the process of democracy and change, the Muslim leadership at all levels should encourage their co-religionists to discard their separatist tendencies and enter the area of competitive polity and its composite problems so as to accelerate the pace of modernisation. Hitting at where it hurts most, an eminent human geographer Moonis Raza (1994) comments that the 'Indianness' and 'Muslimness' of the Indian Muslims are both defining characteristics and neither can be ignored nor underplayed in any nationally sound and scientific assessment of the situation. Thus, Indian Muslims are Muslim Indians as well.

In the past, Muslims had been either rulers or the ruled. Today, in India, they are co-rulers as joint sharers of national sovereignty. As Rasheeduddin Khan (ibid) rightly points out, the majority community is bound to be the first beneficiary of nationalism in a democratic society, therefore the minorities in order to retain their identity depend not merely on the promotion of nationalism, but also on the simultaneous development of subnationalism. Kancha Ilaiah (2003),[3] in his characteristically blunt and ruthlessly honest narration, comments that "Indian nationalism is not the property of Hindus only. It is the property of Muslims, Christians, Buddhists and Sikhs as well." Thus, religious minorities are the natural guardians of a secular state.

[3] Ilaiah Kancha, Buffalow Nationalism, Sage Publications, New Delhi, 2018

SACHAR COMMITTEE REPORT

In the post-independence period, the Government of India, showing concern for the continued educational and economic condition of Muslims, has been gathering information from various sources for taking up remedial measures. Thus, the Planning Commission, National Sample Survey Organisation (NSSO) and Gopal Singh Committee, among others, have been providing inputs.

Not satisfied with the progress in the desired direction, the Prime Minister constituted a high powered committee in 2004 under the chairmanship of Justice Rajinder Sachar, former Chief Justice of Punjab and Haryana high court. For the first time, eminent economists, sociologists and civil servants were taken as its members. The committee is now popularly known as the Sachar Committee.

SALIENT FINDINGS OF THE SACHAR COMMITTEE

(i) Education

(a) The literacy rate among Muslims was 59.1%, which was below the national average of 64.8%.

(b) The mean years of schooling (MYS) is lower compared to the average MYS for all children.

(c) 25% of Muslim children in the 6 to 14-year age group have either never attended school or have dropped out.

(d) The majority of Muslim girls and boys fail in their matriculation examination or drop out before that.

(e) Less than 4% of Muslims are graduates or diploma holders compared to about 7% of the population aged 20 years and above.

(f) There is a strong desire and enthusiasm for education among Muslim women and girls across the board.

(g) Schools beyond primary level are few in Muslim localities. Exclusive schools for girls are fewer.

(h) Lack of hostel facilities is a limiting factor, especially for girls.

(i) Muslim parents are not averse to modern or mainstream education and to sending their children to affordable government schools. They do not necessarily prefer to send children to madrasas. However, the access to government schools for Muslim children is limited.

(ii) Skill Development

(a) Skill development initiatives for those who have not completed school education may be particularly relevant for some sections of Muslims given their occupational structure.

(b) The skill demands in the manufacturing and service sectors are changing continuously and youth with middle school education would meet these needs.

(c) A rehabilitation package for innovative reskilling and for upgrading the occupational structure in the wake of liberalisation is seen as an urgent need.

(iii) Employment and Economic Opportunities

- **(a)** Self-employment is the main source of income for Muslims. They are engaged more in self-employed manufacturing and trade activities compared to others.
- **(b)** The share of Muslim workers engaged in street vending is the highest. More than 12% of Muslim male workers are engaged in street vending as compared to the national average of less than 8%.
- **(c)** Women Muslim workers undertaking work within their own homes is much larger at 70% compared to all workers at 51%.
- **(d)** The share of Muslims in the total workers engaged in the tobacco and textiles/garment-related industries is quite significant.
- **(e)** The share of Muslim workers in production-related activities and transport equipment operation is much higher at 34%, as against 21% of all workers.
- **(f)** More than 16% of Muslims were engaged as sales workers, while the national average was only about 10%.
- **(g)** While the participation of Muslim workers is relatively higher in production and sales-related occupations, their participation was relatively lower in professional, technical, clerical and to some extent managerial work.
- **(h)** Muslims, by and large, are engaged in the unorganised sector of the economy and have to bear the brunt of liberalisation.
- **(i)** The participation of Muslims in regular salaried jobs is much less than workers of other socio-religious categories.
- **(j)** Muslims are relatively more vulnerable in terms of conditions of work as their concentration in informal sector employment is higher and job conditions, even among regular workers, are less for Muslims than those of other socio-religious communities.
- **(k)** The percentage of households availing banking facilities is much lower in villages where the share of the Muslim population is high.

(iv) Poverty and Development

- **(a)** About 38% of Muslims in urban areas and 27% in rural areas live below the poverty level.
- **(b)** Muslims are concentrated in locations with poor infrastructure facilities. This affects their access to basic services like education, health facilities, transport, etc.
- **(c)** About a third of small villages with a high concentration of Muslims do not have any educational institutions.
- **(d)** There is a scarcity of medical facilities in larger villages with a substantial Muslim concentration. About 40% of large villages with a substantial Muslim concentration do not have any medical facilities.
- **(e)** Muslim concentration villages are not well served with *pucca* roads.
- **(f)** Policies to deal with the relative deprivation of Muslims in the country should sharply focus on inclusive development and mainstreaming of the community while respecting diversity.

(v) Social Conditions

- **(a)** A community-specific factor for low educational achievement is that Muslims do not see education as necessarily translating into formal employment.
- **(b)** The Muslim population shows an increasingly better sex ratio compared with other socio-religious communities.
- **(c)** Infant and childhood mortality among Muslims is slightly lower than the average.
- **(d)** There has been a large decline in fertility in all religious groups including Muslims.

CHRISTIANS

Christians constitute the second largest religious minority in India and they are around 3% of the total population of the country. The emergence of Christianity and Christians in India, as per popular belief, has been linked up with the advent of the British colonial rule. However, well-established traditions and historical evidence tell us that Christians have been existing in the state of Kerala right from the first A.D. Therefore, Christians can be considered not only the oldest religious minority, but Christianity is also one of the oldest religions in India. Thus, the 2 crore plus Christian population has been an integral part of India.

Like Muslims, they are widely distributed in the country forming a sizeable proportion of population in several states and Union Territories. The following are some of the important facts and figures about the Christian population in the country:

1. The Christian population is strongly concentrated in the southern states of Kerala, Tamil Nadu, Andhra Pradesh and Karnataka.
2. About 56% of the total Christian population of the country lives in the four southern states mentioned above.
3. Kerala alone has almost one third of the country's Christian population, while Tamil Nadu takes care of about one sixth of the national total.
4. A second major concentration of the Christians is seen in the North-Eastern States which together share 22% of the total Christian population of the country.
5. Though at the national level they form around 3%, at the state level they are in majority in three states, viz. Nagaland (88%), Mizoram (86%) and Meghalaya (65%). There are a few other states with a significant percentage of Christians. These are Manipur (34%), Goa (30%), Kerala (19%), Arunachal Pradesh (10%) and Tamil Nadu (6%). In Assam and Sikkim, they form 3% of the state population. While in the remaining states their population varies between 0.4% and 2%. Among the Union Territories, Andaman and Nicobar Islands has the highest Christian population (24%) and Puducherry has a substantial Christian population (7%). In the rest of the Union Territories, it ranges between 1% and 3%.
6. Among all the religious communities of India, the ratio of female population among the Christians is the highest which is 994 females per 1000 males. Perhaps, that is why they are not only more 'visible', but also constitute a significant segment of the workforce.

7. Contrary to popular belief, Indian Christians too are largely rural. Seventy-one per cent of all Christians in India are of rural background. Interestingly while in the south and the north east the Christians are predominantly rural, in north India, they are predominantly urban.
8. Among all the major religious minorities, Christians have the highest rate of literacy mainly because of the untiring effort of Christian missionaries.

Indian Christians like Indian Muslims do not constitute a 'cultural community'. They speak different languages, maintain different lifestyles and do not occupy a common geographical space. Even in the matter of religion, like Muslims, they are divided into several denominations. Of the multiple Christian denominations in India today, only five could be distinguished as the main groups from which the various sub-branches have emerged. There are the Syrian Christians or the St. Thomas Christians, the Latin or the Roman Catholics, the Protestants, the Tribal and the Dalits. The last two are often fused together since many of their concerns are similar. However, for better reasons, the two should be seen as separate groups. The fact that Roman Catholics constitute a major chunk of the Indian Christian population is also evident from the number of catholic institutions such as churches, schools, colleges and hospitals. The distribution of Catholic Church in India, related as it is with the concentration of catholic population, appears to be an outcome of the long history of diffusion of Christianity. The spread of Christianity owes much to the dedicated social work of missionaries in the areas of education and healthcare.

Two very indigenous offspring of the Christian movement are the tribal and Dalit Christians. Bonita Aleza noted that tribal Christians are spread across various regions of India. However, it is possible to identify two of the largest groups with more geographical specificity. These include the tribals of northeastern India and the Santhals, who are dispersed across Bihar, West Bengal, Odisha, and Assam.

In the remaining tribal areas, Christianity has touched the tribes only marginally. Christianity has been an important agency of welfare and modernisation among tribal societies. It has brought some positive changes in a number of their customs and practices. Among all the Christians in India, the Dalit Christians are the most vocal today. Most of them come from the Hindu untouchable castes who found Christianity as a welcome relief from the tyranny of the caste system. C.B. Webster (1994) has meticulously traced the origin and gradual proliferation of the Dalit Christian movement. He mentions that, on the basis of 1881 census report, four main groups of Dalits could be identified, viz. the Chuhra of Punjab, the Chamar of North India, the Mahar of central and western India and the Paraiyar of South India. Even though these groups were not homogenous, certain common characteristics could still be distinguished among them. These were their main occupation as agricultural labourers, poverty, similar rituals concerning birth, marriage and death and finally lack of sympathy or support to their cause from other social and caste groups. Of course, all of them were also untouchables and suffered from a number of socio-economic disabilities like lack of landownership, lack of services from other castes such as barbers, washermen, priests, etc., bondage, lack of access to education and so on. In the 1920s and 1930s there was a tremendous spontaneous movement of Dalits towards Christianity. The Dalits escaped into the Christian fold to take advantage of upward mobility through economic independence and education. But, discrimination continued to persist, though on a much lower scale, as the descendants of higher caste Christians continued to look at them from the higher pedestal of caste hierarchy. Sometimes even the church resorted to discrimination. As Bonita Aliaz (ibid) points out, even today the church is not free from caste prejudices. In the north, however, caste has been largely replaced by class within the church community. But, the relationship of Dalit Christians with other communities is still defined by caste. In the south, the associational view of caste predominates within the Christian community.

Large numbers of Christians in rural areas, mainly converts from lower Hindu castes, follow their pre-conversion occupational patterns. Rowena Robinson (2001), making an incisive comment on this aspect, says that

> The negotiation of caste differences within Christian groups constitutes an area of considerable historical and sociological interest. Wherever group conversions took place, the converts carried their caste identities with them even as they shed their religious affiliations.

There is a small section of urban middle-class Christians which has experienced upward mobility through the educational facilities made available by the missionaries. TK Oommen,[4] talking about their political status says that

> Christians in India are not organised into a political party and this is due to two factors: First, their socio-cultural fragmentation based on denominations and language to which we have already referred; and, second, their conscious rejection of separate electorates initially and the subsequent non-communal approach they seem to have adopted in political affairs.

There is one area in which Christians dominate in India, notwithstanding their small size and economic disabilities and that is in the area of service institutions, particularly in education and health. The last few decades witnessed large-scale attacks on churches and Christians in Gujarat, Orissa and several other states. The alleged 'large-scale' conversions through 'coercion and fraudulent' means are said to be the root cause of these atrocities. There are more than a million Christians in Bihar, Karnataka and Maharashtra, but significantly, the states targeted for the fundamentalist attack were Gujarat and Orissa having 0.44% and 2.1% Christian population respectively. Though there have always been some cases of conversion of Dalits and tribals, the issue has been blown out of proportion and the hate campaign against minorities, especially Christians and Muslims, is being used as a political tool by a major political party and its various affiliates. B.K. Roy Burman (1999)[5] analysing the facts of conversion tell us that "the followers of Christianity among the tribal peoples of Gujarat were 0.09 percent of the total tribal population of the state in 1961, 0.24% in 1971 and 0.40% in 1981." The percentage of Christians in fact has decreased according to the census of 1991. If Christian missionaries were all the time busy with conversions, why is this decrease in numbers? If a person changes his religion on his own, that is his own choice and such a personal choice is respected all over the world. Yet in a multireligious society like India surrounded by fundamentalist regimes, even microscopic number of conversion to any non-Hindu faiths generates fears, apprehensions, insecurities and ill will. Under such circumstances, it is in the interest of the minorities to keep away from any such activities, however small scale it might be.

[4] Oommen, T K, The Christian Clergy in India, Sage Publications, New Delhi, 2000

[5] Roy Burman, B.K & B. G. Verghese, Aspiring to be tribal/Indigenous, Konark Publication, New Delhi, 1999

SIKHS

Sikhs are the third major religious minority in India. Originated in Punjab, they are found in all parts of the country carrying with them vital elements of the Punjabi culture.

The Sikhs constitute about 2% of the total population of India that comes to 16.26 million people. Significantly, the overwhelming majority of Sikhs are still concentrated in Punjab. Of their total population, 78.5% reside in Punjab, 6% in Haryana and the remaining in Himachal Pradesh, Rajasthan, Delhi, Chandigarh and Jammu & Kashmir. Significantly most of the areas in these adjoining states were once parts of the greater Punjab. The partition of the country in 1947 was a major event in the history of the Sikhs. There was almost a complete exodus of Sikhs from west Punjab (now in Pakistan) and their resettlement on this side of the border. In his analysis of the social geography of the country, Aijazuddin Ahmed remarked that the redistribution of the Sikh population after Partition led to the introduction of Sikh communities in neighboring Haryana and Rajasthan. In these areas, irrigated colonies, such as those in the Ganga Nagar and Kurukshetra districts, became new centers of Sikh resettlement. Sikhs also established themselves in the Terai regions of Uttar Pradesh.

The Sikh Jats became a symbol of irrigation agriculture and perhaps the most active agent of agrarian revolution that followed the construction of canals in Punjab.

The Sikhs are not a **monolith community**. They consist of several sectors such as *Namdharis, Nihangs, Udasis, Nirankaris, Niranjanis, Nanak Panthis*, etc. A Sikh gurudwara is not merely a sacred religious place of worship. It is the religio-cultural hub of the community where so many rituals and ceremonies related to birth, nomenclature, marriage and death are performed. It is the most important place of congregation which has been used even for such secular activities as electoral politics. Though the devout Sikhs visit a village gurudwara or a city gurudwara as a matter of routine, but the most important congregations may be seen on *Baisakhi* which marks the birth of the *Khalsa panth* and the two *Guru Parva* (birthdays of Guru Nanak and Guru Gobind Singh).

> **Quick Fact**
>
> **Monolith Community**
>
> Broken into its roots **mono** and **lithic**, monolithic means 'one stone.' When monolithic is used to describe something societal, it has a slightly negative connotation. A monolithic society is rigid and homogenous, not open to new ideas.

The economic status of Sikhs has always been a matter of envy to others. In rural areas, wherever they live, they are excellent cultivators and a substantial section of them are rich farmers. As stated earlier, these Sikh Jats have played a very important role in the 'Green Revolution' of the country. In urban areas, most of them earn their livelihood in the trade and commerce sector. They have substantial presence in transport, automobile, spare parts and transport service sector such as garage, etc. They have always maintained a larger share in the defence forces, larger in ratio than their population.

Like Muslims and Christians, Sikhs are also internally segmented. They are divided into caste, class and urban–rural divides – the urban Sikh trading community, popularly known as *Bhapas* (Khatris, Aroras, etc.) on the one hand, the daily wage–earning Sikhs, generally of lower castes on the other.

Moreover, there are caste–class divisions among artisans, such as carpenters (*Ramgarhias*), black-smiths (*lohars*), etc. right from the cities to the towns and the villages. Then there are *Mazhabi* Sikhs, the scheduled castes.

After the partition turmoil, the post-Indira Gandhi assassination, anti-Sikh violence was the second event that shook the entire Sikh community. Thousands of Sikhs were massacred in Delhi, Kanpur, Bokaro and elsewhere. But, being a robust and vibrant community, they have recovered from this trauma too. The Sikhs, in spite of their cultural pride, still closely identify themselves with India and except a microscopic minority, they are not tempted by **secessionism**.

Quick Fact

Secessionism

It is the idea of breaking away from a larger group to form a new nation. Many people wanted a separate state, union territory, or an autonomous administrative division within India.

LINGUISTIC MINORITIES

Language is one of the greatest glories and achievements of mankind. It is indeed one of the greatest treasures of human civilisation. It is the most important part of human culture and cultural expression. Language also gives any human group its cultural identity and the preservation of all the components of culture is ensured through language.

India is home to a very large number of languages. In his monumental work Linguistic Survey of India, Grierson enumerated 179 languages and as many as 544 dialects in the country. Even if we take out several languages from this category of languages and put them in the category of dialects, the fact remains that India will be described as a land of great language diversity and linguistic pluralism. Aijazuddin Ahmed describes India's social geography as a linguistic continuum rather than a pluralistic system. Dialects and languages blend seamlessly, with transitional zones where bilingualism is common. This fluid coexistence of languages remains a defining feature of modern India.

When India became independent and different types of groups and communities in pluralistic India were craving for the fulfilment of their aspirations, India's national leaders had to confront several language problems in the first two decades of independence. These problems included the official language issue, demands for the linguistic reorganisation of the provinces of India whose boundaries during British rule did not conform to linguistic division and the status of 'minority languages' within reorganised states. Thus, the issues and problems of 'linguistic minorities' are largely the by-product of the reorganisation of states.

What Do You Think?

How can societies balance the preservation of linguistic minorities' rights and cultural heritage while promoting national integration and unity?

What a Linguistic Minority means is clear from Articles 29 and 30 of the Constitution. Thus, 'Linguistic Minorities' are minorities residing in the territory of India or any part thereof having a distinct language or script of their own.

> The language of the minority groups need not be one of the languages mentioned in the Eighth Schedule of the Constitution. A Linguistic Minority at the state level means any group of people whose mother tongue is different from the principal language of the state the speakers of all the languages become eligible for being included among the linguistic minorities, in one or more states, districts or *taluks*, except for those where the principal language is the same as their own language. (Report of the Commissioner for Linguistic Minorities in India, 1988)[6]

Apart from the constitutional provisions enshrined in Articles 29, 30, 347 and 350 of the Constitution, the bulk of the safeguards for linguistic minorities were formulated during 1956–1961, i.e. immediately following the reorganisation of states on a linguistic basis.

Talking about the prejudices and discriminatory tendencies among the dominant ruling class, Paul R. Brass[7] (1955) rightly points out that

> In contrast to the pluralist policies pursued by the government of India, many of the states have pursued discriminatory policies towards their linguistic (and other) minorities within their boundaries. Moreover, the Centre has been unable to protect such minorities effectively against the opposition of the state governments concerned.

The examples of Bengali-speaking people in Assam; Kannada, Malayalam and Tamil-speaking people of Andhra Pradesh; and vice versa may be cited. Among the worst casualties has been Urdu in the north Indian states and the various so-called 'mother tongues' or 'dialects' of Hindi and other larger languages which have not been granted official recognition by either the central or the state governments. Moreover, even when official recognition has been granted grudgingly in some states, for instance to Urdu in Uttar Pradesh, Bihar and Andhra Pradesh, the discriminatory policies and practices continued unabated. The case of some of these dialects – for example, the Maithili language of north Bihar may also be cited. These are separate languages in all, but have official recognition. To avoid the controversial issue of distinguishing between 'languages' and 'dialects', however, it is best to follow the practice of the Indian census authorities and use the term 'mother tongue' to encompass both terms. Paul Brass (ibid) stretching the argument further says that the languages and mother tongues are, in effect, arranged in a hierarchy of official status. At the top are the two languages, Hindi and English, recognised as official languages of the Union. At the next level are the regional languages recognised as official languages in the linguistically reorganised states (such as Kannada, Marathi, Odiya, Tamil, Bengali, etc.) all of which are also listed in the Eighth Schedule. At a third level are those languages listed in the Eighth Schedule which have no official status in any province, namely Sanskrit and Sindhi, the language of the province of Sindh now in Pakistan.

Since language is the most important marker of identity, the linguistic minorities in different states have to face discriminatory and sometimes hostile attitude of the dominant class in different states, especially in the sphere of job competition and other economic grievances. The speakers of minority languages are always conscious of their cultural identity and when faced with a hostile state tend to come together and become a political force for the redressal of their grievances.

---

6 Report of the Commissioner for Linguistic Minorities, Ministry of Minority Affairs, New Delhi, 1998

7 Brass R Paul, Universe Publishing Company, Mumbai, 2005

While the linguistic minorities are entitled to reasonable safeguards to protect their educational, cultural and other interests, it has to be borne in mind that such safeguards should not operate as to perpetuate separatism. The best interest of both linguistic minorities as also the dominant linguistic majority can be secured only by promoting mutual understanding, goodwill and cooperation between them, rather than by mere insistence on rights and safeguards. After all, in the ultimate analysis, the welfare of the individual or groups of individuals, irrespective of their mother tongue, depends on the progress made by the country as a whole and by defending the national independence.

The case of tribal languages and linguistic groups is also an important issue in any discussion on linguistic minorities. Paul Brass (ibid) taking a holistic view of the situation rightly says that recognition of a mother tongue by a state government is no guarantee that facilities will actually be provided for students in government schools to receive instruction through the medium of their mother tongue. State government rules and regulations generally require that the parents of the children who wish such instruction formally request it and that a certain number of children in each school and classroom must do so in order to receive such instruction. Even then competent teachers and textbooks in the language may not be available. Spokesmen for several other tribal languages, both in the predominantly Hindi-speaking states and in other states with large tribal minorities, have demanded instruction for their children in their mother tongue, but the 'Scheduled Areas and Scheduled Tribes Commission' appointed by the Government of India in 1960 reported that

> In actual fact some of the states have taken this matter very casually. Moreover, the state governments in general have tended to ignore the request of the Commissioner for Linguistic Minorities and for Scheduled Castes and Tribes even for information on the extent to which speakers of tribal minority mother tongues have actually been provided with facilities for instruction in their mother tongues. For example, the government of Bihar claims to have provided facilities for instructions through the medium of Oraon, Ho, Santhali and Mundari, but has not provided any figures to support its claim since 1975–76.[8]

A lot remains to be done for our tribal linguistic groups. The problem of lack of script and the constraints of inadequacy of textbooks need to be tackled at the national level. Early action needs to be taken for evolving a common script for tribal languages/dialects with a view to promoting education among the tribal people, particularly at the primary stage of education. Devanagari (Hindi) may appear to be an appropriate script for adoption for the tribal languages and dialects in the country, as has been adopted by the Bodos of Assam and the Bhils, Munda and Gonds of Madhya Pradesh.

National integration is not possible without emotional integration. Small minorities may be bulldozed into submission for the time being, but in the long run it will lead to separatist tendencies among them. When any minority group feels that its language, religion, customs and traditions are safe in the country and the state is doing all for its conservation, it strengthens the sense of belonging and acceptance of the language and culture of larger society. Cultural pluralism has been the essence of Indian civilisation. India's destiny lies in pluralism and 'unity in diversity'. Moreover, among the determining criteria of any 'civil society' are the way minorities and women are treated in it.

---

[8] Scheduled Areas and Scheduled Tribes Commission, Government of India, New Delhi, 1960

What Do You Think?

How does the promotion of pluralism in Indian society contribute to the upliftment of minorities and women in civil society?

Questions and Indicative Answers

1. Describe the Indic and non-Indic religions along with their distribution in different regions.

- India is home to followers of all the major religions of the world. Religions that originated in India such as Hinduism, Jainism, Buddhism and Sikhism are known as Indic religions.
- Non-Indic religions are those which originated elsewhere, but whose followers brought it to India and now these religions are an integral part of Indian society. These are Islam, Christianity, Judaism and Zoroastrianism.
- Muslims are the largest religious minority and live everywhere in India.
- Christians too are widely distributed, but their largest percentage is in Kerala, Tamil Nadu, Andhra Pradesh, Meghalaya and Mizoram while the concentration of Sikhs may be seen in Punjab, Haryana, Chandigarh and Delhi. Parsees live mainly in Bombay and Gujarat.

2. Discuss the concept of religious minorities and constitutional provisions with respect to them.

- Though a minority is largely determined on the basis of numbers and non-dominant position, the current trend is based on their share in the power structure of society.
- Articles 29 and 30 pertain to the rights of religious minorities to establish and run educational institutions of their choice.

3. Write a note on the socio-economic status of the Muslim minority.

- Right from the days of the Gopal Singh Committee Report and reports of the NSSO, Muslims have always been an educationally and economically backward community. In recent times, the Sachar Committee Report on the basis of hard data reached the same conclusion and made recommendations accordingly.
- Contrary to popular perception, Indian Muslims are not a monolithic population. They also exhibit diversity in terms of their religious beliefs, language, customs, traditions and ethnicity.
- They also live along the caste-like social system.

4. What are the salient findings of the Sachar Committee?

For details, see text.

Previous Years' Questions

1. Discuss the problems faced by religious minorities in India.
(UPSC CSE Mains Anthropology, Paper II, 2015)
2. Write a short note on Endangered Languages **(UPSC CSE Mains Anthropology, Paper II, 2018)**
3. Write a critical narrative on the concerns of religious minorities in India.
(UPSC CSE Mains Sociology, Paper II, 2018)
4. What are the social and political problems of religious minorities in India?
(UPSC CSE Mains Anthropology, Paper II, 2020)
5. Delineate the constitutional safeguard for religious minorities in India.
(UPSC CSE Mains Anthropology, Paper II, 2021)
6. Write a short note on Safeguards for linguistic minorities in India.
(UPSC CSE Mains Anthropology, Paper II, 2022)
7. Discuss the problems of religious minorities in India and suggest measures to solve them.
(UPSC CSE Mains Sociology, Paper II, 2022)

Focus Areas for the Examination

1. Religious Communities and Religious Minorities
2. Social, Economic and Political Status of Religious Minorities
3. Sachar Committee
4. Problems of Linguistic Minorities

CHAPTER 9

Women and Society in India: Different Facets

Chapter Outline

1. Comprehending the historical and contemporary gender disparities in India, particularly through metrics like the sex ratio
2. Analysing how patriarchal structure and cultural norms contribute to gender discrimination
3. Recognising the key constitutional provisions, laws, and policies in India to promote gender equality
4. Examining how caste influences women's status and autonomy
5. Tracing the evolution of feminist movements in India, including their role in addressing issues like dowry, and domestic violence
6. Evaluating the progress and challenges related to women's participation in the workforce, political systems, and decision-making processes
7. Understanding the transformative impact of education on women's empowerment and its importance in addressing systemic inequalities
8. Evaluating the role of media in shaping societal perceptions of women
9. Building Advocacy Skills to advocate for gender justice and equality, leveraging their understanding of societal issues and legal protections

Women constitute half of the earth, but India has shown disproportionate sex ratio whereby the female population has been relatively lower compared to the male population. The growing gap between women and men is evident from the 2001 census data on declining sex ratio for children up to 6 years of age as well as the employment and work trends for women. Based on estimates, there were 986 females against 1000 males in the world in the year 2000; however, in India, the proportion was as low as 933 according to the 2001 census. The following table gives a view of this decline of women's population in India:

Sex Ratio: 1901–2011			
Census	**Sex Ratio**	**Census**	**Sex Ratio**
1901	972	1961	941
1911	964	1971	930
1921	955	1981	934
1931	950	1991	927
1941	945	2001	933
1951	946	2011	943

The states and Union Territories of Punjab, Haryana, Uttar Pradesh, Bihar, Jharkhand, Odisha, Chhattisgarh, Madhya Pradesh, Gujarat, Maharashtra, Tamil Nadu, Delhi, Daman and Diu and Dadra & Nagar Haveli have an extremely adverse sex ratio, going down as low as 874 and 709. In Rajasthan, the sex ratio has fluctuated within a narrow band, but has remained adverse. In West Bengal, the sex ratio improved from 917 in 1991 to 934 in 2001. The 2001 census points out that the number of states and union territories with a sex ratio below the national average has increased, covering a larger proportion of population from nearly 54–60%. Only the states of Kerala and Puducherry with a sex ratio of 1058 and 1001 respectively are comparable to developed countries like Japan at 1041.

Though the sex ratio in India has improved a bit between 1991 and 2001, it may be deceptive because the sex ratio for the age group of 0–6 years has declined from 945 to 927 in the same period. Thus, the phenomenon of 'invisible' girl child is setting in. The most dramatic drop in the child sex ratio seems to have taken place in the states of Punjab (793), Haryana (820), Himachal Pradesh, Gujarat and Maharashtra. It is clear that the juvenile sex ratio has decreased at a much faster rate than the overall sex ratio of the country after 1981. The dramatic fall in the number of girls in the youngest age group is rooted in the underlying bias against the female gender.

The socio-cultural factor responsible for this unfavourable sex ratio is the extreme form of patriarchy that denies even reproductive/fertility rights to women. It leads to a preference for sons and contributes to female foeticide. This preference increasingly manifests in practices like female foeticide and infanticide. The misuse of modern technologies such as ultrasound, scanning, and amniocentesis has become a significant factor in the declining female population. Despite being illegal, it continues in the absence of effective measures. The preference for son is evident in the nutritional and medical neglect of female children. This bias is further reinforced by the growing prevalence of dowry practices and deeply rooted religious superstitions. All these factors have created social perceptions casting girls as liabilities – economically and socially. All this has resulted in such practices as purchasing girls from the poor sections of other states and 'keeping' them as wives (virtually bonded labour), a practice now widely reported in some regions of Haryana and Uttar Pradesh.

STATUS OF WOMEN: CONTINUITY AND CHANGE

Inequality between men and women is one of the most crucial disparities in many societies and this is particularly so in South Asia. Any assessment of the status of women has to start from the social framework. Social structures, cultural norms and value systems influence social expectations regarding the behaviour of both men and women and determine women's role and her status in the society.

The status of women in India is culture, region and age specific. The social status of women in our country is a typical example of the gap between the status and role accorded to them by the constitution and the laws, and those imposed on them by social traditions. Based on the patriarchal institutions and values, women are socialised to be good, obedient and sacrificing daughters, wives and daughters-in-law. They are culturally trained, through the process of socialisation, not to challenge discrimination, subordination, exploitation and subjugation within the social structure. The extreme sense of security, protectiveness and patronising attitude of the males often inhibits the development of their personality and individuality. 'The status of women in the family and society is largely determined by the socio-economic, cultural, political, religious and geographical factors in different regions of the country' (National Profile on Women, Health and Development).

The most common family organisation, the joint family, is composed of a group of patrilineally related males who have equal rights to property, sharing a common residence and hearth. Though considerable changes have come in this pattern of living through the impact of industrialisation, urbanisation and modernisation, joint family norms still prevail to a great extent. A woman is placed under severe restrictions under this type of family structure and has little or no say in decision-making and is directly subordinate to her mother-in law. Her status in the family largely depends on her husband's contribution to the family economy and on the amount of dowry brought by her.

The **cultural autonomy** and status of women have always been controlled by the caste system. This ideology of ritual purity–impurity has been maintained through rules of commensality and marriage, commitment to caste, occupation and lifestyle. Vegetarianism, abstinence from alcoholism and constraints of women have been important determinants of the degree of purity. The National Profile on Women (ibid) says that the ideological and material basis for maintaining the caste system is closely regulated by religious scriptures and the patriarchal, patrilineal and patrilocal family ideology. The control on women is exercised through:

Quick Fact

Cultural Autonomy

It refers to the right of a culturally distinct group to self-govern in matters essential to preserving its identity. This enables such groups to safeguard and promote their language, customs, and traditions.

(i) Disinheritance from property and resources;

(ii) Practicing seclusion or *purdah* whereby women are removed from the public sphere and limited to the domestic sphere;

(iii) Socialisation into customs and values;

(iv) Marriage, ensuring security of the matrimonial home property; and

(v) Menstrual rituals; attitude to the body that inculcates a sense of shame; early arranged marriage; monogamy strictly for woman (polygamy in rare communities); and women's self-worth limited to marriage and family, especially as mother of several sons.

These strictures have been enforced most strictly by the upper castes where women enjoy lesser cultural autonomy than their lower caste counterparts. Largely because of their greater role in family economy, women, among the lower castes and most of the tribal societies, enjoy better rights to visibility and mobility, freedom to choose life partner and to dissolve marriage if it does not work. Through the process of *Sanskritisation*, a number of lower castes have been trying to climb upward in the status hierarchy by emulating the lifestyle, norms and behaviour patterns of higher castes. Consequently, the autonomy of their womenfolk, too, gets eroded. This is the price a lower caste has to pay for achieving upward social mobility.

Emanating from the normative structure of the family where the male maintains the continuity of the lineage, there is a strong preference for sons in most sections of Indian society. The National

Family Health Survey (ibid) has assessed preference for son in 19 populous states on aspects such as immunisation rates, period of breastfeeding, prevalence of three common childhood diseases and likelihood of treatment, prevalence of chronic undernutrition among children under age 4 and infant and child mortality rates. On nearly all these measures and in most states, male children have a decisive advantage over female children. Son preference is observed to be particularly strong in northern and central India and somewhat weaker in the southern and western regions. In tribal populations, discrimination against women is not severe. The practice of female infanticide and foeticide also casts aspersion on the status of women.

Widowhood has also been a 'social curse' in most segments of our population and has been most pronounced among the upper caste Hindus. Among the lower castes, tribal population and Muslims, widow remarriage has been a popular practice. The report of the National Committee on the Status of Women in India (1988) says that social attitudes towards widows differ at different socio-economic levels, but a change in the lifestyle of women after widowhood is characteristic of most sections of Indian society. Traditionally, widows have been considered inauspicious and their participation in auspicious ceremonies is still considered undesirable in substantial sections of the society. In spite of marginal changes in attitudes, the condition of widows continues to be a blot on our society. The committee came across a large number of widows in a state of destitution in Banaras and Mathura: they had been unashamedly abandoned by their families and were eking out an existence through begging or various petty trades.

STATUS OF MUSLIM WOMEN

Status of Muslim women, a matter of intense discussion, is not much different from the rest of the population. Though Islam as ideology talks about gender equality and gender justice, the predominantly patriarchal society has taken away what Islam gave to women. Like Hindu women, Muslim women too have little role to play in the decision-making process at the family level. Moreover, their mobility, especially among the higher social groups, is restricted because of the practice of *purdah* and that is why their share in the workforce is much lower as compared to others. Their overwhelming majority is educationally backward. Their share in productive assets is also low. Though, contrary to popular perception, the percentage of polygamy is very low (lower than Buddhists, Jains and Hindus as documented by several reports, surveys and studies), Muslim males enjoy unfettered rights regarding divorce and get away by paying maintenance after divorce for a short period of time. But, a Muslim woman is entitled to get her *mehar* (dower) in case of divorce. She also enjoys the right to give divorce to her husband. In the midst of reports of the so-called triple *talaaq* (pronouncing talaaq by husband thrice in one sitting) among the lower socio-economic strata, it is ignored that the problem and the consequent results of it are still not rampant among them. Moreover, one hardly comes across a case of 'bride burning' among them. This may be explained by the fact that getting divorce among them is much easier and the male can contract another marriage (at least in theory) without getting divorce from the first wife. As far as widowhood is concerned, there is hardly any problem of widow remarriage. Perhaps that is why the sight of a young marriageable widow is rare in Muslim society. Early marriage is common among the lower caste Muslims and this creates hurdles in women's education among them. In the economic and occupational spheres, the position of Muslim women continues to be one of definite subordination to men. But, the problem of subordination of women in the Muslim community has to be looked at from a larger angle of women of all the religious communities, all of them being victims of male subordination and gender injustice. The need of the hour is not to 'communalise' the situation because it will weaken women's struggle for justice and equality.

CHANGING STATUS

The post-independence phase has witnessed a tremendous upsurge for equality and gender justice. Urban women are showing mass awakening for their rights. The State has been forced to come out against discriminatory practices. Female literacy has increased appreciably. Women have been allowed to enter all professions. Gender issues are emerging strongly. Women of contemporary India have multiple roles to play – at home, in office, factory, legislature. They are fighting back. They are gradually getting a share in the political process. The 72nd and 73rd amendments are the result of the ongoing struggle of women for their rights. They are redefining their role in the family and the larger society. They are gradually rejecting all customs and traditions supportive of gender discrimination. The male-dominated society has decided to play its last card – of religion and God. They have to rise courageously even against religion and God if they create hurdles in their emancipation.

MAJOR PROBLEMS

Although some progress has been made, the basic attitude of Indian society towards women has not changed. This is reflected in problems faced by women even today. In some respects, the intensity of the problems has even increased. Their major problems may largely be categorised into dowry, atrocities and discrimination.

▸▸ Dowry

Dowry, as practiced in present times, has assumed the form of a social menace, as a barbaric practice against woman and her dignity and as a liability to the parents of a girl leading to such consequences as female foeticide and infanticide. In popular terms, it refers to money, gifts, goods or estate that the wife brings to her husband in marriage. It is accepted as a form of marriage payment made by the parents or kin group of the woman to the couple on marriage. It functions as a kind of 'anticipated inheritance': the woman receives on marriage the portion or share of her parent's wealth or property which corresponds to her. However, dowry is not to be confused with the concepts of *Kanyadaan* and *Stridhan*. In Kanyadaan, the bride is given as a gift to the groom. Stridhan refers to the gifts given to a woman by her natal kin or by her husband at or after the wedding and the money she inherits from her parents or earns by her personal efforts. The woman is the full owner of the Stridhan and her husband cannot claim it. It can be inherited by her daughters unless she wills otherwise.

Regardless of the implications of the above-mentioned concepts, with the changes in the society and it's becoming more and more materialistic dowry has become one of the easiest ways of acquiring wealth and thereby elevating one's socio-economic status. Thus, it is also directly related to general corruption in the society and lumpenisation of social values. Unfortunately, dowry which was once given voluntarily as a token of love has now become a financial hurdle to marriage, especially among the middle class. Dowry is now being demanded as a matter of right. The problem of dowry does not end with the celebration of marriage; it continues as a perpetual problem even years after marriage. The bridegroom and his family continue to extort money on every possible occasion such as fairs and festivals. The bridegroom's side continues to demand money whether for business expansion or to supplement the dowry of bridegroom's sisters.

The consequences of not complying with the dowry demand before and after marriage vary. From sheer blackmail at the time of solemnisation of marriage to domestic violence, physical and mental, it may also result in bride burning and other atrocities. Globalisation and increasing impact of market economy have further contributed to the nefarious practice of dowry. The growing consumerism and consumer culture are vulgarising our value system.

Muslims and Christians who, till recent times, were not affected by this malaise are also being afflicted by it. But, significantly, dowry-related atrocities and violence are still confined to a small section of these communities. In the case of Muslims one hardly comes across cases of bride burning mainly because of the reason that divorce among them can be obtained much easily than among Hindus. Moreover, such greedy persons may also go for a second marriage, at least theoretically. Thus, why should they resort to murder of the wife? It amply demonstrates that the status of women in all the communities is low, though in varying degrees.

Under persistent pressure of the women's groups and non-governmental organisations, the government enacted the Dowry Prohibition Act, 1961 which was modified with the Dowry Prohibition (Amendment) Act, 1984 which was further amended in 1986 to provide it more teeth. But, this problem, obviously, cannot be fought with the help of legislation only. It requires a strong social movement against such practices. The problem can be largely attributed to an internalisation of the prevailing patriarchal values which view women as inferior. The burden of tradition, a prevailing ideology of male superiority, an insensitive and sometimes conniving law enforcement machinery, an archaic judicial system and a society that condones violence are all responsible for this situation. Otherwise, how can one explain the remarriage or second marriage of a male responsible for killing his wife for the sake of dowry?

What Do You Think?

Can the issue of dowry in Indian society be effectively addressed through amendments to the Dowry Prohibition Act, or does it require a robust social movement aimed at transforming entrenched patriarchal values?

ATROCITIES AND DISCRIMINATION

Gender discrimination and atrocities against women have been an ugly face of Indian society. If we look at the problem we find that it is the environment of discrimination that is largely responsible for various types of atrocities against her.

> Patriarchy and social milieu that has surrounded the patriarchal society have established an unequal power relationship between men and women. Patriarchy has brought with it inequality, discrimination and deprivation for women on several counts. (Sarala Gopalan and Mira Shiva,[1] 2000)

Discrimination against women persists from 'cradle to grave' and exists in her denial of right to education, denial of nutritious food, medical care, dowry-related problems and sexual harassment.

▸▸ Discrimination and Atrocities through the Life Cycle

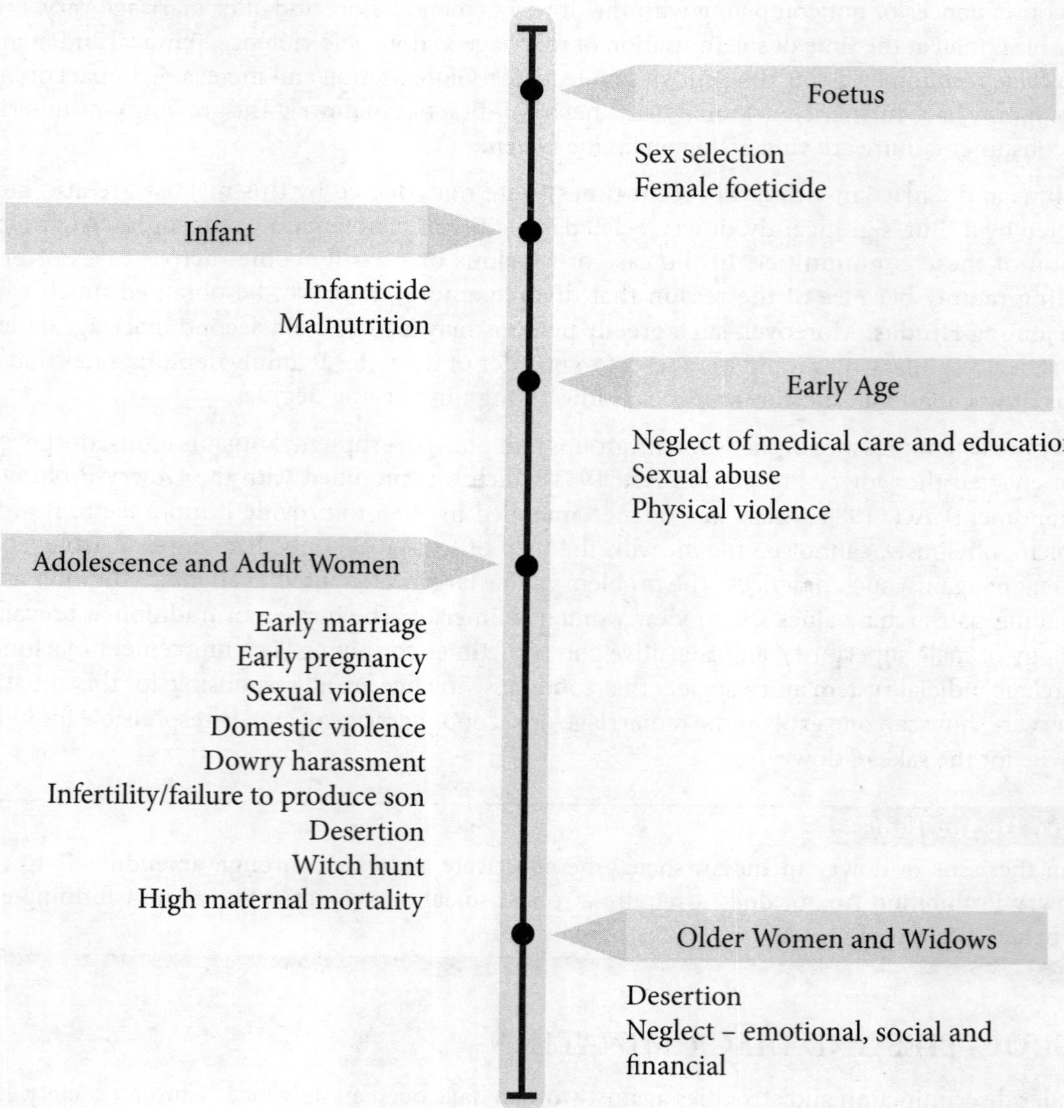

[1] Gopalan Sarala and Shiva Mira, National Profile on Women, Health and Development, Voluntary Health Association of India, New Delhi, 2000

The erosion of traditional values, increasing criminal tendencies in society, poor enforcement of legal provisions, excessive depiction of violence in the media and other factors have contributed to greater atrocities in the society. Women have received a major share of this. The various forms of violence against women are:

- Domestic violence
- Dowry harassment
- Beating and battering which may result in injuries and even death
- Rape
- Sexual harassment at home, public places and workplace
- Eve-teasing
- Kidnapping
- Sex trafficking
- Medical violence

Of all these forms of violence, medical violence remains hidden. It may include needless episiotomy, caesarean sections, unsafe abortions, hazardous drugs, contraceptives, false medico-legal reports, misuse of Medical Health Act, etc. When we analyse the various forms of violence, we notice that most violence risk is from men they know. All the relevant reports reveal that young girls are sexually abused by close male kin. It is important to know that gender violence cuts across all socio-economic groups and most violent men are not necessarily mentally ill; rather they see it as an assertion of their right to dominate.

The caste system is also responsible for violence against women, especially Dalit women. Due to social conditioning resulting from the centuries-old exploitative caste system, Dalit women face the collective threat of physical abuse from men of upper castes. Thus, they have to face the dual problem of gender and caste. Besides these aspects, women become victim of special circumstances too. Atrocities against women in prison or custodial care, widows, single women, women in mental hospitals, handicapped and displaced and refugee women are other less visible aspects of atrocities against women. Thus, crime against women is the most evocative, traumatising and political subject of discussion within India. Though it is not a direct issue of development, it affects women's development.

FEMALE FOETICIDE, INFANTICIDE AND ITS CONSEQUENCES

A tragic fact of modern civilisation is that women being murdered all over the world for different reasons. One of the most brutal forms of killing women may be seen in India and a few other countries. What is more tragic, brutal and condemnable is the denial of opportunity to be born. Female infanticide has been in vogue in India for several centuries though its incidence has increased many fold during the last 4–5 decades. But female foeticide or sex selective abortion of female foetuses is a relatively new phenomenon. Latest advances in medical sciences have developed tests like Amniocentesis and Ultrasonography which are primarily meant to detect any congenital abnormalities of the foetus are being criminally misused by many greedy doctors and paramedics. The objective is to know the sex of the foetus in advance to decide its fate. Though now a criminal offence, such tests are being carried out in large numbers under the very nose of the law-enforcing agencies. Unfortunately female foeticide and infanticide are now socially acceptable in most of the cases across caste, class, religion and region.

In many instances 'son preference' is primarily responsible for female foeticide and infanticide. The devaluation of girls is not only because of economic consideration. It has several dimensions– social and cultural factors, belief that son perpetuates *Kul* and *Vansh* (lineage), provides service, safety and protection to the family. Moreover, as believed by many Hindus, a son's presence is necessary for salvation, for giving *mukhagni* (most important funerary ritual among the Hindus). Thus, the undesirability of having girls for many parents may be because of the following reasons:

- **Economic:** Poverty and lack of resources may lead to inability to afford a girl child.
- **Dowry system:** Though demand for a high dowry has always been troublesome for many parents, rise of consumerism and consumer culture has given further upward push to dowry.
- **Safety and security:** With the growing lawlessness such practices as eve teasing, rape, stalking and acid attacks on unwilling girls make many parents wary of raising a daughter.
- **'Honour killing':** With the growing assertiveness of girls for their rights backed by education and economic empowerment, many girls marry of their own free will, across caste or religion. The highly traditional and patriarchal society does not tolerate it and several parents murder their own daughters for bringing 'dishonour' to the family or community.
- Women producing daughters face humiliation and domestic violence.

The large-scale murder of girls through foeticide or infanticide has disturbed the sex ratio alarmingly. The enormity of the situation may be understood by the fact that the relatively more educated and prosperous states have also emerged as culprits. The following data give some idea of this scary situation based on the last three censuses:

State	1991	2001	2011
Haryana	879	819	830
Punjab	823	798	846
Gujarat	928	883	886
Uttarakhand	948	908	886
Jammu & Kashmir	941	859	–
Uttar Pradesh	927	916	899
Maharashtra	946	913	883
Chandigarh	899	845	867
Rajasthan	916	926	909
Himachal Pradesh	951	896	906
Madhya Pradesh	941	932	912

In a way one may find a large number of 'surplus' men as bachelors because of the skewed sex ratio. Moreover, because of the decreasing number of women, the country is deprived of the contribution of a large productive population which leads to bad economic consequences. A very unfortunate consequence of declining sex ratio is the 'import' of brides. A number of eligible bachelors of Haryana, Punjab, Western Uttar Pradesh and some other states 'explore' the poverty-stricken areas of

Jharkhand, West Bengal, Odisha, Assam and other states, mostly through brokers and middlemen, perform 'marriage' with daughters of poor parents and bring the bride to their villages. This 'pseudo marriage' is largely for the consumption of the local society but in fact it is buying a bride like a commodity. Such 'brides' may be seen in a number of villages in those states serving as domestic slaves or sex slaves being sexually exploited by all the brothers, sometime even others, of the 'bride groom'.

CONSTITUTIONAL PROVISIONS, SPECIAL LAWS AND WOMEN'S EMPOWERMENT

The Indian Constitution has several articles designed to secure gender equality and non-discrimination. In specific terms, they provide for:

- Equality before law and equal protection of laws (Article 14);
- Non-discrimination, inter alia, on ground of sex – specifically in the matter of gaining free access to places of public resort; and State having authority to make special provisions for women (Article 15);
- Equality of opportunity in public employment (Article 16);
- Equal rights for men and women to adequate means of livelihood (Article 39-a);
- State directing its public policy towards securing the health and strength of workers, men and women [Article 39(a), Articles 39(e) &(f)];
- Human conditions of work and maternity relief for women (Article 42);
- State endeavouring to establish a Uniform Civil Code (Article 44); and
- Fundamental duty of every citizen to renounce practices derogatory to the dignity of women [Article 51-A(e)].

In pursuance of the constitutional provisions, the Government has also enacted specific laws for the protection of women and for upgradation of their status.

- **Special Marriage Act, 1954** – Any girl of 18 years of age or boy of 21 years can take recourse to this law irrespective of caste or religious considerations.
- **Hindu Marriage Act, 1955** – Marriage is deemed to be solemnised on the performance of certain rites, especially Saptapadhi; while first marriage subsists, second marriage is forbidden; right to judicial separation and divorce is made available on certain grounds like, for example, unsoundness of mind, conversion to a different religion, incurable or communicable diseases, etc.
- **Dowry Prohibition Act, 1961** – Giving, abetting or taking dowry is a cognisable, non-bailable offence against the State and is punishable with not less than 5 years of imprisonment and a fine of ₹15000 or the amount representing the value of dowry.
- **Child Marriage Restraint (Amendment) Act, 1976** – The age of marriage was raised to 18 years from 15 years in the case of girls and to 21 years in the case of boys.
- **Hindu Adoption and Maintenance Act, 1955** – Unmarried woman, widow or a divorcee of sound mind can also take a child in adoption.
- **Hindu Succession Act, 1956** – It vested women with rights in the matter of inheritance as well as alienation of property at par with males.

Besides these, several laws have been enacted to give labour protection for women workers. The Maternity Benefit Act, 1961 and the Equal Remuneration Act, 1976 are two exclusive and substantive laws providing respectively for (i) leave with wages for 6 months following childbirth; non-exposure to work of arduous nature for 1 month immediately preceding 6 weeks before delivery; and (ii) payment of remuneration equal with men for work of equal value. Protective provisions under other laws provide for facilities such as crèches, time off for feeding the children, separate toilets, etc. The Medical Termination of Pregnancy Act, 1971 permits abortions, if found justified from the medical point of view. Pre-natal Diagnostic Techniques (Regulation and Prevention of Misuse) Act, 1994 regulates investigation for sex determination of foetus. Sex determination tests are often conducted to identify female foetus and abort the same illegally.

WOMEN AT WORKPLACE, SEXUAL HARASSMENT AND VISAKHA GUIDELINES

The year 1997 happened as a turning point for women in India especially those who earn livelihood outside the boundaries of the household. This was the year when the Supreme Court of India formulated and released the Visakha Guidelines and made it mandatory for all the institutions to implement it to prevent and redress sexual harassment of women at workplace. The Visakha Guidelines laid the foundation of the landmark Act known as the *Sexual Harassment of Women at Workplace* (*Prevention, Prohibition and Redressal*) *Act*, 2013. But this piece of legislation did not come out easily and smoothly. It was a long drawn battle.

Briefly tracing the history and background of this Act it may be said that it was the determination and conviction of an ordinary village woman Bhanwari Devi and several NGOs led by an NGO Visakha who persisted with their efforts virtually forcing the supreme court to take this historical step. Bhanwari Devi, a Dalit woman was employed by the Rajasthan government's Women's Development Programme as a *Sathin* as workers in the programme were called. It was her assigned job to spread awareness about hygiene, family planning and the necessity of educating girls, along with campaigning against female foeticide, infanticide, dowry and child marriages. Harassed in the course of her work, Devi was raped by five men belonging to the local dominant caste Gujjar, as 'punishment' in 1992 for stopping the wedding of a nine-month-old Gujjar girl.

The accused were acquitted by the lower court. Led by civil society groups in Rajasthan, the movement held that Bhanwari Devi was attacked at what was essentially her workplace. In the absence of a law that tackled such harassment, some women's organisations filed a writ petition in the Supreme Court asking for guidelines that would help institutions recognise, prevent and redress sexual harassment in the workplace. These groups were *Vishakha*, *Jagori* and *Kali for Women* from Delhi.

> **Quick Fact**
>
> **Vishakha Guidelines**
>
> A set of directives issued by the Supreme Court of India in 1997 to address and prevent sexual harassment in the workplace, forming the basis for subsequent legislation.

Almost 15 years before the implementation of the *Sexual Harassment of Women at Workplace* (*Prevention, Prohibition and Redressal*) *Act*, 2013 it was the Vishaka Guidelines which had put the onus of safe working environment on the employer. It was equally applicable on the private organisations. The court said that such an incident results in a violation of the fundamental rights of 'Gender Equality' and the 'Right of Life and Liberty'. It is a clear violation of the rights under Articles 14, 15 and 21 of the Constitution. The court issued a 'writ of mandamus' and the following directions for prevention:

- It shall be the duty of the employer or other responsible persons in workplaces or other institutions to prevent sexual harassment and to provide for the resolution and settlement mechanism.
- The court defined what constitutes sexual harassment. For this purpose, sexual harassment includes such unwelcome sexually determined behaviour (whether directly or by implication) as:
  (a) physical contact and advances;
  (b) a demand or request for sexual favours;
  (c) sexually coloured remarks;
  (d) showing pornography;
  (e) any other unwelcome physical verbal or non-verbal conduct of sexual nature.

Preventive Steps: All employers should take appropriate steps to prevent sexual harassment. Without prejudice to the generality of this obligation, they should take the following steps:

(a) Express prohibition of sexual harassment as defined above at the workplace should be notified, published and circulated in appropriate ways.

(b) The Rules/Regulations of Government and Public Sector bodies relating to conduct and discipline should include rules/regulations prohibiting sexual harassment and provide for appropriate penalties in such rules against the offender.

(c) As regards private employers, steps should be taken to include the aforesaid prohibitions in the standing orders under the Industrial Employment (Standing Orders) Act, 1946.

(d) Appropriate work conditions should be provided in respect of work, leisure, health and hygiene to further ensure that there is no hostile environment towards women at workplaces.

Criminal Proceedings: Where such conduct amounts to a specific offence under the Indian Penal Code or under any other law the employer shall initiate appropriate action as per the law. The employer should file or assist the aggrieved in filing the complaint with the appropriate authority. In particular, it should ensure that victims or witnesses are not victimised or discriminated against while dealing with complaints of sexual harassment. The victims of sexual harassment should have the option to seek the transfer of the perpetrator or their own transfer.

Disciplinary Action: Where such conduct amounts to misconduct in employment as defined by the relevant service rules, appropriate disciplinary action should be initiated by the employer in accordance with those rules.

Complaint Mechanism: Whether or not such conduct constitutes an offence under law or a breach of the service rules, an appropriate complaint mechanism should be created in the employer's organisation for effective redressal of such complaints. Such a complaint mechanism should ensure the time-bound treatment of complaints.

Complaints Committee: The complaint mechanism, referred to in point (6) above, should be adequate to provide, where necessary, a Complaints Committee, a special counselor or other support services, including the maintenance of confidentiality.

The Complaints Committee should be headed by a woman and not less than half of its members should be women. Further, to prevent the possibility of any under pressure or influence from senior levels, such Complaints Committee should involve a third party, either NGO or other bodies who are familiar with the issue of sexual harassment.

The Complaints Committee must make an annual report to the government department concerned with the complaints and actions taken by them. The employers and person in charge will also report on the compliance with the aforesaid guidelines including on the reports of the Complaints Committee to the Government department.

Workers' Initiative: Employees should be allowed to raise issues of sexual harassment at workers' meetings and in other appropriate forum and it should be affirmatively discussed in Employer-Employee Meetings.

Awareness: Awareness of the rights of female employees in this regard should be created in particular by prominently suitably notifying the guidelines.

Where sexual harassment occurs as a result of an act or omission by any third party or an outsider, the employer and person in charge will take all steps necessary and reasonable to assist the affected person in terms of support and preventive action.

The Central/State governments are requested to consider adopting suitable measures including legislation to ensure that the guidelines laid down by this order are also observed by the employers in Private Sector.

One of the greatest contributions of the Bhanwari Devi case and the consequent Movement is a rethinking of the traditional definition of the 'workplace'.

▸▸ Women's Empowerment

The concept of empowerment flows from that of power. In the popular sense, the term 'power' is understood as the capability to do anything. In the societal context, 'power' is understood as authority, right to command, right to govern or rule, capability to influence, etc. Thus, empowerment simply means vesting power where it does not exist or exists inadequately.

Women's empowerment as a phenomenon is not something new. It has been there throughout the history in all societies. What could be considered new is its increasingly coming out in public, used as a social movement and being looked as an ideology. Now it has been reshaped from women's welfare to their development to empowerment and is being discussed, reported and critically evaluated. What is rather new is the identification of the girl children and women as a special group and the acknowledgement, internationally, of the importance of specific focus on the critical and key issues related to the empowerment of women. What is further new is the increasing realisation and recognition that empowering women is absolutely essential, rather imperative, for familial, societal, national and international development and progress. It has also been realised and accepted that genuine commitment and efforts have to be made at the governmental, non-governmental and individual levels to work towards establishing women's empowerment.

Empowerment of women would mean equipping women to be economically independent, self-reliant, have a positive esteem to enable them to face any difficult situation and to be able to participate in development activities. Empowered women should be able to participate in the process of decision-making. Education would play the most crucial role in empowering women.

What Do You Think?

In what ways can the intersectionality of caste, class, and gender inform more comprehensive policies for women's empowerment?

PROACTIVE INSTITUTIONS FOR EMPOWERMENT

The judiciary also has contributed to furthering the cause of women's empowerment through important judicial pronouncements from time to time. The National Commission for Women (NCW) and it's counterparts at state level are also working to investigate and examine the constitutional and legal safeguards for women and their effective implementation. They also make interventions in specific cases of individual complaints on atrocities against women and recommend remedial action. They also conduct programmes for creating legal awareness amongst women.

Some political parties, especially communist and other leftist parties and their women's organisations such as All India Democrats Women's Association (AIDWA) and Janwadi Mahila Samiti are also fighting and organising movements for womens' empowerment.

In 1992, the 73rd and 74th Constitution Amendments were carried out in respect of Panchayats and Municipalities. Now, more than one million women have secured political space in these bodies. Though, as the reports suggest, men especially husbands, are exercising power by proxy in place of their Pradhan wives, but in days to come women definitely would be asserting their new found political power.

HUMAN DEVELOPMENT PERSPECTIVE

There is no doubt that in the empowerment of women, the human development perspective is very crucial. Concerns of women's nutrition and health, education, employment, environment and above all else, their basic human right to life free from violence need to be factored into public policy.

Education is basic for empowerment of women. It is education that provides knowledge, awareness in regard to social, civic, political, economic and environmental issues and skills for securing gainful employment and means of livelihoods. Through governmental and non-governmental efforts substantial progress has been made in this sector. Some of the vital factors inhibiting education of women are outdated values held by people regarding the role of women consequent on which there is a definite preference for the purpose of imparting education.

As compared to men, women have a significantly lesser rate of work participation, though of late, their participation rate has been increasing faster than that of men. As per 1991 census, women's work participation was 22.27%. The employment of women is mostly in the organised sector. However, the strength of women in the All India Services is not indicative of any significant degree of empowerment of women. While the higher judiciary should stand credit with its landmark judgments, in its structure, it continues to be a **male bastion**.

> **Quick Fact**
>
> **Male Bastion**
>
> A male bastion is a group of people that protects male-dominated way of life or belief. The term can also be used to describe a system that is important and effective in defending a way of life.

▸▸ Women and Media

Media in any society serves as the mirror of the society reflecting concerns for women. Mostly, it is not playing any proactive role in championing their causes. Media persons express their view that they should not adopt the role of advocacy for the sake of objectivity. The mainstream cinema in Hindi and other vernacular languages is still trapped in the stereotyped image of women as weak, submissive and conformist types. With the advent of cable TV and serials being telecast by popular channels, heavy doses of religiosity and ritualism are being pushed down the throat. All sorts of superstitions and anti-emancipation themes are being promoted. It is only the so-called 'parallel cinema' and some television programmes that seem to be interested in women's liberation and empowerment. The saga of women's empowerment has been that of a war in which several battles have been fought against male domination and many more battles have to be fought. India cannot progress without proper and true empowerment of women.

WOMEN'S STUDIES

The discipline of Women's Studies has yet to establish firm roots in Indian academia. Yet, it has made significant progress in the last 10 years with a number of universities and research organisations introducing it as one of the subjects mainly at the postgraduate level. It is interdisciplinary in nature drawing upon the literature of sociology and anthropology, history, political science, psychology, philosophy, social geography, etc. along with oral and visual media.

The concern for public awareness of women's movement and its issues has always been part of the movement. From the 1970s to the 1990s, a number of magazines, information brochures and teaching and research centres emerged. Thus, Women's Studies came into being first as a subject or discipline and then various other disciplines such as history, political science, sociology, literature and philosophy incorporated it in varying degrees. The Indian Association of Women's Studies was also established, which conducts meets from time to time. As Malashri Lal and Sukrita Paul Kumar (2002)[2] rightly point out,

> Women's studies practitioners, inside and outside universities, are becoming increasingly anxious about their academic identity and foresee the imperative to carve out a structural space. Failing this, Women's Studies may be erased out of existence by the mainstream traditional subjects on one hand and the new market oriented variety on the other.

Women's Studies is privileged for being neither the one nor the other and stands to gain immensely by its position as the academic arm of the women's movement in India.

[2] Lal Malashri and Kumar Paul Sukrita, Women's Studies in India, Indian Institute of Advanced Study, Simla, 2002

FEMINISM AND FEMINIST MOVEMENT

Feminism concerns itself with women's inferior position in society and with discrimination encountered by women because of their gender. Feminism is thus a term that emerged long after women started questioning their inferior status and demanding an amelioration in their social position. Even after the word 'feminism' was coined, it was still not adopted as a term of identification. Many of those who campaigned for women's rights organisations in the late 1960s and early 1970s did not call themselves feminist. It is only more recently that the label 'feminist' has been applied to all women's rights groups indiscriminately.

The term 'feminism' embraces a variety of movements and ideologies concerned with the emancipation or liberation of women, the establishment of equal rights for women and opposition to forms of male dominance. It may be looked as a movement to gain for women equal rights with men in social, political and economic fields. It grew in the west as a sequel to the industrial revolution and the tradition in western democracies of denying voting rights to women. In its extremist form, feminism promoted a militant women's liberation movement in the second half of the 20th century based on the premise that all of society is organised along gender lines to ensure male dominance. Some of the liberationist's acts, such as 'bra-burning' and use of such phrases as 'male chauvinist pig', were manifestations of rebellious spirit, but these also proved counterproductive. This women's liberation movement in the west also inspired the oppressed and dispossessed women of the Newly Emerging Economies. Some of the leaders of the western feminist movement such as Gloria Steinem and Germaine Greer became household names among the educated women of Asia, Africa and South American countries.

Most feminist thinking and research draws upon one or more of three related, but distinct perspectives: (i) Liberal, (ii) Socialist or Marxist and (iii) Radical. Within this field there is a great diversity of feminist movements and positions. In the newly emerging economies, feminist movements have also taken a variety of forms, though a similar division into Marxist or socialist feminist ideologies and bourgeois feminism can be made. Marxist or socialist ideologies focus on feminism as a part of overall political programmes opposing the capitalist system; bourgeois feminism concentrates more deeply on ideologies of male dominance and on the subjective liberation of the middle-class women.

ROLE OF WOMEN'S ORGANISATIONS AND WOMEN'S MOVEMENT IN INDIA

Women's movement in India is not of recent origin. It also did not originate on the streets of Delhi and Mumbai. Its beginning may be seen in thousands of places and through hundreds of forms. Yet, this is also true that an organised feminist movement may be traced back to the freedom struggle and the period immediately after we secured freedom.

The period immediately after independence witnessed two leftist movements – Tebhaga Movement in Bengal and Telangana Movement in the undivided Andhra Pradesh. Led by the Communist

Party the poor peasants fought against the landlords and capitalist forces. The women took active part in these movements along with men. The Telangana Movement threw up, for the first time, radical and militant women's leadership. They also organised Andhra Mahila Sabha, Andhra Yuvati Mandal and Mahila Sangam. They fought against not only military power but also against gender inequality, domestic violence, child marriage, polygamy and restriction on their movement outside the four walls of household.

After the promulgation of Indian Constitution and enactment of various laws for women, the women's movement went from strength to strength. The Hindu Marriage Act, the Hindu Succession Act and other legislative measures prepared ground for further struggle. A number of schemes and programmes were formulated for women. The decade of 1960s witnessed a number of economic and political crises. The Naxalite Movement emerged with full force especially in Bihar and Bengal. Though the Naxalite Movement, led by the ultra Marxists and Leninists, was primarily a peasant movement and never led by women but the level of participation of women in the movement was quite high. Many women provided strategic support to the Naxalite revolutionaries. The participation of women in this movement provided them an opportunity to understand the political process in the country and the politics of gender inequality and suppression of women's rights. Even today thousands of tribal women are actively involved with the ongoing 'Maoist Movement' in Chhattisgarh and adjoining regions.

What Do You Think?

To what extent have women's movements in India succeeded in reshaping societal attitudes and breaking down patriarchal structures?

Quick Fact

Chipko Movement

An environmental movement in India with significant involvement from women, emphasizing their role in forest conservation.

Women's movement took new shape after 1970. By this time women's mass movements had realised that women's issues and problems could not be solved through patchwork type of social reform and social welfare and the basic issues had to be confronted head on. This realisation pushed them to the forefront of all the major social-economic, political and environmental issues. Women's involvement in *Chipko* movement focussed on preservation of forests and related environmental issues shows their increasing understanding of core issues. It was followed by similar movements in Karnataka and elsewhere. Between 1970–90 women also fought against liquor and liquor lobby in Kumaon and Garhwal (now in Uttarakhand), Haryana, Andhra Pradesh, Tamil Nadu, Madhya Pradesh, Maharashtra and elsewhere. They had realised that excessive consumption of liquor, especially, among the poor, not only brings economic hardship but also promotes domestic violence.

Gail Omvedt (1993) has traced the origins of the contemporary women's movement and role of women's organisations to the early 1970s when rural and working women were first trained as leaders. "But there were few linkages at that time to the urban, intellectual women who could articulate the oppression of rural and working women in feminist terms" (Geraldine Forbes, 1998).[3] The United Nation declaration of International Women's Year and the International Women's Decade (1975–85) led to the appointment of the Guha Committee and its subsequent report, *Status of Women in India*, a landmark study on women's status in India.

'Emergency' was imposed in the country in 1975. A number of civil liberties and democratic rights groups were organised. Women also played important role in these people's movements. Around the same period, the Progressive Women's Organisation, was created in Hyderabad by some leftist women. The years of working in people's movement had equipped them with an ideology to fight against discrimination and exploitation. On the whole, the period between 1970–2000 saw the emergence of a number of autonomous women's organisations. Though coming from different ideological backgrounds they were unanimous in their view that the membership of such organisations should be restricted to women only and they did not require the patronage and interference of males in these issues. To name a few such organisations – *Forum Against Oppression of Women* in Mumbai, *Saheli* in Delhi, *Asmita* in Hyderabad, *Vimochana* in Bangalore, *Penuramma Eyakkam* in Chennai and many others point to a new found confidence and consciousness. Some other women's organisations with stronger networking and organisational capabilities are related with political parties specially Congress Party and Communist Parties. They may be serving as women's wings of these parties especially the strongest among them – *All India Democratic Women's Association* (AIDWA) related with CPI(M). *Mahila Congress* is an affiliate of the Congress Party and *Durga Vahini* with BJP. Unfortunately women's organisations related with right wing political parties like BJP take up only caste and communal issues, divide the women's power and serve as 'legitimisers' of policies and actions of their parent organisations. The role of Durga Vahini in Ayodhya Movement is a case in point.

What Do You Think?

How can the collaboration between women's organisations and government institutions strengthen advocacy for women's rights?

The decade of 1980, was largely dominated by anti-dowry movement throughout the country. It also included such issues as dowry related atrocities, domestic violence, and commercialisation/commodification of women and lack of property rights. Through writings, *Nukkad Natak* (Street play) rallies and seminars millions of women were mobilised into action. Public debate on sexual harassment and rape was also the result of this movement against dowry. Before 1980 or so girls were very reluctant and hardly vocal on this type of harassment and violence but now such issues may be discussed by many of them without inhibitions. One of the important contributions of leftist women's organisations was to highlight the dangers of communalism in the fight for women's rights. If the society is divided and polarised on the basis of religion, women's movement gets weekend. The decade of 1990's witnessed deep concern for Muslim women and their

[3] Forbes Geraldine, Women in Modern India, Cambridge University Press, New Delhi, 1996

problems along with movement against female foeticide and infanticide. Women's movement in India is now an important part of the worldwide movement of women for justice, equality and empowerment. Now increasing number of women's organisations are actively involved in fighting for justice and equality.

Questions and Indicative Answers

1. How does the disturbed sex ratio reflect on the status of women?

- Because of large-scale female foeticide and infanticide, the sex ratio got disturbed.
- Though sex ratios improved a bit in the 2011 census, the phenomenon of invisible girl child (0–6 years) set in.
- Instead of their value and status improving because of paucity, women were transformed into a commodity and from the poorest areas she was purchased and made to act as a domestic and sex slave.
- The patriarchal society wants total subjugation of women.

2. How does the patriarchal society exercise control over women?

- Women are socialised to be subservient, obedient and sacrificing daughters.
- Joint family was based on submissiveness of women.
- Cultural autonomy was controlled by the caste system.
- Defiance met with disinheritance, seclusion/*Pardah*, arranged marriage, menstrual rituals, sense of shame for body and widowhood as social curse.

3. Is the status of Muslim women different as compared to Hindu women?

- By and large, it is almost similar.
- Gender equality in theory, but not in practice.
- Males enjoy more power in divorce and its gross misuse, but not many cases of bride burning and female infanticide.
- Widow remarriage is very common.

4. What are the major problems being faced by women across castes? Describe discrimination and atrocities on women throughout the life cycle.

- Across caste or community lines dowry (more among Hindus); and
- Atrocities and discrimination, female foeticide and infanticide, neglect of girl's nutrition requirements, early marriage, domestic violence, desertion, etc.

5. What are the issues in women's empowerment?

- Cultural autonomy;
- Equipping her as economically independent; and
- Role in decision-making process.

Previous Years' Questions

1. What are the continues challenges for women in India against time and space? **(GS Mains Paper I, 2019)**
2. Do you think that the constitutional provisions for women have led to their upliftment? Give reasons for your answer. **(UPSC CSE Mains Sociology, Paper II, 2024)**
3. To what have the legal provisions been effective in curbing violence against women in India? Give your argument. **(UPSC CSE Mains Sociology, Paper II, 2024)**

CHAPTER 10

Village India

Chapter Outline

1. Understanding the social structure of Indian villages and examining Village Autonomy
2. Evaluating village's integration with the larger society
3. Jajmani system and its decline due to modernization and industrialisation
4. Evaluating the agricultural and socio-economic consequences of the Green Revolution in rural India
5. Understanding the transition from traditional to modern leadership structures and the role of Panchayati Raj
6. Colonial land revenue systems – Zamindari, Ryotwari, and Mahalwari, and their long-term effects
7. The characteristics and challenges of peasant communities
8. Assessing the causes and outcomes of rural discontent and the role of peasant movements in shaping modern India
9. Understand the historical prevalence of bonded labour and the legislative measures to abolish it
10. Developing an understanding of how rural and urban systems influence each other

India can be characterised as a nation of villages, with approximately six lakh villages where around 64% of its population resides. However, not all villages are the same. These may be classified into different types such as (i) **nucleated villages**, common all over India, which are a tight cluster of houses surrounded by fields; (ii) **linear settlements**, where houses are strung out, each surrounded by its own compound, with little to physically demarcate where one village ends and another begins; (iii) **scattering of homesteads or clusters of two or three houses** where physical demarcation is not clear. Beside these and other types, the size and the density of the population may also represent important types.

Further, India's villages portray an overwhelming diversity of form, style, custom and ritual. Each is a product of a long evolution, an overlapping of separate peoples and cultures over a period of thousands of years. Contemporary village India is a mirror of its past.

The main components of rural social structure in India have been, and still are, despite social change, family and kinship, caste, class and village. Several sociologists while describing village India talk about caste, joint family and village community as forming a trinity. However, on a wider plane, we look at such social institutions rooted in recorded history as described above are longest enduring.

The all-pervading nature of these social institutions may be observed in all spheres of life – social, cultural, economic and political. We get their reflection in social norms and values, statuses and roles and rights and obligations. Within India's rural social structure family, the joint family usually functions as a unit of economic, socio-cultural, political and religious domains.

When we examine the essential nature of India's villages, the issue of **village autonomy** immediately comes to the fore. This has been a controversial issue. Among the earliest scholars, Henry Maine (1881), Charles Metcalfe (1833) and Baden Powell (1896) laid emphasis on the notion of village autonomy in an exaggerated manner. The Indian village was portrayed as a 'closed' and 'isolated' system. Charles Metcalfe (ibid) went a step further and described the Indian villages as 'little republics', almost independent within themselves, monolithic, atomistic, non-changing and self-sufficient. Later research done by historians, sociologists and social anthropologists has demolished this myth. The Indian village was never self-sufficient. It always maintained links with the larger society and centres of Indian civilisation. Migration and movement for work and trade, village exogamy, administrative linkages, interregional markets, inter-village economic ties, caste network, pilgrimage, fairs and festivals and other activities always served as bridges with the neighbouring villages and the larger society. During later years, new forces of modernisation further expanded the inter-village and rural–urban interaction. This was described by Oscar Lewis (1955) as **rural cosmopolitanism**. Despite the increasing external linkages, village remains, by and large, a fundamental social unit and people living in a village have a sense of common identity and loyalty.

Quick Fact

Village Autonomy

The idea that villages in India were once self-sufficient and independent social units. Early scholars described them as 'little republics,' but later studies refuted the notion of complete autonomy.

Quick Fact

Rural Cosmopolitanism

The concept that villages have always been connected to broader societal systems through trade, migration, and social interactions, challenging the idea of village isolation.

TRADITIONAL FEATURES OF VILLAGES AND EMERGING CHANGES

1. **Isolation and Self-Sufficiency:** Historically speaking, till the 19th century, Indian villages were more isolated and self-contained. There was minimal contact with the outside world. There used to be fixed division of labour (because of fixed status and roles as per caste system). Villages consisted of peasants, agricultural labour and artisans. Human labour was the main resource in the absence of mechanisation and use of machines.

   Due to rapid development of transport and communication since the 20th century, villages began undergoing rapid changes in all respects. With increasing use of machines, division of labour has undergone changes. With increased economic and political empowerment of disadvantaged groups and castes, the *jajmani* system has virtually crumbled.

2. **Conservation:** Our villages have always been characterised by a strongly traditional and conservative attitude. Changes may also be seen in their attitudes towards women, youth and social institutions.

3. **Caste Mobility:** Through the process of ***Sanskritisation***, economic and political empowerment, caste system does not remain static. A virtually occupation-free caste system has developed where caste and occupation are now almost delinked.

Quick Fact

Sanskritisation

A process where lower castes adopt the customs and practices of higher castes to elevate their social status.

4. **Joint Family:** Once the hallmark of agrarian society in India, it is now crumbling as a social institution because of rising aspirational level, individualism and assertiveness of educated women.
5. **Marriage:** Decision-making in choosing a spouse is becoming more democratic. Education, economic pursuit and status, beauty and appearance are increasingly now more important than merely social/caste status, though caste endogamy is still very strong.
6. **Living Standard:** Now there is better availability of food, dress and jewellery, more *pucca* houses, toilets and sanitation. With the opening of primary health centres and hospitals, the health status has improved and infant mortality rate has declined appreciably. Small family norm is also picking up.
7. **Economic System:** Preciously private moneylenders were the only source of credit. Now their dependence on *sahukar* (moneylenders) has decreased with the increased availability of institutional finance – cooperative credit societies, self-help groups, rural banks and commercial banks. Plastic money (credit and debit cards) has also entered into villages in most of the states. There is also improved agricultural technology.
8. **Political System:** The traditional village/caste panchayats have declined and under Panchayat Raj, statutory panchayats looking after development work are making rapid inroads. Thus, the democratic decentralisation coupled with reservation for Scheduled Castes, Scheduled Tribes and women has facilitated the emergence of a new leadership with new ideas. The power structure is changing.

INDIAN VILLAGE AS A SOCIAL SYSTEM

System implies an orderly arrangement, interrelationship of parts in which every part has a fixed place and definite role. These parts do not exist in isolation, but are bound by a constant interaction. When this understanding of system is applied to the social system, we get an insight into the working of the social system. The arrangement of social interactions based on shared norms and values provides the basis of the social system. In the practical sense, individuals constitute it, and each individual has a place and function to perform. Talcott Parsons gives a clear understanding of social system by telling that 'Plurality of social actors engaged in more or less stable interaction according to shared cultural norms and meaning' is a precondition. Here the interaction is 'patterned interaction'. He further tells us that the social system is a comprehensive arrangement. It takes under its orbit all the diverse subsystems such as economic, political, religious and others. Moreover, the social system, in itself, neither exists in isolation nor is totally independent. It is also bound by the environment. Thus, geographical factors have also a crucial role to play in the maintenance of social system. By breaking this conceptual understanding into parts, we may get the following information:

- There should be plurality of individual actors, which means there should be a number of interacting individuals.

- Every social system must have certain aims and objectives. It can never be aimless.
- There must be some order and pattern among various functional constituents or units.
- The unity between the constituents of the social system is based on functional relationship.
- Adjustment should be there between the constituents or units.
- Perhaps, the most important aspect of social system is maintenance. The maintenance of the social system is based on socialisation and social control. The former refers to the process through which the children or younger generation learns or adopts the norms, values and behavioural pattern of the family and the larger group while the latter implies the power of enforcement because without social control, social system cannot survive for long.

Now, if we look at the Indian village, we find all the important features of social system in it. There is constant interaction between individuals and there is no anonymity because of small population and high density of population. Indian villages are caste based with a deep-rooted caste system. There is functional relationship and mutual interdependence between different castes as per *jajmani* norms and obligations. Though the *jajmani* system, the socio-economic-political basis of the caste system, has weakened a lot, crumbling or has crumbled in many villages, caste-based interaction is still present. With the enforcement of *Panchayat Raj*, **democratic decentralisation** has been adopted where individuals and castes as units may be competing, but adjustment is also sought and achieved to minimise frictions and conflicts. Joint family and wherever it has disintegrated, nuclear family and caste through caste panchayat supported by statutory panchayat serve as an agency of socialisation and social control for the maintenance of the social system. Since all the important features of the social system are found in the Indian village, it can be concluded that it represents the social system.

Quick Fact

Democratic Decentralization

It involves transferring authority from central governments to local governments, operating on the principle that local administrations are better equipped to address the specific needs of their communities.

THE STUDY OF VILLAGES IN INDIA AND ITS SIGNIFICANCE

The study of small-scale, isolated primitive tribal communities has been the dominant field for social-cultural anthropologists up to 1930s or so. The credit goes to Robert Redfield and his students from Chicago (later prominent anthropologists) for making a significant departure from the past. Redfield initiated the study of civilisation and with this the anthropologists turned their attention towards peasant society and villages and urban centres or cities. Redfield provided a model for village study through his own work – a systematic study of a village in Mexico by the name of Tepoztlán. It was followed by anthropologists all over the world.

In village study, a particular village is chosen as a unit of investigation. It is an ethnographic account of a village written on the basis of data collected, largely through participant observation. In this way, anthropologists utilised their experience and expertise achieved over a century of study of tribal societies through this method.

By the turn of the 20th century in India, being the first among social scientists, some economists had begun village studies. But, obviously, their work and orientation were different. In the 1930s,

William Wiser, though not a trained anthropologist, did two remarkable and pioneering works. His *Hindu Jajmani System*, study of village Karimpur in north India came in 1930 followed by *Behind the Mud Walls* in 1936. These were pioneering works of anthropological tradition as these were based on intensive fieldwork. By the 1950s, a sudden explosion of interest in village studies was witnessed.

In the post-independence period, rural reconstruction and development occupied high priority. American anthropologists were also attracted to village studies and with them anthropologically oriented village studies gained momentum. Morris Opler, Oscar Lewis, McKim Marriott, David Mandelbaum, Bernard Cohn, Allan Beals along with British anthropologists such as F.G. Bailey, A.C. Meyer, Scarlett Epstein, etc. did excellent village studies. They used high levels of scientific method. Now entered Indian anthropologists in a big way. In the late 1950s, M.N. Srinivas published *India's Villages*, S.C. Dube did *Indian Village*, D.N. Majumdar published *Rural Profiles* in two volumes, *Village India*, an edited volume by McKim Marriot and some others heralded a new beginning. S.C. Dube's *Indian Village*, a study of Shamirpet village near Hyderabad is considered a classic in village studies. It provided a complete picture of village life. D.N. Majumdar's *Caste and Communication in an Indian Village* (1958) showed how the introduction of new means of transport and communication impacted caste mobility. *Life in a North Indian Village* by Oscar Lewis and *Caste and the Economic Frontier* by F.G. Bailey was a path-breaking work on the interface of caste and economic pursuit while K.S. Mathur's *Caste and Ritual in a Malwa Village* looked into the dynamics of caste and religious rituals.

The significance of village studies may be understood at two levels – theoretical and practical or applied. In-depth ethnography of villages resulted in the emergence of concepts such as *Sanskritisation* and Dominant Caste developed by M.N. Srinivas on the basis of his study of religion and society of Rampur village. Great and Little Tradition were developed by Robert Redfield on the basis of his study in Mexican villages while the concepts of **Universalisation and Parochialisation** have been given by McKim Marriot to understand the cultural process of Indian civilisation.

Quick Fact

Universalisation and Parochialisation

Universalisation involves adapting global cultural elements into local contexts, while Parochialisation refers to the preservation or emphasis of local cultural uniqueness within the context of broader global influences.

On the practical/applied level, village studies helped the planners involved in rural reconstruction and development. Village studies provided, for the first time, first-hand knowledge of villages in an objective manner. It not only helped in planning – both at the micro and at the macro level – but also helped other disciplines in social science to think of village objectively. It also negated the colonial outlook of villages and in the post-independence period negated the stereotype and image of villages developed by urban people. It helped the government to locate the channels of social change and barriers to change. It also helped to understand the role of communication in the development of new economic pursuit and breakdown of caste prejudices and practices besides understanding the emerging new power structure and leadership. Thus, one can see that village studies are not merely an academic pursuit of anthropologists and sociologists, but may go a long way in its contribution to the nation-building process.

AGRARIAN SOCIAL STRUCTURE AND SOCIAL ORGANISATION OF AGRICULTURE

The study of agrarian social structure has been a matter of serious study in rural sociology and social anthropology. If we go by the dictionary meaning, 'agrarian' pertains to land or its tenure or to a general distribution of lands and organising or furthering agricultural interests. Agrarianism refers to a set of values which holds that agriculture is the most natural and desirable vocation and the farm the ideal place to live.

Thus, an agrarian society may be accepted as "any form of society, especially traditional societies, primarily based on agricultural production and associated crafts rather than industrial production" (Collin's 'Dictionary of Sociology', 1991).[1] As per the Blackwell Dictionary of Sociology, an agrarian society focuses its mode of production on agriculture, particularly the cultivation of vast fields. This distinguishes it from the 'Hunter-Gatherer Society,' which depends solely on foraging for food, and the 'Horticultural Society,' which grows food in smaller gardens instead of large fields.

Besides others, A.R. Desai and Andre Beteille have contributed significantly to the understanding of agrarian social structure in India. Beteille while defining the agrarian social structure is clearly of the view that only peasantry does not constitute it. It means something more than the study of peasant societies and cultures, but all those playing a role in agrarian society from various parts of it. He further says that the study of agrarian social structure revolves around mainly two aspects: (i) technological arrangements and (ii) social arrangements. While the former refers to the ecological conditions and agricultural technology, the latter refers to land ownership and control, power structure, land tenure and related social dimensions.

The understanding of agrarian social structure and the social organisation of agriculture, described as 'Social Framework of Agriculture' by Andre Beteille (1974), is not possible without having a sound understanding of 'peasantry' or 'peasant society' and its various implications and dimensions in the Indian setting.

Talking about the Social Framework of Agriculture, Andre Beteille (ibid) says that the economic activities and economic change cannot be adequately understood in isolation from the social framework within which it takes place. This is particularly true of the underdeveloped (and developing) countries of Asia where economic organisation has a lower degree of autonomy than in the industrial societies of the West. Thus, in such Asian societies, the economic organisation is found to be more closely intermeshed with a variety of social institutions whose functions are partly economic and partly non-economic. He further emphasises upon the relevance of the social framework to economic activities by elaborating that the economic activities involve the mutual interaction of individuals whose rights and obligations are socially defined. The same broad set of activities, as in agriculture, can be socially organised.

[1] Colin's Dictionary of Sociology, Harper Collins, New York, 1991

PEASANT SOCIETY

A peasant society is a small-scale social organisation in which peasants predominate. Anthropologists have defined and explained peasant societies in different ways. A.L. Kroeber was the first anthropologist who tried to provide a formal definition of peasant societies. He described peasant societies as 'part society' indicating its dependence in technological, economic, political, administrative, religious and moral spheres on the larger society. George Foster, taking a cue from Kroeber, described peasant society as a 'half society'. He implied that a larger society, such as a nation may consist of two parts – the first part consisting of cultivating class living in villages and the second part consisting of upper classes living in urban centres. That part of a larger society which is composed of cultivating classes is peasant society or half society. Robert Redfield followed Kroeber and he also defined peasant society as a 'part society'.

Until the 1960s, the peasantry was largely ignored in sociology as having no significant role to play in history. This was despite the fact that peasants have existed for most of recorded history and in many parts of the world. From the 1960s, the publication of key works, such as those by Eric Wolf (1966) and Barrington Moore (1967), began to change this perception, introducing to sociology perspectives developed in anthropology and political economy.

The role of peasantry in the Vietnam war and the growth of peasant political activity in Latin America and Asia raised questions about the assured passivity of the peasantry. There is now a major area of interdisciplinary peasant studies. (Shanin, 1982; Shanin (*ed.*), 1988)[2]

- **(a)** The family farm is the major economic unit around which production, labour and consumption are organised.
- **(b)** Land husbandry is the main activity combined with minimal specialisation and family training for tasks.
- **(c)** There is a particular 'peasant way of life' based on the local village community which covers most areas of social life and culture and which distinguished it from urban life and from those of other social groups.
- **(d)** Peasants are politically, economically and socially subordinated to non-peasant groups against whom they have devised various methods of resistance, rebellion or revolt.
- **(e)** A specific social dynamics involving a cyclical change over generations which irons out inequalities over times via land division and the rise and fall of the availability of family labour through the domestic cycle.
- **(f)** Especially in the contemporary world, a common pattern of structural change, drawing peasants into market relationships, often through the influence of outside bodies such as agribusiness and incorporation into national politics. The precise outcome of these common changes is not predetermined.

[2] Shanin, Theodore, Peasants and Peasant Societies, Basil Blackwell, Oxford, 1987
Shanin, Theodore (ed.), Peasants: Chayanov's Recovered Essays, Practical Action publishing, Rugby, UK, 2024

Robert Redfield[3] in his landmark work 'Peasant Society and Culture' (1956) placing peasant society between folk and urban communities has described the following three as the most important features of a peasant culture:

(a) Highly reverent attitude towards land;

(b) Acceptance of agriculture as the noblest, best and the ideal job; and

(c) A pronounced, industrious attitude of the people demonstrating a firm belief in the dignity of labour.

Among the other important features of a peasant society are as follows:

(i) Family is the primary unit of multilateral social organisation.

(ii) The main source of livelihood is land and agriculture which fulfil almost all the requirements of life.

(iii) They maintain a distinctive, traditional culture in terms of day-to-day life and its schedule.

(iv) Usually, they are dominated by outsiders.

For the peasant societies, agriculture is not an enterprise, but a way of life which cannot be given up in favour of any other activity promising more money or profit. If agriculture becomes an enterprise instead of a way of life, a peasant becomes a 'farmer' like the rich farmers of Punjab, Haryana, Maharashtra or Karnataka. Thus, peasants are subsistence cultivator of agricultural land. They may be owner-occupiers or tenants, participants or non-participants in the market. Some writers (e.g. Chayamov and Eric Wolf) have attempted to isolate a distinctive peasant economy whereas others (e.g. Redfield) stress the notion of a peasant culture.

As the above description indicates, all definitions of the peasantry agree on emphasising the importance of the opposition or contrast between the peasant stratum and the urban elite. The peasantry and the urban centre are two opposing poles of a single socio-economic system and this is reflected not only in their economic interdependence but also in the complex relationship which exists between peasant and urban culture. This may be seen in the concepts of Great/Little Tradition and folk–urban continuum. Among the anthropologists, Eric Wolf (1969), in his *Peasants,* defines the peasants as those whose surplus production is transferred to a dominant ruling group, which employs this surplus both to maintain itself and to redistribute it to other non-agricultural sectors of the population.

Peasants can be most clearly distinguished in agrarian societies. Significantly, cultivators are not the only segment of population constituting a peasant community. People who are not analytically defined as peasants, but still a part of the peasant community are also parts of it. They may be traders, labourers without land and artisans who may have close social and economic links with the peasants. Further, people who are analytically defined as 'peasants', will often engage in some of these activities for part of their time. Thus, while, definitions of the peasantry sometimes rest on the

[3] Redfield, Robert, Peasant Society and Culture, Cambridge UP, 1956

functioning of the household, it is essential to see how this is firmly integrated into a wider social, political and economic network. David Lehmann[4] (1985) stated that

> It seems best to discard the term 'peasants' as a comprehensive descriptor of rural populations of any sort and to use it instead as an adjective describing features of rural production systems without pretensions to exhaustive definition.

CHARACTERISTICS

Anthropologists and sociologists like Kroeber, Foster, Redfield, Wolf, Norback, Thorner, Shanin, Andre Beteille and many more who have written about peasant societies have agreed on the following features as characteristics of peasant societies:

(i) A peasant society has a long history commensurate with that of the city and the state.

(ii) A peasant society has a social system based on face-to-face relationships. It includes village communities. The inhabitants of each village are known to one another through shared experience in work, ritual and leisure activities. This close association entails a social system based on face-to-face relationships. The inhabitants of each village may also have personal ties with individuals outside their village community.

(iii) A peasant society views agriculture as a means of livelihood, not as a business for profit. It is not so much that peasants lack interest in selling a portion of their crops, but rather that such sales are not an end in themselves. These sales can best be understood as transactions that help maintain a given style of life and permit the acquisition of basic necessities. Consequently, peasants are primarily concerned with subsistence production and generally consume a major portion of the food and other articles they produce.

(iv) A peasant society is based on antiquated technology and low agricultural productivity. Its technology in many parts of the world has changed little since Neolithic times. The productivity of peasant agriculture is low. The peasant economy reveals reliance on agriculture, simple technology, an emphasis on subsistence production, a limited range of items produced and a direct dependence on the environment.

(v) A peasant society directs its economic behaviour at a pattern of immediate consumption and at meeting the material demands of **ceremonialism**. First, a peasant society is characterised by lack of deferred gratification, i.e. the tendency to spend rather than to save, to spend now rather than tomorrow. Second, every peasant society directs its effort at meeting the material demands of religious observances and social position in terms of festive foods, fireworks, incense, traditional payments and obligations, taxes, shares and other dues and rents.

Quick Fact

Ceremonialism

Ceremonialism refers to a focus on expressive behaviours like feasting, exchange, and display, which can be either secular or religious. It is most prevalent among the peasant society.

[4] Lehman, David, Agrarian Reform and Agrarian Reformism, Faber & Faber, London, 1974

(vi) A peasant society always maintains communication with the urban centres. It produces some exchangeable surplus food which goes to support towns and cities which in turn provide certain types of manufactured or processed goods and services. These exchanges are frequently organised and carried on through a system of marketplaces, usually in towns or cities. Many of its institutions are local manifestations of national institutions such as the use of a national currency in economic exchange and national educational system. Further, the religious, intellectual and moral life of the urban centres influence the life at the village level and link the peasant community to the wider society.

(vii) A peasant society is resistant or very slow to change. Peasants have survived for thousands of years through a series of techniques designed to make them less tempting targets. It is difficult to convince peasants that they can now discard these defences with impunity. Peasants make the economists sigh, the politicians sweat and the strategists swear all over the world – Moscow and Washington, Peking and Delhi.

POWER STRUCTURE AND CLASS STRATIFICATION

The usual and universalistic way of describing social structure has been through institutions based on birth such as family, kinship and caste. Another way of describing it is through class. Thus, the agrarian class structure may be used to understand the power structure and class stratification in Indian rural social structure. However, both caste and class are necessary to describe the agrarian social structure in India. It also explains the power structure in rural India. In this way, when we talk of agrarian class stratification, we get a better view of rural India which was, traditionally, viewed through caste stratification only. K.L. Sharma[5] (1980), putting the whole issue in proper perspective, made the incisive comment by saying that "caste incorporates the elements of class and class has a cultural (caste) style, hence the two systems cannot be easily separated even analytically."

Broadly speaking, the modern agrarian class structure in India evolved during the British colonial rule. It was the outcome of the land revenue system evolved and enforced by the British rule. There were three classes:

(i) Landowners **(ii)** Tenants **(iii)** Agricultural labourers

Daniel Thorner[6] (1973), in his classical work, describes these three classes as:

(i) Proprietors **(ii)** Working peasants **(iii)** Labourers

In vernacular language, he used the terms *maalik*, *kisan* and *mazdur* for these three classes respectively. The landowners or proprietors traditionally belonged to the upper caste groups. They were tax gatherers and non-cultivating owners of land. Thorner (ibid) understands that the category of proprietors or *maalik* refers to families whose agricultural income is derived primarily (although not necessarily solely) from property rights in the soil. That is to say that whatever other sources of family income may exist, such as from a profession or business, the main agricultural income

[5] Sharma, K L, Indian Social Structure and Change, Rawat Publications, Jaipur, 2008

[6] Thorner, Daniel, The Agrarian Prospect in India, Allied Publishers, Delhi, 1976

is derived from a share of the produce of lands belonging to the family. Typically, this share will be realised in the form of rent. Usually, the rent will be taken in money, but it may be in kind if the tenants are on a crop-sharing basis. Instead of renting out his lands, however, a proprietor may hire labourers to cultivate them for him. He may manage these hired labourers himself or he may hire someone else as manager. He may actually go into the fields and perform some of the work alongside of his hired labourers. The main determinant should be his mode of income – if his agricultural income from that part of his holdings which he cultivates with his own lands is less than the amount he receives from renting out the rest of his lands or having them tilled by hired labourers. Within this group or class of proprietors, it is possible to separate out two subgroups. One consists of large absentee landlords who typically have holdings in more than one village. The second consists of smaller proprietors who reside personally in the village in which they own land and usually exercise some degree of management and control over its cultivation. Most of the members of this class come from the higher castes.

The second class (referred to as kisan) of working peasants have also a recognised property interest in the land (Thorner, ibid). They may be small owners or tenants with varying degrees of security. By and large (but not in every state), their legal and customary rights will be somewhat inferior to those of the *maalik* (proprietors) in the same village. The chief distinguishing feature, however, is the amount of land held. In the case of the working peasant the size of the holding is such that it supports only a single family and then only if one or more members of the family actually perform the field labour. In fact, the produce from the land owned by the kisan may not even provide the entire income required by his family, but at least it provides a larger share than whatever funds he may receive from other agricultural sources, such as doing labour on other people's lands. Kisan as defined here are those villagers who live primarily by their own toil on their own lands. They do not employ labour, except briefly in the ploughing or harvest season, nor do they commonly receive rent. They come from the middle level cultivating or artisan castes, most of them being other backward classes (OBCs) or backward castes as per the current terminology.

The third agrarian class referred to as labourers or *mazdur* comprise those villagers who gain their livelihood primarily from working on the people's land. Families in this class may indeed have tenancy rights in the soil or even property rights, but the holdings are so small that the income from cultivating them or from renting them out comes to less than the earnings from fieldwork. Wages may be received in money or in kind. If the latter, they may be fixed or in the form of a crop share. In practice, the lower ranks of croppers and tenants-at-will are almost indistinguishable from *mazdur*; they will tentatively be included in this category. Most of the members of this class come from the traditionally landless, deprived, untouchable castes or Scheduled Castes and backward castes as per the current terminology.

As Thorner (ibid) rightly points out, the maintenance of this hierarchical structure of interests in the land had required that quite a substantial proportion of the produce be reserved for persons who perform no agricultural labour. What was left to the actual cultivator, after the claims of the various superior right holders were satisfied, might still be subject to collection as unpaid debt by the moneylender. Thus, the power structure in the agrarian class is largely based on exploitation and deprivation. In his landmark work, D.N. Dhanagare (1983) says that although Thorner's categories and subcategories are nearer the realities of the Indian agrarian social structure, there is still a need to read or regroup these categories into such a broader and more comprehensive model and redesignate the commonly used concepts and criteria in the study of peasant societies. Such a model can be drawn from the works of Lenin and Mao, especially those relating to the analysis of agrarian classes in the Russian and Chinese societies respectively:

(i) Landlords
(ii) Rich peasants
(iii) Middle peasants
(iv) Poor peasants
(v) Landless labourers

Dhanagare (ibid) further opines that the social composition of these agrarian classes in terms of specific status groups like castes, religious or ethnic groups, etc. is far too complex in different regions of India to reduce it to any simplistic formulae. However, for a loose and broad classification, this may hold ground. For example, landlords and rich landowners (including non-cultivating urban money lenders/owners) belonged to the upper castes such as Brahmin, Thakur, partly forced labour or Banias in northern India. In Andhra Pradesh the Kammas, Reddys and Raos; in Mysore the Okkaligas and Lingayats; the Patidars in the Gujarat region; while the Kunbi, Marathas and Deshmukhs in Maharashtra could be cited as more examples of the locally dominant land-owing castes. The middle and poor peasantry, mostly debt-ridden, came primarily from the traditional castes of cultivators, artisans and so on. The landless labourers belonged mostly to untouchable castes, the Scheduled Castes.

The post-independence period witnessed significant changes in the agrarian class structure in India. The impact of land reforms and rural development programmes facilitated the emergence of new forces of change. In fact, the challenge to the feudal class structure emerged with the rise of the nationalist movement. Analysing these changes, Yogendra Singh says that the agrarian class structure everywhere in India had a feudal character. The challenge to the feudal class structure came with the nationalist movement when not only was a radical agrarian ideology accepted, but the nationalist leadership also actively undertook the cause of the exploited peasantry and led kisan (peasant) movements in various parts of the country. Following independence, therefore, land reforms were introduced in most states and a beginning was made for transformation in the agrarian class structure. Most sociological studies of the agrarian structure refer to these processes of social change. Moreover, the significant trends mentioned in such studies are as follows:

(i) There is a wide gap between land reform ideology projected during the freedom struggle or even thereafter and the actual measures introduced for land reforms. Consequently, socialist transformation in the class structure of the villages has not taken place.

(ii) This lag could partly be explained by the class character of the Indian political and administrative elite who are resistant to the needed radical reforms.

(iii) The existing land reforms have initiated a process by which the security of tenure and economic prosperity of the rich peasantry has increased, but the condition of the small peasants, both in respect of economic level and tenurial stability, has deteriorated.

(iv) The feudalistic and customary type of tenancy has declined and it has been replaced by a capitalistic form of lease labour or wage labour agrarian system.

(v) A new class of rich middle stratum of peasantry system has come into being and not all of these are from among the ex-zamindars.

(vi) Class inequalities between the top and the bottom levels of the classes have increased rather than decreased.

(vii) The benefits of land reforms have so far not gone so much to the agricultural workers or even to ex-zamindars as to the emergent middle peasantry.

(viii) As a result of these contradictions in the agrarian class structure, tensions in the rural social system have increased and are bound to increase further.

(ix) Finally, the sociological process that is dominant in the current class transformations in the villages is the '**embourgeoisement**' of some and '**proletarianisation**' of many social strata.

Quick Fact

Embourgeoisement

It is the process by which a working-class individual adopts middle-class values through increased wealth or a change in occupation. It reflects the spread of bourgeois values in society and can be seen as the opposite of class consciousness.

Proletarianisation

It is a social process in which individual move from being employers, unemployed, or self-employed to becoming wage labourers employed by an employer.

It refers to the process of deskilling, where the rank of the working class is reduced.

P.C. Joshi[7] (1971), in his celebrated work, made very incisive comments on the trends in the agrarian class structure. Some of these are summarised as follows:

> It led to the decline of feudal and customary types of tenancies and was replaced by more exploitative and insecure lease arrangement. It gave rise to a new market based rich peasant class and decline to feudal landlord class.

Thus, rural India witnessed and is still witnessing the process of social mobility and transformation. Depeasantisation of small and marginal peasants is also a by-product of the transformation of village India.

LAND TENURE SYSTEMS

Land management is the most crucial aspect of agrarian system and agrarian relations. Tenancy in agricultural land refers to leasing out land by an owner to a person who actually cultivates that land temporarily by his personal labour and pays rent in cash or kind to the owner. The owner, generally, has a subordinate interest in that land as he holds it as a matter of social status or to get an unearned income. As such, the owner is less interested in the improvement of the land as it is not the main source for his living. Such a land tenure is far inferior to owner cultivator if we look at it from the viewpoint of tenant's interest. If we look at the land tenure system in India, we find that the land

[7] Joshi, P C, Land Refom and Agrarian Change in India and Pakistan, Vikas Publishing house, Delhi, 1971

problem is a British legacy. The land structure served the colonial-imperialist interests. The main features of land structure in India in the pre-British period were:

(i) It was a self-reliant village economy where there was a system of barter/exchange.
(ii) The farmers produced enough to sustain and pay taxes to the extent of $1/8^{th}$ of the produce.
(iii) The function of the king was to collect taxes to protect the grain and provide proper transport of it from one place to the other (R.P. Dutt,[8] 1979).

With the advent of the British rule, in broad terms, three types of **land tenure systems** came to be established:

(i) Zamindari System: It refers to landlord's tenure. The landlords (Zamindars) were intermediaries between the government and the actual cultivators. This system came into being as a result of the East India Company making a huge payment to Mughal administration in 1765 for Bengal, Bihar and Orissa where they became entitled to realise land revenue. Through permanent settlement in 1793, Lord Cornwallis gave land ownership to zamindars who could give land for cultivation to anybody and evict one as per his wishes. He was obliged to pay taxes to the government. They were non-cultivating owners of land. Zamindari system was run under two types of settlement: (a) Permanent settlement and (b) Temporary settlement. Under the former, the land revenue used to be fixed for a long duration while under the latter, it was for a shorter duration after which the land revenue could always be enhanced. In political terms, the zamindars became their collaborators and stooges.

> **Quick Fact**
>
> **Land Tenure Systems**
>
> Systems introduced during British colonial rule, including Zamindari, Ryotwari, and Mahalwari, defining landownership and revenue collection.

(ii) Ryotwari System: It refers to an independent single tenure. Initially this system was promulgated by Thomas Munroe in 1792 for Madras, but gradually expanded to Bombay, Central Provinces, Assam, Coorg, etc. Under Ryotwari system the *ryot* or the registered holder of the land was recognised as holding the land directly from the government without any intermediaries. His tenure was 'occupancy tenure' and he continued to be landowner as long as he was paying land revenue to the government. Under this system, land settlement used to be determined by the government as per the fertility of the land for a period varying between 20 and 30 years and on that basis land revenues were collected.

(iii) Mahalwari System: It refers to joint village or village community tenure. This system was first introduced in Agra and Oudh Provinces in 1833. Later it was extended to Punjab and parts of Central Provinces. Under this system, the whole *mahal* (village) was vested with land ownership. The communal ownership of land by the entire village community was the basis of this system. The *numberdaar* (village headman) was responsible to collect *maalguzari* (tax) and deposit it in the government treasury. The wasteland, trees, wells, ponds, etc. were common property resources of the entire village community.

[8] Dutt, R P, The Agrarian Crisis in India before Independence, Gambol Books, 2009

With the advent of independence, a number of measures were taken in tenancy reform. In fact, the Indian National Congress, spearheading the freedom movement, was committed to eliminate the intermediaries, parasites and absentee landlords. Though the aspirations of the tiller of the soil could never be fulfilled totally, the agrarian structure underwent important changes. Various measures of land reforms unleashed numerous forces of change.

JAJMANI SYSTEM

It has been the socio-economic basis of the Hindu caste system and an integral part of the agrarian social structure in India. It is said that the term *jajmani* system has been introduced in the vocabulary of Indian sociology and social anthropology by William Wiser through his pioneering work, 'The Hindu *Jajmani* System' (1936). He carried out this study in a village called Karimpur in Uttar Pradesh. In this seminal contribution, Wiser described in detail how different castes interact with one another in the production and exchange of goods and services. Though there are regional variations of this term in different parts of the country, the term *jajmani* system has become a standardised term in sociological literature.

Under the *jajmani* system, each caste group within a village is expected to give certain standardised services to the families of other castes. In general terms, it stands for the exchange of goods and services between the landowning higher castes and landless 'services' castes. These castes have always been occupationally specialised following certain traditional occupations and thus are known also as artisan castes. Those artisan castes such as blacksmiths, goldsmiths, weavers, oilseed pressers, leather workers, barbers, washermen, musicians and a wide range of occupationally specialised groups along with the traditionally landless untouchable castes providing agricultural labour constitute the 'service castes' and are known as either *kamin* or *prajan* and in other terms in different parts of the country. The landed higher castes are broadly known as *jajman* (patrons). These service relations, which are governed by a hereditary tenure, are called the *jajman–prajan* relations.

The *jajmani* system is essentially an agriculture-based system of production and distribution of goods and services. Through *jajmani* relations, these occupational castes get linked with the landowning dominant castes. The landowning castes maintain a paternalistic attitude of superiority towards their occupational or service castes.

Oscar Lewis (1956) rightly points out that under this system each caste group within a village is expected to give certain standardised services to the families of other castes. Pauline Kolenda (1963) looked at it as a system of distribution whereby the higher caste landowning families called *jajmans* are provided services and products by various lower castes. The system, thus, explains the occupational division of labour in an Indian agricultural village with distribution of services and products under a network of role relationship and payments. Tradition approves of such an arrangement and mutual trust and interdependence in the Indian agrarian system based on caste. Talking about the social dynamics of the *jajmani* system, S.C. Dube (1953) says that it is not easy for an agriculturist to remove a family attached to his household and secure the services of another. No one else would be willing to act as a substitute for fear of being penalised by the caste panchayat. David Mandelbaum (1972), a keen observer of village India, emphasises upon the internal functioning of the *jajmani* system and says that the *jajmani* relations essentially operate at the family level. A Rajput landowning family has its *jajmani* ties with one family each from Brahmin, barber, carpenter, etc. and family of service caste offers its services to specific families of jajmans. However, *jajmani* rules are enforced by caste panchayats.

The *jajmani* relations are durable and are of hereditary nature. The *jajmani* rights however may be regarded as a form of property passing from father to son. These relations are in a way informal and governed largely by the local traditions. On the whole, the *jajmani* system carries strong elements of dominance, exploitation and conflict. There is wide difference in exercise of power between landowning dominant patrons and poor artisans and landless labourers who serve them. Another very important feature of the *jajmani* system is that though the *jajmani* relations operate at the village level, they are often not confined to a single village only, because not all the villages have all occupational castes and therefore the services of 'occupations'. Castes from other villages are frequently borrowed. Moreover, for certain occupational castes, such as goldsmiths, blacksmiths and carpenters, a single village may not be adequate to provide sufficient jobs round the year. Such castes, therefore, cater to the needs of a number of villages in a given region. Summarising, one can say that the *jajmani* system is an age-old social institution which refers to the inter-caste and inter-family social, economic, political and ritual ties prevalent in Indian villages. It is one of the most important constituents of social organisation of agriculture in India.

DECLINE OF JAJMANI SYSTEM

Gradual modernisation of Indian economy coincides with the decline of the *jajmani* system. But, its rapid decline was witnessed in the post-independence period. The decline of *jajmani* system can be discussed under the following heads:

(a) Role of the state;

(b) Introduction of technological innovations and industrialisation; and

(c) Political mobilisation of Dalits and the backward classes.

Traditionally, the *jajmani* system-based village economy was primarily a subsistence economy oriented to meet the consumption needs of the local population only. Due to the localised self-sufficiency and immobility of labour and capital, commercialisation and the capitalist transformation of agriculture did not take place. After independence, deliberate and planned attempts were made by the state to link the village economy to the regional and national markets. In order to facilitate it, the government made huge investments towards the expansion of transport and communication networks. The state's policies contributed to rapid monetisation of economy in village India. Increasing productivity in agriculture was very high on the government's economic agenda to feed the huge population.

The process of planned development initiated immediately after independence brought about capitalistic transformation in the agriculture sector. Moreover, the state took initiative in providing various inputs like credit facilities, technical know-how, fertilisers, irrigation, high-yielding varieties of seeds, etc. Now came a sea change in the mindset of landowning classes and the entry of market forces encouraged them to generate surplus for the market rather than sustaining the age-old *jajmani* system. It gave rise to contractual relationship between the landowning classes and agricultural labourers and artisans. The traditional informal ties started giving way to formal relationships as per formal contractual obligations.

Technological innovations and industrialisation also created a situation where there was hardly any need for functional interdependence. With the machine-made goods flooding the market and reaching even remote rural areas, the rural artisan castes were literally made to compete with the machines. Let us take a look at a few ordinary technological innovations. With the growing availability and the consequent increased use of safety razor, the practice of self-shaving became popular minimising the role of the village barber. With the advent of stainless steel utensils, the importance of the village potter declined. And with the availability of hand pumps in the village, the dependence of higher castes on the *Kahars* (drawers and carriers of water to the households) declined. Same was the case with weavers and others. All this rendered the majority of artisan castes jobless. Many of them opted for the market or started providing their services against cash payment in a formal economic transaction. This coincided with the rapidly increasing migration of the service castes to the emerging urban centres and industrial townships. Those who stayed behind became wage labourers working on the lands of the landed elite. Village economy was now being increasingly integrated with the urban and national economy.

Before independence, the nationalist movement took a principled and rather quasi-ideological stand on social equality. The weaker sections – Dalits, tribals and backward classes – were promised an equality-based and injustice/exploitation-free new order. For that matter, the Backward Classes Movement had already made its impact on southern and western parts of India. With the promulgation of the Constitution, the state became committed to their upliftment and empowerment. One of the profound changes in contemporary Indian society has been the emergence of a new sense of identity among Dalits and the OBCs. The democratic assertion of the backward segments of Indian population and their political mobilisation in different parts of the country was a serious blow to the exploitative *jajmani* system based on the monopolistic rights of the landed higher castes controlling the means of production in the traditional agrarian economy. With the new-found confidence and democratic assertion by the backward classes, the *jajmani* system suffered a serious setback. Yet, it also seems to be true that whatever the weaker sections gained, the new economic policy and globalisation threaten to take it away from them.

GREEN REVOLUTION AND ITS SOCIAL CONSEQUENCES

One of the most significant and laudable achievements of post- independent India is in the field of agriculture where revolution was brought in. When India announced in 1984 that it would provide to the drought-hit countries of sub-Saharan Africa 1 lakh tonnes of wheat as its contribution to the alleviation of human suffering, the gesture evoked universal praise and admiration. This pronouncement was particularly significant since not long ago India itself was struggling with food shortage and was depicted as a country which can survive only with a begging bowl. All this transformation was possible because of forward looking policies of the government, its enterprising and hardworking farmers, committed scientists, extension and developmental workers, inputs, agencies and the country's sheer determination to transform itself from a food deficit and importing country to a self-sufficient nation.

While these achievements are significant, India has to go a long way to provide its people with the amounts of food, sugar and other commodities comparable to what is consumed in the more developed countries.

The Green Revolution has brought changes in the agrarian relations. It has been successful in realising production in large land holdings, but has increased economic disparity among rich farmers, small and marginal farmers and agricultural labour. One of the effects of the Green Revolution has been the swelling of the bulk of agrarian proletariat in some parts of the country. The landless have been getting organised; the organisation of the landed is also emerging as a counter to this. It also resulted in large-scale migration of labour to the enclaves of prosperity. Large migration of agricultural labour from Bihar and eastern Uttar Pradesh to Punjab and Haryana is a case in point.

The emergence of new dominant castes is, to a great extent, linked with the advent of Green Revolution. This is more obvious in the case of a number of backward castes placed in the middle or lower rungs of the local caste hierarchy. Several studies by sociologists and social anthropologists have shown that it is the socially backward castes (OBCs) and not the traditionally landless Scheduled Castes that have really benefited from land reforms. Since these backward peasant castes were excellent cultivators, when more land was added to their kitty, they became very enterprising. Moreover, they were already numerically strong in their respective regions. The only criterion left to be achieved by them to become dominant castes was higher status in the local social hierarchy which they achieved by going for *Sanskritisation*. The Jats of Punjab, Haryana and western Uttar Pradesh; the Ahirs, Kurmis and Gujjars of Uttar Pradesh, Bihar and parts of Madhya Pradesh; the Marathas of Maharashtra; the Patels and Patidars of Gujarat; the Reddys and Khammas of Andhra Pradesh; the Vokkaligas and Lingayats of Karnataka; and several other peasant castes from other parts of India may be cited as examples of this phenomenon. These upward climbing castes took full advantage of the Green Revolution and through a plethora of cash crops and commercial agriculture, accumulated wealth and property not only in villages but also in the adjoining urban centres. Thus, Green Revolution played an important role in the altered social structures of different regions of the country.

Another interesting and significant fallout of the Green Revolution is a shift of authority from the older generation to the younger generation. Since the Green Revolution involved a new technology, economic transactions, institutional finance for credit, a little knowledge of English language and new varieties of seeds and plants, the well-entrenched older generation found itself ill equipped to handle this situation. Thus, the younger generation got a better and stronger role in the decision-making process.

The Green Revolution, by pushing the commercial crops to the forefront, invited and facilitated the entry of new market forces. It greatly affected the *jajmani* relations between the traditional *jajmans* (patrons) and client or service castes. Those owning land were no more interested in sharing the agriculture produce with the service castes in lieu of services provided by them. They preferred to pay in cash rather in kind. Thus, the tradition-based exchange between goods and services started giving way to the formal economic transaction through wages. Thus, the inter-caste relations in village India could never be the same again.

AGRARIAN UNREST

The roots of unrest and discontent in rural India may be traced to the agrarian structure. If we analyse the Indian agrarian structure, we find that differences have always been there in the areas of land ownership, land control, income and standard of living. Though social and economic inequalities always persisted, in earlier times these were contained through traditional values and religious beliefs and practices.

The doctrine of *karma* and *dharma* functioned as safety valve along with *bhagya* or fate: The divine decree was all pervasive. People, including the deprived and exploited, were reconciled to their fate. Inequalities were accepted as normal and natural. Over a period of time, the working class attained a level of awareness, which proved instrumental in radicalising their analysis – about their life and society. Political movements made poor peasants and agricultural labour aware of their exploitation, mechanism and dynamics of exploitation and gave them strength and voice.

Agrarian unrest is primarily related to the material conditions of the people living within agrarian structure. With every decline in material conditions, unrest increases. If we look at the pre-independence scenario, we find that it was after 1918 that peasants began to develop political consciousness, took part in organised national struggles and subsequently built up their own organisations. The Moplah Rebellion of 1922, formation of agricultural and labour unions in Andhra Pradesh in 1923, in Punjab, Bengal and Uttar Pradesh in 1926–1927, eruption of peasant struggles of Bardoli (Gujarat) in 1928–1931 and similar other events gave voice to agrarian unrest. The Congress Socialist Party, Communist Party and various groups along with the Left to the centre's nationalist leaders like Nehru contributed significantly to the formation of *kisan* (peasant) organisations. When the First All India Kisan Congress met at Lucknow in 1935, it was for the first time in the history of India that an all India organisation of Indian peasantry was formed with a programme of common demands giving expression to the aspirations of the Indian peasantry.

Unfortunately the Congress governments formed in different provinces before independence failed to take any radical steps to fulfil the aspirations of the peasantry. This gave rise to cynicism and disillusionment among the poor peasants suffering under the existing agrarian systems.

At the heightened levels of political awareness some of the biggest organised peasant struggles were waged between 1946 and 1950. The struggles of Warli in Maharashtra, the Tebhaga Movement in East Bengal and the Telangana Movement in Hyderabad State (now Andhra Pradesh-Telangana) represent the most revolutionary phase of peasant struggles waged against the backdrop of simmering agrarian unrest. In these struggles, communists provided the leadership and played the key role. In the post-independence period, the Naxalbari (Naxalite) Movement represents the most vocal and radical face of agrarian unrests.

The agrarian unrest is not distributed uniformly throughout the country. It has been and still is more vocal in the paddy-growing regions of Andhra Pradesh, Tamil Nadu, West Bengal and Kerala. Incidentally, these regions have a comparatively higher density of population and higher ratio of poor peasants and agricultural labour. The Left Front governments of West Bengal and Kerala have been able to carry land reforms and take steps to protect the interest of tenants and sharecroppers.

The main causes of agrarian unrest may be summarised as follows:

(a) Uneven and unjust distribution of sources of income in the rural areas and the widening gap in this sphere.
(b) High incidence of unemployment and underemployment coupled with low wages.
(c) Increasing indebtedness and land alienation, especially among the tribal peasantry.
(d) Displacement and lack of rehabilitation measures.
(e) Increasing awareness among the depressed and deprived sections about their miserable material conditions and socio-economic disabilities. The majority of the poor peasants and landless agricultural labour come from Scheduled Castes, tribal communities and the Other Backward Classes (OBCs) including poor Muslims.
(f) Political mobilisation of Dalits and backward classes.

Andre Beteille[9] (1974) holds the agrarian structure with the following features responsible for the prevailing agrarian unrest:

(a) Presence of two opposite poles of social and economic inequalities.
(b) Strengthening belief, especially after independence, that these inequalities can be reduced if not totally removed.
(c) Failure of administrative and political efforts to change the prevailing patterns of inequalities, especially at its lower rungs.

For centuries, the subaltern population was thriving in India without whispering anything about their 'felt needs' and real conditions. Now the widespread discontent and unrest gets itself manifested in violent as well as non-violent means.

BONDED LABOUR

Exploitation of man by man created debtor–creditor and master–slave relationship sustaining prevalent socio-economic inequalities in India. Caste system, in league with the seat of power, religion and the legal system glorified and sustained it uninterruptedly through centuries by enabling its transmission from generation to generation.

Perhaps, no other society in the world is as burdened by the memories and material survivals of its ancient past as is the Indian society. There is a long history of oppression and bondage right from the

[9] Beteille, Andre, Studies in Agrarian Social Structure, Oxford University Press, New Delhi, 1974

ancient times to the present. Debt bondage has been the most prevalent form of bonded labour in India. Bonded labourers are known by different names in different states and regions in India. Known as Jeeta in Himachal Pradesh; Sevak in Uttar Pradesh and Haryana; Kamia, Baramasya and Janour in Bihar; Hali in Gujarat; Halia and Muliya in Orissa; Padiyal, Paniyal and Pannyal in Tamil Nadu; Adiammar, Paniyan, Kattunaikan in Kerala; Jassigula, Gothi and Vethi in Andhra Pradesh; Baramasi and Solkari in Madhya Pradesh; Jeetha in Karnataka; Chakar and Halia in West Bengal; Sagari in Rajasthan; Vela, Begar and Salkavi in Maharashtra, the practice of bonded labour has been prevalent throughout rural India and parts of tribal India.

The cultural environment of exploitation under which the practice of bonded labour flourished witnessed all forms of exploitation and oppression ranging from child labour to the sexual exploitation of bonded women. Though the Constitution prohibited *begaar* (forced labour), it continued to flourish. Through Bonded Labour System (Abolition) Act, 1976, the Government of India tried to tackle debt bondage head on. Section 2, clause (g) of the Act, defined bonded labour system as the system of forced or partly forced labour under which a debtor enters, or has or is presumed to have entered into an agreement with the creditor to the effect that:

(i) In consideration of an advance obtained by him or by any of his lineal ascendants or descendants (whether or not such advance is evidenced by any document) and in consideration of the interest, if any, due on such advance; or

(ii) In pursuance of any customary or social obligation; or

(iii) In pursuance of any obligation devolving on him by succession; or

(iv) For any economic consideration received by him or by any of his lineal ascendants or descendants; or

(v) By reason of his birth in any particular caste of community he would:

- **(a)** Render, by himself or through any member of his family or any person dependent on him, labour or service to the creditor or for the benefit of the creditor, for a specified period or for an unspecified period, either without wages or for nominal wages; or
- **(b)** Forfeit the freedom of employment or other means of livelihood for a specified period or for an unspecified period; or
- **(c)** Forfeit the right to move freely throughout the territory of India; or
- **(d)** Forfeit the right to appropriate or sell at market value any of his property or product of his labour or the labour of a member of his family or any person dependent on him; and includes the system of forced or partly forced labour under which a surety for a debtor enters, or has or is presumed to have entered, into an agreement with the creditor to the effect that in the event of the failure of the debtor to repay the debt, he would render the **bonded labour** on behalf of the debtor.

Quick Fact

Bonded Labour

A system where labourers are tied to their employers due to debt. It is a practice historically tied to caste and economic inequality.

Thus, we find that by very definition the practice of bonded labour is similar to that of slavery. Debt bondage has been most prevalent among the landless agricultural labour or farm labour followed by brick kiln workers, stone quarry workers/handloom weavers and so on. In the case of agricultural labour, it is mostly prevalent among the landless and to a lesser extent even among the marginal and pauperised peasants. Among many socio-economic disabilities, the untouchables have been suffering from their customary landlessness; the Scheduled Castes of today are the worst victims of debt bondage. Nadeem Hasnain (1981) in his pioneering work on the Kolta bonded labour of Jaunsar-Bawar (Dehradun), Jaunpur (Tehri Garhwal) and Rawain (Uttar Kashi) has shown the dynamics of bondage and exploitation. The Kolta, being untouchables, were barred by custom from owning land. It was further compounded by the social ban on keeping or touching gold, thus making him totally vulnerable to any economic exigencies when a Kolta would be having nothing except his body which becomes a ready object of mortgage.

The most unfortunate aspect of the practice of bonded labour is its presence in the Green Revolution areas, especially Punjab and Haryana, where the migrant farm labour is trapped in debt bondage. Despite several administrative and legislative measures, the chains of servitude manifesting in debt bondage and slavery persist, though, to a lesser extent.

LEADERSHIP AND FACTIONALISM

The structure of rural leadership may be understood at two levels:

(i) Traditional leadership

(ii) Emerging contemporary/modern leadership

Traditional leadership in rural India has been based on caste status, size and prestige of the family, age, economic status, traditional or indigenous knowledge, contact with the larger society and with the wider world and manifold personality. The traditional leadership exhibits primacy of blood relations, heredity, informal control and reciprocity. The village panchayat and caste-based panchayat leadership are the most obvious expressions of traditional leadership.

In the post-independence period, especially with the promulgation of statutory Panchayati Raj and democratisation of rural life, new patterns of leadership have emerged. The processes of democratisation and democratic decentralisation have led to the emergence of democratic leadership. The traditional power structure in villages has been undergoing radical changes. Yet, at the same time, it is also true that in several regions the traditional elite has transformed itself into modern elite through the democratic process. It is through the democratic process that the leadership under the traditional dominant castes has given way to backward castes in several parts of the country. In the new emergent modern leadership, education has become an important determinant. Increasing representation of the youth and middle class are also important dimensions of modern leadership. Moreover, trends of collective leadership instead of single autocratic leaders have also added a new dimension.

When we look at rural **factionalism**, the very spirit and essence of faction should be understood first. By its very nature, a faction is a political group geared for conflict situations for the attainment of its goals. The recruitment to a faction is done largely by the factional leader and loyalty to the leader and faction are the main determinants. Factions have always been an important part of the rural political structure under which not only the relations between members of the local society are determined, but also serve social, economic and political goals. Like other groups, a faction is also a social group, small sized and geared to fulfil certain common goals and interests. Oscar Lewis (1953) in his landmark study of village life in North India had enumerated the following factors in the formation of a rural faction:

> **Quick Fact**
>
> **Factionalism**
>
> Divisions and conflicts within villages, often based on caste, kinship, or economic interests, influencing local politics and leadership.

(i) Dispute over succession of land
(ii) Dispute over adoption of child
(iii) Disputes related to land and irrigation
(iv) Clash over sex-related crimes
(v) Murders
(vi) Inter-caste conflicts

Paul Brass has described factionalism as an integral feature of traditional Indian society because of which it has not been able to coordinate with the contemporary politics. On the basis of his study of five districts of Uttar Pradesh, he identified three main reasons for continued factionalism:

(i) Lack of external pressures and threats
(ii) Lack of unanimity over ideological issues
(iii) Lack of effective authority

Briefly speaking, the causes and the consequences of factionalism may be enumerated as the changing face of caste system and *jajmani* system, religious differences, differing political loyalties, growing class consciousness and Panchayati Raj and cooperatives. Though factionalism is not a bad thing in itself, if it goes beyond manageable limits it becomes detrimental to social harmony and attainment of economic and political goals.

DEMOCRATISATION AND LEADERSHIP

The traditional power structure in rural India had three bases, viz. zamindari system, village panchayat and caste panchayat. The power structure was dominated by the higher castes and the leadership ran, by and large, on a hereditary basis. Despite an overwhelming majority, the lower and middle level castes did not wield power and had an insignificant role in the decision-making process.

After independence, the zamindari system was abolished and the polity was democratised. The process of rural democratisation began. The ensuing land reforms after zamindari abolition led to the emergence of changes in social and economic power structure. Rural development programmes and welfare measures for the weaker sections of the society, especially education promoted social mobility in rural India. The influence of ascribed status declined and the legitimacy of achieved status started adopting new forms. From the point of view of leadership there have been two major sources of power structure in rural life – superiority based on birth and ritual status and numerical strength. Democratic norms obviously focused on numerical strength, yet the traditional power structure continued to wield substantial influence even in the democratic environment. The higher caste groups continue to have enormous clout in electoral politics and leadership. Yet, at the same time, the situation is undergoing rapid changes.

When we take a look at the emerging pattern of rural leadership, we come across the increasing role of democratisation and these patterns may be categorised as follows:

(a) **Emergence of democratic leadership:** Under the new democratic dispensation a new democratic leadership has emerged. The traditional rural leadership was based on an individual's heredity or ascribed status, landownership and caste affiliation. The influences of all these factors have declined. Now an individual's contribution and popularity or his factional strength is a major determinant in the democratic set-up. Moreover, the democratisation process has also promoted a leadership on secular lines. Thus, the entire traditional power structure is undergoing a radical change.

(b) **Education as an important factor in mobility:** Till recent decades education was not the important determinant of leadership in the midst of rampant illiteracy. Now education is considered as an important qualification of a leader. The importance of education has increased manifold as a major attribute of leadership.

(c) **Specialisation as a major element in leadership:** With increased socio-economic mobility the variety and pluralism in rural life have increased appreciably. Now the same leader is not considered suitable for a variety of jobs.

(d) **Emergence of youth power:** In the traditional stratification model and power structure, age was a very important criterion. The 'council of elders' was a case in point. The dominant belief that experience and age were crucial attributes of leadership has declined. Education and the process of westernisation, especially knowledge of English language, have strengthened youth leadership. Besides these patterns, mobility in leadership, rise of collective leadership backed by political parties, etc. may be seen as other important ingredients of democratised leadership in rural India. Increasing political awareness and democratic assertion by the Dalits and OBCs have also introduced a new climate in rural leadership and power structure.

EMPOWERMENT OF PEOPLE

▸▸ Panchayati Raj and 73rd Amendment

Self-governing village communities that survived the rise and fall of empires are an important feature of pre-colonial India. Moreover, in a country like India where more than 65% of the population lives in villages, it is necessary to have an efficient system of decentralised democracy. Land reforms, cooperatives, Panchayati Raj and community development movements were intended to bring about a prosperous, dynamic and genuinely democratic rural social system.

The philosophy of Panchayati Raj is largely based on Mahatma Gandhi's vision that democracy through people's participation could be ensured only by way of 'Gram Swarajya' in which the management of the affairs of the village would be done by people themselves. It was laid down in Article 40 of the constitution that 'the state shall endow such power and responsibilities to the panchayats so as to make them institutions of self-government.' In pursuance of the Directive Principles also, it was conceived to decentralise powers and functions to the Panchayati Raj Institutions (PRIs).

When rural development programmes were taken up in the early 1950s, they hardly took cognisance of Mahatma Gandhi's idea of Gram Swarajya. The community development projects were taken up without effective people's participation and hence lost direction. In order to review the situation, the Balwant Rai Mehta Committee was set up in 1957. The study team opined that without an agency at the village level which could represent the entire community assuming responsibility and provide the necessary leadership for implementing development programmes, no significant rural development could take place. Its recommendation that public participation in community works should be organised through statutory representative bodies had implications of far-reaching importance.

It recommended the establishment of Panchayati Raj in 1959. The recommendations of Mehta study team, favouring democratic decentralisation through setting up of PRIs, accelerated the pace of constituting PRIs in all the states. Subsequently, the National Development Council also affirmed the basic principles of democratic decentralisation enunciated in the Mehta report and left it to the state governments to work out structures as suitable to each state.

Broadly speaking, Panchayati Raj or local self-government, is an exercise in decentralisation of administrative authority. The system is based on the following principles:

- **(a)** There should be a three-tier structure of local self-governing bodies from the village to the district level with an organic link from the lower to the higher ones.
- **(b)** There should be a genuine transfer of power and responsibility to these bodies.
- **(c)** Adequate financial resources should be transferred to these bodies to enable them to discharge their responsibilities.
- **(d)** All development programmes at these levels should be channelised through these bodies.
- **(e)** The system evolved should be such as to facilitate further decentralisation in the matter of power and responsibility in the future.

There are three main organs in the framework of Panchayati Raj – Gram Panchayat, Panchayat Samiti and Zila Parishad. There are regional variations in these terms in different states. Broadly speaking, Panchayati Raj is a complete process of governance and it refers to a system organically linking people from the Gram Sabha to the Lok Sabha. A report of the Ministry of Community Development (1964–1965) stated that younger and better leadership was emerging through the PRIs and there was a fairly high degree of satisfaction among the people with their working. The establishment of PRIs had given a boost to the emergence of local leadership by creating new seats of power to be filled by the competitive mechanism of democratic elections. This had enabled a large number of people to acquire leadership at the local levels whereas in the earlier traditional set-up, they had no access to political or administrative organs because of *status quoist* socio-political factors.

The appointment of the Ashok Mehta Committee in 1977 marked a turning point in the concept and practice of Panchayati Raj. This was set up to enquire the working of the PRIs and to suggest measures to strengthen them. The PRIs, which came into being in certain states after the Ashok Mehta Committee recommendations, may be termed as the second-generation panchayats. West Bengal was the first state to take the initiative in 1978 to give a new life to its panchayats on the lines of the Ashok Mehta Committee recommendations. Karnataka, Andhra Pradesh and Jammu & Kashmir followed either revising their existing Panchayat Acts or passing new acts since what the second-generation Panchayati Raj gave were powers to local bodies. Moreover, its orientation was more political. It evoked widespread enthusiasm both at the level of implementation of schemes as well as their working. The West Bengal pattern was considered a success story.

However, the second phase of Panchayati Raj in India could not go much further as state governments could not establish full-fledged Panchayati Raj without adequate Constitutional safeguards. It was against this backdrop that the constitution (64th Amendment) Bill was introduced in parliament in 1989. But, because of technical reasons it fell through. The Congress government, in 1991, introduced the 73rd (Panchayat) and 74th (Nagarpalikas or Municipalities) Constitutional Amendment Bills.

▶▶ 73rd Amendment

After a long-drawn-out compromise process, finally in 1993, the 73rd and 74th Amendments to the Constitution were passed. The amendments prescribed a uniform three-tier system: district, taluk/block and village levels in the rural areas and town panchayats in smaller urban centres besides the existing municipalities and corporations in the larger urban centres. The local self-government institutions were to have a uniform 5-year term and in the event of dissolution, elections were to be held within 6 months. SC/ST representations proportionate to the population and one-third reservation for women were introduced at all levels.

Reservation for OBCs was left to the state legislatures and most of them provided for their reservation. A state finance commission was to be appointed by every state government institution.

The XI Schedule, added after the 73rd Amendment, contains the following subjects.

1. Agriculture including agricultural extension;
2. Land improvement, implementation of land reforms, land consolidation and soil conservation;
3. Minor irrigation, water management and watershed development;
4. Animal husbandry, dairy and poultry;
5. Fisheries;
6. Social forestry and farm forestry;
7. Minor forest produce;
8. Small-scale industries including food-processing industries;
9. Khadi, village and cottage industries;
10. Rural housing;
11. Drinking water;

12. Fuel and fodder;
13. Roads, culverts, bridges, ferries, waterways and other means of communication;
14. Rural electrification including distribution of electricity;
15. Non-conventional energy sources;
16. Poverty alleviation programmes;
17. Education including primary and secondary schools;
18. Technical training and vocational education;
19. Adult and non-formal education;
20. Libraries;
21. Cultural activities;
22. Markets and fairs;
23. Health and sanitation, including hospitals, primary health centres and dispensaries;
24. Family welfare;
25. Women and child development;
26. Social welfare, including welfare of handicapped and mentally retarded;
27. Welfare of weaker sections and in particular SCs/STs;
28. Public distribution system; and
29. Maintenance of community assets.

After the 1993 constitutional amendment, various states have delegated powers out of the 29 functions listed in Schedule XI of the Constitution. Though functions have been transferred by many states, funds have effectively been transferred by a few of them only.

As far as women are concerned, the 73rd Amendment is an important landmark in the history of women participation in the democratic institutions at the grassroots level. Apart from one-third membership, they head one-third panchayats and lakhs of them will be performing leadership roles. Though it is true that a traditionally highly patriarchal Indian society has not taken kindly these efforts of empowerment of women and women representatives often have not been treated with the dignity they deserve, the fact remains that with their growing confidence in themselves and through democratic assertion they are bound to succeed.

IMPACT OF MARKET ECONOMY ON INDIA'S VILLAGES

When we look at India's villages, we find that traditionally, rural economy was primarily a subsistence economy oriented to satisfy the consumption needs of the local population. The *jajmani* system served as the basis of the economic organisation under which local people belonging to different castes were involved in exchange of goods and services as per local traditions. However, it is also true that within this subsistence economy, there was some role of the market. There used to be local, informal markets with varying periodicity, but they served social-cultural functions more than a place of formal economic transactions. These periodically held markets provided avenues for interrelationship between the clusters of villages. Significantly, the economic exchange in such markets was predominantly either redistributive or reciprocal type. Thus, we can say that a limited degree of cash economy and market exchange did exist in the pre-industrial urban centres in India from the medieval period onwards.

What Do You Think?

How can traditional knowledge and practices be integrated with modern economic systems to achieve a balanced growth model?

With the advent of the British rule and the consequent process of modernisation, the pace of change increased rapidly. The colonial vested interests of the British rule pushed a new kind of capitalistic economy in agriculture. Land became a commodity and property. A new kind of land revenue system was introduced promoting monetisation. Simultaneously, the process of peasantisation and de-peasantisation was witnessed, especially in the case of tribal communities. The system of land revenue settlement introduced by the British rulers required the payment of revenue in cash. This became instrumental for a rapidly increasing tendency of raising more cash or commercial crops. In this way, the village economy got linked to the urban and later to the national economy. This was the beginning of monetisation and extension of market economy to Indian villages.

After independence, modern means of transport and communication were introduced by the government as part of massive economic development programmes resulting in full-fledged extension of market economy to village India. Now the commodities of daily use in urban markets such as soaps, toothpaste, hosiery, etc. are also available in village and town markets. In contrast, poultry items from a village in northern India have reached the markets of metropolitan cities of far-off regions. The emergence of a rich class of peasantry created enormous demand for luxury goods in villages. A.R. Desai in his pioneering contribution identified four major trends of change in village India:

(a) Rapid transformation of agrarian society from subsistence economy to market economy;
(b) Rapid transformation followed by the introduction of modern technology;
(c) Abolition of intermediaries such as *Zamindars* and *biswedars*; and
(d) Emergence of associations and institutions having linkages with urban and national organisations.

With the introduction of market economy, there was a change in the nature of production and consumption. Now the prime motive behind agricultural production was to generate a surplus for the market, thus facilitating the entry of more and more market forces. It also promoted a consumption-oriented life style among rural folks. The demand for urban, machine-produced items increased rapidly. Consumption and possession of these items became status symbols. Thus, the rural transformation promoted by the market economy may be summarised as follows:

(a) The new market economy created a new class of rich peasants, big traders, petty officials and political workers.

(b) It promoted a large number of new facilities, especially related to credit. Now, even credit cards have entered rural society.

(c) It facilitated the entry of improved implements such as tractors, water pumps, threshers, etc.

(d) Polarisation of peasants into rich landowning class and extremely poor landless labourers increased manifold.

(e) Monetisation has expanded the avenues of social mobility. It had a deep impact on such traditional social institutions as joint family. The differential capacities of various members of the joint family to generate income led to a tendency towards nuclear families.

(f) It led to occupational mobility and diversification.

(g) An occupation-free caste structure started emerging, providing a big blow to the traditional *jajmani* system.

(h) Caste barriers to economic mobility are crumbling. New avenues of healthcare and education have entered rural life.

(i) It indirectly promoted empowerment of women.

Among all these features, the most glaring phenomenon of recent origin is the agrarian distress and the resultant suicides of peasants even in regions of green revolution such as Punjab, Haryana, Karnataka, Andhra Pradesh, etc. A.K. Vasavi (1999), analysing the phenomenon of suicides among peasants, has identified certain general trends and factors. He rightly points out that the promotion of commercial agriculture based on the utilisation of hybrid seeds, chemical manures and pesticides in a predominantly semi-arid region has had severe repercussions. As a whole, there is a lack of compatibility between the ecological specificity of the region and commercial agricultural practices and climatic changes, especially changes in the rainfall pattern, compound the conditions of uncertainty and risk in agriculture subjecting agriculture to an ecological crisis.

Along with the ecological crisis, the economic crisis worsens the situation further. Though commercial agriculture is promoted on the basis of utilisation of external inputs, institutional credit facilities to purchase these inputs are available to a limited number of agriculturists (mostly large landowners). Most agriculturists incur heavy debts in order to engage in commercial agriculture. Small and marginal cultivators for whom institutional credit is not readily or easily available resort to non-institutional debts at high rates of interest in order to take to modern cultivation or to remain in cultivation. The local moneylenders and *sahukars* are the most easily available sources of credit who thrive on usury. In times of ecological crises such as an outbreak of pests or diseases, such peasants incur more debts.

The introduction of commercial agriculture in a predominantly dry agriculture belt has its impact on the social fabric too. This type of agriculture no longer draws on the established principles of local or indigenous knowledge and caste-and kin-based ties. The agri-business agents and agencies along with the agriculture extension workers enter the scene at the cost of the traditional institutions of dissemination of knowledge. They are not always congenial to the interests of hopeless peasantry.

Sharp fluctuations in prices, a part of market economy, compound the problem. Increased cost of production without assured procurement or support prices from the government agencies push the cultivators into a corner. Cultivators also complain of the large-scale dilution of pesticides and lack of guarantee of many commercial seed varieties. The loss of crops for two successive seasons has been devastating. Under such conditions of changing agricultural practices, minimal state and administrative support, increasing subordination to market forces, high risks in agriculture and declining community support, it is not hard to imagine the personal distress that cultivators experience. The subordination of cultivators to market and capital forces without any safety net to support them in terms of crop loss or radically fluctuating prices beyond their control accounts for the devastation and pauperisation of small farmers. Just as the suicides are symptoms of passive distress in the region, the loss of staple food grains in the region must also be considered a serious issue. As Susan George (1985) had rightly commented, the loss of staple grains in any specific region without a substantial alternative economic base indicates a threat to the food security and hence the fragility of the local communities. Thus, the phenomenon of suicides is directly related to the economic factors as part of the market economy.

What Do You Think?

What policies can ensure sustainable development while preserving the cultural and environmental fabric of rural India?

IMPACT OF GLOBALISATION ON VILLAGES

1. Though forces of market economy had entered Indian villages before the advent of globalisation, it has further increased after globalisation has set in.
2. Globalisation has facilitated greater mobility and faster connectivity mainly because of faster means of transport and communication. Easy availability of cell phone and Internet is transforming villages.
3. This has contributed to rapid migration to nearby and distant places in search of better employment.
4. With increasing mechanisation and improved varieties of seeds, fertilisers and pesticides, agricultural production has increased substantially.
5. Cropping pattern is changing rapidly and more and more peasants are taking up commercial crops, though it has also added hazards. In case of repeated crop failures, the farmers get trapped in distress and many of them commit suicide.
6. Globalisation has created markets outside the states and even countries, but the big, rich farmers are the main beneficiaries.
7. There is increased use of plastic money.
8. The aspirational level of the educated youths has increased.
9. The self-sustaining nature of villages has been destroyed.

CHANGING MODE OF PRODUCTION IN INDIAN AGRICULTURE

'Mode of Production' is a central concept in the Marxist analysis. It is understood as the way a society is organised to produce goods and services. Mode of production has two major aspects:

- Forces of production
- Relations of production

'Forces of production' or productive forces include manpower or human labour power. It also includes means of production that is, tools, productive machinery, other infrastructure, technical knowledge, materials, plants, animals and land. In the 'relations of production' or social and technical relations of production include property, power and those controlling productive assets and relations between social classes. Allan G. Johnson in *The Blackwell Dictionary of Sociology* (1995) writes that since production is a social activity, any mode of production must also include a set of social relationships. Karl Marx's own conception revolved around the key idea that people produce not only 'linen and flax' but in so doing also produce definite social relations.

In the light of this understanding let us examine the changing mode of production in Indian agriculture.

What Do You Think?

1. How does the changing labour dynamic, with increased migration to urban areas, influence the agricultural mode of production in rural India?
2. Can sustainable farming practices be effectively integrated with modern agricultural techniques to address the changing modes of production?

An analysis of caste-based system of production represented by *Jajmani System* needs to be understood. In the traditional caste system land ownership was vested in higher castes only. This system of production developed an elaborate system of exchange of goods and services. The landed higher castes were called *Jajman* (patron) and the service providers – the occupationally specialised lower castes such as carpenters, barbers, blacksmith, oilseed pressers, landless untouchable castes and poor Muslims etc were called *Prajan* or *Kamin* or by some other names as per regional languages. The landless service castes were providing their services and in exchange got a share in the harvest. The *Jajmani* relations were permanent and hereditary in nature. In the post-independence period the *Zamindari* and *Jagirdari* system was abolished by the Indian State. With this, the *Jajmani* system also declined. Now a number of traditionally landless castes got some land. Further, with the advent of democracy and adult franchise untouchable and backward castes mobilised themselves politically and the entire gamut of relationship in the production system underwent change in most parts of the country. In many regions technological innovations such as safety razor and hand pumps freed such castes as barbers and *kahars* (carriers of water) from *Jajmani* obligation. Moreover, with the introduction of new tools and mechanised agriculture, manual labour did not remain the only input in agriculture. This altered the very nature of relationship between the land holders and agricultural labour. With the increasing avenues of transport and communication rural to urban migration increased many fold. Now those who remained in the village and were either landless or had small and unproductive land holding insisted and got wages in cash. It became cash-based wage transaction and that is how mode of production in Indian agriculture changed.

MIGRATION

Migration may be understood as the physical movement of the people from one place to another. Thus, it is a form of spatial mobility from one geographical area to the other. Migration has international dimension too but here we are concerned with the migration of rural population. Migration also affects the social composition of populations. In its popular connotations migration is understood as the more or less permanent movement of people across a social and geographical boundary. Migration may also have psychological effects upon the individual.

India has experienced mainly rural to urban migration. Because of high rate of unemployment, landlessness, lack of income generation opportunities or adverse social condition and similar other factors, people decide to migrate. Thus rural to urban migration may be understood through two types of factors.

- 'Pushed out' factors
- 'Pulled into' factors

Starvation, economic hardship, natural calamities and hostile social environment (especially in case of Dalit castes) may force one to leave one's village or geographical region and migrate to an urban centre to lead a life of '**urban anonymity**'. If only the head of the family migrates, he may continue to remit high proportion of the income to family members back home in village. In this case persons live in dormitory like, densely populated housing to achieve maximum possible savings. In most of the cases, the local governments do not feel it necessary to provide basic amenities to such places such as sanitation, water, electricity, primary school, health centre etc. If the entire family migrates to an urban centre, able members of the family may also take up job like domestic help, courier and messenger, rickshaw puller or any such sundry job to save enough for a one-room tenement or may take advantage of government sponsored housing schemes for the poor. In metros like Delhi, after a passage of time, the whole cluster of houses take the form of resettlement colonies and get legalised thanks to the political interests of the local politicians. In such cases the social ties of the migrants with their native villages decline and wither away. Moreover, the children brought up in metros or big cities will not like to go back to their villages.

Quick Fact

Urban Anonymity

It refers to the sense of isolation or being unnoticed in a city, despite being surrounded by others. People feel disconnected from the space they inhabit.

Under 'pulled into' factors we include mainly the attraction of cities, its glamour, promise of better living conditions, better income free from the oppression of the caste system. In this case nobody is pushing them out. In the wake of COVID-19 pandemic many myths regarding migration lie exploded when millions of migrant labour mainly from Uttar Pradesh, Bihar, Jharkhand, Chhattisgarh and Orissa took to 'reverse' migration, back to their native villages and roots. Only those of them who had settled firmly with some assets did not move. It was heart breaking to see thousands and thousands of migrant labour going back on their feet, by bicycles, by auto-rickshaw while dozens of them are losing their lives in accidents, exhaustion or starvation.

Questions and Indicative Answers

1. What are the main components of rural social structure?

- Despite diversity, rural social structure has family (mostly joint family), kinship, caste, class.
- Caste, joint family and village communities form a triad and any change in any of these shall induce change in the social structure.
- Family/joint family forms economic unit in rural social structure.

2. Why did some British administrators describe India's villages as 'little republics'?

- Charles Metcalfe and others exaggerated the autonomy of Indian village and described these as little republics.
- This was far from the truth.
- As Oscar Lewis, an eminent American anthropologist, showed Indian villages form 'rural cosmopolitanism', meaning one village is linked to several other villages through kinship ties, religion, fairs and festivals, etc.

3. How are India's villages also a social system?

- Enumerate all the key features of social system.
- Since all the features of social system are found in a typical Indian village, it may always be described as a social system.

4. What is meant by a Village Study? In what way it is significant?

- Village and peasant study are a later development in anthropology.
- In-depth and intensive study through fieldwork employing participant observation makes a village study. This is nothing, but a village ethnography.
- At the theoretical level, village ethnography led to the emergence of new concepts such as *Sanskritisation*, dominant caste, universalisation and parochialisation.
- At the applied level, village study helped planners and development administration to make suitable programme for rural development.
- Village studies have negated stereotype of villages.

5. **Discuss the key features of peasant society.**
   - Write Krobber's description of peasant society as 'part society' and provide Redfield's and Shanin's description.
6. **Discuss the power structure and class stratification in India's villages.**
   - Briefly give the classification by the British administrators.
   - D.N. Dhanagare gave a detailed classification based on pre-independence and post-independence changes.
7. **Write a note on the jajmani system and its decline.**
   - *Jajmani* system forms socio-economic and political basis of the traditional caste system.
   - William Wiser initiated its study.
   - *Jajmani* system refers to the elaborate system of exchange of goods and services between castes.
   - It explains the functional interdependence between different castes in a village.
   - Because of zamindari abolition, technological innovations, political mobilisation of Dalit and backward castes and role of state, it declined. It has disappeared from the cities and started crumbling in the villages.
8. **Describe the impact of globalisation on India's villages.**

   Important factors are:
   - Increased role of market,
   - Better connectivity and mobility, rapid migration, changes in cropping pattern, introduction of plastic money (debit and credit cards); and
   - It adversely impacted the self-sustaining nature of villages.

Previous Years' Questions

1. Examine the contribution of village studies towards the understanding of Indian Social System. **(UPSC CSE Mains Anthropology, Paper II, 2015)**
2. Discuss the main features of farmers' movement in India. **(UPSC CSE Mains Sociology, Paper II, 2015)**
3. Write a short note on the Jajmani system and contemporary market economy. **(UPSC CSE Mains Anthropology, Paper II, 2019)**
4. Identify the theoretical concepts that have emerged out of village studies in India. **(UPSC CSE Mains Anthropology, Paper II, 2019)**
5. Write a short note on Jajmani System: Continuity and Change **(UPSC CSE Mains Anthropology, Paper II, 2020)**

6. Discuss the challenges during village studies in India.
(UPSC CSE Mains Sociology, Paper II, 2022)
7. The decade of 1950s was the golden period of village studies in Indian Sociology. Explain the statement. (UPSC CSE Mains Sociology, Paper II, 2023)
8. Despite the efforts of the government, bonded labour still continues in India. Discuss.
(UPSC CSE Mains Sociology, Paper II, 2024)
9. Identify different forms of inequalities associated with agrarian social structure in India.
(UPSC CSE Mains Sociology, Paper II, 2024)

CHAPTER 11

Urbanisation

Chapter Outline

1. Urbanisation and its significance in societal transformation
2. Recognising features like high population density, heterogeneity, social mobility, and predominance of non-agricultural occupations
3. Analysing the positive effects of urbanisation, including economic growth, increased employment opportunities, and improvements in living standards
4. Understanding the relationship between urbanisation and industrialisation
5. Examining the factors contributing to urban poverty and the need for inclusive development
6. Knowing smart cities, and how they aim to address urban challenges
7. Exploring how urbanisation influences gender roles, providing more opportunities for women while also highlighting new challenges

Urbanisation is a process through which people change their lifestyles, occupations, behaviour, workplaces, organisation of work and leisure, housing, modes of transport and communication and become drastically different people from what they were in the rural areas. In terms of spatial mobility, it refers to the population shift from rural areas to urban areas. It is also a process by which towns and cities are formed and become larger as more people begin living and working. A number of disciplines such as geography, sociology, anthropology, economics, urban planning, architecture and public health find it relevant to their disciplines. Urbanisation is not a modern phenomenon.

An area is classified as rural or urban depending upon various criteria such as population size, density, occupational composition and civic status. Since the 1961 census, an urban area was determined based on two important criteria, namely (i) statutory administration and (ii) certain economic and demographic indicators. The first criterion includes civic status of towns and the second entails characteristics like population size, density of population and percentage of workforce in the non-agricultural sector. Processes like industrialisation also facilitate urbanisation in setting its direction and speed.

According to a number of experts, the following are the characteristics of urban area:

- Large size and high density of population;
- **Heterogeneity** in several respects;
- **Anonymity:** Because of larger population, many people become anonymous to many. Thus, urban anonymity gets reflected in social relations;
- More individualism, superficiality and organic nature of relationship;
- **Transiency:** where people keep on making new acquaintances and forgetting the older ones;
- Differentiation along class lines;
- High pace of life and **social mobility**;
- Specialisation of functions and standardisation of behaviour;
- Specialised services; and
- Predominance of non-agricultural occupations.

Quick Fact

Heterogeneity

Diversity in population composition and lifestyles in urban areas.

Social Mobility

The ability of individuals to move up or down the social hierarchy, often facilitated by urban environments.

IMPACT OF URBANISATION

Urbanisation has impacted our society in both ways, positive as well as negative. It has a *positive* impact on the rural economy since large urban systems consume enormous amount of primary agricultural products. Urbanisation helps agricultural development, non-farm development and contributes to poverty alleviation. An additional facilitating role is played by industrialisation which generally takes place only in urban centres. Industrialisation and urbanisation create an incredible number of economic opportunities. These include production of a wide variety of products and services which, in turn, employ a large number of people giving them higher income and affording a better standard of living.

What Do You Think?

How does urbanisation reshape traditional social structures and cultural identities, and what measures can ensure sustainable and equitable growth in rapidly urbanising areas?

Compared to rural India, women in cities enjoy much more freedom and cultural autonomy which include the right to visibility and mobility and freedom to choose a spouse. Thus, urban working and non-working females are far more emancipated. We also witness urbanisation of family in urban India. Among its features the important ones are decline in fertility, rise in the level of female literacy, greater work opportunity for women outside the family, primacy of nuclear family and rise in the age of marriage of females.

Among the *negative* impacts of urbanisation, the most pronounced is haphazard growth. Such urban growth comes with enormous strain on resources. India's big cities are already bursting at the seams and are clamouring for more of basic infrastructure. Human cost of urban growth cannot be ignored; it is the poorest sections of population that had to repeatedly bear the human cost of successive waves of urban development. Given large-scale migration of the poor and agonisingly slow provision of civic, social, economic and infrastructural facilities in the cities, slums have proliferated in urban India where people are forced to live with minimal resources and under subhuman conditions.

PROBLEM AND FUTURE SCENARIO

In the recently held Davos Economic Forum, it was clearly in view that the development of cities is now being considered as the pivot of development in India. Presently, urbanisation has emerged as the symbol of development as it has more possibilities of employment in comparison to the rural areas and thus contributes to the national income. If we look back, we find that till 2001 only 27.81% of India's population was living in cities. By 2011 it climbed to 31.6% and as the reports suggest, it increased to 33.6% by 2018. As per the 2001 census, the number of towns-cities was 5161 which registered a sharp increase and became 7936. The present scenario reveals that today one out of every three Indians lives in towns/cities. Moreover, the latest reports of the United Nations reveal that today almost half of the world's population now lives in urban areas and by 2050 almost half of the Indian population too shall be living in urban areas. By that time, around 70% of the world's population might be living in cities.

Globalisation has also posed a number of challenges to the world, especially to developing countries such as India. Moreover, the process of urban development in India is posing an existential problem for our villages.

The pace at which urbanisation is swallowing villages is creating problems of far-reaching importance. Cities are emerging as a threat to the preservation of our environment because large green belts and regions are being sacrificed for the development of cities. This has also threatened the existence of cities by creating climatic changes, especially cities situated along coastal regions. Such cities now face the threat of man-made disasters and calamities. Moreover, cities have given rise to a number of temporary housings and slums whose inhabitants fulfil the needs of the upper and middle classes, but are themselves steeped in poverty and deprived of basic requirements of a decent living. Moreover, rapid technological development has also threatened the groups of people living by their traditional occupations. The haphazard transport system in cities causes an increasing number of deaths on roads. Public transport system, in most of the cities, has crumbled along with the decaying public health services. Thus, increasing privatisation and corporatisation in public health and education sectors are contributing to more inequalities. Corruption in public life, though affecting everybody, hits the poor harder. Potholes on roads, lack of sewer lines and not so efficient supply of water and power are now a familiar feature in a large number of cities.

As Jyoti Sadana (2019) rightly points out, in the model of civilisation presented by Europe, it is impossible for the village and city to coexist. Mahatma Gandhi had rejected this model of modern civilisation based on consumerism. **Neo-liberalism** and globalisation have virtually converted the village as merely the suppliers of foodgrain, labour and raw material.

Quick Fact

Neo-liberalism

Neoliberalism is a political and economic philosophy that emphasizes free trade, deregulation, globalisation, and a reduction in government spending.

Besides rural to urban migration, urban to urban migration is also likely to accelerate in India due to changing labour market demand, but this would have no impact as far as urban growth is concerned. According to a report published by Mckinsey Global Institute,[1] By 2030, 590 million people in India will live in cities. Mumbai and Delhi will be among the five largest cities in the world. The rapid pace and scale of urbanisation has been witnessed anywhere barring China. By 2025, India and China shall have mega cities whose population is above 10 million.

SMART CITY

A new concept by the name of Smart City was launched in 2015 under Smart Cities Mission (SCM) as a centrally sponsored scheme as part of urban rejuvenation. The government plans to develop 100 smart cities during 2015–2020. The concept of smart city is based on 'smart solutions'. Its features will be as follows:

- E-governance and citizen services;
- Waste management;
- Water management;
- Energy management;
- Urban mobility; and
- Others include telemedicine, trade facilitation centres, skill development centres, etc.

What Do You Think?

1. What measures should governments implement to ensure that smart cities cater to all socioeconomic groups and do not become islands of privilege?
2. How can the ethical use of technology in smart cities be ensured to protect privacy, prevent surveillance misuse, and foster trust among citizens?

An important question being raised by many is what would be the fate of the poor and the marginalised sections of society? Will these smart cities be meant only for those who will be well versed and equipped with computer and Internet technology? Would such cities be a jungle of multi-storeyed buildings where individualism shall prevail and human relations shall be replaced by technology? The very concept of smart cities should be open for public debate.

Questions and Indicative Answers

1. What are the characteristics of urbanisation?

- Non-agricultural occupation, high density of population, heterogeneity, anonymity, differentiation along class lines, high pace of life, social mobility, etc.

[1] Mckinsey Global Institute Report, India's Urban Awakening: Building Inclusive Cities, Sustaining Economic Growth, 2010

2. Discuss the impact of urbanisation.

- High consumption of primary agricultural products, non-farm occupations, generation of more employment, increased air and water pollution, poorest sections hard hit, rise of slums; and
- In the model of civilisation presented by Europe and followed by us, it is almost impossible that villages and cities might coexist.

Previous Years' Questions

1. Does Urbanisation lead to more segregation and marginalisation of the poor in Indian metropolises? **(GS Mains Paper I, 2023)**

Focus Areas for the Examination

1. Impact of Urbanisation on the poor
2. Smart City

CHAPTER 12

Social Movements in India

Chapter Outline

1. Identifying key elements of social movements and examining different approaches
2. Analysing the role of the state in responding to movements and its strategies, such as repression or co-option
3. Recognising the contributions of reform movements to societal transformation
4. Analysing how Dalit movements address caste-based discrimination and aim for social justice
5. Know the causes and typologies of tribal movements
6. Exploring the radical shift in post-independence peasant movements

The study of social movements is a comparatively late development in social sciences. The growth of such studies has been remarkable in the last four decades not only in India, but also in other parts of the world. Sociology, social history and social anthropology took the lead in research studies of social movements. While political science took a long time to accept social movement as a genuine subject, social anthropology took interest only in tribal movements.

There is no precise definition of the term 'social movement' accepted by scholars of all disciplines or even scholars belonging to the same discipline. According to The Blackwell Dictionary of Sociology, it is described as a continuous, structured, and collective endeavor directed toward achieving a particular aspect of social change. Social movements have always been of great sociological interest because they are a major source of social change and social conflict. Martin Fuchs & Antje Linkenbach (2003) say that social movements by definition are an unstable, transitory phenomenon. They do not have a clear beginning or, in many cases, a clear point of termination and cannot be easily and precisely separated from the process of social interaction at large. The term 'social movement' refers to a diverse spectrum of collective social and political phenomenon, as heterogeneous as revolutions, religious sects, political organisations or single-issue campaigns or anti-colonial resistance and resistance against inroads by alleged outsiders. Given the heterogeneity they give a 'provisional' definition of social movements – 'A social movement takes the forms of collective self-organisation for the attainment of social recognition and the assertion of rights or existential interests hitherto denied to a group or category of people. It engages in distance against the threat of a group's or category of people's rights and basis of existence.' The main criterion for judging which kinds of inequalities or injustices is being addressed may be inferred only from a situational appraisal of the concerned actors in a movement. The term 'social movement' is used by many researchers 'in a natively descriptive manner' to refer to a supposedly unified collective subject. Touraine (1995) says that two aspects are generally implied in this point: first, the 'anti-establishment social content, a reference to ideas of autonomy, equity, human dignity or fundamental rights and second, the link to social change especially modernisation, as a triggering cause or an objective of social movements'. Ghanshyam Shah[1] (2002) asserts that "Objectives, Ideology, Programmes, Leadership and Organisation are important components of social movements. They are interdependent, influencing each other. The objectives of the movement change from narrow particularly local issues to broad aims of social transformation." Sometimes, a movement which begins with broad objectives may, in the process, get bogged down to one or two particular issues. Ideology also undergoes change. Various strategies and programmes are evolved to mobilise the people. They sustain the movement for a long period. Leadership which initiates or emerges in the course of the growth of the movement plays a crucial role in articulating ideology and objectives, evolving strategies and programmes and maintaining the spirit of the participants.

APPROACHES

There may be several approaches, but as Shah points out, generally studies on social movements follow either a Marxist or non-Marxist framework for analysis. Scholars following the Marxist approach are primarily interested in bringing about revolutionary change in society. According to them, the causes for social movement are located in the economic structure of society. Antagonistic interests between the propertied and labour classes are inherent in a class-based society which generates contradictions. Though to Marxists, structural causes of conflicting economic interests are central to their studies, a number of Marxist scholars have begun to pay attention to ethnic, religious and other cultural factors. Now, a group of Marxist historians known as '**subaltern** scholars' have also emerged and they are studying 'history from below'. They criticise the 'traditional' Marxist historians for ignoring the history of the masses, as if subaltern classes do not make history of their own, depending solely on the advanced classes or the elite for organisation and guidance. These subaltern studies are strongly criticised by other Marxist scholars for ignoring structural factors and viewing 'consciousness' as an independent structural contradiction. The non-Marxist scholars have also shown variations in their approach to analysing social movements. It is argued by most of them that mass movements are the products of mass societies.

> **Quick Fact**
>
> **Subaltern**
>
> A sociological category based in a complex socio-political context, subaltern refers to that section of the population who is socially, geographically, or politically excluded from the hierarchy of power established during the colonial times and centred on the metropolitan majority of the nation.

[1] Ghanshyam Shah, Social movements in India: A review of Literature, Rawat Publications, Jaipur, 2002

STATE AND MOVEMENTS

The role of the state is very important in any analysis of social movement. Shah (ibid) is empirically correct when he says that the immediate response of the state to all movements pressuring or challenging its authority is negative. It has a tendency to resist any collective action which, by nature, "either exerts pressure on the authority for certain policy and action and/or protest against the decision and action of the state. The state looks at social movements as a challenge to its legitimacy of governance. Neither the capitalist state, overtly representing propertied classes, nor the communist state, claiming to be the state of the working class, prefers to face the movements of the classes it supposedly represents." The state is somewhat softer with those movements which have reformist demands within the institutional framework than those movements which aim at overthrowing and replacing state power. The strategy of the state varies from situation to situation. When the brutal and repressive force of the state fails, the leaders and opinion makers of the movement may be co-opted, who then serve as 'legitimisers' of the state's policies and action. The state may also take to deceit, indoctrination and sabotage. All these actions and counteractions are obviously because of the fact that most of the social movements are anti-establishment in nature.

TYPOLOGIES OF SOCIAL MOVEMENTS

Serious researchers of social movements have tried to understand the nature of social movements through different typologies. Shah (1977) classifies movements into (i) Revolt, (ii) Rebellion, (iii) Reform and (iv) Revolution. While a revolt is an open challenge to political authority, a rebellion is an attack on existing authority without any intention to seize state power. A revolution may be taken as an organised struggle to overthrow the government and the socio-economic structure which sustains it and replaces it by an alternative social order. Reform does not challenge the political system per se, but tries to bring about certain desired changes within the existing socio-political structure. That is why the state shows a lenient attitude towards such movements. M.S.A. Rao (1978) classifies the movements into Reformist, Transformatory and Revolutionary, while T.K. Oommen (1977) classifies them as Ideological, Charismatic and Organisational. Specific issues may also be the main determinants in the classification of social movements. Such issues may be linguistic, civil rights or rights in natural resources such as tribal struggles for their forest rights. A common practice of classifying the movements on the basis of the actors/participants is too obvious. That is why naming the movements as peasant movement, tribal movement, Dalit movement, women's movement or student's movement is now a popular practice.

In the Third Survey of Research (ICSSR, 2000), Rajendra Singh made a review of 'Old' and 'New' social movements taking into consideration the changing paradigms and conceptual frameworks. He says that the conventional 'old' themes of peasant, tribal, working class, students and the religious and sectarian movements persist in and continue to be the main concern of a number of social movement studies in India. But, side by side, perhaps in an ascending order, a large number of studies on 'new' themes have emerged, such as the environment and ecology, farmer's agitation, feminist assertions, identity-oriented ethnic and of the multiple and plural expression of collective actions of the movements of grassroots organisations and action groups and human right and civil liberty movements. The 'old' and 'new' themes, in their many empirical impressions, often show overlaps and some elements of the 'old' do achieve entry in the 'new' and vice versa. However, while the 'old' and the classical movement's studies generally revolve around the less complex and relatively simple forms of core conflicts, the contemporary 'new' movements, on the other hand, reflect widely differentiated and increasingly complex and expanding nature of social conflicts in India. "As such, the analytical separation between the 'old' and the 'new' movements is a helpful exercise."

SOCIAL MOVEMENTS IN INDIA

Though new themes have entered into the realm of social movements in India, the best studied ones have been Social and Religious Reform Movements, Backward Classes Movement, Dalit Movement, Tribal Movement, Peasant Movement and to a lesser extent, Women's Movement. A brief description of these movements is given here leaving out women's movement which has been discussed in the chapter on 'Women and Society'.

SOCIAL AND RELIGIOUS REFORM MOVEMENTS

As the name suggests, reform movements seek to introduce certain reforms or changes in norms and values and consequently, even in the existing social relations within the larger framework of the society. Usually, reform movements use legitimate means and the changes are sought to be brought about without disturbing the existing framework of the society. The Brahmo Samaj Movement led by Raja Ram Mohan Roy and others during the 19th century, Arya Samaj Movement led by Swami Dayanand Saraswati, Aligarh Movement led by Sir Syed Ahmed Khan and the **Tablighi Jamaat Movement** led by Moulana Ilyas in the 20th century are some of the important examples of social and religious reform movements.

> **Quick Fact**
>
> **Tablighi Jamaat Movement**
>
> An international Islamic religious movement that asks its followers to be more observant of their religion and arduously practice it by following Prophet Muhammad while preaching to non-Muslims.

The Brahmo Samaj Movement may be considered as the harbinger of social reform in modern India. As a result of modern, western education, a liberal intellectual class emerged who tried to reinterpret Hinduism in a wider liberal, rational and humanistic framework. They found the traditional Indian social system steeped in a number of aberrations and social evils which needed to be corrected and reformed. Gender injustice and cruelty towards women were perpetrated through such practices as *Sati* and polygamy especially among the higher, *Kulin* castes of Bengal. Untouchability was an accepted and socially-religiously sanctioned practice. The widespread and blind idolatry supported by deeply rooted dogmatism was the order of the day. The westernised, liberal intelligentsia viewed such practices as socially retrogressive and obnoxious. Reacting strongly against the prevailing evils of the Hindu society, Raja Ram Mohan Roy supported by similar enlightened persons launched a reform movement in 1829. It was known as the Brahmo Samaj Movement. Its major objective was the purification of Hinduism and preaching the worship of one God. The movement was largely based on Reason, Rationality and the Vedas. It also sought to incorporate relevant teachings of other religions too. It promoted the idea of human dignity and severely criticised and condemned Sati and untouchability. It laid emphasis on modern secular education. In fact, Raja Ram Mohan Roy was instrumental in the passage of legislation banning Sati. The Brahmo tradition was promoted, after Roy, by Debendranath Tagore and Keshub Chandra Sen. The movement also promoted widow remarriage and the cause of women's education. It propagated against the rigidity and orthodoxy of the caste system and worked against child marriage. The major weakness of the movement was its restricted influence only among the urban-based Bengalese. Yet, it had a profound impact on the socio-cultural, political and intellectual life of Bengal and adjoining areas in the 19th and early 20th century. The internal dissensions and squabbles weakened the movement, but it continued to inspire the future generations of reformers.

The scope and range of the Arya Samaj Movement was wider than the Brahmo Samaj Movement. Its founder was Swami Dayanand Saraswati who initiated it in 1875. The Arya Samaj Movement was revivalistic in character. The Vedas were regarded by the movement as infallible and the source of all knowledge. Swami Dayanand's burning reformatory zeal held the 'ignorant priest' in contempt and made the slogan 'Back to the Vedas' as the face of the movement. He condemned the 'useless' rituals as the source of bread and butter. Arya Samaj Movement's programme of social reform included the abolition of hereditary caste system and its replacement by the four varna system. It attacked the practice of untouchability and promoted a scheme of social status not based on birth, but on merit. The importance of the Vedas in its ideology may be gauged from the fact that it not only rejected all the later religious thoughts, but also regarded them infallible and the source of all knowledge – religious and secular that included philosophy, science and technology. The movement promoted gender equality and women's education, but opposed co-education. The Arya Samajis started a network of DAV (Dayanand Anglo-Vedic) Colleges throughout India and a university (Gurukul) near Haridwar to propagate their ideas of education. The movement was able to attract a wide segment of nationalists including Lala Lajpat Rai. Although the Arya Samaj Movement represented a form of national awakening, it generated a negative and hostile attitude towards Islam and Muslims. In the 1920s, the Shuddhi campaign (a purification movement) was launched to reconvert various **neo-Muslim groups** in Northern India to Hinduism. This initiative sparked significant communal tensions and became highly controversial. Consequently, it could never become truly national or cosmopolitan in character and in fact became a hindrance to the growth of secular nationalism by alienating the minorities.

Quick Fact

Neo-Muslim Groups

Neo-Muslims are those Muslims who converted to Islam in recent times. The Meo of Mewat region is the most obvious example.

Two best-known reform movements among the Muslims are the Aligarh Movement and the Tablighi Movement. The Aligarh Movement, led by Sir Syed Ahmed Khan, holds a special place in the realm of social reform among the Muslims of India. Sir Syed was a great visionary who was able to look beyond his times. He had the background of English education and was tremendously impressed by modern scientific thought and favoured reconciliation between modernity and Islam. He accepted

Quran as an authoritative work and rejected all other sources if they went against modern scientific thought. He worked for the interpretation of Quran in the light of rationalism and scientific thought. He believed that Quranic teachings were based on reason and hence rejected any interpretation of the Quran that came into conflict with reason, science or nature. Throughout his life he fought against obscurantism and irrationality. He strongly advocated for a critical approach and freedom of thought. He campaigned against **fanaticism** and **separatism** and championed the cause of Hindu–Muslim unity citing Hindus and Muslims being 'two eyes of the beautiful bride called India'. He exhorted Hindus and Muslims to adopt an attitude of mutual tolerance and goodwill. He hated intellectual backwardness. As the founder of the Aligarh Movement, he promoted modern education and got several books from western education translated into Urdu language for the benefit of north Indian Muslims. Though he was instrumental in establishing several schools in different towns of north India, his efforts culminated in founding the Mohammedan Anglo-Oriental College at Aligarh (Uttar Pradesh) in 1875 which later grew into Aligarh Muslim University, now a major central university. He ensured that this college was run on non-communal lines and students of all castes and communities were also freely admitted. His idea of social reform had no place for retrograde medieval customs. The Aligarh Movement strongly promoted women's education, discouraged the *Purdah* system, condemned polygamy and easy divorce. That is why he was always in confrontation with the orthodox section of Indian Muslims. Some of his critics severely criticised him for his affinities with the British rulers and some of his separatist ideas during the last days of his life. Unfortunately, the Aligarh Movement could not be sustained vigorously after his death, but continues to inspire the reformative elements in Muslim society of the Indian subcontinent.

Quick Fact

Fanaticism

Excessive enthusiasm, unreasoning zeal, wild notions on some subject.

Separatism

The pursuit of political, cultural, or religious independence by a group, aiming to create a distinct identity or separate state.

Contrary to the progressive nature of Aligarh Movement, the Tablighi Movement was religious, oriented and revivalist in several aspects. The Tablighi Jamaat is the most widespread, yet least studied, Islamic Movement in the contemporary world. Today, it is active in more than hundred countries of the contemporary world. It had its origins in the 1920s in the villages of Mewat, a culturally distinct region spread over Haryana and Rajasthan, home of a tribal community known as Meo. The Tablighi Jamaat (literally meaning a group of religious preachers) as we know it today, was started in the 1920s by a charismatic Islamic scholar Moulana Muhammad Ilyas. Yoginder S. Sikand (2000), who has studied this movement intensively, is of the view that the immediate cause behind the launching of the movement was the shuddhi campaign of the Arya Samaj to reconvert to the Hindu fold numerous neo-Muslim groups in Northern India, most notably the Malkana Rajputs of the western districts of the then United Provinces. In the wake of the shuddhi movement it dawned on Maulana Ilyas that the only way that the neo-Muslims, who till then continued to practice many customs derived from their Hindu past, could be saved from being absorbed into the Hindu fold was to instil in them a firm consciousness of being Muslims, along with teaching them the basics of Islam. He chose the Meos, a neo-Muslim group, as his initial field for missionary efforts. Ilyas wanted to restore the 'purity' of

Islamic practices among the Meos through 'Islamisation' of the Hindu customs and practices. No doubt, this heightened their Islamic identity and consciousness, but weakened the traditional ties between the Meos and their Hindu neighbours. Sociologically speaking, the 'Great Tradition' of major religions may be different from each other, but the 'Little (local) Traditions' are shared at the local level by people following different religious systems. In fact, it is the commonly shared Little Traditions which serve as the cultural bridge between different religious communities occupying the common geographical space. Thus, in a way, there is every possibility that the work of Tablighi Jamaat may be promoting cultural exclusiveness which may not be in the interest of social and national integration despite the fact that it may be understood as the work of religious reform.

BACKWARD CLASSES MOVEMENT

In loose and broad terms, backward segments of Indian population include the 'Scheduled Castes', 'Scheduled Tribes' and 'other backward classes' and in terms of broader social organisation the usual description may include all the lower castes (backward castes), but in contemporary sociological discourse the Dalits (largely untouchable castes/Scheduled Castes) and backward castes (non-untouchable middle level or lower castes) are dealt with separately. Thus, usually, the Dalit movement includes largely untouchable castes and backward classes movement incorporates the non-untouchable lower castes. In these terms, the movement of backward classes/castes has also been described as Non-Brahmin Movements.

Significantly, all the backward castes never enjoyed a uniform socio-economic status. In his study on the backward caste movements, M.S.A. Rao (1979) divided non-upper castes into three categories. The uppermost category of the backward castes consists mostly of landowners. There are several such castes in different parts of the country, such as the Jat, the Ahir, the Gujjar in Punjab, Haryana and Uttar Pradesh; the Maratha in Maharashtra; the Vellala in Tamil Nadu; the Kamma, the Kapu and the Reddy in Andhra Pradesh; the Vokkaliga and the Bant in Karnataka; the Yadav and the Kurmi in Uttar Pradesh and Bihar, etc. Ranking below them are tenant cultivators, artisans and other service castes. They include the Ahir and the Kahar in Bihar, the Koli in Gujarat and the Vaddar in South India. Such caste groups are considered caste Hindus, located above the pollution line. Despite this they did not enjoy political power. They were under the economic and political control of the landowning castes. "The latter often extorted forced labour from the former as domestic servants and palanquin-bearers and expected several customary payments (free gifts) on various festivals" (Rao, ibid).[2] At the bottom are the untouchable castes who are designated Scheduled Castes under the Constitution of India. The socio-economic conditions of most of the Scheduled Castes and other backward castes are qualitatively different, though some of the non-upper caste movements also known as anti-Brahmin movements included untouchables. Most of the studies on the untouchable movements do not include the movements of the other backward castes.

[2] M. S. A. Rao, Social Movements in India: Studies in Peasant, Tribal and Women's Movement, Manohar Publishers, New Delhi, 2002

Most of the non-Brahmin or backward caste movements occurred in the erstwhile Madras and Bombay Presidency. The 19th-century social movements made significant inroads in Indian society and shook the traditional caste order. Jyotiba Phule of Pune was one of the first to have revolted against the tyranny of caste in general and of the Brahmins in particular. In 1873, he organised an association called the Satyashodhak Samaj (Truth Seeker's Association) and asked his followers not to engage any Brahman priest. He started schools for the children of non-Brahmin castes (Omvedt, 1971). While Phule started the Non-Brahmin Movement in Maharashtra and mobilised the Malis (gardener caste), it was Sahuji Maharaj of Kolhapur who injected new life in the movement by advocating the right of communal representation. He may be regarded as the chief architect of the anti-Brahmin ideology.

Though seeds of the Non-Brahmin Movement had been sown, it took a systematically organised form only in 1920s in the Madras Presidency where the South Indian Liberal Federation popularly called as Justice Party was formed in 1916. It formulated the Non-Brahmin's Manifesto directed against the dominance of Brahmins in the fields of education, public service and politics. It is important to note here that the upper non-Brahmin castes such as the Vellalars, Naidus, Nayars and Mudaliars took a lead in building up an anti-Brahmin ideology and organisation to subvert Brahmin dominance. The Non-Brahmin Movement of Madras spread to the princely state of Mysore. The major players here were the Lingayats, the Vokkaligas and the backward Muslims. The Non-Brahmin Movement in Mysore differs from its counterparts in Madras in two respects. First, the movement in Mysore did not alienate the lower non-Brahmin castes and the Muslims and second, the anti-Brahmin ideology here did not assume the form of a pro-Dravidian and Anti-Aryan image. The orientation of the Non-Brahmin Movement in Kerala was different from those in Bombay, Madras and Mysore. It was oriented towards the immigrant non-Malayali Brahmins, especially the Tamil Brahmins and the major actors here were the Nairs. Significantly, there were no significant anti-Brahmin movement in the North.

While the conflict between Brahmins and the upper caste non-Brahmins became the centre of anti-Brahmin movements, the conflict between the upper non-Brahmin castes and the lower non-Brahmin, but non-untouchable castes gave birth to a number of social movements in different parts of India. Four such movements with different ideological overtones are the Yadava Movement, the Vanniyakula *Kshatriya* Movement, the Nadar Movement and the Self-Respect and D.K. Movement.

The Yadavas are a generic name for a category of castes called by different names in different regions. In Uttar Pradesh, Himachal Pradesh, Punjab, Haryana, Delhi, Bihar, Gujarat, Madhya Pradesh and Rajasthan, they were known as Ahirs. They are known as Golas and Sadgops in Bengal and Orissa, Gavli and Gopala in Maharashtra, Golla in Andhra Pradesh and Karnataka, Idayan in Kerala and Konar in Tamil Nadu. They are not homogenous even occupationally and follow such diverse occupations as selling milk and milk products, cattle herding and cultivation. In the early 20th century they developed a new Yadava identity. They traced their lineage to the Yadu dynasty and Krishna. The Krishna mythology also gave legitimacy to pastoral occupations. The majority of them were economically weaker, deprived and exploited being cattle herders, small cultivators and agricultural labourers. After coming under the influence of Arya Samaj, especially in Northern India, they started participating in Vedic Hinduism gaining self-respect, but in the process had to bear the wrath of

Thakurs, Bhumihars and Brahmins, who looked at these attempts of upward social mobility through *Sanskritisation* with suspicion. The latent hostility became open violence when the Ahirs started wearing *janev* – the sacred thread – in public. It was followed by the formation of caste associations and a call to add Yadav after their names. However, the national identity of the Yadavas emerged in 1923 with the formation of the All India Yadava Mahasabha led by modern, educated Yadav elite. The Mahasabha started a whole programme of social reforms. It pleaded for vegetarianism, teetotalism and for the removal of such practices as dowry and untouchability. The 1960s was a turning point in the Yadav movement. It agitated for the creation of a separate Yadav regiment in the Indian army and later assumed the leadership of the backward castes fighting for the preferential treatment in education and employment. It brought about a high degree of social awakening regarding their status as a relatively deprived group and formulation of an ideology on the basis of mythological and historical sources. Education achieved a high priority among them and their recruitment to the defence forces and the police rose substantially. Through the democratisation process the political elite among them also got a share in the political power in different states, especially Uttar Pradesh, Bihar and Madhya Pradesh.

When we look into the social processes in Indian society we find that the process of **Kshatriyasation** has been the most popular. In the backward caste movements, along with the Yadav, mention may be made of the Nadar and Vanniyakula *Kshatriya* movements in Tamil Nadu. Hardgrave (1969) has given an extensive account of the history of the Nadar Movement. He showed that the Nadars, traditionally a caste of toddy tappers, claimed *Kshatriya* status in the last quarter of the 19th century. They donned sacred thread and got Brahmin priests to conduct the sacred thread ceremony and other rituals. They also formed the Nadar *Kshatriya* Mahajana Sangam at Madurai in 1895 and emerged as a strong political force in Tamil Nadu after independence.

Quick Fact

Kshatriyaisation

It is a social and cultural transformation, where groups adopt the lifestyle and values of the Kshatriyas. It is similar to Sanskritisation, where groups emulate the Brahmin way of life.

In the late 19th and early 20th centuries, the Rajbansi community sought to establish themselves as Kshatriyas.

The Pallis, an agricultural caste, experienced a similar situation as part of the Vanniyakula *Kshatriya* movement. After attaining the awareness of their status as a deprived group, they organised themselves in 1830s. They claimed descent from the Pallava dynasty of the *Kshatriyas,* but supported anti-Brahmin movement.

Unlike the case of the above-described castes, the Jogis, a caste of traditional weavers from West Bengal, adopted the Brahminical model as a form of protest. They attained consciousness of their deprived status in the late 19th century and set up the Jogi Hitaisini Sabha in 1901 and started a journal Jogisika. Then they took to wearing sacred thread in order to assert their ritually pure status. Similarly, another caste of agriculturalists, Namasudra, claimed Brahmin status.

Another ideology of protest, more articulate with wider socio-political implications, was the Self-Respect Movement. The leader of the Movement, Periyar EV Ramasamy, protested against the accident of birth as the one and the only criterion of status and worth. He sought a new value system in which people irrespective of caste and creed could enjoy equal self-respect. By directly attacking the Brahmins and puranic Hinduism, he derived support from the wider system of Tamil and Dravidian culture which he considered superior to the Brahminical Aryan culture. Since the late 19th century the intellectual foundations and superiority of Tamil Dravidian culture over Sanskrit Aryan culture were established and Periyar succeeded in raising the self-respect of low caste Hindus and untouchables. Around the same time, the conflict between the emerging non-Brahmin urban middle class and the established Brahmin middle class and upper castes took a sharp turn. The non-Brahmin castes started uniting themselves and the 'Non-Brahmin Manifesto' was published in 1916 followed by the formation of the South Indian Association in 1917 which was later converted into the Justice Party to counter the political influence of the Congress Party. Finally, the Justice Party and Self-Respect Movement were merged in 1914 to form the Dravida Kazhagam (D.K. Party) under Periyar. Later on, in 1949 it was split and Dravida Munnetra Kazhagam (DMK Party) was formed under the leadership of C.N. Annadurai. After Annadurai's death, the whole ideological content of the Dravidian movement degenerated and declined and the rest is now part of history.

DALIT MOVEMENT

The Dalit movement may largely be looked at as the movement of untouchable castes or, as per the constitutional arrangement, Scheduled Castes. Tracing the history of the Dalit movement, Ghanshyam Shah (2002) says that the anti-caste movement which began in the 19th century under the inspiration of Jyotiba Phule and was carried on in the 1920s by the Non-Brahmin Movements in Maharashtra and Tamil Nadu developed under the leadership of Dr. B.R. Ambedkar. But, social movements of Dalits show a particular character. This cannot be explained satisfactorily by reference to economic exploitation or political oppression, although these dimensions are of great importance. As Martin Fuchs & Antje Linkenbach[3] (2003) point out, "class analytic approaches have been tried on Dalit movements, but have not been successful in accounting for the extra-economic oppressive factors... What, furthermore, distinguishes the case of Dalits or 'untouchables' is the fact that they are always a minority.

Dalit movements have set themselves with wider and fundamental aims. Their inner motive can be conceived best as a 'struggle for recognition' as fellow human beings. On the one hand, it is a struggle for self-confidence and space for self-determination. On the other hand, it is a struggle for an overhaul of the social system. Its larger target has been the "abolition of stigmatisation (inadequately condensed in the notion of untouchability) and of all discriminations derived therefrom or connected with it (atrocities and physical violence), sexual harassment, forced labour, landlessness, public 'disabilities' and exclusion from certain occupations and certain spaces or from religious congregations" (ibid).

Studies on Dalit movements are very few. Ghanshyam Shah (1980) classifies Dalit movements under the following:

(i) Reformative Movements
(ii) Alternative Movements

[3] Martin Fuchs & Antje Linkenbach, Religious Individualisation, Taylor & Francis, Vol. 1, 2003

The reformative movements are further divided into (a) Bhakti Movements, (b) neo-Vedantic Movements and (c) *Sanskritisation* Movements. The reformative movement tries to reform the caste system to solve the problem of 'untouchability'. The alternative movement attempts to create an alternative socio-cultural structure by conversion to some other religion or by acquiring education, economic status and political power. Before independence, the Dalits were embracing Islam or Christianity, but after the promulgation of the Constitution, conversion to Buddhism has been the main channel so that they continue to enjoy the Scheduled Caste status and the consequent advantages. Both types of movements use political means to attain their objectives. The Bhakti and neo-Vedantic movements were not confined to the Scheduled Castes. They were initiated by Hindu religious and social reformers. According to the pioneers of these movements, untouchability was not an essential part of Hinduism and, for that matter, of caste system. Dayanand Saraswati, the founder of the Arya Samaj, believed that 'the caste system was a political institution created by the rulers for the common good of society and not a natural or religious distinction'. The Satyashodhak Samaj in Maharashtra, the Self-Respect Movement in Tamil Nadu and the Adi-Dharma Movement in Bengal are important anti-untouchability movements launched in the last quarter of the 19th and early 20th century.

Modern Dalit social movements reached their peak in the first half of the 20th century. "They used the space provided by an emerging, restructured public sphere for regional self-organisation and trans-regional networking." Dr Ambedkar's movement occupies the most important place in the modern Dalit movements. Tracing its history, Shah says that Ambedkar made his entry into political and social life of India in the period immediately after the First World War and the Russian Revolution. It was an era marked by social and political upheaval and the increasing hegemony of Marxist socialism in movements of social liberation. Though Ambedkar organised and led one of these movements, popularly known as the Mahar Movement because it was largely confined to a lower untouchable caste Mahar, as an autonomous movement for Dalit liberation, rejecting the leadership and ideological hegemony of non-Dalit socialists, he was influenced by Marxism throughout. His movement continues to inspire the Dalit leadership even today and the entire political mobilisation of the Bahujan Samaj Party (BSP), which became the ruling party in Uttar Pradesh, was based on it. Significantly, Ambedkar concluded that the only way of improving the status of the untouchables was to renounce Hindu religion. He, himself, became a Buddhist and Dalits continue to move towards this goal.

Building on Ambedkar's policies and the new identity provided by '**Ambedkarite Buddhism**', the Dalit Panther Movement and the Dalit Sahitya (Dalit literature), Movement gave expression to Dalit experiences of oppression. As Robert Deliege (1999) rightly suggests, the name of the Dalit Panthers Movement is typical of the increased aggressiveness of untouchables who are proud to be called Dalit while the term 'panther' which is itself significant, is obviously an echo of the American Black Panthers, with whom the young Dalits sometimes identify. This organisation was born in 1972 in Bombay. Its best-known founders J.V. Pawar and Dhasal emphasised the need to fight

Quick Fact

Ambedkarite Buddhism

Bhimrao Ramji Ambedkar, a Dalit leader and scholar of Buddhism, started this socio-religious movement in India. It was launched in 1956, when nearly half a million Dalits joined him and converted to Navayana Buddhism.

It rejected Hinduism, challenged the caste system in India and promoted the rights of the Dalit community.

for their basic rights and held that every atrocity must be avenged. By 1971, it gathered an estimated 25,000 members, the majority of whom were neo-Buddhist Mahars. Although its manifesto contained a certain number of radical positions, the movement soon began to suffer from its weak ideological foundations. It finally broke up in 1974, under the strain of rivalry between two of its loaders Dhale and Dhasal. By 1977, nothing remained of this organisation, which had never tried to reach out the rural areas. But, it left an indelible mark on the Maharashtrian Dalit consciousness. Several writers in the Dalit Panther current became the harbingers of a Marathi literary movement known as 'Dalit Sahitya' ('literature of the downtrodden'). Once again neo-Buddhist Mahars dominated this remarkable movement. Their ideology is openly militant and often aggressive: the wretched untouchable becomes a proud Dalit, sure of his rights and strength. Like the Dalit Panthers, these authors have no intention of hiding; rather, they claim their revolt loud and clear. Their weapon is the pen and many of their poems express these sentiments. Some of the writers and poets have a more militant, even aggressive style. Recent translations of many Dalit poems and other writings give a much more detailed idea of this movement.

TRIBAL MOVEMENTS

Tribal people are ethnic groups. Different tribes have their own territory, history, social structure dialects and experiences. Research into tribal movements has traditionally been the domain of social anthropology and commenced in the 1940s. Though systematic research into tribal movements in India started with the publication of a special number of the journal 'Man in India' (1945), most academic work on this topic came in the 1960s.

The tribes of India have exhibited signs of restlessness ever since the inception of colonial rule. The centrality of tribal movements lies in the fact that most of these signify resistance and revolt against the state. Turning to the specific manifestations of the restlessness among the primitive and post-primitive tribes, B.K. Roy Burman[4] (1984) has envisaged the following parameters:

1. Response to threats to the privacy of habitat;
2. Response to threats to access to and control of resources;
3. Response to disruption of traditional roles in the total interaction set-up;
4. Search for new meanings of the relationship between man and nature;
5. Search for new meaning of the relationship between individuals and society;
6. Search for new frontiers of identity;
7. Search for a more satisfactory system of control of resources; and
8. Search for a more satisfactory system of organisation of community power at all levels.

It is obvious that while the first three possible origins of restlessness are responses to challenges emanating primarily from outside, the last five are responses to challenges primarily from within, though there may be a degree of arbitrariness in the delineation of these responses.

[4] B.K. Roy Burman, Social Dimensions of Development, Vol. 14: 2, pp. 9–19, Sage, 1984

Some scholars of tribal movements have evolved different typologies of tribal movements. L.K. Mahapatra (1972) has applied the typologies widely used for social movements to tribal movements: (1) reactionary; (ii) conservative; (iii) revisionary or revolutionary. The reactionary movement tries to launch a movement to bring back 'the good old days', whereas the conservative movement tries to maintain the status quo. The revisionary or revolutionary movements are those which are organised for 'improvement' or 'purification' of the social or cultural order by eliminating 'evil' or 'low' customs, beliefs or institutions. Surajit Sinha[5] (1968) classified the movements into:

(i) Ethnic rebellion
(ii) Reform movements
(iii) Political autonomy movements within the Indian state
(iv) Secessionist movements
(v) Agrarian unrest

Santhal revolt/rebellion comes under the category of ethnic rebellion, Tana Bhagat Movement of the Oraon tribe may be a good example of reform and revitalisation movement, Jharkhand and Bodoland movement come under the third category, the Naga and the Mizo movements of 1910s and 1950s come under the fifth category and the Naxalbari Movement is a good example of agrarian unrest among the Santhals. In his two volumes on Tribal Movements in India, K.S. Singh (1982, 83) makes more or less the same classification except that he uses the term *Sanskritisation* instead of reform movement. The major tribes of Central Indian tribal belt such as Gonds, Bhils, Oraons and Mundas have adopted the process of *Sanskritisation* to elevate their social status vis-à-vis the larger society. The process of Kshatriyasation has been a familiar process among the Gonds who have laid claim over *Kshatriya* status for them.

Tribal movements have predominantly been located in the so-called 'tribal belt' in middle India. Some of these movements have also incorporated elements of Christianity (Birsa Munda Movement 1895–1901) and of the Bhakti tradition (Bhagat movements of the Oraons) into their vision. The movements of the tribes of north-east India (Naga, Bodo, Mizo), which are documented in case studies, occupy a special position as they "developed into armed struggles for political autonomy and separate nationhood, which started in pre-independent India, but continued after independence". Martin Fuchs and Antje Linkenbach (2003) identify three main approaches to the study of tribal movements especially during British India.

▶▶ (1) Tribal Movements as a Reaction to a Clash of Cultures and Relative Deprivation: The Messianistic Movements

This approach was followed by Stephen Fuchs (1905). Two homogenous, but unequal cultures, one rather underdeveloped and retarded, the other at least technically vastly superior, are seen as abruptly confronted. The members of the marginal cultural group are said to be emotionally and intellectually incapable of dealing with the new situation. Then they began to search for a solution by imagining a future society in which the present state of deprivation will be fully reversed. The desired ideology and actions depend heavily on the figure of a charismatic leader, a messiah or prophet, who claims to be the recipient of divine and magical powers. Although the movements

[5] Surajit Sinha, Tribal Solidarity and Messianic Movements, Vol. 2: 1, Contributions to Indian Sociology, 1968.

often show a 'revolutionary' character, interpretations and actions of leader and subjects are regarded as 'irrational' and the uprising necessarily is doomed to failure.

▸▸ (2) Tribal Movements as Expressions of Social Disorganisation: The Revitalisation Movements

This concept was adopted in his study of East Indian tribal movements by Edward Jay (1961). In Jay's approach, society or culture is seen as an organism or system which regularly has to undergo periods of cultural distortion and social disorganisation to reach a new equilibrium through an adaptive or acculturative process. Under colonial conditions, the revitalisation movements of Indian tribals functioned as 'catalysts of acculturation and means for the creation of new moral order, in which elements of the opposing culture were integrated'.

▸▸ (3) Tribal Movements as Resistance of the Subaltern

A central concern of the subaltern school of history was to give recognition to the peasant (i.e. subaltern) as a subject of history. In the context of subaltern studies, tribal movements are looked upon as a particular case of peasant movements. For the subalternists, tribal as well as peasant movements originate in social opposition and cultural conflict. Moreover, economic issues involved in the tribal movements were often somewhat similar to those affecting non-tribal peasant movements.

PEASANT MOVEMENTS

Peasant movements and agrarian struggles continue to be one of the central themes of the 'old' movement study tradition of sociology and social anthropology in India. Systematic interests in peasant movements can be traced back to the 1960s largely because it was a period when the 'agrarian question' and unequal distribution of land in the 'global south' were prominent political issues. Peasants came to represent a possible alternative revolutionary subject (Alavi, 1965). However, Erick Stokes (1978) finds that peasant rebellions look strangely absent in Indian society. This situation is attributed to the peculiar Indian social structure, i.e. the caste system and the village structure. However, the 'passive' and 'docile' character of Indian peasants has been challenged by Kathleen Gough (1974), A.R. Desai (1979), D.N. Dhanagare (1983), Ranajit Guha (1983) and others. They argue that historians have overlooked a number of peasant rebellions before and during the British rule. Furthermore, according to Andre Beteille (1974), the areas with a larger number of agrarian revolts are predominantly rice-producing regions. These regions not only have a large proportion of agricultural labourers, but land is also unequally divided among the cultivators.

Peasant movements in India are generally classified in terms of pre-British/pre-Colonial, British/Colonial and post-independence periods. In terms of classification, A.R. Desai (1986) classifies colonial India into ryotwari areas under British territory, zamindari areas under princely authority and tribal regions. Kathleen Gough (1974) classifies peasant revolts on the basis of their goals, ideology and methods of organisation. The five types suggested by her are:

1. restorative rebellions to drive out the British and restore earlier rulers and social relations;
2. religious movements for the liberation of a region or an ethnic group under a new form of government;

3. social banditry;
4. terrorist vengeance with the idea of meting out collective justice; and
5. mass insurrection for the redress of particular grievances.

Talking of issues, Ghanshyam Shah (1990) says that there was a tendency among British officers and historians to depict some of the revolts as communal riots or mere banditry. The Moplah rebellion of the 19th century and the early 1920s in Malabar was interpreted primarily as Hindu–Muslim communal clashes rather than as a conflict of economic interests between tenants and landlords, merely because the two groups happened to belong to different religious communities. It was the revolt of Muslim peasantry against the non-Muslim landed gentry. Dhanagare (1983), Pannikar (1979) and Namboodiripad (1943) argued that the uprisings were mainly related to agrarian conflicts between tenants and landlords. Moreover, some of the leaders of the Moplah rebellion were Hindus. Shah further argues that in most of the cases the peasants revolted against exploitation and oppression when their economic condition deteriorated. These changes may be classified under the three heads:

1. deterioration of their economic condition due to price rice, famine, etc.;
2. structural changes, which cause an increase in the exploitation of peasants, consequently deteriorating their condition; and
3. rising aspirations of peasants to improve their condition.

Famine was almost a regular feature of rural India in the 18th and 19th centuries and it continued to be so in isolated pockets to some extent even after independence, though it is now called 'drought' and not famine. *Begaar*, *veth* or *vethi* (forced labour) was widely prevalent in the last century as well as today. During the peasant movement in Oudh (1919–1922), the peasants took a pledge that they would not work as labourers without payment. Eviction of tenants as cultivators by moneylenders, landlords or government officers was one of the causes for widespread resistance and revolts in the 19th century.

It is generally believed that the Bhoodan Movement, launched by Vinoba Bhave in the early 1950s, was largely to counter the leftist movements and also focused the issue on the distribution of land. "Changes in the mode of production in agriculture have disturbed the traditional agrarian relationships which also led to peasant unrest. Under the British rule, land became a marketable commodity and commercialised agriculture developed during the late nineteenth century" (Shah, ibid).[6] Barrington Moore argues that "where a large-scale commercial agriculture has resulted in proletarianisation of peasantry and consequently in snapping of the old traditional bonds of caste, etc. the possibilities of insurrection are much greater." The demand for higher wages has been a central issue in the struggles of agricultural labourers in the 19th as well as the 20th century.

KISAN SABHA

Kisan Sabha, the leading leftist organisation, played a very important role in organising peasants and has been in the forefront of peasant struggles in the country. Born on 11 April 1936 and carrying a membership of more than a crore, it was instrumental in pushing the peasant's agenda to

[6] Shah Ghanshyam, Social Movements and the State, Sage India, New Delhi, 2001

the centre. The first meeting of the Kisan Sabha was held along the 49th Convention of the Indian National Congress. It was presided over by the legendry peasant leader Sahajanand Saraswati. On this occasion, it released a 'peasant's manifesto'. Reviewing the plight of the peasantry in India, it said that the peasants were leading a life of slavery and back-breaking poverty. The Zamindars, Taluqadars, Malguzars, Inamdars and other landowners were exploiting the peasants. The main reason for this condition was the prevailing land revenue system and the system of debts and credit developed by the British imperialist. With the passage of time, the peasants were attaining more and more economic and political consciousness. This declaration presented the following four basic demands of peasants:

(i) The prevailing condition of landownership with all its forms should be abolished.

(ii) All the old debts and interest should be cancelled and the administration should formulate new schemes of credits for the fulfilment of immediate needs of the peasants.

(iii) All the cultivable barren land should be distributed among the landless and those peasants having less than 5 acres of land.

(iv) A new land tax system should be promulgated in place of the prevailing land revenue system. The new system should be applied on those peasant families enjoying the net income of more than 5000 rupees and having family members up to five.

Among the other major demands, exemption of uneconomic landholdings from tax, security of tenure, declaration of all types of feudal and traditional extortions as unlawful, stay on repayment of loans for 5 years formed the nucleus of the charter of demands. Though in the initial stages the Kisan Sabha supported the Congress government before independence, the peasant movements in Bihar, Bengal, Punjab and Andhra Pradesh created a major rift between the rightist and leftist elements in the Congress Party and most of the leftists sided with the Kisan Sabha and carried the peasant struggles through the Kisan Sabha and communist parties. The rest is now part of history.

TELANGANA MOVEMENT

The attainment of independence was marked by two mass uprisings of peasants who had become quite politicised by this time largely because of the involvement of the leftist leaders. The Tebhaga Movement (1946–1947), a struggle of sharecroppers in Bengal for a two thirds share of the produce (instead of the customary half), had the support of the Kisan Sabha and the Communist Party of India. The Telangana Movement (1946–1951) was largely against the feudal conditions in the princely state of Hyderabad and it was launched by the Communist Party under its leadership. It was an organised movement against the feudal conditions and ruthless exploitation by the musclemen of the feudal lords, police and the Razakars (volunteers) of the Nizam of Hyderabad.

The Telangana region comprised almost half the area of the erstwhile Hyderabad State. The Telangana revolt began in the middle of 1946 and lasted for over 5 years till it was called off in October 1951. In order to understand the Telangana Movement, we should have a clear idea of the prevailing agrarian social structure in Hyderabad State. There were two main types of land tenure: Khalsa or Diwani tenure was on the lines of Ryotwari – the peasant proprietary system. The landholders in this type of land tenure were not called 'owners per se, but were treated as pattadars (registered occupants)'. D.N. Dhanagare (2002) analysing the intricacies of this type of land tenure says that the actual occupants within each patta were shikmidars, who had full rights of occupancy, but were not registered. As the pressure on land grew, the shikmidars, previously the cultivators of lands, began to lease out lands to subtenants (asami shikmis) for actual cultivation. They were tenants at will having neither legal rights in land nor any protection against eviction. The second main type of land tenure was called *jagirs*: one, sarf-e-khaas was obviously the most important of them being assigned to the Nizam himself as 'crownlands'. Scattered in several parts of the state, the sarf-e-khaas covered a total area of 8,109 square miles (1,961 villages) and fetched revenues totalling about 20 million rupees which met the Nizam's household, retinue and other expenses and partly met the cost of his army. The *jagirdari* system of land administration was the most important feature of the political organisation of Hyderabad. Over the years, the number of *jagirdars* steadily multiplied. In the 1922, there were 1,167 *Jagirdars* in the Nizam's dominations; in 1949, their numbers had gone up to 1,500.

Nowhere in Hyderabad was feudal exploitation of the peasantry more intense than in Telangana district. Here, some of the landlords, whether *jagirdars* or deshmukhs, owned several villages and thousands of acres each. The vetti system, the symbol of exploitation of poor peasantry, was such that the landlord could force a family from among his customary retainers to cultivate his land and to do one job or the other including domestic, agricultural or official, as an obligation to the 'master'. It symbolised the dominance of landlords and subjugation of the peasantry. In terms of social composition, most of the agricultural labourers on whom the vetti obligations fell were from the lower and untouchable castes such as the Mala and the Madiga. A similar system known as bhagela serfdom was also prevalent, especially in Warangal and Nalgonda districts. "It seems that the vetti and bhagela arrangements were perversions of the traditional Hindu jajmani system which was based on the principle of reciprocal exchanges" (Dhanagare, ibid).[7] Brahmins were once predominant among the substantial landowners and Pattadars in Telangana region. With the rise of the Reddys and Khammas – the two notable castes of peasant proprietors – the influence of the Brahmins as a landowning caste declined. From the turn of the 19th century, however, Marwari Sahukars gradually penetrated rural Telangana and established their ascendancy as moneylenders. The bulk of the rural masses – the poor peasants, unprotected tenants, sharecroppers and agricultural labourers – came either from the lower untouchable castes or from the tribal groups like the Hill Reddys, Chenchus, Lambadis and Banjaras. The tribal communities had long-standing grievances against the government on account of its taxes and levies, against moneylenders and revenue officials who usurped their lands and also against private contractors who exploited the tribal labourers in the forests, on construction sites or in mines and collieries. Dhanagare is of the view that two important aspects of the agrarian should not be lost sight of. First, the development of irrigation facilities and cultivation of commercial crops had been taking place since the late 19th century. The main commercial crops of Telangana – groundnuts, tobacco and castor seeds – were grown in Nalgonda, Mahbubnagar, Karimnagar and Warangal districts. Second, the development in commercial farming was not, however, matched by any corresponding growth of towns, of industrial enterprise and markets, not even of transport and communication facilities. Consequently, cultivators had to depend almost entirely

[7] Dhanagre, D N, Peasant Movements in India 1920–1950, Oxford University press, New Delhi, 1983

on urban moneylenders, traders, merchants and businessmen who controlled the few and highly centralised markets in Telangana for the sale of their produce. Local retailers, agents and village sahukars helped urban commercial interests in securing the produce from the cultivators and thus managed to have a share in the profits of the marketing enterprise.

Growing land alienation compounded the situation further between 1910 and 1940 when a large number of peasants including tribal peasants lost their lands to non-cultivating urban interests, mostly Brahmins, Marwaris, Komtis and Muslims. The sudden increase in food prices in the wake of the Second World War made the situation unbearable for the poor, exploited and oppressed peasantry. The suffering peasantry did not have any channels of democratic protests as the despotic rule of the Nizam permitted neither political freedom nor any representative 'institutions'.

The above-described situation served as the background of the Telangana Movement. The Andhra Conference, set up in 1928, operated in Telangana districts and mobilised public opinion on issues like administrative and constitutional reforms, schools, civil liberties, recruitment to services, etc. The Hyderabad unit of the Congress started a satyagraha in 1938 for political reforms. But, the agitation came to be dominated by the Arya Samaj and the Hindu Mahasabha – the militant Hindu nationalist organisations – and the Congress, acting on Gandhi's advice, abandoned it to lessen political confusion. The communists arrived on the Telangana scene only during the latter half of the Second World War. Their arrival was a jolt to the communal politics of both Hindus and Muslims.

The movement began rather modestly in 1946, under the leadership of the Communists, in Nalgonda district and then spread to Warangal and Bidar districts. As Hamza Alvi (1968) points out, the initial aims of the Telangana Movement reflected the broad demands of the whole of the peasantry against illegal and excessive exactions of the Deshmukhs and the Nawabs. One of the most powerful slogans of the movement was for writing off all peasant debts. The repression let loose by the feudal lords and their governments was met by armed resistance by the peasantry. The movement then entered a new revolutionary stage. "Local communists participated in the movement vigorously, although it did not receive the official sanction of the communist leadership until later. By the time of the Second Congress of the CPI in March, 1948, the Telangana Movement had already entered its revolutionary phase" (Alvi, ibid).[8] By 1947, the Telangana Movement had a guerrilla army of about 5,000. The peasants killed or drove out the landlords and the local bureaucrats and seized and redistributed the land. They established governments of peasants. Peasant rule was established in an area of 15,000 square miles. The government of the armed peasantry continued until 1950 and was crushed by the so-called Police Action and Indian army.

The movement had been crushed, but continues to inspire the exploited peasantry even today.

NAXALBARI MOVEMENT

When we look at the peasant movements in the post-independence period we should not miss the fact that certain issues which had dominated in colonial times lost their significance in independent India, when land reforms, zamindari abolition, declining importance of land revenue and a public

[8] Alvi, Hamza, Capitalism and Colonial Production, Routledge, New Delhi, 2023

credit system began to alter rural conditions. The period after 1947 was characterised by two major social movements: the Naxalbari Movement and the New Farmer's Movements.

Some idea about the political background and the prevailing political situation is essential to understand the Naxalbari Movement, now popularly known as the Naxalite Movement. On 2 March 1967, a non-Congress, United Front government was sworn in West Bengal. The government was dominated by the CPI(M), CPI and other leftist groups and a breakaway group from the Congress, the Bangla Congress. The United Front government was pledged to bring about the long overdue land reforms in favour of the poor and landless peasants and release from the burden of chronic indebtedness to the sahukars and moneylenders. After assuming power, the CPI(M) found itself in a difficult situation. The bureaucracy, the judiciary and vested interests were found to be hurdles in any smooth and quick implementation of this agenda.

Meanwhile the euphoria generated by the left front government, especially among the downtrodden peasantry, was fast giving way to disillusionment. At Siliguri, Charu Majumdar and Kanu Sanyal, two very popular leaders representing the 'ultra-left' within the CPI(M), were quietly explaining to their followers that the measures for land redistribution of announced by the revenue ministers Hare Krishna Konar of CPI(M) would not only fail to satisfy the landless, but also prove to be detrimental to the interests of the future peasant movements. "They reiterated the need for moving beyond economism towards the task of politicising the peasants" (Sumanta Banerjee, 2002).[9]

Thus, it is clear that the peasant uprising shows the existing schism within the CPI(M). The 'extremist radical groups' were either expelled or they disassociated themselves from the party.

The Darjeeling District Committee had to be dissolved. The most conspicuous among the breakaway groups was the Naxalbari O Krishak Sangram Sahayak Samiti. Though the impact of the Naxalbari Movement was felt throughout the country and a number of urban, educated youth joined it as part of the Naxalite Movement, it was in the states of West Bengal and Andhra Pradesh that its impact was maximally experienced. In Bihar, the Naxalite Movement came face to face with the Sarvodaya Movement. "The fact that all this could happen within three years of Naxalbari – no matter how miniscule the scale, intensity and spread and the composition of the leadership and cadre – is sufficient reason not to dismiss the phenomenon as transient and ephemeral" (Partha N. Mukherji, 1984).[10]

The succeeding Congress government resorted to the brutal suppression of the movement and consequently led to the unusual phenomenon of mass emigrations from the Communist Party to other parties, especially the Congress Party. Thousands of bright and educated young boys and girls were arrested and tortured to death. The still committed leadership and cadre formed a breakaway CPI(ML) party which remained underground for some time and is now functioning as a revolutionary democratic party in several states and also fights elections.

The consequences of the Naxalbari uprising are of far-reaching importance. Naxalbari movement had a profound impact on not only the agrarian scene in India but also on the political situation.

[9] Sumanta Banerjee, In the Wake of Naxalbari, Sahitya Samsad, Kolkata, 2009

[10] Mukherji, P N, From Left Extremism to Electoral Politics, Manohar Publication, New Delhi, 1983

The radical elements involved with the movement posed a challenge to the mainstream left political forces. Thus, the Telangana and Naxalbari Movements continue to inspire the revolutionary zeal of the tribal and non-tribal peasantry and a section of the urban masses.

WOMEN'S/FEMINIST MOVEMENT

The feminist movement in India is not of recent origin. It also did not originate on the streets of Delhi and Mumbai. Its beginning may be seen in thousands of places and through hundreds of forms. Yet, this is also true that an organised feminist movement may be traced back to the freedom struggle and the period immediately after we secured freedom.

What Do You Think?

How have women's and feminist movements evolved to address intersectionality, and what challenges remain in ensuring inclusivity across diverse social, cultural, and economic contexts?

The social reform movements of the 19th century calling for widow remarriage, ban on sati and child marriage and promotion of women's education may be taken as the first wave of feminist movement. The active participation of women in the freedom movement and the emergence of several national level women's organisations such as All India Women's Conference, National Federation of Indian Women and Women's India Association may be seen as the next wave of feminist movement. They raised the issues of women's education, right to franchise, *Purdah* and individual rights. The third wave of the movement began after 1947. As Deepti Priya Mehrotra (2001) rightly points out, women's movement between 1947 and 1970 was characterised by lethargy as compared to the period before and after it. Perhaps, most of the women activists thought that with India getting independence their problems would be solved. Organisations such as the All India Women's Conference thought that they had nothing to do with political issues and hence turned their attention to social welfare. During this period, most of the women's organisations worked in the field of social service and welfare.

The period immediately after independence witnessed two leftist movements – Tebhaga Movement in Bengal and Telangana Movement in Andhra Pradesh. Led by the Communist Party, poor peasants fought against landlords and capitalist forces. Women took active part in these movements along with men. The Telangana Movement threw up, for the first time, radical and militant women's leadership. They also organised Andhra Mahila Sabha, Andhra Yuvati Mandal and Mahila Sangam. They fought against not only military power, but also against gender inequality, domestic violence, child marriage, polygamy and restriction on their movement outside the four walls of the household.

After the promulgation of the Indian Constitution and enactment of various laws for women, the feminist movement went from strength to strength. The Hindu Marriage Act, the Hindu Succession Act and other legislative measures prepared the ground for further struggle. A number of schemes and programmes were formulated for women. The 1960s witnessed a number of economic and political crises. The Naxalite Movement emerged with full force, especially in

Bihar and Bengal. Though the Naxalite Movement, led by Marxists-Leninists, was primarily a peasant movement and never led by women, the level of participation of women in the movement was quite high. Many women provided strategic support to the Naxalite revolutionaries. The participation of women in this movement provided them an opportunity to understand the political process in the country and the politics of gender inequality and suppression of women's rights.

Women's movement took new shape after 1970. By this time women's mass movements had realised that women's issues and problems could not be solved through patchwork type of social reform and social welfare and the basic issues had to be confronted head-on. This realisation pushed them to the forefront of all the major socio-economic, political and environmental issues. Women's involvement in the *Chipko* movement focussed on the preservation of forests and related environmental issues shows their increasing understanding of core issues. It was followed by similar movements in Karnataka and elsewhere. Between 1970 and 1990, women also fought against liquor and liquor lobby in Kumaon and Garhwal (now in Uttarakhand), Haryana, Andhra Pradesh, Tamil Nadu, Madhya Pradesh, Maharashtra and elsewhere. They had realised that excessive consumption of liquor, especially among the poor, not only brought economic hardship, but also promoted domestic violence.

Gail Omvedt (1993) has traced the origins of the contemporary women's movement to the early 1970s when rural and working women were first trained as leaders. "But, there were few linkages at that time to the urban, intellectual women who could articulate the oppression of rural and working women in feminist terms" (Geraldine Forbes,[11] 1998). The United Nations declaration of *International Women's Year* and the *International Women's Decade* (1975–1985) led to the appointment of the Guha Committee and its subsequent report, Status of Women in India, a landmark study on women's status in India.

'Emergency' was imposed in the country in 1975. A number of civil liberties and democratic rights groups were organised. Women also played an important role in these people's movements. Around the same period, the Progressive Women's Organisation was created in Hyderabad by some leftist women. The years of working in people's movement had equipped them with an ideology to fight against discrimination and exploitation. On the whole, the period between 1970 and 2000 saw the emergence of a number of autonomous women's organisations. Though coming from different ideological backgrounds, they were unanimous in their view that the membership of such organisations should be restricted to women only and they did not require the patronage and interference of males in these issues. To name a few such organisations, Forum Against Oppression of Women in Mumbai, Saheli in Delhi, Asmita in Hyderabad, Vimochana in Bangalore, Pennurimai Iyakkam in Chennai and many others point to a new-found confidence and consciousness. Some other women's organisations with stronger networking and organisational capabilities are related to political parties, especially the Congress Party and Communist Parties. They may be serving as women's wings of these parties; especially, the strongest among them – All India Democratic Women's Association (AIDWA) – is related to

[11] Geraldine Forbes, Women in Modern India, Cambridge University Press, New Delhi, 1996

CPI(M). Mahila Congress is an affiliate of the Congress Party and Durga Vahini is related to BJP. Unfortunately, women's organisations related to right-wing political parties like the BJP take up only caste and communal issues, divide women's power and serve as 'legitimisers' of policies and actions of their parent organisations. The role of Durga Vahini in the Ayodhya Movement is a case in point.

> The new visibility of women in the right-wing movement appropriating the issues of the contemporary feminist movement in their demonstrations against Muslims and Christians is disturbing. (Forbes, ibid)[12]

The 1980s was largely dominated by the anti-dowry movement throughout the country. It also included such issues as dowry-related atrocities, domestic violence, commercialisation and commodification of women and lack of property rights. Through writings, *Nukkad Natak* (Street play) rallies and seminars, millions of women were mobilised into action. Public debate on sexual harassment and rape was also the result of this movement against dowry. Before 1980 or so, girls were very reluctant and hardly vocal on this type of harassment and violence, but now such issues may be discussed without inhibitions. One of the important contributions of leftist women's organisations was to highlight the dangers of communalism in the fight for women's rights. If the society is divided and polarised on the basis of religion, women's movement gets weakened. The 2002 carnage in Gujarat and communal violence in other parts of the country provide ample evidence of it. The 1990s witnessed deep concern for Muslim women and their problems along with the movement against female foeticide and infanticide. In the present scenario empowerment – social, economic and political – is the dominant theme in women's rights movement supported by hundreds of women organisations. Women's movement in India is now an important part of the worldwide movement of women for justice, equality and empowerment.

Questions and Indicative Answers

1. Name and briefly describe the social movements in India.

- These are social and religious reform movements;
- Backward class movement, Dalit movement, tribal movement and peasant movement; and
- The readers are expected to give equal attention to all types of movements.

2. How does the state look at the social movements?

- Role of state is very important in the analysis of social movements.
- State looks at movements with suspicion and may take it as a challenge to its legitimacy.
- Significantly, the state takes a relatively softer stand on reformist demands.

[12] Geraldine Forbes, Women in Modern India, Cambridge University Press, New Delhi, 1996

Previous Years' Questions

1. What is identity Politics? Discuss the main trends in Dalit Movement in India?

(UPSC CSE Mains Sociology, Paper II, 2021)

2. Trace the social and historical origins of Dalit Movement in modern India.

(UPSC CSE Mains Sociology, Paper II, 2024)

3. Highlight the major contributions of the reform movements in pre-independence India.

(UPSC CSE Mains Sociology, Paper II, 2024)

Focus Areas for the Examination

1. Social Movements in India
2. Dalit and Backward Class Movement and their impact on Indian Society

CHAPTER 13

Social Empowerment and Indian Society

Chapter Outline

1. Identifying key disadvantaged groups in India-Dalits, Scheduled Tribes, Other Backward Classes, women, and minorities
2. Gaining familiarity with Constitutional Provisions
3. Understanding the legal frameworks-reservation policies and anti-discrimination laws
4. Analysing the root causes of social inequalities in Indian society, including the role of the caste system and patriarchy
5. Exploring how modernisation, technological advancements, and political mobilisation have influenced the empowerment of marginalised communities
6. Evaluating the effectiveness of government policies

The concept of empowerment and social empowerment have never been more in vogue in the analysis of society, including Indian society, than in the post-independence period. Empowerment, in general terms, is the process designed to increase the degree of autonomy and self-determination in the lives of people in order to enable them to represent and protect their interests, to overcome their sense of powerlessness and to use their resources and chances. Empowerment has emerged as a key concept for all the 'weaker sections' of the society. Obviously, the disempowered or those lacking power in comparison with others need empowerment. In the Indian context empowerment is the key requirement for the Dalit, Adivasi (tribal communities), Women, all types of minorities – religious, linguistic, ethnic and sexual, and others lacking power and facing discrimination in a variety of ways. Empowerment has several dimensions – social, cultural, economic, and political.

Quick Fact

Disempowered

Individuals or groups lacking power and facing discrimination due to societal structures.

Social empowerment is largely understood as a process of assessing opportunities and resources in order to make personal choices such as what to eat, wear, how to live, etc. It is understood as the process of developing a sense of autonomy and self confidence, and acting individually and collectively to change the social relationships and the institutions that exclude them.

Social empowerment is indispensable to improving quality of life for the people suffering from disadvantages. It is implemented at the following levels to meet the desired goals:

- Individual level
- Family level
- Community level
- Social policies level to promote social inequity and inclusion of the disempowered or disadvantaged

Social empowerment is geared to remove socially-induced inequalities, disadvantages and discrimination. It also helps getting easy access to basic minimum services. The founding fathers of the Indian Constitution were well aware of all types of inequalities including institutionalised inequality and discriminations being faced by large segments of Indian society. The Constitution of India has provisions – some of general nature applicable to all the citizens, while others for specific sections of the society:

- **Article 14** is directed towards equality before law. It guarantees Right to Equality as the fundamental right to all Indian citizens. India has never been a society based on equality because of the caste system. The Constitution did not abolish the caste system but, in one stroke, delegitimised all inequalities and inferiority/superiority based on birth, religion, race and gender. It clearly declares that the state shall not deny to any person equality before law, the equal protection of the laws within the territory of India.
- **Article 16(4)** declares that 'nothing in this Article shall prevent the State from making any provision for the reservation of appointments or posts in favour of any backward class of citizens which, in the opinion of the state, is not adequately represented in the services under the state'.
- **Article 46** is the key constitutional provision which declares that the "state shall promote with special care the educational and economic interests of the weaker sections of the people, and in particular, of the Scheduled Castes and Scheduled Tribes, and shall protect them from social injustice and all forms of exploitation."

Let us first review the constitutional safeguards for the socially excluded and marginalised communities, such as scheduled castes and backward castes, which contribute to the social empowerment of these segments of the Indian society.

SCHEDULED CASTES AND OBCs

Article 366(24): 'Scheduled Castes' means such castes, races or tribes or parts of or groups within such castes, races or tribes as are deemed under Article 341 to be Scheduled Castes for the purpose of this Constitution.

Article 341(1): The President may with respect to any State or Union territory, and where it is a state after consultation with the Governor thereof, by public notification, specify the castes, races or tribes or parts of or groups within the castes, races or tribes which shall for the purpose of this Constitution be deemed to be Scheduled Castes in relation to that State or Union territory, as the case may be.

Article 341(2): Parliament may by law include in or exclude from the list of Scheduled Castes specified in a notification issued under Clause (1) any caste, race or tribe or part of or group within any caste, race or tribe, but save as aforesaid a notification issued under the said clause shall not be varied by any subsequent notification.

The safeguards provided to the Scheduled Castes are grouped in the following broad heads:

- **Social Safeguards** – Articles 17, 23, 24 and 25 (2b)
- **Economic Safeguards** – Articles 23, 24 and 46
- **Educational & Cultural Safeguards** – Article 15(4)
- **Political Safeguards** – Articles 243, 330 and 332
- **Service Safeguards** – Articles 16(4), 16(4A) and 335

▶▶ Statutes and Legislations

A number of legislations have been enacted for implementation of the Constitutional safeguards to the SCs and STs. Illustrative lists of such legislations are given below:

- The Protection of Civil Rights Act, 1955.
- The Scheduled Castes and the Scheduled Tribes (Prevention of Atrocities) Act, 1989 and Rules thereof.
- The Scheduled Castes and the Scheduled Tribes (Prevention of Atrocities) Amendment Act, 2015 and the Scheduled Castes and the Scheduled Tribes (Prevention of Atrocities) Amended Rules 2016.
- The Employment of Manual Scavengers and Construction of Dry Latrines (Prohibition) Act, 1993.
- Prohibition of Employment as Manual Scavengers and their Rehabilitation Act, 2013.
- Acts and regulations in force in different States to prevent alienation of land belonging to SCs/STs. In some States such provision exists in the Land Revenue Code.
- Acts in different States for restoration of alienated land to SCs and STs.

The following safeguards are meant exclusively for the **OBCs**:

Article 340 of the Constitution provides for the appointment of a Commission to investigate the conditions of and the difficulties faced by the socially and educationally backward classes and to make appropriate recommendations. The article reads as under:

Appointment of a Commission to investigate the conditions of backward classes–

1. The President may by order appoint a Commission consisting of such persons as he thinks fit to investigate the conditions of the socially and educationally backward classes within the territory of India and the difficulties under which they labour and to make recommendations as to the steps that should be taken by the Union or any State to remove such difficulties and to improve their condition and as to the grants that should be made for the purpose by the Union or any State and the conditions subject to which such grants should be made, and the order appointing such commission shall define the procedure to be followed by the Commission.

2. A Commission so appointed shall investigate the matters referred to them and present to the President a report setting out the facts as found by them and make such recommendations as they think proper.
3. The President shall cause a copy of the report so presented together with a memorandum explaining the action taken thereon to be laid before each house of Parliament.
4. In pursuance of the Article 340 of the constitution the Government of India first constituted the Kalelkar Commission (First National Commission for Backward Classes) and then Mandal Commission (the Second National Commission for Backward Classes). Most of the states have appointed the State Backward Classes Commissions to identify the socially and educationally backward castes within the states and do the needful for them.

Abolition of untouchability and the related measures are supposed to go a long way in the journey of social empowerment of the scheduled castes while elimination of social and educational backwardness shall be the core issue for the backward castes.

SOCIAL EMPOWERMENT IN VILLAGE INDIA

Jajmani System has been the socio-economic basis of the Hindu caste system and an integral part of the agrarian social structure in India. Under the Jajmani System each caste group within a village is expected to give certain standardised services to the families of other castes. In general terms, it stands for the exchange of goods and services between the landowning higher castes and landless service castes. These castes have always been occupationally specialised following certain traditional occupations and thus are also known as artisan castes. Gradual modernisation of Indian economy coincides with the decline of the jajmani system. But its rapid decline was witnessed in the post-independence period. In loose and broad terms, the decline of jajmani system may be discussed under the following heads:

Quick Fact

Jajmani System

A traditional socio-economic arrangement in rural India involving the exchange of goods and services between higher and lower castes.

(a) Role of the State
(b) Introduction of technological innovations and industrialisation
(c) Political mobilisation of the Dalits and the backward classes

The decline of Jajmani System in Village India freed the Dalit castes, backward castes and poor and landless sections of minorities and contributed most significantly to their social, economic and political empowerment. They were now free to pursue any occupation of their choice and their aspirations and dreams. The Bonded Labour Abolition Act, 1976 freed most of these disadvantaged groups contributing to their social empowerment.

What Do You Think?

How can traditional social structures and modern development initiatives coexist to promote meaningful social empowerment in village India, particularly for marginalized groups?

SCHEDULED TRIBES

Tribal communities have never been a part of the caste system and hence their problems are entirely different from SCs and OBCs. Rather social empowerment, the core issue with them is economic empowerment. Their problems are primarily related with the erosion of their rights in *jal, jangal, zameen* (water, forests, land). (Their major problems may be seen in another chapter of this book). Women among the tribal communities enjoy much more cultural autonomy and rights in comparison with the rest of the population.

Article 46: Promotion of Educational and Economic Interests of Scheduled Castes, Scheduled Tribes and Other Weaker Sections. This is the key constitutional provision for the STs and all other constitutional safeguards emanate from it.

WOMEN

The principle of gender equality is enshrined in the Indian Constitution in its Preamble, Fundamental Rights, Fundamental Duties and Directive Principles. The Constitution not only grants equality to women, but also empowers the State to adopt measures of positive discrimination in favour of women. Within the framework of a democratic polity, our laws, development policies, Plans and programmes have aimed at women's advancement in different spheres:

Article 42: The State to make provision for securing just and humane conditions of work and for maternity relief.

Article 243 D(4): Not less than one-third of the total number of offices of Chairpersons in the Panchayats at each level to be reserved for women.

To uphold the Constitutional mandate, the State has enacted various legislative measures intended to ensure equal rights, to counter social discrimination and various forms of violence and atrocities and to provide support services especially to working women. Although women may be victims of any of the crimes such as 'Murder', 'Robbery', 'Cheating' etc., the crimes, which are directed specifically against women, are characterised as 'Crime against Women'. These are broadly classified under two categories.

1. The Crimes Identified Under the Indian Penal Code (IPC)
   - **(i)** Rape (Section 376 IPC)
   - **(ii)** Kidnapping and Abduction for different purposes (Section 363–373)
   - **(iii)** Homicide for Dowry, Dowry Deaths or their attempts (Section 302/304-B IPC)
   - **(iv)** Torture, both mental and physical (Section 498-A IPC)
   - **(v)** Molestation (Section 354 IPC)
   - **(vi)** Sexual Harassment (Section 509 IPC)
   - **(vii)** Importation of girls (up to 21 years of age)
2. The Crimes identified under the Special Laws (SLL)

   Although all laws are not gender specific, the provisions of law affecting women significantly have been reviewed periodically and amendments carried out to keep pace with the emerging requirements and changing social realities.

Some acts have special provisions to safeguard women and their interests like:

(i) *The Family Courts Act, 1954*
(ii) *The Special Marriage Act, 1954*
(iii) *The Hindu Marriage Act, 1955*
(iv) *The Hindu Succession Act, 1956 with amendment in 2005*
(v) *Immoral Traffic (Prevention) Act, 1956*
(vi) *The Maternity Benefit Act, 1961 (Amended in 1995)*
(vii) *Dowry Prohibition Act, 1961*
(viii) *The Medical Termination of Pregnancy Act, 1971*
(ix) *The Contract Labour (Regulation and Abolition) Act, 1976*
(x) *The Equal Remuneration Act, 1976*
(xi) *The Prohibition of Child Marriage Act, 2006*
(xii) *The Criminal Law (Amendment) Act, 1983*
(xiii) *Indecent Representation of Women (Prohibition) Act, 1986*
(xiv) *Commission of Sati (Prevention) Act, 1987*
(xv) *The Protection of Women from Domestic Violence Act, 2005*

National Commission for Women: In January 1992, the Government set-up this statutory body with a specific mandate to study and monitor all matters relating to the constitutional and legal safeguards provided for women, review the existing legislation to suggest amendments wherever necessary, etc.

Thus, various constitutional, legal and administrative measures have been taken towards the empowerment of women. At the same time it is also true that social change may not come merely through law. The strongly patriarchal Indian society does not allow socio-cultural autonomy to women ungrudgingly. Backed by the State, women are trying hard for their social empowerment and fighting for every inch of the social space.

Education, Health, Productive Rights, and Sexual Rights shall define their social empowerment. Though it is a long journey but they have to win.

Questions and Indicative Answers

1. What are the objectives of social empowerment?

- Human societies, in general, are based on inequalities. Social inequalities in Indian society are institutionalised where a number of groups are traditionally disempowered.
- Social empowerment aims at empowering the disempowered.
- Dalits, backward castes, tribal communities and a large section of religious minorities are grossly underrepresented in power structure of the society.
- Thus, through social empowerment such vulnerable sections may be empowered to enjoy the resources – social, cultural, economic and political, and also to contribute to their as well as the society's betterment.

2. How does the Constitution of India, directly and indirectly, promotes social empowerment of the weaker sections of the society?

- The Constitution of India has provisions–some of general nature applicable to all the citizens, while others for specific sections of the society. It has proclaimed equality in all respects for every citizen thus demolishing, in principle, the very structure of inequalities characterising the Indian society.
- The Constitution has special provisions for the weaker sections that include SCs, STs, OBCs, Minorities, and Women.
- In pursuance of these constitutional provisions, the State took a number of legislative measures and supervisory organisations for the implementation of these measures. Moreover, the law courts may always be approached for the redressal of grievances.

3. In what way social empowerment is operational vis-a-vis caste system in Village India?

- The caste system, especially in Village India, operated through the *Jajmani System*, the socio-economic basis of caste system.
- The Jajmani System has been based on an elaborate system of exchange of goods and services between the land owning higher castes and the landless lower castes. This traditional landlessness kept the dalits and other weaker sections powerless.
- In the post-independence period, the Indian State took a number of measures including land reforms for the redistribution of land to the landless. Several technological innovations and the Dalit/backward class movement empowered the weaker sections and the discriminatory Jajmani System crumbled thus paving the way for their social empowerment.

Focus Areas for the Examination

1. Social Empowerment and Indian Society
2. Social Empowerment of the Scheduled Castes
3. Legislations For Women Empowerment

CHAPTER 14

Globalisation and Indian Society

Chapter Outline

1. Understanding globalisation and its economic, social, and political dimensions
2. Recognising the effects of globalisation on women, the LGBTQ community, Dalits, and tribal communities
3. Examining how globalisation influences social structures like the joint family, caste system, and marriage practices in India
4. Analysing the emergence of new societal phenomena, such as live-in relationships and LGBTQ rights, under the influence of globalisation
5. Identifying changes in food habits, clothing, and festivals due to globalisation (e.g., the proliferation of fast food and international cuisines)
6. Exploring the role of mass media, OTT platforms, and online education in accelerating global connectivity, the growth of medical tourism, and its impact on India's healthcare system

Every nation and society, in the course of its history, is confronted with issues that dominate the concerns and preoccupations of its people. India has been confronted by the problems of casteism, communalism, regionalism and ethnic conflicts, tribalism and linguism. But, of late communalism along with globalisation and violation of human rights in the form of mob lynching and other violent acts have emerged as dangerous forces affecting the health of the Indian society.

CONCEPT OF GLOBALISATION

'Globalisation' has emerged as one of the most important and talked about phenomena of the present age with its social, economic and political dimensions. According to The Blackwell Dictionary of Sociology, Globalisation is characterised as a process, where social life within societies is increasingly shaped by international influences, including political and trade relations, as well as shared music, fashion, and mass media. Perhaps, the most powerful form of globalisation is economic in which planning and control expand from a relatively narrow focus such as a single firm doing business on a regional or national basis to a broad global focus in which the entire world serves as a source of labour, raw materials and markets. As James Petras and Henry Veltmeyer (2001) point out, globalisation is both a description and a prescription and as such it serves as both an explanation and an ideology that currently dominates thinking, policy-making and political practice. As a description, 'globalisation' refers to the widening and deepening of the international flow of trade, capital, technology and information within a single integrated global market. As a prescription, 'globalisation' involves the liberalisation of national and global markets in the belief that free flow of trade, capital and information will produce the best outcome for growth and human welfare. Significantly, when the term 'globalisation' is used, whether to describe or prescribe, it is usually presented with an air of inevitability and overwhelming conviction, betraying its ideological roots.

Analysing the necessity of international economic and socio-political management in the face of globalisation, Samir Amin (1997), a renowned and strong voice on the issue of globalisation and its implications for the Third World countries, says that globalisation of the capitalist system is certainly nothing new, but it has undeniably taken a qualitative step forward during the most recent period. 'Moreover, this deepening economic interdependence between nations occurs at a time when there is a crisis of accumulation, and the post-war boom has given way to stagnation. The advance of globalisation has not been confined to trade; it also affects productive system, technology, financial markets and many other aspects of social life. The new globalisation erodes the efficiency of economic management by nation-states, though it does not abolish their existence. Rise of ethnicity as a political response to economic globalisation is yet another important dimension of globalisation.'

The passive acceptance of the inevitability of globalisation in its present polarising form – equation of development with the expansion of the market – is a dangerous fallout of the current scenario. Marginalisation is a necessary precondition of liberalisation, privatisation and globalisation.

IMPACT OF GLOBALISATION ON WOMEN, DALITS, AND TRIBAL COMMUNITIES

When we look at the impact of globalisation on various segments of Indian society in concrete terms, we are confronted by a scenario where it will, and it has already had an adverse impact on all the social groups which have been suffering silently different forms of oppression, exploitation, deprivation and marginalisation – women, Dalits, tribal people, minorities, etc.

Women in India have been badly affected by globalisation – economically and socially. Because of scarcity of food and other necessities of life, the poor in India, for sheer economic reasons, feed their girl children less than their boys, as boys are perceived as major breadwinners. This also contributes to the widening gap in the sex ratio. With decreasing subsidy on food, the security has been shrinking rapidly and the poor women have to spend more 'women hours' on unproductive and meaningless labour. With growing retrenchment of their menfolk, women workers previously working as agricultural labour are mostly consigned to the organised sector in urban areas at starvation or less than starvation wages. Hiring women workers seems to be more convenient for the employer because women workers face more difficulties in getting organised than male workers get and hence are more susceptible to exploitation.

What Do You Think?

How has globalisation influenced the economic opportunities, cultural identities, and social empowerment of women, Dalits, and tribal communities, and to what extent has it reinforced or challenged existing inequalities in these groups?

While globalisation is making people more materialistic and money minded, the greed for dowry is also increasing rapidly and the poor parents of girls are being further pushed to different and humiliating conditions. With increasing globalisation, a frenzy was created over the so-called 'beauty contests'. As Arvind (2002)[1] rightly pointed out "While the benefits of this frenzy are reaped by the corporations who advertise their products via these phenomena, the entire display has had its impact on the minds of urban women, particularly middle and lower middle class young women." The vast proliferation of 'beauty parlours', 'facial creams' and other cosmetics which promise to increase 'fairness' bears witness to the notions being inculcated. Equally, by the logic of the 'market economy', prostitution is a perfectly legitimate activity – one more industry of the 'service sector'. In this age of globalisation, girls from even well-to-do families are taking to prostitution and call girl professions either directly or through the so-called beauty parlours, massage parlours and 'make a friend' industry through telephonic communication.

Unfortunately, the so-called liberal westernised culture promoted by the media, especially cable TV, has not helped the process of democratisation of social relations and decrease in patriarchal value system. In fact, feudal values and patriarchal system have increased under the impact of globalisation supported by Hindutva. Thus, with globalisation, women are being further marginalised, patriarchal values are sought to be strengthened and **'commodification'** of women is increasing leaps and bounds. When we try to understand genuine democratisation in men-women relationship we must know that it comes only through sustained struggle against the feudal and patriarchal values. It should also oppose the imperialist culture promoted by the ruling classes in India.

Quick Fact

Commodification

The transformation of relationships and entities, including cultural and social aspects, into marketable commodities.

Dalits in India belong to a large section of the society, who have been subjected to inhuman indignities on account of caste differentiations perpetuated for centuries and millennia. They still bear the burden of acute poverty and the worst types of social degradation. They, usually, fall at the bottom of almost any parameter relating to economic well being or quality of life. B.L. Mungekar[2] in *State, Market and the Dalits: Analytics of the New Economic Policy* in a lucid analysis of Dalit plight says that "the effects of the birth based occupational distribution on different castes were entirely opposite in nature. Thus, the absence of freedom of occupation, low earnings (mainly in kind), implicit restrictions of needs and stigma on menial labour destroyed the economy of the lower castes. They came to be wholly dependent on the upper castes for their economic existence.

[1] Arvind Subramanian, The Missing Globalization Puzzle, IMF working paper, Washington DC, 2002

[2] Mungekar, B L, India's Economic Reforms and the Dalits, Dr. Ambedkar Institute of Social and Economic Change, Bangalore, 2003

The main elements of current economic reforms as a part of globalisation are:

(i) liberalisation of external trade;
(ii) liberalisation and opening up of domestic financial markets;
(iii) direct foreign investments;
(iv) cuts in subsidies; and
(v) gradual privatisation.

While the richer sections tend to gain, the poor ones have to suffer during the **'structural adjustment' programmes**. The lower allocations to social sector are likely to adversely affect the poor and the Dalits, being the overwhelming majority of the poor, are the worst sufferers. It is the poor who depend largely on public services and any reduction in budget allocations contributes to the reduction and availability of social services and their consequent higher costs.

Quick Fact

Structural Adjustment Programs (SAPs)

Economic policies involving reduced government spending, privatisation, and liberalisation to encourage market-driven economies.

In socio-economic terms, the small gains made by the Dalits through reservations are being reversed. More than 75% of Dalit workers are still connected with land; only 25% are marginal and small farmers while the rest earn their livelihood as landless labourers. In urban areas, they mostly work in the unorganised sector. Under the impact of the new economic policy, land reforms, the key question for their development is being pushed out of the agenda and is being substituted with corporatisation of farming for the global agricultural market. The policy thrust of the World Bank-IMF-WTO combination has always been clearly for the abolition of land ceiling laws and for liberalising investment into agriculture. "Thus, inflation and the slow growth process are squeezing the poor while the expenditure on poverty alleviation programmes and social services are declining in real terms because of the fiscal crunch. Admittedly, the main burden of adjustment is likely to fall on the poor and the Dalits." (P.G. Jogdand, 2000)[3]

The tribal population of the country shares a number of features of the impact of globalisation with the Dalits. This is mainly because of the reason that both these segments have been and still are the deprived and marginalised populations. As with Dalits, the systematic cuts in welfare expenditure, the privatisation of public sector, drop in investment in agriculture, dismantling of the public distribution system, etc. have also hit the tribals very hard. In the name of 'development', tribal people are being driven off their lands, their forests are being submerged, their sources of income are being sapped and they are thus being virtually pushed to death.

The entry of multinational companies (MNCs) into industrial mining and commercialisation of forest products is likely to increase inequalities of income and consumption between regions and people. The new agricultural policy enunciated by the government is capital intensive. Improved seeds, pesticides and fertilisers are costly and subsidies are being withdrawn. There is also encouragement for mechanised farming. This is harmful to the tribal interests.

[3] Jogdand, P G (ed), New Economic Policies and Dalits, Jaipur, Rawat Publications, 2000

Globalisation policies threaten to disturb the biodiversity of forest areas preserved for millennia by the tribal communities. The MNCs are going to steal the gene resources of plants, herbs and trees or seeds. They will claim intellectual property rights on those items, which are under the nurture and control of the tribal people. Globalisation is also promoting overconsumption of industrial and consumer goods, thus changing the lifestyle of the tribal and other deprived people to their disadvantage. Disruption of traditional crafts and small-scale industries is predictable as capital efficiency factor is throwing out small-scale units. There will be more unemployment as traditional labour-intensive small-scale industries are being displaced by new technologies.

The tribal population of India as per the 2011 census is 8.6% of the total population. More than half of the scheduled tribe population is concentrated in the states of Madhya Pradesh, Chhattisgarh, Maharashtra, Orissa, Jharkhand and Gujarat. Tribal communities inhabit about 17% of the country's geographical area where around 70% of the country's forest and mineral resources are found. They live in different ecological and geo-climatic conditions ranging from plains, forests, hills and inaccessible areas. They are living at different techno-economic and educational levels of development, but the overwhelming majority derives its livelihood from agricultural sector. Because of their vulnerability to all types of exploitations, constitutional guarantees have been provided to them and the President of India has been made directly responsible for their wellbeing. Article 46 directs the State to promote, with special care, the educational and economic interests of the weaker sections and protect them from social injustice and all forms of exploitations. The Fifth Schedule provides an ideal frame for tribal administration in which the executive was vested with unlimited powers to adopt the legal frame so as to become consonant with the tribal situation. As B.D. Sharma (2001)[4] rightly pointed out, "the objective was the process of fast changes should not create strain for the tribal system. Instead, the institutional structure should adapt itself to the demands of a smooth transition. The prime consideration being the wellbeing of the tribal people." This was not only the constitutional obligation, but also the civilisational obligation.

Here is an attempt to show as to how the forces and factors of globalisation have been unleashed on the vulnerable tribal populations without empowering and preparing them resulting in their further marginalisation and pauperisation.

Until the early 1990s, the country was guided by the socialist model of development where the role of the state was clearly welfare and social justice was its fundamental mandate. The new economic policy and the process of globalisation threaten to reverse the earlier goals and for the vast multitude of masses, especially the tribal population, it has emerged as the demon of neo-colonialism being promoted by the capitalist system. Under the impact of liberalisation and globalisation, the state is abrogating its social responsibilities. It seems that the goal of the neo-liberalist agenda is to paralyse the nation-states or at the most it should act as policeman. Those having an unflinching faith in the liberalist agenda want to have such a flexible nation-state that

Quick Fact

Neo-liberalism

An economic philosophy advocating minimal state intervention, promoting privatisation and market-driven economies.

[4] Sharma, B D, Tribal Affairs of India, New Delhi, Sahyog Pustak Kuteer, 2001

should support the capitalist forces whenever demanded to do so and for the remaining period should stay silent in a corner.

When we look at the tribal situation we find that the majority of the tribal population have been caught in the whirl of development – industrialisation, urbanisation, etc. uprooted and displaced them with nothing to fall back upon. Most of their land is unirrigated and they are living at relatively lower techno-economic levels of agrarian economy. The majority of them are living within their subsistence economy, dependent on their habitat – land, forest and water. In their traditional cultural ethos and value system, the habitat is accepted as a common heritage of the community where individuals had limited rights.

Thus, the tribal people are fast losing command over their resources. Article 39 is not an ordinary guiding principle of state policy. It clearly defines the limit of the state's brief with regard to community resources. As pointed out by B.D. Sharma (ibid), the attempted dispensation of the state in allowing alien command over community resources under the new sacrament is not authorised under the covenant. The experience of indigenous and tribal communities in other Third World countries too, invaded by liberalisation and privatisation, show that livelihood, land and forests have been ruthlessly overridden. Whenever the state transferred control over resources from the community and even from itself to private institutions, commercialisation and commoditisation of resources became primary concern giving little thought to its long-term consequences. It has been proved beyond doubt that the tribal ethos and value system had inherent mechanisms for sustainable development of natural resources. For instance, in central India and in the north-eastern regions, tribal communities dedicate large chunks of forests to their gods and goddesses – it becomes god's abode from where not even a twig of grass could be removed. The endangered species of flora and fauna are declared totems, which help their protection and preservation in today's globalising economy. The neo-colonialists are interested only in immediate gains; otherwise, how can one justify natural forests being turned into economic plantations such as teak, eucalyptus, pine, etc. serving the global market. First, they came with teak, which does not provide even shade during the scorching summer. Then came eucalyptus under which not even grass grows. Thereafter it was the turn of pine which would burn like torch. That is how after the destruction of the life support system, the struggle in many areas is now confined to mere physical survival or for the next meal. In a globalising economy, it is the market and not community which is the focal player. The laws and policies are aimed not at social justice and welfare, but maximisation of profits and optimum exploitation of resources. As people lose command over their habitat, the nutritional status declines. There will be many more Kalahandis and Sargujas because these are the necessary consequences of the new economic regime.

Under the impact of globalisation and free market, land use in tribal areas is being changed drastically. Lot of land has already come under industrial and mining complexes. The draconian Land Acquisition Act has already acquired millions of hectares of land at throwaway prices in the name of 'national interest' and 'public interest' without bothering to train and absorb the affected people in these projects or taking any rehabilitation measures. In any case, even if the tribal people were able to get a higher market price for the land acquired, many of them will not be able to handle the money. Moreover, agriculture in the tribal areas is being made a losing proposition so that small cultivators may voluntarily opt out and made to realise that wage labour is more remunerative.

The impact of globalisation on the Scheduled Areas should be a major area of concern for the tribal population. In order to adapt to globalisation, policymakers are preparing to make a complete reversal of the Indian Constitution wherever people's rights and control of resources is concerned. In a globalised situation, it is the market and not the community, which is the chief player. All laws and policies relating to the Scheduled Areas – the Land Transfer Regulations, the Forest Act, the Environmental Protection Act, the Land Acquisition Act – are under immediate threat of repeal, dilution or amendment. These laws were meant for the protection of people and resources while the new policies call for exploitation of resources at the cost of people. Now all these 'bottlenecks' are being removed to promote globalisation. The tribal population has always been known for their strong community life and collective spirit and they used it as a part of their 'survival strategy'. This is rapidly being eroded through the promotion of private rights at the cost of 'community rights'. Thus, the tribal people are going to be the worst sufferers, the sacrificial lamb for globalisation.

Besides its effects on the specific sections of Indian society as described above globalisation has influenced and impacted the entire Indian society in a variety of ways:

SOCIAL STRUCTURE

Globalisation has not only affected the Dalits, tribal people and women but all the segments of society in a variety of ways and in varying degrees. If we look at the social structure in India, we find that Joint Family, Caste, and Village Communities are the most important social institutions. Though all of these have been changing but the process of globalisation has hastened the process of change. Some of the most important changes in the caste system are:

- Emergence of an occupation-free cost structure. Now occupations are almost totally delinked from the caste system. It has freed the landless occupational castes (mostly coming from the SCs and OBCs) to pursue any occupation of their choice.
- Disintegration of caste-based system of production.
- Emergence of **Dalit entrepreneurship**. Though it is still in rudimentary stage, it is giving a new identity to the Dalit castes and providing strong motivation to them.
- Caste endogamy (the norm of marrying within the caste) has been weakened though it is still a strong practice.
- Caste as a system is dying but individual castes are thriving and competing to grab as much resources as possible.

Quick Fact

Dalit Entrepreneurship

The emergence of businesses and entrepreneurial ventures owned and operated by members of Dalit communities.

FAMILY AND MARRIAGE

Joint family has been a strong institution of Indian society serving the requirements of the agrarian society. It represented a collective life suppressing the individual rights. With the advent of new professions the rural population now has many alternatives to choose from. With the disintegration of joint family in urban India and its continued weakening in village India the very scheme of statuses and roles are changing. The educated and aware women are now asserting their rights. The mass media has also hastened this process.

The institution of marriage, once very sacrosanct, now shows signs of crack. Though the *Hindu Marriage Act*, enacted immediately after independence, gave a lot of relief to the suffering woman but it's dissolution through divorce carried social stigma. Moreover, the grounds for divorce did not include the factor of 'incompatibility' between the husband and wife. Now a couple, especially women, may apply for divorce on this ground too. With 'Live-in Relationship' getting legal approval from the Supreme Court of India, a new chapter has been added to the 'life and liberty' domain. For a strongly traditional society like India, it has shaken the very foundation of the institution of marriage.

Mushrooming growth of matrimonial websites and dating websites are by products of globalisation. Though a number of persons have been arranging their marriage through matrimonial websites but these were only a few and the overwhelming majority of people preferred to explore spouses through the tested channel of priests and middlemen when contacting strangers. Now the high-tech matrimonial sites are facilitating marriages across the continents. This was unthinkable till recent times.

SEXUAL MINORITIES

The majoritarian idea of binary sexual relations e.g. between males and females only was considered normal and natural. Any thought of 'sexual orientation' has been 'blasphemous' and virtually a sin in the traditional Indian society. Even a feeble murmur of LGBTQ (lesbian, gay, bisexual, transgender and queer) was always pushed under the carpet. Same sex relationship was an anathema to the Indian society. This attitude had ruined thousands and thousands of lives and had resulted in failed marriages.

- Decriminalisation of Section 377 of the Indian Penal Code opens a new, though narrow, window socially. It is not only a great victory for the LGBTQ Community but also portrays the growing open and liberal attitude of the Indian judiciary. The Supreme Court mentioned that 'consensual sex between adults in a private space, which is not harmful, cannot be denied as it is a matter of individual choice.' This verdict has been described as the 'dawn of a new era' and globalisation has definitely played an important role in making people aware of different sexual orientations.

Though, by and large, the majority of people in Indian society are still not reconciled to the same sex relationship and consider it as 'immoral' and social nuisance yet its legal validity shall go a long way in reducing hostility of the society if not acceptability.

FESTIVALS AND NEW EVENTS

Different types of festivals, though mostly religious in nature, have been an integral part of the Indian society. Since India is a multi-religious and multi-cultural society, festivals of different religious groups and tribal societies add spice to the social-cultural life of India's population. Increasing exposure to western societies and cultures, largely through the mass media, as part of globalisation has facilitated the entry of new festivals and events in the Indian society. The most notable of these is Valentine's Day. Also called Saint Valentine's Day or the Feast of Saint Valentine, it is celebrated on 14 February every year. Regarded as the day of love and lovers, it is now an important event in India. The liberals hail it while the conservatives and right-wing persons hate it, humiliate and attack the young couples celebrating it. Cards and gifts exchanged between lovers are now a large part of its global market.

The purely Indian and religion-oriented festivals have also been transformed by the forces of globalisation. The market forces unleashed by the **liberalisation** of economy and globalisation are pushing out spirituality from religion and transforming religion into a saleable commodity. Even the local festivals and deities are getting universalised. Major festivals of all religious communities have become part of the market and have been commercialised.

Quick Fact

Liberalisation

Opening domestic and international markets, reducing trade barriers, and encouraging free-market principles.

FOOD AND CLOTHING

Indian cuisine now has a big market in US, Canada and Europe. On the other hand, even the relatively smaller cities in India, not to speak of the metros, can boast of having food joints and restaurants serving Chinese, Continental, and Middle-eastern cuisine. Pizzas, burgers, noodles, etc. are now household names. McDonald's, Domino's, Kentucky Fried Chicken (KFC), Baskin Robbins ice cream, etc. may be seen throughout India. Thus, the 'junk food' is now a part of Indian food.

The branded clothes from US and Europe are now available in single brand and multi brand stores throughout the country. The faded and 'torn' jeans are now part of India's dress culture. Expensive brands of perfumes are easily available in variety stores along with expensive 'imported' cell phones and watches.

CONSUMER CULTURE AND NEW BUSINESS CULTURE

With the adoption of New Economic Policy and the advent of globalisation, consumerism and consumer culture have arrived in India. Multinational companies and Indian corporates have generated high paid jobs and a new disease called **'Affluenza'**. Those afflicted with this disease are the carriers of consumer culture and have hardly any social concern. The consumer culture has pushed the amount of dowry upward and the hard pressed parents along with their daughters are facing further pressure.

Quick Fact

Affluenza

A social condition arising from consumerism, where individuals prioritise material wealth over social and ethical responsibilities.

A new business culture is also emerging largely through the advent of multinational and foreign companies. A new work culture backed by hard competitiveness and efficiency are the hallmarks of the new business ethics. In this business environment stability and security of job are virtually gone. The 'Hire and Fire' policy is now the buzz word.

SOME OTHER FEATURES

The forces of globalisation have facilitated a number of changes. Some of these may be mentioned below:

- High cost new health care system
- **Medical tourism** in which citizens of several countries find it easier and cheaper to get specialised medical treatment in India.
- Indian performing arts getting global audience
- Hundreds of new TV channels, streaming sites and OTT such as Netflix, Prime Video, Disney + Hotstar etc.
- Online international education
- Religion online

Quick Fact

Medical Tourism

A practice where individuals travel internationally to seek affordable and specialized medical care.

Globalisation has also created **'Bicultural identity'** in which one's local or native identity and westernised identity may go together. This may be seen in a variety of ways such as a number of traditional Indian cultural features getting mixed up with western lifestyle. This phenomenon may also be described as **'Sandwich Culture'** in which a person gets sandwiched between two different cultures.

Quick Fact

Bicultural Identity

A phenomenon where individuals simultaneously embrace local and global cultural identities.

Another by product of globalisation is 'globalisation' – a mix of global and local. This shows the highly flexible nature of the forces of globalisation. For instance during such festivals as *Navratri* during which a number of people go on fasting and avoid non-vegetarianism, some food outlets either drop non-vegetarian items from their menu or open a separate counter for their 'Navratri Special' cuisines. Fusion music, Indipop, Rap Bhangra and such other music and dance styles may also be taken as examples of the phenomenon called globalisation.

Quick Fact

Sandwich Culture

A mix of traditional and modern (Westernised) cultural traits creating a hybrid identity.

Questions and Indicative Answers

1. Discuss the impact of globalisation on women.

- Women adversely hit by globalisation; among the poor, because of scarcity of food, girls are fed insufficiently and badly;
- Globalisation making people more materialistic and greedy and demand for dowry has increased;
- Commodification of women; and
- Increase in call girl business as legitimate activity – one more industry of the service sector.

2. How does globalisation promote consumerism and consumer culture?

- Rise of new affluent middle class;
- High-pressure advertisement through audiovisual mode; and
- Adverse effect on economically weaker sections who cannot afford expensive goods, especially consumer goods.

Previous Years' Questions

1. Discuss the impact of Globalisation on Indian Villages.
   (UPSC CSE Mains Anthropology, Paper II, 2014)
2. Discuss the positive and negative effects of Globalization on women in India.
   (GS Mains Paper I, 2015)
3. Discuss the impact of Globalisation on village economy in India.
   (UPSC CSE Mains Anthropology, Paper II, 2015)

Focus Areas for the Examination

1. Impact of Globalisation on Dalit and Tribal Communities
2. Globalisation and Sexual Minorities

CHAPTER 15

Secularism, Communalism and Regionalism

Chapter Outline

1. Understanding the concept of Secularism
2. Analysing secularisation as a modernising process
3. Identifying the ideological opposition between secularism and communalism
4. Recollecting the causes and impacts of communal violence and evaluating the role of education in combating communalism
5. Examining the concept and the causes of regionalism
6. Exploring the relationship between regionalism and communalism

Not only in social science discourse, but also in day-to-day affairs of the society and state, people use these concepts not necessarily in their correct implications and meanings. Yet even the popular meaning and understanding of these concepts of secularism, communalism and regionalism are important in a way. Following is a brief narration and analysis of these concepts in both its academic as well as populist connotations.

SECULARISM AND SECULARISATION

In purely sociological terms, secularism stands for an ideology and has strong ideological connotations, but the usage of this term in India does not conform to this ideological position. First, let us take up the ideological implications of this term in pure sociological terms. On a theoretical plane, as Emile Durkheim puts it, all that is there in the world – beliefs, myths, dogmas, actions, persons and beings – are either sacred or secular. All that is related to religion is covered under 'sacred' and according to this scheme of things all traditional societies are basically 'sacred societies' because they are governed, in crucial segments of social life and in varying degrees, by laws of religion. It is religion that controls the activities of the members of such societies. Among the characteristics of secularism, the following are the most important ones:

(i) Separation of authority between 'church' (religion) and the 'state';
(ii) Emphasis on 'this world' as opposed to the 'other world'; and
(iii) Rationalism and scientific outlook.

Secularism implies that the state will not be governed by the religious principles or church, i.e. by religious authorities such as *Bishop, Pundit, Mullah* or *Khalifa*. The doctrines promoting social inertia such as fatalism and divine retribution have no place in secularism. A secular mind is characterised by rationality. A secular (modern) society is not against religion as such, but it has to fight superstition and intolerance as well as bigotry and obscurantism. Societies are not born secular. Instead the societies that are practicing varying degrees of secularism had to undergo transformation from traditional (religious/sacred) to secular. The process of secularisation has played its part in this transformation. Secularisation is, thus, a process of social change through which the public influence of religion and religious thinking declines as it is replaced by other ways of explaining reality and regulating social life. A number of western societies are examples of this phenomenon where religion still survives, but is largely confined to the private domain of individuals.

Secularism is inscribed into the preamble of our constitution together with democracy. But, two concepts of secularism have been operating side by side. The 'western' concept of the separation of religion and politics, especially separation of religion and the state, which virtually relegates religion to the realm of the private and on the other hand *Sarva Dharma Sambhava* (equal respect to all religions) go together. 'True Hinduism' promises and pays equal respect to all religions, but 'political *Hindutva*' thinks and acts otherwise. Thus, secularism in the Indian context is opposed to communalism ideologically. It signifies religious non-discrimination and equal liberty for all citizens – believers and non-believers. A secular polity is one in which the state does not discriminate between citizens on the basis of their religious conviction. It grants equal civil rights to all citizens, respects the religious liberty of each and protects even the liberty of those who do not believe in religion.

Secularism today is facing a crisis worldwide. In India, as Gurpreet Mahajan (former professor of Jawaharlal Nehru University, New Delhi) points out, the critics of secularism make two arguments: (a) the concept of secularism, a separation of religion and politics, is alien to Indian society and way of life, hence it has no place in the Indian context; (b) separation of religion from politics is an idea that comes with the Protestant ethic – as a 'gift of Christianity', it has limited applicability. The advocates of secularism regret the fact that the Indian state is not sufficiently secular as it allows the use of religion in the public domain. The critics of secularism, on the other hand, feel that this concept has no relevance for India as religion cannot be separated from politics in this country. But, to what extent the intermixing of religion and politics can play havoc with the peace and prosperity of the country is amply clear from the politics of *Hindutva* using Ayodhya as a means of achieving political power. The prevailing conditions in our neighbour country Pakistan should be an eye-opener and a lesson to us.

Secularism is understood as the antithesis of communalism. This view also promotes the protection of minorities from a dominating majority. Indian society, since its beginning, was able to set traditions under which an integrated social, cultural and political life was possible in a multireligious, multi-ethnic and multilingual framework. Imposing its own cultural and religious ideas and symbols on *others* has been alien to Hindu tradition and true Hinduism. This is amply demonstrated by one of its greatest exponents Swami Vivekananda.

Broadly speaking, the process of secularisation operates through three factors:

(i) Education
(ii) Legislation
(iii) Social reform

Education, when imparted on scientific and rational lines, gives rise to rationality in the thinking process. If we take the case of India, education was imparted through religious institutions – *Pathshala, Madrasa* and seminaries – attached to *temples, maths, mosques* and *churches.* When the scope of acquisition of formal education was widened and secular educational institutions were opened, it brought about a sea change. The change in the content of education and medium of instruction was largely responsible for it. That is why the role of formal education in social transformation cannot be minimised. The legislative action is also a crucial factor in the process of secularisation. But, mere legislative action not supported by proper motivation and social environment may not achieve the desired results. Many developing countries may be cited as examples of this situation. Take the case of India. Our country has gone secular by legislative fiats without the backing of sufficient infrastructure for the emergence of true secularism. Behind our country's facade of secularism and national unity lurks a bewildering variety of parochial, narrow-minded, obscurantistm and unscientific feelings that threaten to tear the fabric of our 'secular' country apart. Casteism, tribalism, linguism and religious communalism are painful facts of our day-to-day existence. The so-called 'do gooders', 'godmen' and religious bigots are flourishing at will. In the face of these factors, secularism is reduced to just a paper tiger. In reality, secularism should be a way of life. It is not a slogan, but an article of faith. Social movement for social reform is a potent weapon for the promotion of the process of secularisation. It does mental conditioning. It prepares us to accept social change. Whatever degree of secularism our society has achieved and absorbed owes a lot to various social reform movements launched from time to time.

Two subsidiary factors in the secularisation process are urbanisation and industrialisation. Both these factors owe a lot to technological innovations. It has been observed that as the area of scientific knowledge and technology widens, the area of religion shrinks. This hardly means that religion and science are incompatible. As S.C. Dube (1974)[1] rightly pointed out:

> On a higher spiritual and moral plane, religion is not necessarily inconsistent with the idiom of science and the ethos of progress. Moreover, urbanisation and industrialisation help loosen the grip of 'in group' feeling and present newer alternatives to man.

The State of India seeks to promote the secularisation process by:

(i) abolishing such symbols of ritual inequality as untouchability, the practice of which has been declared a penal offence;
(ii) throwing open all religious places and institutions to all classes and sections of the people;
(iii) reform of the Hindu Personal Law eventually aiming at evolving a common personal law for all communities in the country;

[1] Dube, S C, Contemporary India and its Modernization, Vikas Publishing House, New Delhi, 1974

(iv) forbidding all such agencies as shops, public restaurants, hotels and places of public entertainment from discriminating against any citizen of the state;

(v) throwing open all educational institutions to members of all communities;

(vi) secularising the content of textbooks by including such material as could be helpful in the promotion of a scientific-rational outlook by deleting such material as was likely to poison young minds, which smacked of traditionalism, obscurantism and religious orthodoxy; and

(vii) developing a sound economic base so as to eradicate poverty and ensure an equitable distribution of wealth among the people.

Secularism is one of the basic elements in the process of modernisation. Thus, if our society is to become modernised to cope with the worldwide changes, we are left with no other option, but to adopt 'secularism in practice' by speeding up the process of secularisation.

COMMUNALISM, FUNDAMENTALISM AND COMMUNAL VIOLENCE

The most striking feature of India's current socio-political scenario is the 'explosion' of communalism in the face of new economic policy and globalisation. It is threatening the very social fabric of Indian society.

Communalism is a highly complex phenomenon in pluralistic India. Academics from different disciplines in social sciences have produced a variety of definitions – some vague, some based on certain static preconceived notions, while others on the basis of the ever-changing socio-political dynamics. In some of these definitions communalism has been explained as 'above all an ideology', to some others, 'a false consciousness', 'a struggle for scarce resources', 'competition for jobs', 'an instrument of ruling class politics' and so on. On the basis of its highly intolerant and anti-democratic nature, it is also seen as a precursor to fascism. Among the plethora of definitions, W.C. Smith's (1979)[2] definition presents a fairly generalised and popularly accepted scenario:

> Communalism is that ideology which has emphasised as the social, political and economic unit the group of adherents of each religion and has emphasised the distinction, even antagonism, between such groups.

Even at the risk of being seen as an oversimplification of a complex phenomenon, the same definition may be rephrased as Communalism is an ideology based on the belief that society is divided into religious communities whose interests differ and are opposed to each other and hence antagonistic in nature. The rephrasing makes Smith's definition clearer and more understandable in the context of India's experiences of religious communalism carrying social, economic and political dimensions. Here, since religion and religious identity (or may be communal identity) is central to the understanding of communalism and India being a traditional society having religion as the highest value in life, no discussion on communalism shall be worthwhile without the role of religion and religious identity. Here, one can say that the sense of religious affiliation, which has commonly been central to one's identity, is ordinarily acquired during childhood in the course of socialisation.

---

[2] Smith, W C, Religious Diversity: Essays, New York City, Harper Collins, 1976

Let us go back to the basis of communalist ideology that the society is divided into religious communities whose interests differ and are opposed to each other to see the empirical and logical fallacies the communalist organisations are proud of and their misinterpretation of the past. Are the problems of poverty, unemployment and lack of education and healthcare not common to all the religious communities? Do their interests in these matters differ or are they opposed to each other?

Communalism can be said to have had more than a 100-year-old history, affecting aspects of the socio-cultural and political life of India in myriad ways. During certain times, it lays dormant, while being potentially explosive. Bipan Chandra (1987)[3] in his acclaimed work on communalism argued that "communalism was the false consciousness of the historical processes of the last one hundred fifty years, because, objectively, no real conflict between the interests of Hindus and Muslims existed." It was a false view of history.

K.N. Panikkar (1991)[4] said that "communalism is a state of consciousness which primarily draws upon certain assumptions of distinct cultural identity for members professing the same religion." Gyanendra Pandey (1990)[5] suggested that "communalism is a form of colonialist knowledge, which in its Indian usage, means a condition of suspicion, fear and hostility between members of different religious communities." All these definitions broadly touch upon the antagonistic relationship whether 'imagined' or real between the two major religious communities such as Hindu–Muslim, Hindu–Christian, Hindu–Sikh and Muslim–Sikh relations.

History and narrative of the past plays an important role in communalism. Perhaps that is why it may be said that the chemistry of history is very dangerous. It is like a double-edged weapon. When used in a particular way it may keep the wounds fresh. As a tool, history may also be distorted to serve a particular purpose.

COMMUNAL VIOLENCE

Violence between religious communities in the form of riots, pogroms or terrorism draws our attention in a dramatic manner, but the underlying and long-term cause of this violence is the spread of communalism. As Bipan Chandra (ibid) remarks, while the communal riots give credibility to the basic communal ideological precepts among the ordinary people and enlist further support for communal politicians, it is communal ideology and politics, which the communal politicians and ideologues preach in normal times, which form the real basis on which communal tensions and violence occur. In other words, communal ideology and politics are the disease, communal violence only it's external symptom.

> Communal riots and other forms of communal violence are only a concrete conjectural manifestation of the communalisation of society and politics. Communal ideology leads to communal politics and psychology of differentiation, distance and competition along religious lines. (Chandra, ibid)[6]

[3] Chandra, Bipan, India's Struggle for Independence, Penguin Random House, New Delhi, 1987

[4] Panikkar, K N, Communalism in India: A Perspective for Intervention, People's Publishing House, New Delhi, 1991

[5] Pandey, Gyanendra, The Construction of Communalism in Colonial India, Oxford University Press, New Delhi, 1990

[6] Chandra, Bipan, India's Struggle for Independence, Penguin Random House, New Delhi, 1987

Communalism and communal violence are the products of the overall social, economic and political situation of the society. Communal violence has been, by and large, an urban phenomenon where the deprived and poor people have been involved. But, more than religion, it is communal propaganda, rumour mongering and communal mobilisation that have been responsible. Any type of violence and lawlessness provides an opportunity to the interested people to indulge in loot and plunder largely for economic reasons. The happenings in Gujarat (2002) shook all the sensible, justice-loving, democratic and secular people of the country. The alleged involvement of the state in a communal violence has never been so blatant and naked. Significantly, the dirty work of violence is left to a certain type of communalised militant youth, especially belonging to the Dalit and backward castes and sometimes to the tribal groups, while the ideological work evolves with great subtlety. This may be an intelligent tactic on the part of communal leadership to divert the attention of the traditionally deprived sections from their problems. It may also be a ploy of blocking the deprived sections of the society from finding a rightful place in the power structure which till now has been tightly held by the upper social strata. But, in the Gujarat carnage, the involvement of the upward mobile, prosperous middle class in loot and plunder is a phenomenon that requires an urgent analysis by sociologists.

COMMUNALISM: THE NEW FACE OF INDIAN POLITIES

The Indian state was conceived in a secular, non-communal manner. In the secular-democratic state, an important role was assigned to politics and the political parties. Unfortunately, elections in independent India became ends in themselves and narrow self and political interests rather than larger national interests became more important. In this scenario, the communal implications of the numbers game in a pluralistic society became apparent. The political parties conceive of their interests in terms of caste and religion.

> Such an ethnic orientation of the numbers game has two prominent features. One is the rise of new political organisations that are sometimes blatantly and sometimes not so blatantly communal. This happens on the local levels or starts at that level and then moves up. (Rajni Kothari, 1998)[7]

He looks at Shiv Sena as a blatant example of this, but there are many others too. The capture of political organisations by cultural and sectarian organisations is also a case in point. What starts as a non-political organisation takes on political roles. Rajni Kothari gives the example of Rashtriya Swayamsevak Sangh and Jamaat-e-Islami for this phenomenon or process. Such organisations declare that they have nothing to do with politics, but they go on spreading their tentacles. In the course of time, political organisations like parties, trade unions and professional associations like those of students and teachers, even women's organisations, become increasingly dependent on sectarian and communal organisations which are not supposed to be political.

[7] Kothari, Rajni, Communalism in Indian Politics, Rainbow Publishers, Noida, 1998

Lumpenisation of politics also ultimately gets linked to communalism. But, the role of the middle class in communal politics is an alarming phenomenon. Substantial sections of middle class become the torch bearers of communalism and get involved in communal politics as activists or supporters.

Quick Fact

Lumpenisation of politics

It refers to the infiltration and dominance of individuals or groups characterised by a lack of ideological depth, commitment to democratic values, or concern for the public good.

FIGHT AGAINST COMMUNALISM

The long-term remedy for fighting communalism lies in initiating the process of de-communalising the people at all levels. This means waging a continuous and intense ideological-political struggle against communalism. If communalism is basically an ideology, then it cannot be suppressed by force. An ideology is to be fought at the level of ideas. An honest educational and cultural policy along with the use of media is required to educate the members of the society towards the danger of communalism. That is why controlling the departments of Education, Home and Information has been central to the scheme of things of the communal political parties whenever and wherever they are able to have their share in running the government.

What Do You Think?

How can we move beyond reactive responses to communal incidents and instead build proactive, long-term strategies that foster inter-community harmony and dismantle the systemic roots of communalism?

Sometimes, even the positive factors of development such as literacy may be exploited by an interested ideology and its practitioners. Illiteracy, combined with traditional/folk culture, protected the mass of Indian people from the ideologies of hate.

"Literacy has also exposed them to the influence of communalism, obscurantist and irrational ideals purveyed through newspapers, pamphlets and posters; even in children's books communal interpretation of Indian history, particularly of the ancient and medieval periods, forms the bedrock of communal ideology in India" (Chandra, ibid). Communalisation of law enforcement agencies is becoming a major problem in India today. In a landmark study, Vibhuti Narain Rai, a senior IPS officer of Uttar Pradesh cadre in his study 'Perception of Police Neutrality in Communal Riots', has come out with the partisan role of police personnel especially at the lower levels in various communal riots. The role of the media is immensely heightened during communal violence. They can greatly contribute in checking the inflamed tempers as well as adding fuel to the fire. Communalism has to be fought right from the socialisation of children in the families and here parents would be playing a crucial role.

REGIONALISM

Like communalism, regionalism beyond a point also poses a threat to the well-being of Indian society. In order to understand regionalism we must have some idea about 'region.' In fact, region, regionalism and state are interrelated concepts. Though there is no universally acceptable definition of region, a fairly acceptable one may be that a region is a homogenous area with physical and cultural characteristics distinct from those of neighbouring areas. It is a permanent and definite area. Region is a multidimensional concept encompassing the geographical as well as economic and social-cultural factors such as language.

Because of generations of living in a region, people develop a strong sense of affinity and emotional attachment with it – the territory, language, culture and history, overall a sense of belonging. Because of all this people give more importance to their region. Thus, regionalism involves a strong sense of loyalty and affinity with one's region. In this way regionalism is not a bad thing in itself. But, if it promotes separatism and clash with other regions, it becomes detrimental to national unity. Development of one region is fine, but it should not be at the cost of others. Regionalism in India is largely because of a high degree of diversities – geographical, economic, historical, linguistic, ethnic and socio-cultural. These diversities have led to different worldviews and ideologies. In the field of politics regionalism may also be understood as a political ideology. Regionalism also embodies a quest for self-identity and self-fulfilment on the part of the inhabitants. There are several causes of regionalism, foremost of these are:

1. **Geographical and linguistic causes:** Because of lack of transport and communication, some regions may be relatively isolated and difficult to reach. Thus, because of relative isolation, loyalty to language may become too strong.
2. **Historical experiences:** Due to certain historical reasons, there may be a deep-rooted belief among the people of a particular region that they are different from others, even with their neighbouring populations. This thinking becomes stronger if the people were also dominated politically by others.
3. **Uneven or lopsided development:** Markedly uneven economic development in the country is the most striking and common reason for regionalism. People of relatively underdeveloped regions, lagging others, have a nagging complaint against it. They also develop a sense of victimhood and get trapped in **'relative deprivation'**. Regional movements in Jharkhand, Chhattisgarh, Uttarakhand and Telangana resulting in separate states are the glaring examples of this. Two more movements of regionalism – Vidarbha in Maharashtra and Saurashtra in Gujarat – demanding separate states because of the same reasons have been going on for quite some time. There are also feeble voices for further division of Uttar Pradesh into Purvanchal (eastern part), Awadh (central part) and Harit Pradesh (western part).

   The problem of uneven development may be increasing more after the adoption of the new economic policy and liberalisation of economy. The corporate sector is not interested in investing in the economically backward regions. Instead they prefer regions where there is sufficiently strong infrastructure. This means that it is left to the government only to invest more and more in such backward regions. Regional imbalances are to be kept minimal if regionalism is to be checked and curbed.

Quick Fact

Relative Deprivation

A perception of being worse off than others, which can lead to dissatisfaction, grievances, and collective movements.

4. **Cultural identity:** Language plays a very important role in cultural identity. In Indian society, language and religion have always been strongly emotive issues. In regionalism, religion or religious identity, like the case with communalism, hardly plays an important role, thus language assumes the most important role (after Independence, state reorganisation was done on the basis of language). In the 1960s, because of certain steps taken by the central government, southern states, especially Tamil Nadu, had erupted on large-scale anti-Hindi agitation.

Regional parties and local leaders exploit the regional sentiments sometime magnifying the grievances. The ultimate aim is to capture political power. Some of these such as the Shiva Sena exploit local sentiments by promoting **'son of the soil' sentiments**. During the 1970s and 1980s they were targeting South Indians, now their violence and abuse are directed at people from North India, especially those from Bihar and Uttar Pradesh. From time to time they also promote animosity and hatred against Muslims (as a group coming from any state), thus preparing a heady mix of regionalism and communalism. Economy's failure to create enough employment opportunities gives such parties and organisations handle to attack the so-called 'outsiders'. When this does not work as effectively as they wish, they promote the feelings of 'relative deprivation' by comparing the plight of the local people with the affluent elite of the 'outsiders'. Issues such as interstate water disputes are also magnified fuelling regional sentiments.

Quick Fact

Son of the Soil Sentiments

A regionalist ideology promoting the interests of local inhabitants over those perceived as outsiders, often used politically to gain regional support.

Development of transport and communication provides more avenues for spatial mobility so that the people may realise that there are other people too facing the same problems of paucity and deprivation. Increase in social-cultural contacts will definitely promote feelings of friendship and harmony. Regional imbalances and lopsided development of different regions is the bedrock for regionalism. The pace of economic development must increase. Mass media, especially television and radio, should go a long way in curbing regionalism, but it is a double-edged weapon. Vested interests have also used it to serve their purposes. Regionalism by the people is not a bad thing in a federal structure as it is meant to attract the attention of the centre towards their problems, but no regional movement should be allowed to go on for a long time because the longer it continues the sense of grievance, even when it is not based on reality, the more it gets strengthened and deeply embedded.

Questions and Indicative Answers

1. **What do you understand by secularism? Discuss the role of secularisation as a modernising process.**
   - The sociological explanation is different from its common usage, that is, separation of religion from state affairs;
   - Equidistance from the followers of different religions;
   - Religion as private affair within private domain;
   - Rationalism and scientific outlook; and

- No society is born as secular; it is through the process of secularisation that these become secular. It is through this that even traditionally religious societies become modern societies. This may be advanced through education, legislation and social reform.

2. What do you understand by communalism? How does communalism in a pluralistic society act as a divisive force?

- It is a highly complex phenomenon.
- Communalism in the Indian context, religious communalism, may be explained as based on the belief that various religious communities have their own interests and are antagonistic to each other.
- This is a misnomer because all communities have a lot in common – poverty, lack of education, healthcare and there is no clash of interest.
- In the Indian context, communalism was promoted by British rulers as divide and rule policy and post-independent rules have also been using it in varying degrees. It is divisive and leads to communal violence.
- Communalism is by and large an urban phenomenon, especially among the educated urban middle class.

3. What is regionalism? What are the factors promoting regionalism?

- Regionalism is rooted in India's diversity. It is a multidimensional concept.
- Deep attachment with one's region is the basis of regionalism because a geographical region may also be seen as a cultural region, common language, customs and traditions, common history.
- Religion barely plays any role in regionalism unlike communalism. In most of the cases, lopsided and uneven development of different regions triggers feeling of regionalism. Take the example of Uttarakhand separating from Uttar Pradesh, Telangana separating from Andhra Pradesh and regional movements for a separate Vidarbha (from Maharashtra) and demand for further division of Uttar Pradesh into three states.
- Shiv Sena's animosity towards non-Maharashtrians is also a case of regionalism as it promotes 'sons of the soil' feeling.
- Under the new economic policy and liberalisation, private investors will not invest in backward regions because of lack of infrastructures. In such cases, the State has to, but the State has been retreating and withdrawing in favour of the private sector.

Previous Years' Questions

1. What is the basis of Regionalism? Is it that unequal distribution of benefits of development on regional basis eventually promotes regionalism? **(GS Mains Paper I, 2016)**
2. Is religion playing an important role in increasing fundamentalism? Give reasons for your answer. **(UPSC CSE Mains Sociology II, 2016)**

3. Distinguish between religiousness/religiosity and communalism giving one example how the former has got transformed into the latter in independent India. **(GS Mains Paper I, 2017)**
4. How the Indian concept of secularism is different from the western model of secularism? Discuss. **(GS Mains Paper I, 2018)**
5. Communalism arises either due to power struggle or relative deprivation. Argue by giving suitable illustrations. **(GS Mains Paper I, 2018)**
6. Anthropological Understanding of Communalism. **(UPSC CSE Mains Anthropology, Paper II, 2019)**
7. Regionalism as an opportunity and threat to national integration. **(UPSC CSE Mains Anthropology, Paper II, 2022)**
8. Examine the different understandings of secularisation in India. **(UPSC CSE Mains Sociology Paper II, 2022)**
9. What is regional disparity? How serious is this issue of regional disparity in India? **(GS Mains Paper I, 2024)**

Focus Areas for the Examiantion

1. Understanding Secularism and Secularisation
2. Communalism and Indian Politics
3. Regionalism as the manifestation of relative deprivation and lopsided development

CHAPTER 16

Some Current Social Issues/Problems

Chapter Outline

1. Critically evaluating the impact of the Internet and investigate the socio-cultural effects of the Internet
2. Understanding Cyber Crimes and Cyber Terrorism and analysing their impact on individuals, institutions, and national security
3. Studying elderly care including health issues, social security, and changing family dynamics
4. Analysing the rise of Consumerism and understanding the impact of globalisation and consumer culture on societal values, economic behaviours, and environmental sustainability
5. Assessing key legislations, such as the Land Acquisition Act and the National Policy on Older Persons
6. Understanding problems and adverse impact for the sexual minorities and LGBTQ in Indian Society
7. Understanding the socio-legal implications related to MeToo Movement, Triple Talaaq Law, and Anti-CAA Movement
8. Knowing New Farmer's Movement and the difference of opinion between Farmers and the Government
9. Exploring social impact of Covid-19 pandemic

India, like any other country and society, is confronted with multiple problems. Some of these have been continuing for decades, but some others are new ones. Following are some such issues being grappled by the Indian society.

SOCIAL IMPACT OF INTERNET

The Internet is the latest in a series of technological breakthroughs in interpersonal communication following the telegraph, telephone and television. The Internet is a global system of interconnected computer networks that use the Standard Internet Protocol (IP) to serve billions of users worldwide. The Internet can now be accessed almost anywhere by numerous means, especially through mobile Internet devices, data card through wireless network supporting this technology. Internet telephony is another common communications service. With the advent of multimedia, Internet communication is no more restricted to text messaging. One can also see images and videos. The Internet has enabled or accelerated new forms of human interactions through instant messaging, Internet forums and social networking. It now contains unlimited information and has proved itself as a boon to students, researchers and social activists. It is also being used for political mobilisation, friendship enhancement as well as hate speeches and mails.

What Do You Think?

How has the widespread availability of the internet reshaped societal interactions, and does it enhance community building or contribute to greater social isolation?

Perhaps no other modern technology has affected our social life as the Internet. The human-computer interaction is now impacting various aspects of our social life and its socio-cultural impact has been a matter of research throughout the world. Increasing individualism has made us lonely as never before. Text, music and videos together have filled the loneliness or perhaps many have become lonelier affecting one's capacity for socialisation.

INTERNET AS A SOCIAL TECHNOLOGY

Having studied the communication contexts of people, psychologists have discovered how the Internet has the potential of changing social relationships. Though the Internet is being used for several objectives, interpersonal communication is the most important of these. Online communication has badly affected face-to-face relationship. Our urge or capacity to meet and talk and understand each other's feelings has decreased substantially resulting in decreasing warmth in relationships. This has badly affected the psychological health of our society. Thus, online communication is less beneficial than offline communication, though online communication is inevitable in a number of circumstances. Some recent studies reveal that the increasing use of the Internet does not necessarily expand our social network or mutual support system. A number of heavy users of the Internet have reported an increase in social tension as it has decreased the level of dialogue between family members, shrinking the social circle and increasing frustration. Some analysts have described it as the 'lonely world in cyberspace'.

Internet has also hit hard at our privacy. Privacy has an important role in our social life. At a click, one may know where a person lives or works, what is his/her phone number and how to reach his/her home. The increasing abuse of a much useful social site Facebook is an example.

INTERNET AND SOCIAL BEHAVIOUR

People meeting and interacting with each other is a necessary prerequisite for a healthy society. Cyber relationship can never be a substitute for real relationship. Its negative impact on children can be seen easily. A number of children, instead of meeting and playing with each other and spending time together in games or gossips, prefer to sit with an internet-enabled device. Many of them do not prefer to eat with parents and siblings and instead confine to their rooms playing with the computer mouse. This weakens social or kinship bonding. Previously, in most of the homes, dinner used to be a time for all family members to share their day's experiences and benefit from parental guidance, thereby strengthening family solidarity. Watching TV together also used to be such an occasion. Gradually, these practices are vanishing from a number of homes having multiple Internet connections or data cards. It has adversely affected social engagements and psychological benefits. Children may be very competent in using the Internet, but not on how to live in the real world. Children need friends and they need to play and spend time with them to learn how to behave and how to interact with others. Excessive use of the Internet may be responsible for social disconnect. Thus, Internet addiction may lead to social disconnect.

INTERNET AND INTELLECTUAL TRAINING

It is true that the Internet gives us access to unlimited and infinite sources of information and knowledge, but it is also true that it may close the doors of deep thinking and may affect analytical capabilities. A number of students and researchers have stopped thinking and reflecting and instead insert and use the material available on the Internet without thinking and questioning. The increasing practice of 'cut and paste' is detrimental to the generation of knowledge. Different types of material available on the Internet are replacing standard textbooks and adversely affecting our original thinking. Moreover, growing intellectual piracy shall also not lead us to original research. This is not good for any knowledge society.

OBSCENE AND VIOLENT VIDEOS

One of the most damaging effects of the Internet is the easy availability of obscene and offensive videos depicting violent and perverse sex. It is largely impacting children and young adults. Pornographic videos are now a multimillion-dollar industry. The National Coalition to Prevent Child Sexual Abuse and Exploitation (2011) has studied the impact of 'pornified culture' on children and young adults. Sexual urge and its satisfaction is natural and normal, but constant exposure to sexually explicit materials contributes to an earlier onset of sexual behaviour in children and contributes to several psychological aberrations and distortions, especially before one achieves mental and physical maturity. Thousands of pornographic texts and videos are available on the Internet depicting violent sex that glorifies physical violence against women. We will have to accept that pornography can never be a substitute for sex education.

Exposure to such videos for a prolonged period may give rise to such a pornified culture where there is no space for natural and normal relationship between male and female. Psychologists are of the view that it promotes distorted and perverse sexual values such as group sex, sodomy and bestiality. Developing sexually deviant tendencies – committing sex offences experiencing difficulties in one's intimate relationships and accepting myths such as a rape victim deserved to be raped because of how she dressed – may be the result of exposure to such videos. Unfortunately, CDs depicting such sexual acts are also available in all cities at cheap and affordable prices. Behind the alarming frequency of sexual harassment of women, pornography too plays a part besides aggressive patriarchy.

CYBER TERROR AND CRIMES

As we know, the Internet has unique, even transformational qualities as a communication channel, including relative anonymity and the ability to easily link with others who have similar interests, values and beliefs. However, it has also immense possibilities of being misused and responsible for serious problems for the society. With the astronomical expansion of the Internet in India during the last decade or so, we have also become vulnerable to its misuse in a variety of ways. It is like a double-edged sword which has immense use as well as abuse. Harassing and terrorising people, exploiting them and committing frauds are the main aspects of its misuse. Following is the brief description of its misuse which has posed grave social problems:

(i) 'Tagging' has emerged as a big nuisance. Tagging refers to a way attaching a person's name to an online image so that the person's name is displayed with it. If it is done without permission, it is unethical and may be a source of embarrassment if the image is objectionable and offensive. It may also cause distress or ridicule. This is perhaps the commonest and least harmful abuse of Internet. It is a big nuisance.

(ii) Spamming may be another nuisance. It is sending in bulk unsolicited commercial messages. Though highly irritating, it is not illegal. It is like email bombing.

(iii) Cyberstalking is also a common abuse of Internet. It is like following or stalking somebody in cyberspace for the purpose of harassment. It may involve throwing false accusations, threats, etc. to harass somebody. In most of the cases, the stalkers are men and the majority of the victims are women. This may be very disturbing to the mental peace of the victim.

(iv) Phishing and hacking are counted as cybercrimes. Phishing is an act of sending an email requesting for sensitive information such as username, password, credit card details by posing as an authorised agent of an establishment or agency. It is a criminally fraudulent process of acquiring such information to access a bank account or using a credit card to rob the innocent victims. Most of the banks and credit card companies keep warning their customers not to divulge any such information to anybody as they are unauthorised to acquire any such information.

Hacking, a serious cybercrime, is a process through which someone seeks and exploits weaknesses in a computer system or computer network and gets access to a website or personal email account. A hacker possesses advance understanding of computers and computer network. Many of us keep receiving false messages from our friends and relatives seeking financial help because of an emergency. When a website of a sensitive nature is hacked, it may pose a security threat to an institution or a government agency.

(v) Cyber terrorism has now emerged as a big problem for India and other countries. It is the intentional use of computer networks and public Internet to cause destruction and harm for personal objectives. The objectives may also be political or ideological. It may also be understood as disruption attacks against information systems for the primary purpose of creating alarm or panic.

In order to handle Internet abuse, the Government of India has legislated the Information Technology Act, 2000. Amended several times to cover more and more areas and adding more provisions, there is at least some way to deal with the misuse of cyberspace and promoting use of Internet for a variety of purposes. It has also laid down penalties for cybercrimes.

AGEING AND THE AGED

Ageing is a natural process that begins at birth and continues throughout one's life till death. This natural process may be divided into infancy, childhood, adolescence, adulthood and old age. To understand the problems of the elderly people, a new and specified branch of knowledge named gerontology was developed. It studies the social, psychological and biological aspects of ageing while geriatrics is the branch of medicine that studies the diseases of older adults.

In most of the gerontological literature, people above 60 years of age are considered as 'old' and constituting the 'elderly' segment of the population. In academic research, retirement age is often taken as an index of aged status. The boundary of old age cannot be defined exactly because it does not have the same meaning in different societies. The Government of India adopted 'National Policy on Older Persons' in 1999 and it identifies 'senior citizen' or elderly as a person who is of age 60 or above.

The aged population in India is currently the second highest in the world and it constitutes around 8% of the total population. Both the share and size of the elderly population are increasing over time as a result of rising life expectancy and longevity largely due to better medical facilities and healthcare.

By virtue of spectacular medical progress, the grey population throughout the world including India is rising rapidly because of delayed death. But, additional life will bring little cheer if it is burdened with sickness and suffering. Developing societies like India are on the verge of entering an ageing society where economic resources are inadequate and the modernisation process is changing the value system in which the care of the aged is slipping lower and lower in the priorities of the families.

CHANGING SCENARIO

In the traditional Indian society, old people were treated with respect, honour and authority because of norms and values embedded in religious scriptures and the ethical system. Older people played an important role in the joint family system as the *karta* or head of the family. Since the second half of the 20th century things began to change. Rapid urbanisation, industrialisation and westernisation (in urban society) have created several problems for the aged. A new value system started impacting the traditional Indian society. The joint family in urban areas started disintegrating. It has been serving as an important means of social security for the aged in the absence of any state support.

The aged in our society, in most of the cases, feel rejected and neglected as our society is getting more and more youth oriented. As the famous poet W.B. Yeats[1] once wrote:

> That is no country for old men. The young
> in one another's arms, birds in the trees

[1] Yeats,W B, Collected Poems of WB Yeats, Scribner, North Carolina, 1996

In many cases, more in the urban areas and comparatively less in rural societies, the old are increasingly being relegated to loneliness and discomfort. The young in our society show lack of character vis-à-vis older ones and one wonders how is it that while parents could take care of three, four, five or more children, several children together cannot take care of one parent.

> The migration of younger people from rural areas to towns and cities increases the vulnerability of the old who stay behind, particularly those living in families which do not have independent production sources like land, livestock or household industry and are dependent primarily on their labour. (P.H. Reddy, 1996)[2]

The spread of education among women, accompanied by their employment outside the home, in offices and factories, leaves no time for such women to take care of old people at home. Moreover, there is now a greater investment by the family in the education and upbringing of children. The higher cost of living and changing priorities are also affecting the intra-family distribution of income in favour of children. The wealth flow is turning downward. All these socio-economic changes have adversely affected the situation of the elderly in India. As Aparajita Chattopadhyay (2004) rightly points out, social exchange theory establishes that people will maintain stable relationships only if they find it profitable to continue their exchange. With advancing age, old people have less to offer to the relationship, which makes them feel awkward and ultimately adversely affects their well-being. It is the responsibility of the younger generation to respect the aged and to remind them that they still have a productive and useful role to play in society. A good interaction between family members is significant for safe old age, but reduced family size, as an outcome of demographic evolution, is indeed a matter of concern for the aged. Thus, the dilution of the family support system for the elderly, mobility of the younger generation, paucity of government funds, incapability of NGOs or private organisations to provide elderly care and the importance of the elderly learning to take care of themselves through cooperatives have posed serious problems for the quality of life of the aged in India.

There is now an increasing need to ensure social security for elderly people, especially women. The population of women in the 60 plus age group is higher than the male population and they are an extremely marginalised group of people.

> The dependency of widowhood is most vulnerable as it is women who mostly outlive their spouses. Further, the fragility of their existence is accentuated when compared to the dependency of older couples living with their spouses. Men who were widowed almost always obtained a companion compared to their destitution that forced the widows. (Meera Gopal, 2006)[3]

Widows are disadvantaged more within families compared to their male counterparts. Apart from the several socio-economic insecurities that widows alone face, threat to life and injury to person is, in particular, always present when there are claims to property and land. Reports about abuse of elderly people by the family are frequently cited, especially in urban areas.

---

[2] Reddy, P H, The Health of the Aged in India, Health Transition Review, 1996

[3] Gopal, Meera, Caste, Sexuality, and Labour, Current Sociology, 60:2, 2012

HEALTH PROBLEMS

In old age, physical strength deteriorates and mental stability diminishes demanding greater coping skills on the part of the aged persons to adjust to the changing environment. Research into ageing tells that economic development and urbanisation have brought lifestyle changes that have led to unhealthy nutrition and physical inactivity contributing to the prevalence of diabetes. Almost half of the elderly Indians have at least one chronic disease such as asthma, arthritis, depression or diabetes. Senility, Alzheimer, Parkinson and mental disorders are frequent. Visual impairment and vision loss increase dramatically with age. Senility refers to changes in behaviour caused by structural changes in the brain and is used derogatively to describe the old and their behaviour in general. It is an impoverished environment, poor nutrition and diseases that break down the nervous system's resistance against deterioration. Aspects of physiological deterioration in old age can be reduced through measures of healthcare and through other strategies that improve quality of life. However, a sense of deprivation, marginality and loneliness is also instrumental in creating several medical problems.

ELDERLY CARE AND SOCIAL SECURITY

Loss of regular assured income and emotional insecurity resulting in the creation of void in life, loss of spouse, friends and relatives coupled with frailty accompanied with advancing age increases dependency. According to Helpage India, as many as 70% of the aged depend on others for their day-to-day maintenance. The situation is worse for elderly females where 85–87% are economically dependent, either partially or fully, on others. The situation is compounded by the almost nonexistent geriatric care facilities.

Care for the aged is also known as 'elderly care'. It emphasises the social and personal requirements of senior citizens who need some assistance with daily activities and healthcare, but who desire to age with dignity. Traditionally, elderly care has been the responsibility of family members and was provided within the extended family home. In the face of weakening or disintegration of the joint family, it has to be provided by state or charitable institutions. Unlike American and European societies, there is scarce institutional support for the care of the aged in India. However, the aged do not require healthcare only from the state or charitable organisations, but wish to be with their near and dear ones. They wish to be respected and loved and not to be treated as unproductive human resources. Family life is necessary for senior citizens to lead a life of security, care and dignity.

Some social security measures in vogue in India are directed mostly at workers in the organised sector. The important ones are the Employees' Provident Fund Act, 1952, Family Pension Scheme 1971, Maternity Benefit Act, 1976, etc.

Since the 1990s, most of the states have been implementing old age pension to the economically weaker sections of the society. Though it is only paltry (ranging from ₹30 to 100), amounts have been paid and this scheme is more of a symbolic value. Even an average pension of ₹150–200 may prove to be adequate for the food requirements if they lived with their kin, but grossly inadequate when one has to pay house rent, water, electricity charges, medical bills, etc. Some states like Kerala introduced progressive measures such as Agricultural Workers Pension Scheme, Special Pension Scheme for the Handicapped and Destitute Old and Widows Pension Scheme.

LEGAL RIGHTS OF SENIOR CITIZENS

Article 41 of the Constitution says that the State shall, within the limits of economic capacity and development, make effective provision for securing the right to work, to education and to public assistance in cases of unemployment, old age, sickness and disablement and in other cases of undeserved want.

- The aged people have also been provided legal protection under various personal laws of Hindus, Muslims, Christians and Parsees.
- Prior to 1973, there was no provision for maintenance of parents under the Code of Criminal Procedure. A new provision was introduced for the first time in section 125 of the Code of Criminal Procedure in 1973 making sons and daughters responsible for the maintenance of aged parents if they are not in a position to maintain themselves.

A National Policy on Older Persons was announced in 1999 which identified a number of areas of intervention that included financial security, healthcare and nutrition, shelter and protection of life and property for the well-being of the older persons. It was followed by the creation of a National Council for Older Persons (NCOP) by the Ministry of Social Justice and Empowerment to operationalise the national policy.

PRIORITY ISSUES

Helpage India has identified the priority issues to be addressed by the State. It covers a wide range of ameliorating measures such as:

- Non-contributory pensions to older persons in below poverty line (BPL) families;
- Income generation opportunities for the able-bodied and willing older persons;
- Imaginative schemes for contributory pensions for those older persons who can afford to save in their prime years;
- Special schemes for women, Dalits, rural poor, destitute and disabled older persons and widows;
- Accessible and affordable geriatric health facilities to all older persons;
- Provision of infrastructure and trained personnel; and
- Development of facilities in public health arena for the poor.

It is estimated that by 2020 the number of senior citizens would be more than ten crore. The State and non-State response to this great challenge is grossly unsatisfactory. Needless to say, if this problem is not addressed urgently and on a war footing, the aged people shall be in a miserable state.

RISING CONSUMERISM, CONSUMER CULTURE AND THE 'NEW MIDDLE CLASS'

Rapid advancement of consumerism and consumer culture is changing the Indian society in a variety of ways. This is closely related to the emergence of a 'new' middle class, in a way a by-product of consumerism and consumer culture. The process of globalisation, in several ways, is responsible for this shift.

Consumerism may be understood in terms of effects of equating personal happiness with purchasing material goods and consumption in excess of one's needs. Traditionally, it has been associated with capitalism, western culture and compulsive buying. Now it is a worldwide phenomenon. Consumerism may also be described as 'affluenza', a metaphor for describing the tendency of overconsumption or mindless consumption. The craving for material possession is limitless. It is socially transmitted. The result of this is painful, infectious, overload, stress, debt anxiety and wastage.

All consumption is not bad. It is a necessary condition of human existence, but consumption without need is bad. It has its positive aspects too. It leads to increased industrial production, higher growth rate of economy, increased employment not only in manufacturing sector, but also in marketing, advertising, etc. But, overconsumption causes a lot of negative consequences – overwork, high debt, anxiety and stress, sometimes leading to suicide.

The 'culture of overconsumption' may be described as consumer culture. It may be defined as a culture in which the majority of consumers avidly desire, purchase, acquire and display goods and services that may be for non-utilitarian reasons such as status enhancement, envy provocation and novelty seeking.

I am using the 'middle class' as a category of people who have one third or more surplus/saving after expenses on food and housing. Our traditional middle class could be seen up to the 1960s or 1970s. Most such people were men of integrity, honesty and humility. They came mostly from economically secure families, maintaining high standards of morality; they also supported social and religious reforms, promoted nationalist sentiments and were bound by a certain *Lakshman Rekha*, the boundaries of which most of them rarely crossed. With the advent of the new economic policy, economic liberalisation and globalisation in the 1990s, a 'new' middle class emerged. Most of the people from this class come from an urban background, highly educated and fiercely competitive and conversant with English as a medium of expression. They have high salaries, possess professional and managerial skills and are restless to move upward as rapidly as possible. Presently, those earning an annual income of 10–15 lakhs may be put in this category and they may number somewhere around 20 crore people. In fact, they are the torchbearers of consumer culture.

After the 1990s, India became one of the favourite destinations of multinational companies and corporate houses because after China, India has emerged as the largest market for consumer goods. The new wave of economic reforms also created new avenues of employment beyond the borders of India – Gulf countries, Saudi Arabia, Canada, etc. This new middle class seeks to construct its identity through good employment, handsome income/salary and acquisition of status symbols. 'Mall and multiplex culture' is an integral part of this class. They may be seen spending a lot on expensive western-style branded cloths, cosmetics, international cuisine, expensive electronic goods, cell phones, health and beauty parlours, holiday resorts, clubs, etc. and expensive goods are exchanged. Never before did young men and women in the 21–30 age group have so much money and disposable income. When a new lifestyle becomes 'mainstream culture', nonparticipation in it makes people frustrated and they may think that they have been marginalised. Flaunting multiple credit cards is a status symbol for many such people.

The phenomenal rise in demand for dowry is directly related to consumer culture. All regions coming under the 'green revolution' have also witnessed the emergence of this new middle class. Our media, especially electronic media and popular TV channels, are promoting consumer culture. Most media houses are controlled or run by corporate houses and multinational corporations and they have a vested interest in promoting consumerism.

The impact of consumer culture is proving disastrous for economically weaker sections of our society. Their craving and aspirational level have been enhanced by the consumer culture and high-pressure advertising, but they do not have the means to fulfil their desire. Some of them take to criminal activity to earn more money while several others spend their hard-earned income on unnecessary and unproductive items instead of consuming nutritious food. They have become more vulnerable to all sorts of diseases. The consumer culture has come to stay in our society and its size is expanding day by day.

SEXUAL MINORITIES: LGBTQ IN INDIAN SOCIETY

Indian Constitution recognises only two types of minorities-linguistic and religious but it recognises the right to equality and right to life and dignity and does not allow any discrimination. Needless to say, the Indian society is strongly patriarchal and exhibition of 'masculinity' is accepted a virtue among the majority of people.

Among all the minorities in Indian society, sexual minorities are least understood and discussed. Moreover, the traditional Indian society, till recent times, has been avoiding this issue or pushing it under the carpet. In order to have a comprehensive understanding of sexual minorities there should be a clear understanding of 'Sexual Orientation'. This very concept defies the majoritarian idea of binary sexual relations e.g. between males and females, as normal and natural. Thus, those who refused to be fitted within this framework had to fight a long battle. 'Sexual Orientation' is a relatively new notion in human rights law and practice and one of the controversial ones in politics. Formally speaking, sexual orientation "is an enduring emotional, romantic, sexual or affectional attraction to another person."

Thus, the sexual orientations manifest themselves in the form of Lesbians, Gay, Bisexuals and Transgender. Sexual orientation, largely, "refers to a person's sense of identity based on those attractions mentioned above, related behaviours and membership in a community of others who share those attractions" (American Psychological Association). Despite all the advances in medical, biological and behavioural sciences, scientists cannot say for sure the exact reason or cause of sexual orientation. They believe that these orientations are caused by a complex interplay of genetic, hormonal and environmental influences. Primacy is given to non-social biological causes of social orientation than social ones. This is true that across regions and cultures overwhelming majority of people are heterosexual and only a minority of people are of homosexual or bisexual orientation. On the basis of sexual orientation, the following categories of persons may be identified.

- *Asexuals* are not sexually attracted to anyone and/or no desire to act on attraction to anyone. They are not sexless. Asexual persons sometimes do experience affectional/romantic attraction.
- *Gays* are the people whose physical, romantic and emotional attractions are to people of the same sex. Gay people (both men and women) are sometime also referred to as homosexual but in the current discourse on sexuality this is considered offensive and hence avoided.
- *Lesbians* are women whose physical, romantic and emotional attraction is to the other women.
- *Bisexuals* are those persons who have physical, romantic and emotional attraction to more than one gender.
- *Transgenders* are people whose gender is different from the sex (male or female) they were assigned when they were born. This also depends how they feel inside and how they express themselves. Some such persons decide to undergo surgery or other medical treatment, so their outward appearance matches their true self. The traditional societies described them as eunuch.
- *Queer* may be referred to such persons whose identity is not strictly heterosexual. Once considered an offensive term the rights movement has reclaimed it and use it with pride while describing themselves and their movement.

Some other commonly used words are:

- *Homophobia* refers to negative attitudes and feelings towards people who are not of heterosexual sexualities. It may express itself through dislike or discomfort and sometime hostility.
- *Biphobia* is aversion of and/or prejudice towards the idea that people can be attracted to more than one gender.
- *Gender Binary* may be described as a system of classifying sex and gender into strictly distinct and disconnected forms of masculine and feminine. Mostly, it is a social construct.
- *Androgyny* refers to the mixing of masculine and feminine gender expressions.

Thus, all such people described above are described as sexual minorities. Though a number of terms have been coined such as GSM (Gender and Sexual Minorities), GSSM (Gender, Sexual and Romantic Minorities), and GSD (Gender and Sexual Diversity) but it is SGM (Sexual and Gender Minority) that has gained widest acceptance, since the last decade. Moreover, it may be said that Sexual and Gender Minority is a generic or umbrella term that includes all the groups and populations accepted under LGBTI (Lesbian, Gay, Bisexual, Transgender and Intersex). *Study Guide: Sexual Orientation and Human Rights* (ibid), an advocacy group for LGBTQ, has comprehensively taken up rights of the sexual minorities:

- *The right to non-discrimination* and to be free from *violence and harassment* is usually denied by omitting sexual orientation in anti-discrimination laws, constitutional provisions or their enforcement.
- The *right to life* is violated in states where the death penalty is applicable for sodomy.

- The *right to free from torture or cruel, in human or degrading treatment* is infringed upon by policy practices, investigations or in the case of lesbians, gays and bisexuals in detention.
- *Arbitrary* arrest occurs in a number of countries with individuals suspected of having a homo/bisexual identity.
- The *freedom of movement* is denied to bi-national couples by not recognising their same sex relation.
- The *right to a fair trial* is often affected by the prejudices of judges and other law enforcement officials.
- The *right to privacy* is denied by the existence of 'sodomy laws' applicable to lesbians, gays and bi-sexuals, even if the relation is in private between consenting adults.
- The *rights to free expression and free association* may either be denied explicitly by law or lesbians, gays, and bisexuals may not enjoy them because of the homophobic climate in which they live.
- The *practice of religion* is usually restricted in the case of lesbians, gays and bisexuals, especially in the case of churches advocating against them.
- The *right to work* is the most affected among the economic rights, many lesbians, gays and bisexuals being fired because of their sexual orientation or discriminated in employment policies and practice.

Besides these, there may be several other areas of discrimination and most of these may be observed in not only traditional Indian society but also in USA and several other western countries. Muslim countries, perhaps, give the harshest treatment to gay and lesbians who may be considered 'anti-social'.

▶▶ Indian Scenario

Despite general lack of understanding and appreciation of the Queer groups, the western societies are much more tolerant than the third world countries. Yet, "Queer studies is an extremely dynamic field which is expanding almost every day to include new histories, new cultures of intimacy and kinship, and the new ways of being queer" (Kaustav Bakshi et al 2019). The LGBTQ movement in the Third World is faced with several obstacles and challenges: traditionalists, nationalists, and religious, among many others. In India, the queer movement is only at a nascent stage as yet. Indian democracy has to go through the 'litmus test' of not only tolerating but respecting the rights of minorities:

> Would Indian democracy be a place where the majority tramples over the voices and concerns of the minorities, in other words, would it degenerate into crass majoritarianism or would it be sensitive to the voices and aspirations of those on the margins and perhaps not powerful enough to get their voices heard? (Menon & Subberwal, 2019)[4]

Till the last few decades LGBTQ were largely invisible and people avoided talking about it or talking with shame. This attitude of Indian society had ruined the lives of thousands of men and women who were forced to marry persons of opposite sex by the family elders resulting in failed marriages.

[4] Menon, K & Ranjana Subberwal, Social Movements in Contemporary India, Sage Publication, 2019

Surprisingly and unfortunately, even the women's movement in India did not take up this issue for a long time focusing on the oppression and exploitation of women by the patriarchy, dowry and female feticide, infanticide and related issues. People of other sexual orientations were also not coming forward to assert their rights. Even in the mass media the queer were largely invisible. Here at least two examples are worth mentioning. When the famous feminist Urdu novelist Ismat Chughtai published her short story *Lihaaf* (quilt) in 1942 depicting lesbian relationship she was hauled to the law court and the lower court described the short story vulgar and obscene but she was not imprisoned though a number of her readers, both men and women, shamed her for this story. Another instance of relatively recent times is the movie Fire (1996) by Deepa Mehta which, beside other issues, also depicted a lesbian relationship between two female characters portrayed by Shabana Azmi and Nandita Das. A number of rightwing Hindu organisations violently protested against the film and the director Deepa Mehta for 'corrupting' the *Bhartiya Sanskriti* (Indian Culture) forgetting that there are irrefutable "evidences from various regional and religious cultures including Muslim, Buddhist, Jain and Hindu to argue how they sustain a range of cultural practices which do not succumb to the gender normative. Such cultural practices have been documented in the Mughal era too" (Ghosh, 2020)[5]. Vanita and Kidwai (2000) in their outstanding work *Same Sex love in India: Readings from Literature and History* have argued that our ancient texts tried to subordinate non-penetrative as well as non-heterosexual sex to penetrative hetero sexual sex. Many of them also tend to take a somewhat pejorative view of those who are homo erotically motivated. Nevertheless, the examples of ancient texts have often been cited by members of the queer community later to forward their claim and gain respect, dignity and opportunities.

Section 377 in The Indian Penal Code

377. Unnatural offences.—Whoever voluntarily has carnal intercourse against the order of nature with any man, woman or animal, shall be punished with 1[imprisonment for life], or with imprisonment of either description for a term which may extend to ten years, and shall also be liable to fine. Explanation.—Penetration is sufficient to constitute the carnal intercourse necessary to the offence described in this section.

Decriminalisation of Section 377 of the Indian Penal Code

Decriminalisation of this section of IPC is not only a great victory for LGBTQ but also portrays the growing open and liberal attitude of the Indian judiciary. Section 377 was introduced in 1861 during the British colonial rule which made sexual activities "against the order of nature" illegal. First decriminalised by the Delhi High Court in 2009, the judgment was overturned by the Supreme Court of India in 2013. In 2018, the Supreme Court agreed to hear a petition to review the 2013 verdict by a smaller bench. On 6 September, 2018, the Supreme Court gave a unanimous verdict and declared the Section 377 unconstitutional. The court mentioned that "consensual sex between adults in a private space, which is not harmful to women or children cannot be denied as it is a matter of individual choice." This verdict has been described as the 'dawn of a new era.'

[5] Ghosh, B, Social Movements: Concepts, Experience, and Concerns, Sage Publication, New Delhi, 2020

After the decriminalisation of Section 377, the LGBTQ movement has become more visible and has attained more confidence with the result that besides the metros even relatively smaller cities like Lucknow has seen 'pride parades' and more meetings offline and online. During the last five years a number of Indian movies being shown in cinema halls have exhibited movies on gay and lesbian themes. With the advent of Netflix and several other streaming services that allow the people to watch TV shows and movies without commercials on an internet-connected device, the Indians are now more exposed to the queer themes especially based on gay or lesbian characters. Thus, such portrayals no more creates 'embarrassing' movements that used to be till sometime back. Significantly, general masses are now more curious to know about the 'abnormal sex' as against the hostility and contempt for the queer.

▶▶ Major Problems

The LGBTQ, despite decriminalisation of Section 377, are still facing serious problems. Do they have all the rights of an ordinary Indian citizen? The landmark judicial verdict is a beginning for a long battle of complete freedom as they are now sanctioned all the constitutional rights and liberties protected by the Constitution.

S B Math and S P Seshadri highlighted disparities in healthcare access for sexual minorities in *The Invisible Ones: Sexual Minorities, Indian Journal of Medical Research*, drawing on the WHO constitution and analysing existing situations.

They wrote, sexual minorities face significant challenges across physical, mental, and social dimensions of well-being. They are at high risk for STDs, HIV/AIDS, and violence, including physical, sexual, and emotional abuse. Transgenders often face denial of hormonal therapy and sex reassignment surgery (SRS) and lack access to dedicated healthcare facilities, heightening their vulnerability to physical and mental illnesses. Stigma and discrimination further contribute to emotional disorders, elevated suicide risks – particularly for men in same-sex partnerships – and increased substance abuse, including heavy alcohol and drug use, as a means of coping. Social exclusion and societal pressures lead many into coerced heterosexual marriages, resulting in discord or poor quality of life. Housing discrimination adds to their struggles, forcing frequent relocations and challenges in proving residency, compounding their marginalisation.

Media, by and large, played a negative role in depicting the sexual minorities. The vernacular and regional press and non-English TV Channels particularly, spread canards and negativity about them.

▶▶ Adverse Impact on Mental Health

Most of the sexual minorities tend to live within their narrow shell because of experiences that negatively impact their mental health. Following are some such reasons:

- Harassment, ridiculing and bullying at school
- Dropping out of school
- Humiliating and sarcastic attitude of neighbours and colleagues
- Verbal harassment and harssment at workplace

- Indifference and hostility leading to rejection by the loved ones or co-religionists
- Difficulty to find regular jobs
- Lack of family and social support
- Lack of opportunities to make social contributions
- Strong prejudices around sexual orientation
- Secret 'honour killings'

Indian society is still bound by rigid set of social-cultural norms that refuse to accept a different sexual orientation. For sexual minorities especially for gays and lesbians, family may be most helpful and in cases where family is appreciative and supportive a person with a different sexual orientation feel happy, confident and may contribute to the society at large. It is true that homosexuality is now more acceptable to the present generation but is mainly in cities especially big cities. Rural India is still frozen in time. Forced marriages and family sanctioned 'corrective rapes' are one of the responses by the rural society. Thus, we may say that India lives in different centuries simultaneously. A large number of Indian people are living in 19th century, many in 20th century and a few in the 21st century. Same may be said about villages, towns, cities and metros. Behavioural variations may also be seen in different classes and politico-economic strata and status groups. Needless to say, change cannot be achieved overnight. Law and administrative measures have their own limitations. Social change does not come merely through legislation.

MeToo MOVEMENT: A BLOW TO PATRIARCHY

Global MeToo Movement is the first mass movement against sexual abuse. The phrase 'MeToo' was initially used in 2006 on *My space,* by a sexual harassment survivor and activist Tarana Burke of New York. It spread like wildfire in different parts of the world. Millions of people started using the phrase in English and different languages of the world. Recently, Burke herself described it as an international movement for justice for marginalised people especially of marginalised communities.

MeToo Movement is related with the concept of consent. In a hard hitting and ruthlessly honest analysis Shalu Nigam (2018)[6], a lawyer and right activist, says that "sexual assault or rape has been used as a weapon since ages to control, conquer, and terrorise women." In her acclaimed work Against Our Will: Men, Women and Rape (1975), Susan Brownmiller argues that rape is fundamentally a deliberate tool of intimidation used by men to instil fear in women collectively. She further says that rape is primeval and ultimate act of subjugation where the rapist asserts his power with the urge to dominate. Thus, "sexual assault is a weapon of force and an act of dominance, a principal agent of man's will and women's fear, a triumph of manhood and is easier to comment in situation where the aggressor has an advantage which persists due to structural domination such as feudalism, slavery, work, war or in custody situations where the victim could hardly resist and is over awed by the power and authority of the assaulter." Toxic masculinity is used as a weapon to humiliate the women – the vulnerable and the week.

[6] Nigam, Shalu, Women and Domestic Violence in India: A Quest for Justice, Routledge, 2020

Any generalisation is dangerous. In the heat of MeToo Movement we should not get carried away and look at all the men with suspicion. Not all sex in patriarchy is rape or sexual assault. So, not all men are rapists and not all sex is rape. The majority of men do not rape. Robert Jensen, in his book The End of Patriarchy: Radical Feminism for Men, urges us to broaden our understanding of harmful behaviours by considering categories of men who, while not committing rape, contribute to a culture of sexual violence. This includes men who would be willing to rape if they were assured of no punishment, those who refrain from intervening when witnessing rape, and men who buy sex from women, believing payment entitles them to act without restraint. He also highlights men who are sexually stimulated by pornography depicting scenarios resembling rape, those who find the idea of rape sexually arousing, and those whose sexual gratification relies on dominance and power over women.

'These men are not rapists. But should we take comfort in the fact that the men in these categories are not, in legal terms, guilty of rape? Are we advancing the cause of ending men's violence against women by focusing only on the acts legally defined as rape. .... If we can't talk about patriarchy– if we can't face the myriad ways that we men are socialised to seek domination in sexuality and everyday life – then let's admit that we are giving up on the goal of a world without rape and harassment.' Socialisation of men within their families, peer groups and communities is to a great extent, responsible for the sexual harassment and assault. We should also accept that MeToo is not a man versus women issue. It is women versus patriarchy. Religion too plays an important role in strengthening patriarchy and archaic behaviour towards women.

▶▶ MeToo and Indian Society

The entry of MeToo Movement in a highly patriarchal and traditional society like India where women are conditioned to accept discrimination and harassment as part of their lives was not a sudden rage. It was the years of oppression and abuse that was built-up. It finally cracked. The international MeToo movement definitely inspired and encouraged a section of women in India to break the age old 'culture of silence'. It gathered momentum in 2018 in the cinema industry of Bombay when a couple of female actors publicly accused some male actors and directors of sexual harassment and assault. This led to many other women in the news media and various other fields to come out openly against the perpetrators of sexual harassment. The movement got the boost further after a female journalist won a criminal defamation case against an editor turned politician whom she accused of sexual harassment.

What Do You Think?

How has the MeToo movement influenced the cultural and legal landscape of gender equality in Indian society, and what challenges remain in achieving true empowerment for women?

For centuries women in Indian society have been socialised and conditioned to remain silent and bear the agony. Overwhelming majority of women suffer all sorts of harassment – stalking, molestation, rape and verbal abuse, virtually every day. There is outrage for selective rape cases, whenever extreme brutality has been perpetrated, when it is widely reported in media. In such cases large number of women and justice- loving men in the cities and towns take to the street. However, in 2018 the entire social media was taken by storm and MeToo became a buzz word. This was an act of defiance against the deeply rooted patriarchal power structure. The movement sent a strong message to the perpetrators, would-be perpetrators and potential perpetrators who refused to understand the meaning of 'consent'. Moreover, MeToo movement shall definitely force a number of men to have some respect for women. It will also definitely give more courage to women to give up the notion of 'shame' in the wake of sexual harassment.

However, at the same time, our patriarchal society makes every effort to blame the victims, accuse them of maligning the perpetrators despite the fact that in many instances people around the culprits are well aware of the character of the culprit and their track record in sexual harassment. Sometime, the women going public on their experience of sexual harassment are accused by the supporters of the culprits of doing it for vested interests or just seeking attention. Sometime even the family member or friends of the victims urge them to 'forget' as the whole legal process is too cumbersome and time and money consuming.

Due to ignorance, illiteracy and lack of access to internet vast multitude of masses are not aware of the movement in village India and small towns. Even if it percolates to some villages it fails to enthuse the women, especially the Dalit women, who cannot afford to go to the police or a legal court. Generally speaking, the character of the police, especially at the lower levels, is so heavily patriarchal and misogynist that they may justify such incidents as normal and scare away the victim. It gains some force and voice only in those villages or towns where some good and committed NGO has been working. Even in cities, years of apathy towards the Supreme Court's Visakha Guidelines failed to provide a safe and women-friendly environment.

▸▸ What Is to Be Done?

Sexual assault and harassment have always been the norm. Women who have tried to fight back have always done it as individuals making it much easier for them to be dismissed or targeted themselves as 'money grabbers' or attention seekers. Sexual harassment and abuse by men in positions of power will not stop until there is an organisation formed to fight this, in the courts and in mainstream and social media. Barbara Maclean, an academic and career counsellor in California suggested the following tactics and support which may also be applied in India:

- Provide legal aid for individuals and groups in their claims against abuse.
- Educate women about their legal rights and best ways to confront abuse in the work place.
- Groups of women could show up to protest at worksites that have been accused of abuse.
- Form emotional support groups for women who are going through the fallout from abuse.
- Bombard social media with complaints about organisations and companies that are harbouring abusers.
- Bombard HR departments with phone calls demanding they take action against claims of harassment or abuse.
- Share ideas with each other through private online groups for defending and taking action against sexual predators in the workplace.

Some women's organisations such as All India Democratic Women's Association (AIDWA) an affiliate of CPI(M) and some NGOs are using similar or some other innovative methods to get justice for the victims.

Unfortunately, the LGBTQIA have been left out from the purview of the law on sexual abuse, harassment and assault. They are silent sufferers of abuse and humiliation and most of the members of the society do not show any sympathy for them or stand by them.

The *Prevention of Women Against Sexual Harassment Act* was enacted in 2013 after, much pressure and sustained campaign by the progressive women's movement. Yet, acts of harassment and violence are not being taken seriously either by the law makers or implementers of such laws.

Women and supportive men have to unite to create a powerful organisational network to raise consciousness against sexual harassment of women, do strong advocacy and protect the victims. Needless to say, this will be a long journey in a strongly patriarchal and tradition-bound society like India but such battles are fought with determination.

BANNING TRIPLE TALAAQ LAW AND ITS SOCIO-LEGAL IMPLICATIONS

Marriage is a universal social institution and so is the dissolution or termination of marriage. Perhaps, barring Hindu's marriage everywhere is a social contract with the provision of dissolution by seeking divorce. Adultery, barrenness and incompatibility of temperament are some common grounds for seeking divorce. Divorce is always a public affair.

The issue of '*triple talaaq*' (pronouncing divorce thrice in one go) has always been a debatable issue in Indian society. A number of NGOs and women's rights groups have been demanding a total ban on this procedure of divorce because the lives of many Muslim women have been ruined. Before proceeding further we must know that:

- the provision of instant triple talaaq is not followed by all Muslims
- there are several ways of effecting divorce in Islam
- a number of Muslim-majority countries have already declared triple divorce illegal and invalid

Triple divorce is followed only by the Sunni Muslims following *Hanafi* School of Islamic jurisprudence. It is visible in India because a large number of Indian Muslims follow this school of jurisprudence. Because of its 'news value' triple divorce gets a lot of public and media attention, while other forms of divorce available to both Muslim men and women are hardly spoken about and discussed. Moreover, not every Sunni Muslim belonging to the Hanafi School uses triple divorce way to dissolve his marriage. Only a small number of them go by it but even this cannot be justified.

In response to a petition filed by a divorced Muslim woman, a victim of triple divorce, a Constitution bench of the Supreme Court declared that the practice of instantaneous Triple Talaaq is unconstitutional by a 3:2 majority. Following up this verdict The *Muslim Women (Protection of Rights on Marriage) Act, 2019* was passed on 26 July, 2019.

The key features of this Act are:

- Any pronouncement of *talaaq* by a Muslim husband following the earlier practice of pronouncing it three times for the instantaneous divorce in any manner-spoken or written, in text, SMS, or any electronic channel will be void and illegal
- Any Muslim husband who communicates the *talaaq* orally or in writing may face a punishment of up to three years in jail which may be further extended
- If a Muslim husband pronounces *talaaq* in this way, the women and her children are entitled to receive an allowance for subsistence to be determined by a judicial magistrate
- The divorced woman is entitled to the custody of her minor children.

Theoretically and from the point of view of gender justice this Act is fine but it has generated some questions crying for solutions.

- If the erring husband is sent to jail will the parents and other family members of the husband (if the couple lives in joint family) allow the wife and the children (if any) to continue to live in the household?
- Who would maintain and look after the wife and the children?
- After the completion of the imprisonment when the husband returns will he be again living with the same wife whose complaint sent him to jail?
- Moreover, if the divorce has not occurred since it is illegal and invalid, marriage continues, so why all the fuss?

Divorce in Islam: There is no unanimity among the different Schools of **Islamic jurisprudence** and Islamic scholars regarding the status of triple divorce. Though the dominant juristic view did hold triple divorce in one setting as valid, there were enough dissenting voices in each school of Islam which considered three pronouncements in one go as just one revocable pronouncement. Indeed, the incidence of triple divorce has been quite low. It should be made clear to those who do not agree with this legal ban on triple divorce that divorce is not like 'two-minute noodles' or 'instant coffee'. It suits the patriarchal mindset which does not look at the wife as 'equal partner' in matrimonial alliance. Tahir Mahmood[7], an eminent expert on Islamic jurisprudence says that the background of the tradition of triple divorce should be made clear. Going into the history he says that the

> "blatantly anti-women divorce customs prevalent in the pre-Islamic Arabia had been given a serious blow by the teaching of Prophet Muhammad, who was indeed a great social reformer. Demonstrating the truth of the saying 'old habits die hard', unscrupulous men innovated, in course of time, ways and means to circumvent the Prophets teachings."

Quick Fact

Islamic Jurisprudence

Jurisprudence is the study and theory of law, exploring its principles, philosophy, and applications.

Islamic jurisprudence is the interpretation and application of Islamic law (Sharia) based on scholarly consensus.like Quran, Hadith etc.

[7] Mahmood, Tahir, Muslim Law in India and Abroad, Universal Law Publishers, Allahabad, 2016

This self-contradictory concept remained in vogue for centuries in Muslim societies across the globe. Country after country in Asia and Africa abolished by legislation the "detestable" practice of triple talaaq.

The Shia Muslims believe that pronouncement of such divorce is unjust is not valid under the Shia jurisprudence (*Fiqh Jafari* School of jurisprudence). Accordingly, only one pronouncement can be made in one month or one menstrual cycle. Three successive pronouncements in three separate months lead to a final divorce. The whole process is to be conducted in the presence of two witnesses. Thus, such a procedure, also shared by many Sunni Muslims, gives ample time to both the parties to think and ponder over the whole issue. This provides sufficient space for reconciliation. It is to be noted that during the entire process the husband and wife should not have any physical relations and, if possible, should live separately thus giving them time to feel the possible absence of each other in separation.

Zia us Salam (2018)[8] in his popular book *Till Talaq Do us Part* explains the relevant facts in a simple rather layman's language for the general readers. A Muslim woman's right to dissolve marriage is well protected by the *Muslim Personal Law (Shariat) Application Act, 1937* and the *Dissolution of Muslim Marriage Act, 1938*. "They, in addition, enjoy atleast five other ways of getting rid of incompatible, viplent or slanderous husbands. The condition for this cover everything from dowry demands to casting aspersions on the character of the wife, or simply the inability to fulfil marital obligations. Various permissible methods of divorce in Islam, practically common to all Muslims are:

- *Khula*: *Khul*, an Arabic word, also called *khula,* is a procedure through which a woman can give a divorce to her husband by returning the 'Dower' (*mehar*) or something else that she received from her husband or without returning anything, as agreed by the spouses.
- *Talaaq-e Tafweez*: It is a way of divorce under which the husband vests in his wife the right to divorce him. This condition should ideally be written down in the *Nikaahnama* (nikaah document) at the time of marriage.The wife may lay down several conditions in this document including the husband not taking out another wife in her lifetime.
- *Mubarat*: This is out of court divorce by mutual consent.This provision finds mention in the *Muslim Personsl Law (Shariat) Application Act*, 1937. It is almost the same to what modern day courts often advice to the quarreling couples.

Further, if a husband charges his wife with adultery, and is not able to prove it with evidence, she is entitle to obtain divorce whis is also recognised by the *Shariat Act*, 1937.

▶▶ Social-legal Implications

First, let us see the key points of the judgement delivered by the majority and minority of judges. Two judges came to the conclusion that triple talaaq is now part of statutory law and it is therefore subject to the discipline of fundamental rights. It is not protected by the right to freedom of religion.

[8] Salam, Ziya, Till Talaq Do Us Part, Penguin Books, Delhi, 2018

Indira Jaisingh, an eminent legal expert says that "This is the most important advance made in the judgement. For the first time a law governing family matters has been subjected to the discipline of the Constitution.

The other two judges have come to the opposite conclusion.
They have opined that

> "We have arrived at the conclusion that *talaaq-e-biddat* is a matter of 'personal law' of Sunni Muslims belonging to the Hanafi school. It constitutes a matter of their faith. They have practiced it for at least 1400 years. We have examined whether the practice satisfies the constraints provided for under Article 25 of the Constitution, and have arrived at the conclusion that it does not breach any of them. We have also come to the conclusion that the practice, being a component of personal law, has been protected by Article 25[9] of the Constitution".

One of these two judges, the Chief Justice, goes on to say that "religion is a matter of faith, and not of logic. It is not open to court to accept an egalitarian approach over a practice which constitutes an integral part of religion. The fifth judge, Justice Joseph Kurian whose vote proved decisive in setting aside instant triple talaaq came up with a memorable statement:

> "What is held to be bad in the Holy Quran cannot be good in *Shariat* and, in that sense, what is bad in theology is bad in law as well….. Merely because a practice has continued for a long time, that by itself cannot make it valid if it has been expressly declared to be impermissible."[9]

Indira Jaisingh[10] taking a relevant stand on the verdict of the Supreme Court comments that "the big question is, why did the court once again dodge the question of whether the law violated the rights of women since it discriminates against women based on sex?" There is no discussion in the judgement on what gender justice means for women. She further says that the law is indeed manifestly arbitrary but it is also manifestly discriminatory based on sex and hence there is no reason why it should not have been struck down on that ground, laying the foundation for a 'gendered understanding' of the Constitution. Since the 1950s, the Supreme Court of India has avoided and dodged the question of whether family law is beyond purview of the constitution– this judgement makes a breakthrough. Such a ruling would benefit not just Muslim women but all women. Justice Rohington Nariman's ruling that triple talaaq violates the right to equality under Article 14 of the Constitution is extremely significant. It means that we can now test and challenge the discriminatory personal laws of other religious communities especially of Hindus, against fundamental rights.

It is to be noted that though the Muslim women have also the right to get divorce from their husbands, they have to go to a court but if a Muslim man wants a divorce, he can just pronounce any of the other two forms of divorce, which have not been declared unconstitutional. This is discriminatory. Moreover, there are a large number of Hindu men who simply desert their wives and go away

---

[9] Supreme Court of India, Writ petition(c) No. 118 of 2016
[10] Jaisingh, Indira, Supreme Court Observer, 6 September, 2017

leaving the poor wives to fend for themselves. But the wives still retain the status of married women and they can claim, much more easily maintenance.

Equipped with this legislation women in India belonging to all religious communities may unite to fight against discriminatory practices in Indian society.

FARMER'S MOVEMENT

The recent farmer's protest may be said to be the largest ever mobilisation of the peasantry in independent India revealing a deep crisis in the agrarian life in India. The farmers' movement was triggered by the three Acts passed by the parliament in September 2020. These Acts are:

1. **Farmers Produce Trade and Commerce (Promotion and Facilitation) Act, 2020.**
    - It expands the scope of the trade areas of farmer's produce from select areas to any place of production, collection and aggregation.
    - Allows electronic trading and e-commerce of scheduled farmer's produce
    - Prohibits state governments from levying any market fee, cess or levy on farmers traders and electronic trading platforms for the trade of farmers produce conducted in an 'outside trade area'.
2. **Farmers (Empowerment and Protection) Agreement of Price Assurance and Farm Services Act, 2020**
    - It provides a legal framework for farmers to enter into pre-arranged contract with buyers including mention of pricing
    - Defines a dispute resolution mechanism.
3. **Essential Commodities (Amendment) Act, 2020**
    - It removes food stuff such as cereals, pulses, potato, onions, edible oil seeds and oil from the list of essential commodities, removing stock holding limits on agricultural items produced by horticulture techniques except under extraordinary circumstances.
    - Requires that imposition of any stock limit on agricultural produce only occur if there is a steep price rise.

When the farm bills were passed and became Acts a number of farmer's unions such as Samyukt Kisan Morcha and All India Kisan Sangharsh Coordination Committee gave an all India call to oppose these Acts which, according to them, were against the interests of the farmers. Though the mobilisation and protest occurred in many parts of the country the focus and nerve centre of the movement was the border areas of Delhi, Punjab, Haryana, Western Uttar Pradesh and Rajasthan. The farmers insisted on repealing these farm laws.

In several ways it is a different, a new peasant movement. Shail Mayaram[11] rightly says that there is a "phenomenal difference between present movements then and now. In colonial India, peasant movements were largely against the British Empire or the states under princely rule often involving

[11] Mayaram, Shail, How different are the ongoing Farmer's protests from those of Colonial India? The Wire, 30 December, 2020

the same combinations of *Zamindar, Sahukar, Sarkar* (landlord, usurer and state)." The protests would be against the rise in revenue rates and other kinds of obligations that elites demanded, such as *begaar* (forced labour without remuneration in cash or kind), oppressive cesses and repayment of loans with high interest rates. The colonial bureaucracy was primarily a revenue bureaucracy, hence the appreciation appellation "Collector" who was tagged with other roles. The Institution of the Indian Railways facilitated the deep penetration of the state and market, the extraction and movement of agrarian produce would become a mode of colonial control over the "*wild*".

The post-independence period saw various types of land reforms most salient of which was zamindari abolition which was a big relief to the peasantry. The institutional finance in the agricultural sector, though not sufficient, freed many from the clutches of moneylenders.

If we look at the post-independence peasant movements, the first striking difference between then and now is that the earlier movement was mainly confined to Western Uttar Pradesh because the senior Tikait's influence was largely confined to a few districts in this region. It was mainly spearheaded by the Jat farmers growing sugarcane. Their main demands were higher prices for sugarcane, reduced charges for electricity and prompt payment for their cane crop. The present movement spread across the country. Another difference was the absence of brutal force by the state to prevent any mobilisation. But the most striking difference is the presence of large number of women though the trend was visible in the long march of the peasants in Maharashtra in 2019-20 when they were marching, sometime barefooted, covering hundreds of kilometers to Bombay. Another striking feature of the present movement was the absence of a single messiah like leader. Instead, it is a collective leadership devoid of leaders of political parties. It reflects the strong bonds between diverse groups of peasants.

▸▸ Difference of Opinion Between Farmers and Governments

The following demands of the farmers reflect the serious difference of opinion between the government's stand (reflected through the Acts and negotiations with the farmers) and farmers' leadership.

- Farmers call for a special session of the Parliament to repeal the farm laws altogether
- The government should make minimum support price (MSP) and state procurement of crops a 'legal right'
- The conventional procurement system should continue
- Honest implementation of Swaminathan Committee Report that recommended MSP at least 50% more than the cost of production
- Reduction of diesel prices, an important input in the present-day mechanised agriculture, for agricultural use by at least 50%
- Centre should not interfere in state subjects

Some other demands pertain to stubble burning in Punjab and Haryana and repeal of provisions of air quality management in NCR (National Capital Region), withdrawal of Police cases against the farmers etc.

For the agitating farmers the new law on 'contract farming' is very problematic as it neither protects nor provides support to farmers, especially small farmers. Commonly referred to as Contract Farming

Act, 2020, the Farmers (Empowerment and Protection) Agreement on Price Assurance and Farm Services Act, 2020, is one of the key legislations passed by the Parliament. As Sukhpal Singh (2020)[12] writes, "the stated purpose of the new Acts is to create 'one nation-one market' and provide choice to farmers in selling their produce by better price 'discovery', besides attracting private investment in agricultural markets". Singh says that there is no doubt that contract farming generally benefits farmers who can undertake farming activities through this agreement, compared with selling in the existing open market (wholesale) or direct purchase channels, though it involves higher cost of production and higher investments generally. But, the exclusion of small land holders remain a key challenge as contracting agencies prefer large farmers to reduce their transaction cost, with a few exceptions in some regions and for some crops.

In the view of some of the top experts, exposing agriculture with the state not interfering in the functioning of the agricultural markets may not be a pro-farmer policy. A well-known 'people's economist', Prabhat Patnaik says that these farm laws, for the first time since Independence, would allow encroachment into agriculture by unbridled capitalism, of which, naturally, the big players, i.e. corporates and multinational agribusiness firms would be the main beneficiaries. He further says that this will bring about at least three fundamental changes:

- It would open up the country's land resources to the dictates of the world market, which means in effect the dictates of imperialism, since the superior purchasing power of the advanced countries would then determine the pattern of the of land use.
- Since in the present context the demand of the advanced countries is for tropical crops other than food grains, full-fledged commodity production would mean a diversion of land away from food grain production, i.e., a substitution of other crops and other ways of using land for food grains production, which would mean India's becoming food-import dependent in the event of domestic food demand exceeding food protection.
- As already mentioned, it would mean leaving the peasantry to the mercy of the corporates, and a loss in the economic status of the peasantry.

Patnaik further says that issues involved in the peasant protest, therefore, go far beyond this or that clause of the three Acts. They concern the very survival of the peasantry.

Going into the nitty gritty of these farm laws, one of the top experts of the rural economy and problems, P. Sainath[13] digs out some shocking details from these farm laws:

No suit, prosecution or other legal proceedings shall lie against the Central Government or the State Government, or any officer of the Central Government or the State Government or any other person in respect of anything which is in good faith done or intended to be done under this Act or of any rules or orders made there under.

Welcome to Section 13 of The Farmers' Produce Trade and Commerce (Promotion and Facilitation) Act, 2020 (the one aimed at gutting the Agriculture Produce Marketing Committees, better known as APMCs).

[12] Singh, S., Doubling farmer's Income: A Critical Review of Policy, RAS, 10:2, 2020

[13] Sainath, P, Time for Non-Farmers to Join Protests Against New Agricultural Laws, Press Trust of India, December 3, 2020

And you thought the new laws were only about farmers? Sure, there are other laws that also exclude prosecution of civil servants for carrying out their legal duties. But this one goes way over the top. The immunity given to all those *in respect of anything,* acting 'in good faith,' whatever they do, is sweeping. Not only can they not be taken to the courts for a crime they may have committed 'in good faith' – they are protected against legal action for crimes they are yet to commit ('in good faith' of course).

Just in case you missed the point – that you have no legal recourse in the courts – Section 15 rubs it in:

'No civil court shall have jurisdiction to entertain any suit or proceedings in respect of any matter, the cognisance of which can be taken and disposed of by any authority empowered by or under this Act or the rules made thereunder.'

Who is the 'any other person' doing things 'in good faith' who cannot be legally challenged? Hint: try listening to the names of corporate giants that the protesting farmers are chanting. This is about the ease of business – of very, very Big Business.

"No suit, prosecution or other legal proceedings shall lie…." It's not just farmers who cannot sue. Nobody else can, either. It applies to public interest litigation too. Nor can non-profit groups, or farm unions, or any citizen (driven by faith good or bad) intervene.

These are surely among the most sweeping exclusions of a citizen's right to legal recourse in any law outside of the Emergency of 1975–77 (when we simply suspended all fundamental rights).

The usurping of judicial power by an arbitrary executive will have profound consequences.

Every Indian is affected. Translated into English, the legal-lingo of these laws also convert the (low-level) executive into a judiciary. Into, in fact, judge, jury and executioner. It also magnifies the already most unjust imbalance of power between farmers and the giant corporations they will be dealing with."

SOCIAL IMPACT OF COVID-19 PANDEMIC

The Outbreak of pandemic disease has been a part of civilisation largely because of technological changes and their consequent impact on ecology. When COVID-19 pandemic hit the world including India, the world tried to recollect the last widespread pandemic popularly called 'Spanish Flu' considered as the most-deadly disease event in human history. It took heavy toll of life from 1918 for almost two decades and according to estimates around 100 million people died including 7–8 million from India.

The present pandemic that engulfed India too has impacted the Indian population and society in multiple ways. It has affected virtually all the social institutions of Indian society from family and kinship to economy and religion. Let us take a view of its effects on our lives.

▸▸ Family and Kinship Relations

With the promulgation of complete lockdown in March 2020, life of all sections of the society underwent changes. With the closure of schools and colleges the children were restricted within the four walls of their homes. This was a new experience for them. The school going children and adult students had never spent so much time in their homes since they started going to schools and colleges. This totally disrupted their life. The everyday routine was totally disrupted. Their privacy was gone. The constant interaction with the parents, especially mother, resulted in increased tension and the 'generation gap' which otherwise, had any how been managed was now fully exposed with all its ramifications resulting in arguments and tensions. The situation was more serious where the children did not have the luxury of an exclusive room. The grown up sons and daughters who in many cases, never participated in domestic chores were expected, and sometimes forced, to take some responsibility in the absence of domestic help.

On another level the restrictions and lack of mobility also demanded participation of husbands and grownup sons in those areas of domestic life they were not used to. They were also forced to adopt new habits.

- Most of us are now doing new things not done before.
- Those not used to cleaning their own dishes or rooms are forced to do so now.
- Those not used to working from home are now forced to do so now.
- A new division of labour in the households jolted the traditional structure of household. Cases of domestic violence increased and women in many families have to bear the brunt of it. As reported in the media a new spurt may be seen in women going for separation or divorce because of domestic violence.

Elderly persons and parents in many instances experienced a new form of neglect and discrimination. It may be summarised through the following points:

- Being mentally disturbed a number of sons showed discourtesy to their old parents
- Because of financial crunch and insecurity the necessities of the old parents were also neglected
- Sometime a silent snub was sufficient to convey the message
- The quality of food and medicines being provided deteriorated
- *Helpage India*, a well-known organisation devoted to the welfare of the old people testifies these events and incidents.
- In some cases, instances of parent beating also occurred.
- The plight of old people living alone was miserable in many instances.

The Indian society has always been known to maintain strong kinship ties and kin solidarity. COVID pandemic exposed the fragility of our kinship system. Joint families, wherever it is still being maintained, tended to behave a little differently. Nuclear families (consisting of husband, wife and unmarried children) forming the structure of joint family showed a trend of narrowness and insulation which could be described through a quote– *living together separately*, meaning that though they are living under a common roof but their lives were going in different directions. Kinship ties between first or second cousins or kinship ties based on marriage also suffered. COVID made people more selfish and self-centred.

In many instances there was total disassociation with each other to the extent that they feared to attend the last rites of close kins even in cases of death not related with corona virus or not willing to see the face of the deceased for the last time despite the fact that *antim darshan* (seeing the face for the last time) has been an established social practice.

▶▶ Neighbourhood, Racism/Ethnic Prejudices

Unlike most of the western societies, villages, towns and even smaller cities have been maintaining inter-personal and community relationship which may be viewed as extension of kinship network. COVID-19 has affected this nature of relationship adversely. Neighbours avoided each other and with just a suspicion of corona infection to any of them virtually shut their doors to even those with whom they have been maintaining good relations for years. In the case of death of any member of the family in the neighbourhood there was a stoic silence and sometime even a formal condolence was missing as if even this gesture could invite infection.

It was observed in several cities that the neighbourhood showed hostility and opposed the burial or cremation of the dead in the burial/cremation ground and the grieving members of the deceased family escorted by some policemen had to go from one place to the other to perform the last sites. Another unfortunate part of the story is the hostility shown by the neighbours to the 'corona warriors' – doctors and paramedics, who endangering their lives were fighting to save the lives of others. In many instances either these corona warriors were under threat or forced to vacate their rented premises by a hostile landlord or neighbourhood.

In metros such as Delhi and Banglore where a large number of people from north-eastern states live, the ignorant and hostile local people humiliated and threatened them believing that they were Chinese because of their mongoloid physical features. This is one of the most painful, unfortunate and tragic episodes threatening the very idea of India as a nation of diversities. In many cases several of these people from the north-east went back to their states carrying bitter memories.

When the news broke of the alleged spread of corona virus from the headquarters of the Muslim organisation *Tablighi Jamaat* near Nizamuddin in Delhi the newspapers and social media were flooded with hate mail and stories against the Muslims in general. The **Xenophobia** and stigmatisation of a whole religion and community was very unfortunate. It had its repercussions in several towns and cities where social relations of generations were disturbed and damaged. After sometime when the truth came, the hostility against the community subsided but the damage had been done and the social fabric disturbed.

Quick Fact

Xenophobia

Xenophobia is the irrational fear or hatred of people perceived as foreigners or outsiders.

▶▶ Mass Migration

It is believed that the migration from the cities to the villages pushed by the pandemic was the biggest after the partition-induced mass migration in 1947 from both sides of the border. Lakhs of people working at lower levels as workers after losing their jobs and shelter decided to leave these cities and embarked on a journey back to their towns and villages. It was a total lockdown. There was no transport-roadways or railways and thus in extreme desperation they were walking and cycling covering distances of hundreds of kilometers. Dozens of them were crushed and killed by the fast-moving vehicles on the highways. It was a pathetic scene.

Many of these migrants, after reaching their native villages had to encounter a different type of problem. The old inter-caste and inter-family tensions and disputes erupted again. Many of them got bare livelihood in the form of wages in MNREGA schemes and they survived but could not bear with the tensions and disputes described above and when the movement through roadways and railways was resumed, most of them went back to those cities. In some cases even, their employers arranged transport to bring them back.

▶▶ Economy and Employment

The pandemic jolted the economy and shook its very foundation. Millions of people lost their livelihood, production was adversely affected and the market suffered heavy losses. The impact of COVID-19 on the economy with its social implications, may be summarised through the following points:

- Reduced workforce across all economic sectors
- Joblessness on large scale, loss of employment to the low wage-earning sections such as delivery boys, cab drivers, domestic help etc. resulting in severe conditions for survival
- Large number of people had to sell their stocks or investments and used their savings such as fixed deposits, provident fund, etc.
- Decreased demand for commodities and manufactured goods
- People deferred large purchases; slump in real estate
- Panic buying and hoarding of essential commodities led to artificial shortage and pushing their prices upward.
- Decreased demand for petrol, diesel and electricity
- Hospitality sector lost heavily. Small hotels faced closure while the big ones survived with reduced workforce and reducing room tariff.
- Tourism industry was virtually shattered because even after the lockdown was relaxed the potential tourists were not willing to spend money on vacations during the prevailing uncertainty.
- Pandemic also resulted in life-style modification for a number of people
- One sector of economy that did brisk business was pharmaceutical industry. Even the relatively neglected Ayush sector flourished because of increased demand for medical supplies. Those manufacturing 'immunity boosters', sanitizers, masks etc. earned lot of money.
- Poor people, homeless, refugees and migrants are disproportionately affected
- Crushing debts and mounting bills for many

▶▶ Education

During the prolonged lock down and later people's reluctance to send their wards to schools and colleges, 'online education' was introduced. Online classes gave a big boost to the sale of tablets, laptops, desktops and even smart phones. In this scenario, the teachers had to bear the brunt of double or even triple shifts of classes to accommodate large number of students. In towns and villages, the internet is not very efficient and the power erratic, even those students who were fortunate to have these resources suffered not to speak of the less fortunate ones who did not have even a smart phone. In the areas of research, COVID-19 virtually monopolised which some scholars described as 'covidisation of economic research' while the other areas of research were neglected.

▶▶ Psychological Repercussions

The pandemic adversely affected the people not only socially and economically but also psychologically. A number of people suffered from sense of loneliness and isolation, despondency, social ostracism, physical distress along with depression. A number of people also suffered from comorbidity, social phobia and deep-rooted paranoia. In most of the hospitals, especially governmental ones, neglect of patients other than corona infected, has been a general complaint. It was a traumatic situation and there are a number of patients with PTSD (Post-Traumatic Stress Disorder). Overall, it was a severe psychological crisis.

▶▶ Social/Physical Distancing

The traditional Indian society has never been an individual oriented society but living in collectivity. There has always been a lack of privacy and people were used to take interest in each other's life, participating in all the gatherings from birth related rituals, marriage, death and post-death congregations. The fear of corona virus and the restrictions imposed by the government authorities resulted in limited number of people participating during such occasions. Moreover, maintenance of physical distance popularised as 'social distance' is a new phenomenon in Indian society. This has been alien to our culture leading to a new form of untouchability.

With the restriction imposed on congregation in places of worship and closure of these places for a long time a new form of religiosity emerged. The priest driven religiosity was replaced by a 'Good centred' and 'priest free' religiosity as most of the religious people were performing the religious rituals within their homes. Thus, we observe so many changes in our social values, cultural ethos and behavioural patterns. Now, the moot question is, will the people go back to their earlier life style or shall be continuing with several changes incorporated in their lives after the pandemic goes away?

ANTI-CAA MOVEMENT AND ITS IMPLICATIONS

The passage of Citizenship Amendment Act (CAA) passed by the parliament in December 2019 triggered the most intense and longest mass movement in recent times. This may be termed as one of the most popular movements attracting participation of millions of people across the country and may have parallels only with Nav-nirman Andolan of 1974 (JP movement), the Mandal Agitation in 1990 and Anti-Corruption Movement of 2012–14. The spontaneity and politically independent nature of the protest surprised many. It would have continued had the COVID-19 pandemic not struck the whole country.

Let us examine the crux of the matter in the protest and mass movement. The Citizenship Act, 1955 provided six different methods to acquire Indian citizenship:

- By Birth (Section 3)
- By Descent (Section 4)
- By Registration (Section 5)
- By Naturalisation (Section 6)
- Persons covered by the Assam Accord (Section 6a)
- By Incorporation of territory (Section 7)

The CAA,2019 amended the Citizenship Act,1955, by inserting the following provisions in Section 2, sub-section (1) after Clause (b):

- Provided that any person belonging to Hindu, Sikh, Buddhist, Jain, Parsi or Christian community from, Afghanistan, Bangladesh or Pakistan, who entered into India on or before 31st day of December, 2014 and who has been exempted by the Central Government by or under Clause (c) of sub-section (2) of Section 3 of the Passport (entry into India) Act, 1920 or from the application of the provisions of the Foreigners Act, 1946 or any rule or order made thereunder, shall not be treated as illegal migrant for the purposes of this Act.

A new section 6B was inserted (in the section concerning naturalisation), with four clauses, the first of which stated:

1. The central government or an authority specified by it in this behalf may, subject to such conditions, restrictions and manner as may be prescribed, on an application made in this behalf, grant a certificate of registration or certificate of naturalisation to a person referred to in the the provision to Clause (b) of sub-section (1) of Section 2.
2. The "exempted" classes of persons were previously defined in the Foreigners (Amendment) Order, 2015 (issued under the Foreigners Act, 1946).
3. A Exemption of certain class of foreigners– (1) Persons belonging to minority communities in Bangladesh and Pakistan, namely, Hindus, Sikhs, Buddhists, Jains, Parsis and Christians who were compelled to seek shelter in India due to religious persecution or fear of religious persecution and entered into India on or before 31st December 2014.
   - **(a)** Without valid documents including passport or other travel documents and who have been exempted under rule 4 from the provisions of rule 3 of the *Passport (entry into India) Rules, 1950* ; or
   - **(b)** With valid documents including passport or other travel documents and the validity of any such documents has expired, are hereby granted exemption from the application of the provisions of the Foreigners Act, 1946, and the orders made thereunder in respect of their stay in India without such documents or after the expiry of those documents, as the case may be:
     - The rules had been further amended in 2016 by adding Afghanistan to the list of countries.
     - Exemptions were granted to northeastern region of India in the Clause (4) of Section 6B:

4. Nothing in this section shall apply to tribal areas of Assam, Meghalaya, Mizoram or Tripura as included in the sixth schedule to the Constitution and the area covered under "The Inner Line" notified under the Bengal Eastern Frontier Regulation, 1873.

Moreover, under Section 5(1) (c), a person married to a citizen of India and residing in India for at least seven years has the option to apply to register as an Indian citizen. The Citizenship (Amendment) Act, 2019 (CAA) amends the Citizenship Act of 1955 to grant a faster and smoother path to Indian citizenship under the assumption of religious persecution to any person belonging to the specific minorities-Hindus, Sikhs, Buddhists, Jain, Parsis, and Christians from Pakistan, Bangladesh and Afghanistan who entered India on or before 31st December, 2014. The Act also seeks to relax the requirements of residence in India for citizenship by naturalisation from 11 years to 5 years for illegal migrants covered under the Act.

On the face of it, looks fine and in consonance with India's stand.

However, an analysis and holistic view of this unfolds several uncomfortable realities.

The CAA includes followers of all religions except Muslims. However, protests started in Assam and other states of the north-east. In these states people did not want Indian citizenship to be granted to any refugees or immigrants regardless of their religion. In their case a large number of Bengali speaking Hindus,Muslims and Buddhists from Bangladesh have been entering into these States since the Partition of the country. They feared that acceptance of Bengali Hindus, Muslims and Buddhists would alter the demographic balance and cause erosion in their political and cultural rights. They also feared that it will encourage and motivate further migration from Bangladesh that could violate Assam Accord.

The common point of criticism against the CAA is that it is exclusionary in nature and violates the spirit of the Constitution as the amendment promotes the idea of religion-based citizenship. Religious identity has never been the basis for granting citizenship. Justice A.P. Shah[14] says that "there is no legislative basis for singling out persecution of religious minorities as the basis for granting Indian citizenship. The CAA is projected as a 'fast-track' means of granting citizenship by naturalisation to what it describes 'persecuted minorities' (Hindus, Sikhs, Buddhists, Jains, Parsis and Christians) from only three neighbouring countries– Afghanistan, Bangladesh and Pakistan. Those belonging to these communities from these countries will not, as per the law, be regarded as "illegal immigrants".

The CAA gives rise to some uncomfortable questions that need to be answered:

- Why does the list of (persecuted) minorities include only from Pakistan, Bangladesh and Afghanistan?
- Why not from other neighbouring countries such as Sri Lanka, China and Myanmar despite the fact that Hindu Tamilians from Sri Lanka and Tibetan Budhists are also persecuted minorities leave aside the persecuted Muslim minorities from China and Myanmar?

[14] Shah, Justice A P, CAA violates Secularism, Basic Structure of Constitution, The Wire, 31 January, 2020

As pointed out by an eminent scholar Prof. Mamdani, whether intended or not, it makes CAA suspect behind the curtain of its benign nature. He says that the most obvious reason could be because the ruling powers in Sri Lanka, China and Myanmar are not officially Muslims and the legislation intends to present the perpetrator as Muslims, and only Muslims. In that case persecuted Muslim minorities of Pakistan namely Ahmediya and the Shia should also have been included. The persecuted Rohingya Muslims of Myanmar and the Uighur Muslims of China along with the Buddhists from Tibet also deserve our sympathy.

▸▸ CAA and Its Relationship with National Register of Citizens (NRC)

The Prime Minister and the Home Minister asserted again and again that CAA was not intended "to take away citizenship of any Indian citizen but to give citizenship to those coming from the three countries" could not give assurance and healing touch to the people of marginalised communities especially the Muslims who very apprehensive about the use of National Register of Citizens. When it was implemented in the state of Assam, lakhs of people who had been living there for several generations were excluded from it, declared 'stateless' and detained in detention centers. They were Bengali speaking Hindu and Muslims. Bharatiya Janata Party in its election manifesto promised to implement it throughout the country and the Home Minister kept emphasising that it would be implemented throughout the country to identify illegal settlers and infiltrators. The experience with Assam NRC shows that many people were declared "foreigners" because their documents were deemed 'insufficient'. This included several Muslim ex-servicemen and decorated defence personnel who had earned name in defending the motherland.

The Assam NRC fuelled apprehensions in the minds of people especially Muslims that they may also face the same fate. There was such a panic response that millions of them rushed to the municipal and other local bodies and panchayats to obtain copies of their birth certificates and land revenue records (if those owned some land). There was a general apprehension that there was a 'grand design' to declare millions of them as 'stateless' and disenfranchise them and deprive them of their democratic rights. It is an open secret that Indian Muslims have always been apprehensive of the intentions of BJP towards the minorities and there has been an uneasy relationship between BJP and Muslims-Christians.

This is true that a large number of 'Bangladeshis' are living in different parts of the country and earning their livelihood as rag pickers, sanitation workers, construction labour and in a variety of odd jobs. This also includes Bengali speaking Muslims from West Bengal and Assam. This should be an easy job to identify the people from Bangladesh and deport them. Why the entire Indian population should be targeted and disturbed because of a few lakhs of illegal immigrants from Bangladesh? The legislation itself is problematic and is compounded by the linkages with the National Register of Citizens.

▸▸ Massive and Widespread Protests

The above-mentioned reasons were largely responsible for the widespread mass protests in almost all parts of the country. Besides some Muslim organisations, a number of NGOs, Human Rights activists and students from different universities participated in this movement. This was an spontaneous non-political and non-violent movement. Those taking active part in this movement ensured that the political parties are not allowed to grab space and take advantage of this mass movement to further their political interests though almost all non-BJP political parties supported it from outside. The most salient feature of the movement is the massive mobilisation and participation of women. Perhaps, this was the first time in post-independence India that the very face of the movement was women and women participated in a movement in such large numbers. "*We the people of India.....*" became a clarion call among the participants especially students protesters. The repeated public reading of the preamble of the Constitution and display of the pictures of Mahatma Gandhi, Nehru, Patel, Azad and Ambedkar ensured that the movement did not degenerate into a sectarian one. Shaheen Bagh, a locality in Delhi inhabited by the lower middle class Muslims became the idea of India.

Questions and Indicative Answers

1. **In what way the Internet technology is impacting the Indian society?**

   Of all the technologies of communication , Internet is the latest. It has brought about a revolution in Indian society ... Quick transmission and access to hitherto distant areas of knowledge is rapidly changing the Indian society in a variety of ways.

   People becoming lonely as many of them are so heavily invested in it that they are not socializing ... Cyber crimes have become common ... Children, apart from gaining more and more information and knowledge are also getting access to undesirable channels such as pornography.

2. **What are challenges of care for the elderly population in Indian society?**

   Breakdown of joint family as a mutual support system ... Changing value system in which parental care was an integral part ... Lack of preparation on the part of the State to take care of the elderly people

3. **Explain consumerism and consumer culture and the rise of middle class in Indian society.**

   Consumerism, in the Indian context, comes with the surplus income after spending on food and housing. Consumer culture signifies the tendency to spend and consume when it is not required. After the liberalisation of economy in the 1990s, multiple new occupations emerged. Corporate sector and multinational companies offered exorbitant salaries and perks to their employees and the young generation in their 20s and 30s had money they never had before. This new middle class had a different value system.

4. **Who are sexual minorities? Discuss the implications of decriminalisation of Section 377 of Indian Penal Code.**

   LGBTQ may also be described as sexual minorities.

   In the Indian society existence of gays and lesbians was never acknowledged. With the society opening up and liberal ideas entering into it the LGBTQ gathered enough courage to stand up and fight for their rights. In big cities 'Rainbow Processions' and rallies could be seen for the first time after the Supreme Court decriminalised Section 377 of IPC

On the one hand the dominant conservative sections of the society do not like it, but the socially progressive sections support the rights of LGBTQ-the right to happiness

5. **What do you mean by 'Me too Movement'? Is it a blow to patriarchy in Indian society?**

   'Me too movement' is related to the concept of consent. Global Me-Too Movement is the first mass movement against sexual abuse.

   The entry of Me-Too movement in a highly traditional and patriarchal society like India is a whiff of fresh air because in the traditional Indian society where women are conditioned to accept gender discrimination and sexual abuse silently.

   This movement opened a door of protest and thus a big blow to the strongly patriarchal Indian society.

6. **What do you mean by 'Triple Talaaq'? Do you think that merely banning it will solve the problem?**

   'Triple Talaaq' is one of the ways of divorce among the Muslim societies ... As the very term suggests a substantial section of Muslim society accepts as legitimate pronouncement of divorce three times simultaneously. It is not permissible among all sections of Muslims. Giving its verdict in a petition filed by a divorced Muslim woman, Supreme Court legally banned it and made it criminal offence with the provision of fine and imprisonment. But failed to provide any provision for the maintenance of the divorced women and her children.

7. **What are the main causes behind the eruption of the recent farmer's movement?**

   The recent farmer's movement may be said to be the biggest ever mobilisation of farmers in Independent India – It was against the three Acts passed by the parliament in September 2020 – The farmers were of the view that these Acts were not in their interests and would lead to corporate farming

8. **How do you asses the social impact of Covid-19 pandemic on Indian society?**

   Covid-19 pandemic proved fatal for millions of Indians – It was not only a health hazard but also impacted the social, economic, cultural life of Indian people as it tried to redefine social relationships, mode of education, and employment pattern.

9. **What were the reasons behind the large-scale Anti-CAA Movement?**

   This mass movement was in response to the amendments made by the Government of India in the conditions of granting Indian citizenship to all religious communities except the Muslims – many people had the apprehension that they may be deprived of Indian citizenship if followed by National Population Register. Moreover, when persecuted minorities – Hindus, Sikhs, Christians, Buddhists-of Pakistan, Afghanistan, and Bangladesh were covered by this amendment, why the persecuted Tamil Hindi Minority of Sri Lanka was left out? Was it just to show that religious persecution takes place only in Muslim majority countries?

10. **What do you mean by ethnicity? Examine the ethnic conflicts in the north-eastern region of India.**

    See the formal definition and explanation of ethnicity – India's northeastern region had been geographically closed for a long time giving rise to multiple ethnicities with their exclusive regions – After independence two types of separatism erupted – some of the ethnic groups demanded internal autonomy within Indian Union while the Nagas and the Mizos wanted to have independent sovereign states.

Previous Years' Questions

1. Discuss the problems of elderly in India. What are the different perspectives to solve their problems? **(UPSC CSE Mains Sociology, Paper II, 2015)**
2. Discuss the issues relating to the entitlement of transgender in Indian Society. **(UPSC CSE Mains Sociology, Paper II, 2018)**
3. Elaborate the 'MeToo' movement and its impact on India. **(UPSC CSE Mains Sociology, Paper II, 2018)**
4. Assess the impact of ban on 'Triple Talak' on marriage and divorce among the Muslim community in India. **(UPSC CSE Mains Sociology, Paper II, 2018)**
5. What do you understand by LGBTQ? Comment on the issues concerning their marriage rights. **(UPSC CSE Mains Sociology, Paper II, 2019)**
6. Covid-19 pandemic accelerated class inequalities and poverty in India. Comment. **(GS Mains Paper I, 2020)**
7. Is 'ageing' an emerging issue in Indian society? Discuss the major problems of old age people in India. **(UPSC CSE Mains Sociology, Paper II, 2021)**
8. Child cuddling is now being replaced by mobile phones. Discuss its impact on the socialization of children. **(GS Mains Paper I, 2023)**

Focus Areas for the Examination

1. LGBTQ in Indian Society
2. Social impact of Internet
3. Ageing and the aged in Indian Society

CHAPTER 17

Concepts Used

Chapter Outline

1. The significance and application of foundational terms such as globalisation, postmodernism, ethnicity, and diaspora
2. Evaluating how globalisation affects economies, cultures, and societies
3. Understanding the role of ethnicity and analysing the factors that define ethnic identity
4. Investigating the experiences of diasporic communities, their cultural persistence, and their contributions to host and origin countries
5. Exploring Civil Society and its Importance while learning the differences between acknowledging diversity (pluralism) and advocating for equality and integration of minority groups (multiculturalism)
6. Examining the Rural-Urban Continuum and address Social Exclusion
7. Connecting sociological concepts to practical issues
8. Exploring the challenges and opportunities posed by modernisation, urbanisation, and technological advancements in shaping social structures

Some important basic concepts being used to describe and analyse different social, cultural, economic and political situations come from social science discourse, but have also been used effectively in our day-to-day life. Most of these are used in the analysis of postcolonial situations in different parts of the world, including India, in different contexts and situations. These are fit to be used in Indian society that is highly stratified, and demonstrate glaring social inequalities.

GLOBALISATION

'Globalisation' has emerged as one of the most important and talked about phenomena of the present age with its social, economic and political dimensions. According to The Blackwell Dictionary of Sociology, globalisation is a process, where social life within societies becomes increasingly influenced by international factors, including political and trade connections, as well as shared cultural elements like music, fashion, and mass media. Perhaps, the most powerful form of globalisation is economic, in which planning and control expand from a relatively narrow focus – such as a single firm doing business on a regional or national basis – to a broad global focus in which the entire world serves as a source of labour, raw materials and markets. When business is conducted on a local level, for example, problems of dealing with workers, obtaining raw materials and other goods, transportation and selling the final product all take place within the same social framework. In a globalised economy, however, transnational corporations operate in many different countries at once and exploit variations in local conditions to their own advantage. If workers in a more affluent industrial society such as Britain or the United States, for example, go on strike in order to improve pay or working conditions, a transnational corporation can simply shift work to another country where workers are more compliant and have lower expectations.

Analysing the necessity of international economic and sociopolitical management in the face of globalisation, Samir Amin (1997), a renowned and strong voice on the issue of globalisation and its implications for Third World countries, says that the globalisation of the capitalist system is certainly nothing new, but it has undeniably taken a qualitative step forward during the most recent period. Moreover, this deepening economic interdependence between nations occurs at a time when there is a crisis of accumulation and the post-war boom has given way to stagnation. The advance of globalisation has not been confined to trade; it also affects productive systems, technology, financial markets and many other aspects of social life. The new globalisation erodes the efficiency of economic management by nation-states, though it does not abolish their existence.

Rise of ethnicity as a political response to economic globalisation is yet another important dimension of globalisation. Samir Amin[1] (ibid) says that the

> Present epoch is surely characterised by an awakening or reawakening, marked by collective social identifications which are starkly different from those defined by membership of a nation-state or a social class.

In Africa, the dissolution of national unity sometimes seems to have given way to ethnicity as a basis for the legitimate renewal of competing forces. In India, Afghanistan, Eastern Europe, the former Soviet Union and the former Yugoslavia, even in Western Europe and in Spain, national unity has come into question. When we take a close look at the thesis put forward by the advanced and dominant countries and the system in support of globalisation, we find that the management of the political and social systems by the single virtue of the market is a utopia. Concerned at the rise of ethnicity and religious fundamentalism in Third World countries, Samir Amin (ibid) puts forward an alternative agenda of action – the question of ethnicity should be replaced in the strategic framework by an action one can sum up thus: respect diversity, unite in spite of it. Respecting diversity means renouncing the empty discourse of power which pretends to act 'in the national interest' (which this power more often than not betrays) by pretending to interiorise the ideology of the nation-state. The rise of *Hindutva* forces in India pretending to be 'nationalist', but in fact opposed to pluralism and consequently anti-minority in nature, the emergence of Muslim fundamentalism in Pakistan, Bangladesh and some Arab nation-states exhibiting similar trends has been strengthened by the process of globalisation.

The passive acceptance of the inevitability of globalisation in its present polarising form, that is equation of development with the expansion of the market, should be fought. Each society should be allowed to negotiate the terms of its interdependence with the rest of the global economy.

---

[1] Amin, Samir, Capitalism in the Age of Globalization, Bloomsbury Academic, 1997

National development can be pursued in a pluralistic world. The very goal of homogeneity may also be divisive, especially in the case of the pluralistic Third World countries.

Ethnic violence of the worst type is an alarming trend in the face of globalisation. Arjun Appadurai[2] (2001), in a UNESCO-sponsored study on keys to the 21st century, puts forward a thought-provoking agenda of action.

> There should be a concerted effort to delink ethnicity from citizenship: State policies should be developed to move away from monoethnic and majoritarian forms of citizenship to forms of citizenship that are dual, serial and multiple, so as to accommodate a world of growing hybridity and diversity in cultural identities.

POSTMODERNISM

Like globalisation, 'postmodernism' too has emerged as an omnipresent phenomenon present in every discourse concerning human society today. There is hardly a single field of intellectual activity which has not been touched by the spectre of postmodernism. From architecture to zoology, forestry, geography and from law to history, literature, arts, medicine, politics, philosophy and sexuality, it has not left any field untouched. The term was probably first used by Arnold Toynbee, the great British historian, in 1939 in his monumental work, *A Study of History*. In this work, he suggested that the modern period ends more or less in the third quarter of the 19th century – that is, sometime between 1850 and 1875. This suggests that there is from that moment a kind of break into a period 'after modernism', a postmodernity located not in the 20th century, but rather in the 19th. By the time he wrote volume V of this work published in 1939, he used the term 'postmodern'. At this point, he had shifted the chronology a bit, suggesting that the modern now comes to an end during the First World War, 1914–1918 and the postmodern begins to articulate and shape itself in the years between the two wars, between 1918 and 1939. But, the term 'postmodern', from its very inception, is characterised by an ambiguity.

Marvin Harris[3] (1999), while elaborating postmodernism, displays a high degree of clarity. According to him

> Post-modernism is an intellectual movement or orientation that promotes itself as the anti-thesis of modernism. The term itself was introduced by architects in the late 1940s. While the themes of post-modernism actually originated long before anyone started to design post-modern buildings.

Extending the elaboration further, he identified the disparagement of western science and technology as the most prominent intellectual strand. Other strands that follow from this central tenet include:

(i) The representation of social life as a 'text';
(ii) The elevation of text and language as the fundamental phenomenon of existence;
(iii) The application of literary analysis to all phenomena;

[2] Appadurai, Arjun, Globalization, Duke University Press, 2001
[3] Harris, Marvin, Theories of Culture in Postmodern Times, AltaMira Press, 1999

(iv) The questioning of reality and of the adequacy of language to describe reality;
(v) Disdain for, or rejection of, method;
(vi) Rejection of broad theories or metanarratives;
(vii) Advocacy of polyvocality;
(viii) Focus on power relations and **cultural hegemony**;
(ix) Rejection of Western institutions and achievements; and
(x) Extreme relativism and tendency towards **nihilism**.

> **Quick Fact**
>
> **Cultural Hegemony**
>
> It refers to the dominance of one group's cultural values, beliefs, and norms over others, shaping societal consensus and maintaining power structures.
>
> **Nihilism**
>
> **Nihilism** is the philosophical belief that life lacks inherent meaning, purpose, or value, often rejecting established moral and societal norms.

The concept of postmodernity belongs in social thought because it alerts us to some tremendously important social as well as cultural shifts taking place at the end of the 20th century. In order to understand the main currents of postmodern thought, it helps to step back and interrogate those thinkers who anticipated postmodernity. Undoubtedly, the single most significant figure is Friedrich Nietzsche. He announced that 'nihilism stands at the door'. Nietzsche achieved notoriety for proclaiming the 'death of God'. His slogan, 'the death of God', means that we can no longer be sure of anything. Morality is a lie, truth is fiction. While these lies may seem abstract, a generation before Nietzsche, Karl Marx viewed the same process in a much more mundane light. What Nietzsche saw as 'a predicament for science, rationality and metaphysics', Marx attributed to the 'banal everyday workings of the bourgeois economic order'. In other words, under capitalism, people allow the market to organise life, including our inner lives. By equating everything with its market value – commodifying – we end up seeking answers to questions about what is worthwhile, honourable and even real, in the marketplace. Nihilism can also be understood in this practical, everyday sense.

David Lyon[4] (2002) taking a refreshing look at postmodernity says that big questions remain unanswered.

> The post-modern may refer to the exhaustion of modernity, but does this invite obituaries or merely a call to make a room for a fresh appraisal of modernity? Is logocentrism dead or dormant?

ETHNICITY

The intellectual history of the term 'ethnicity' is relatively short: prior to the 1970s, there was little mention of it in anthropological literature and textbooks contained no definition of the term. Since the mid-1970s, the concept has acquired strategic significance within anthropological theory partly as a response to the changing postcolonial geopolitics and the rise of ethnic minorities' activism in many industrial states. This has resulted in a proliferation of theories of ethnicity, explaining such diverse phenomena as social and political change, identity formation, social conflict, race relations, nation-building, assimilation, etc.

[4] Lyon, David, Surveillance as Social Sorting, Routledge, 2002

Among a variety of definitions, the most generalised one may be as given in 'The Blackwell Dictionary of Sociology' (1995), which describes ethnicity as a concept referring to a shared culture and way of life, especially as reflected in language, folkways, religious and other institutional forms, material culture such as clothing and food and cultural products such as music, literature and art. 'The collection of people who share an ethnicity is often called an ethnic group, although technically the use of 'group' is inappropriate in sociological usage because a group is a social system with some degree of regular interaction among its members.' An ethnicity, however, typically includes far too many people for regular interaction. "Etymologically speaking, the term 'ethnic', derived from the Greek word 'ethnikos', refers to: (a) nations or peoples not converted to Christianity; (b) races or large groups of people having common traits and customs; or (c) groups in an exotic primitive culture." But, in sociological-anthropological parlance, an ethnic group can be defined as a historically formed aggregate of people having a real or imaginary association with a specific territory, a shared cluster of beliefs and values connoting its distinctiveness in relation to similar groups and recognised as such by others The definition thus has five components:

(i) a subjective belief in real or assumed historical antecedents;
(ii) a symbolic or real geographical centre;
(iii) shared cultural emblems, such as race, language, religion, dress and diet or a combination of some of them which, though variegated and flexible, provide the overt basis of ethnic identity;
(iv) self-ascribed awareness of distinctiveness and belonging to the group; and
(v) recognition by others of group differentiation. It is thus a self-defined and 'other-recognised' status.

Barth (1969) says that an ethnic group refers to that population which (a) is largely biologically self-perpetuating; (b) shares fundamental cultural values realised in overt unity in cultural forms; (c) makes up a field of communication and interaction; and (d) has a membership which identified itself and is identified of others as constituting a category distinguishable from other categories of the same order. While race is a biological concept, culture is purely social in nature.

By concentrating on what is *socially* effective, ethnic groups are seen as a form of social organisation. There are three competing approaches to the understanding of ethnicity. They could be roughly categorised as

(i) Primordialist
(ii) Instrumentalist
(iii) Constructivist

Sergey Sokolovski and Valeny Tishkov (1996) commenting on these three approaches say that primordialist theories assert that ethnic identification is based on deep, 'primordial' attachment to a group or culture; instrumentalist approaches treat ethnicity as a political instrument exploited by leaders and others in pragmatic pursuit of their own interests; and constructivist approaches emphasise the contingency and fluidity of ethnic identity, treating it as something which is made in specific social and historical contexts, rather than (as in primordialist arguments) treating it as a 'given'.

Furthermore, if we take a close look at these three approaches, we find that the primordialist view asserts that ultimately there is some real, tangible foundation to ethnic identification. It accepts that ethnicity should be viewed as a predominantly biological phenomenon closely related to culture and history. Pierre Lvan den Berghe (1981), an exponent of this approach, has explored the contribution of sociobiology to the explanation of ethnic phenomena and suggests that these are rooted in a genetic predisposition for kin selection or 'nepotism', which in the long run leads to primordial loyalties. Clifford Geertz is also a known exponent of this view who conceives ethnicity as an inchoate, but powerful characteristic of human life. To him, these congruities of blood, speech, custom and so on are seen to have an ineffable and, at times, overpowering coerciveness in themselves.

Unlike the primordialists, the instrumentalists define ethnicity "as an instrument for the pursuit of material interests by competing cultural groups within complex societies" (Jean Popeau, 1998).[5] The extreme stand, taken by some instrumentalists, conceives of ethnicity objectives in the contemporary world and therefore needs no historical or cultural explanations. Sergey Sokolovski and Valeny Tishkov (ibid) stretching this point further say that for instrumentalists, claims to ethnicity are a product of political myths, created and manipulated by cultural elites in their pursuit of advantage and power. The cultural forms, values and practices of ethnic groups become resources for elites in competition for political power and economic advantage. They become symbols and referents for the identification of members of a group, which are called up in order to ease the creation of a political identity. Thus, ethnicity is created in the dynamics of elite competition within the boundaries determined by political and economic realities.

The constructivist approach found the first voice in a seminal contribution of Fredrik Barth and his colleagues titled as 'Ethnic Groups and Boundaries' (1969). They treated ethnicity as a continuing ascription which classifies a person in terms of their general and inclusive identity, presumptively determined by origin and background, as well as a form of social organisation maintained by intergroup boundary mechanisms.

Besides the three approaches described above, sociologists refer to some more approaches such as Marxist and Neo-Marxist approach and Weberian approach. For the former, ethnic conflict emerges at two levels: (i) at a general level in which ethnicity is viewed as a device detracting from the consciousness of class interests and (ii) in a situation where there has been a 'cultural division of labour', when members of an ethnic group are placed in a subordinate position within a given state (internal colonialism) or in the global context (international division of labour). For them, ethnic relations are antithetical to the development of class solidarity. Mobilisation on an ethnic basis evokes false consciousness. It weakens class solidarity. In the latter approach, ethnicity does not constitute a group; it only facilitates group formation of any kind, particularly in the political sphere.

As Sergey Sokolovski and Valery Tishkov (ibid) rightly point out, all approaches to understanding ethnicity are not necessarily mutually exclusive, so one possible avenue of research is the integration of the soundest aspects of existing approaches into a coherent theory of ethnicity. There are

[5] Popeau, Jean, Core Sociological Dichotomies, Sage Publications, 1998

reasons to believe that a constructivist conceptualisation could serve as the nucleus of such a synthesis. Another direction for ethnicity research is the assimilation of relevant knowledge from other social sciences.

DIASPORA

Diaspora is another new field of study in sociology and social-cultural anthropology. Derived from a root word from Greek, it means dispersion or scattering. In sociological-anthropological literature, it refers to dispersion or scattering of a population to far-off places. This term was initially used in the context of exile of the Jews to different parts of the world explaining the protracted exile of the Jewish people and cultural contacts with different regions and populations, cultures, philosophies and ways of life. Richard Marienstrasse (1989) says that this interpretation is somewhat metaphorical. It will be understood that the idea of diaspora implies or may be held to imply the idea of 'centre' and 'periphery'; the idea of a relationship or lack of relationship to the soil and the territory; the ideas of 'majority' and 'minority'. But, it is only recently that this term has come to describe minority groups whose awareness of their identity is defined by a relationship, territorially discontinuous, with a group settled 'elsewhere' (e.g. the Chinese diaspora, the Indian diaspora, etc.).

Quick Fact

Diaspora

The dispersion of people from their homeland to multiple regions, maintaining cultural identity and connections to their origin.

The diasporic community may be occupying an ambiguous status of being both an ambassador and a refugee.

> Further, categories emerge, through the use of such words as immigrant, exile, refugee. Their use attempts to give some indication of the ideologies, choices, reasons and compulsions which may have governed the act of migration. (Jaabir Jain, 1998)[6]

Right from its very inception, there has been a search for a theoretical framework to integrate this area of study. Ravindra K. Jain, in his seminal volume 'Indian Communities Abroad' (1993) provides an important discussion on several frameworks to deal with cultural persistence. This is the retentionist view of Indian culture overseas and the studies falling under this category have recorded the ability of Indians to retain, reconstitute and revitalise many aspects of their culture in an overseas setting. One of the best examples of this perspective is Morton Mass's (1961) study of East Indians in Trinidad. Studies of cultural persistence fall under the general rubric of acculturation processes. The second perspective is purely and simply an adaptationist one. Studies falling under this category are chiefly concerned with the question of the adaptation of the social group or an immigrant society into the social environment of the host society. R.K. Jain's (1970) work on South Indian migrants in a typical Malaysian setting is a study of the process of adaptation of the people of Indian origin to conditions of life and work in a particular Malayan environment, namely rubber plantation. The third perspective is that of the plural society, first advocated by Furnivall (1948) in the context of colonial society of Southeast Asia.

[6] Jain, Jaabir, Writers of Indian Diaspora, Rawat Publications, Jaipur, 1998

According to him, this kind of society possessed three characteristics – cultural, economic and political. Culturally, a plural society consists of incongruous and incompatible cultural sections between which communication is hampered. Economically, the relationships between the cultural sections are those of the marketplace. Politically, this kind of plural society is held together only by the fact of being dominated by an external colonial power. R.K. Jain has argued (1986) that the concept of plural society in the sense used by Furnivall is applicable only to 'settlement societies' and not to civilisations.

With the globalisation of ethnicity as the postmodernist phenomenon of our times, diaspora studies have assumed further importance. From an Indian angle, such studies are of immense importance in assessing not only the implantation of Indian society and culture in all parts of the world, but also the economic and symbolic capital which non-resident Indians may contribute to the development of India. From a purely academic point of view, the Indian diaspora is one of the most varied, representing several religions, regions and castes.

CIVIL SOCIETY

'Civil society' is one of the most used and abused concepts in current sociopolitical thinking. Civil society (from the Latin *Sociatas civilis*) is not a new concept. It entered European discourse in the 15th century. Contrary to modern use, it did not denote a natural or pre-state type of society. The concept of civil society, though highly popular and much revived in recent years, remains intensely contested and debated. As Susanne Rudolph (2000) rightly points out, civil society is defined variously by different theorists, but a minimal definition would include:

- **(i)** the idea of a non-state autonomous sphere;
- **(ii)** empowerment of citizens;
- **(iii)** trust building associational life; and
- **(iv)** interaction with, rather than subordination to, the state.

Moreover, according to conventional notions prevalent in the social sciences, civil society refers to the space in a given society that

- **(i)** exists between the family level and the state level;
- **(ii)** makes inter-connection between individuals and families; and
- **(iii)** is independent of the state.

Elaborating it further, Ashutosh Varshney (2002) says that many, though not all, of the existing definitions also suggest two more requirements: that the civic space be organised in associations that attend to the cultural, social, economic and political needs of the citizens and that the associations be modern and voluntaristic, not ascriptive.

Going by the first requirement, trade unions would be part of civil society, but informal neighbourhood associations would not. The modernity of civil society is, of course, qualified since not all modern political systems have civil societies. In the opinion of a number of scholars of 'civil society', the communist polities were not civil society (though it has generated lot of debate) despite the fact that they were modern, attacked ascriptive statuses, hierarchies and privileges, undermined religion and instituted a secular order. This was largely because the state penetrated all sites of organisational life: hospitals, universities, theatre and literary societies. The idea of associationalism is central to the concept of civil society. Associations empower citizens, each of whom, in isolation, could not confront the state as agent and participant, not create consequences within society.

Hegel is the pivotal figure in shaping contemporary understanding of the idea of civil society. Hegel's question concerned the possibility of creating and sustaining a community under modern conditions. It was in response to this problem that he introduced the distinction between 'state' and 'civil society'. His solution tries to integrate the individual freedoms specified by the natural law tradition (from Hobbes to Rousseau and Kant) with a rich vision of community, existing under conditions of modern exchange.

As Joseph Femia[7] (2002) points out, modernity was crucial to the development of the concept of civil society.

> Customary models of authority were progressively undermined by the commercialisation of land, labour and capital; by the growth of the market economy; by great scientific discoveries, such as the Copernican system; and by the Protest Reformation.

When we look at the ramifications of civil society with reference to India, we may at once refer to the much-acclaimed work of Ashutosh Varshney on ethnic conflict and civic life in the context of Hindu–Muslim relations. He calls for the strengthening of civil society and integrated civic networks. Towns where Hindus and Muslims continue to be integrated in business, political parties unions, professional associations of lawyers, teachers, doctors, students and clubs; riots remain either absent or rare despite the attempts by vested interests. "An integrated organisational and civic life makes the state behave better than intellectual and political exhortations that it do so" (ibid). It follows that citizen action in India has to take two forms: (a) while continuing to pressure the state of its dereliction of constitutional duty, it should (b) focus on building integrated civic structures. The first has been the primary strategy for citizen action in India so far (of course by concerned citizens). Such action is necessary, but not sufficient. Varshney then proceeds to conclude by saying that citizen initiatives should follow a two-track strategy, combining (a) and (b). The state, otherwise, will continue to get away with its utter misconduct and gross disrespect for human lives as we witnessed in the post-Godhra, anti-minority violence in Gujarat in 2002. Civil society, which by and large, tends to be local or regional, is the missing variable in available theories, to which researchers of ethnic conflict should pay increasing attention. Associational civic engagement is necessary for peace in inter-ethnic urban settings.

MULTICULTURALISM

'Multicultural' and 'multiculturalism' are words frequently used to describe the ethnic diversity that exists everywhere in the world today. However, there is some confusion about what precisely they signify. Do they simply describe diversity or are they advocating particular response to that diversity? We must be very clear as to why multiculturalism has overtaken pluralism as the dominant concept. Cultural pluralism is not a modern phenomenon. History provides many examples

[7] Femia, Joseph, Machiavelli Revisited, University of Wales Press, 2002

of different communities and cultures existing side by side within the same society, co-existing peacefully and many times amicably. Cultural plurality, thus, has been a hallmark of many societies for a long time.

This is a very useful concept to understand and analyse the social situation in countries of diversity. It has been fashionable to describe Indian society in terms of pluralism – social-cultural, linguistic, religious, environmental and racial/ethnic.

Thus, pluralism is merely an acknowledgement of diversity. Multiculturalism is a step forward. It denotes not only the acknowledgement of diversity, but also recognition of the contribution of various groups to the various spheres of life and it also demands their special protection under the law. Several such minority groups even in modern democracies suffer discrimination, oppression, exclusion and marginalisation in different ways and in varying degrees. Multiculturalism calls for not only protection of interests of such minority groups, but also equal share in power structure. Their contributions are not only to be recognised, but should also not be denigrated. Their identities are also to be respected and not to be mocked at as different from the dominant population. Many minority groups around the world, including those in India, have been facing these problems.

What Do You Think?

How can societies promote true multiculturalism that celebrates diversity while fostering a shared sense of identity and belonging?

Multiculturalism does not support cultural assimilation into the dominant majority, but a respectful integration so that they may feel to be an integral part of the larger society. Thus, intentional homogenisation is not considered desirable. Multiculturalism looks at the society with diversity, not as a 'melting pot', but as a 'salad bowl' or 'cultural mosaic'. Some of the theorists are firmly of the view that minority cultural groups should not only enjoy equal rights, but also special group rights. It requires the majority dominant population to be educated and trained to not only accept it, but also advocate for it whenever they come across any deviance or departure from this desired goal. This leads to an ideology in which no specific or particular community values may be treated as 'central' including the dominant groups. Now if we look at the Indian society, we are constrained to conclude that although the Indian Constitution goes near the ideals of multiculturalism, the Indian society, in practice, cannot be described as multicultural. At the most, it may be said that it is a plural society trying to be multicultural. The present status of Dalits, tribal communities and religious and linguistic minorities bear testimony to this conclusion.

Multiculturalism as a coherent theory, with its distinct conception of democracy and citizenship, has emerged only in the recent past. As Gurpreet Mahajan[8] (2002) points out

> The simultaneous presence of many cultures and communities within the same social space points to a plural social fabric, but it does not betoken the presence of multiculturalism. The latter entails something more than the mere presence of different communities or the attitude of tolerance in society. Multiculturalism is concerned with the issue of equality

[8] Mahajan, Gurpreet, The Multicultural Path, Sage Publication, 2002

Thus, it is this emphasis on equality that distinguishes multiculturalism from pluralism. Within the framework of plurality, the major concern is peaceful coexistence and amity. Pluralism, in other words, indicates the presence of differences and marks a departure from policies aimed at annihilating the other, but that is all. It remains silent about the public status of these communities.

The multicultural condition, like the condition of postmodernity, cannot be reductively defined. Rather, it can be described phenomenologically. David Theo Goldberg,[9] in his seminal work *Multiculturalism: A Critical Reader*, writes

> Multiculturalism stands for a wide range of social articulations – ideas and practices that the '-ism' reduces to a formal singularity, fixing it into a cemented condition, the ideology of 'political correctness'.

Multiculturalism has a history. One needs to be clear about monocultural commitments to which multiculturalism arose in response. The term multiculturalism has come to be used primarily in connection with demands on behalf of black and other minority groups for equal representation in the United States.

Unlike multiculturalism, pluralism and tolerance often become most apparent when one community's dominance is clearly acknowledged. The dominant community asserts its supremacy by prominently displaying its symbols in public spaces, and any challenge to these symbols is perceived as rebellion, met with strong resistance. In India, sixth century A.D. onwards, rulers demonstrated their authority by replacing local deities' idols with those of their own gods.

In contrast, multiculturalism makes a value statement. It asserts that the many cultural communities that are present in our society must live as equals in the public domain. Multiculturalism thus speaks of issues that are central to democracy and egalitarianism. Any discussion on multiculturalism should take place along with an assessment of its core agenda. In the case of India, it has always been characterised by pluralism or cultural mosaic, but the post-independent Indian polity based on its constitution is trying to reach the ideal of multiculturalism. Anthropologists have been 'reluctant' students of multiculturalism. As Terence Turner[10] rightly points out

> There are a number of ways that anthropologists could contribute constructively and critically to multiculturalist thinking and practice and a number of ways also that they might expand their own theoretical and practical horizons by doing so.

RURAL–URBAN CONTINUUM

Discussing the distinctiveness and difference between a village and city or rural and urban has been an old pastime of a number of scholars of human and settlement geography, anthropology and sociology. The concept of 'continuum' in the present context was first developed by the cultural anthropologist Robert Redfield in the wake of his study of the Mexican rural society, 'Folk Culture of Yucatan' (1941).

[9] Goldberg, David, Theo Multiculturalism: A Critical Reader, Wiley-Blackwell, 1995

[10] Turner, Terence, Anthropology and Multiculturalism, Cultural Anthropology, Vol. 8, No. 4, 1993

Let us first look at the literal meaning of the term continuum. It is anything that goes through a gradual transition from one condition to a different condition without any abrupt changes. This may also be a continuous sequence in which adjacent elements are not perceptibly different from each other, although the extremes are quite different. The underlying idea obviously is about continuity. Thus, in this context, the process of continuity between rural and urban societies is being sought to be understood. A civilisation consists of both rural and urban societies. A village of today gets transformed into a town and city. Thus, it is not a total break in culture and traditions. Though one may find a strong distinction between rural and urban in terms of occupation, environmental factors, size of the community, density of population, pace of social mobility or change, migration pattern, social stratification, level of literacy or education and systems of interaction between people (including levels of anonymity). When Robert Redfield was studying Yucatan people, he encountered the problem of differentiating between folk culture and urban culture. He noticed that beyond a point, folk culture (beliefs, social practices, values, etc.) and urban culture were merging with each other and thus he found it impossible to tell where the folk culture comes to an end and the urban culture began. Then he concluded that both of these should not be considered as two totally disjointed, independent and separate entities. Rather it would be prudent and logical to treat both in terms of continuum.

What Do You Think?

How can we bridge the rural–urban divide while preserving the unique cultural and social identities of rural communities in the face of urbanisation?

Thus, we find that it is almost impossible to draw a clean and sharp line of demarcation between rural and urban culture and society. There is always some overlapping and commonality between the two. Every rural society possesses some elements of urban society and every urban society carries some elements of rural society. In most of the cases, urban people maintain an attitude of superiority by describing the rural as 'rustic', superstitious, crude, unsophisticated and lacking refinement. This superiority in terms of technology may be true, but in terms of beliefs, faith and rituals, the urban population exhibits the same amount of 'superstition' and sometime even more. Are urban people rationalists par excellence? Moreover, in the process of urbanisation and expansion of city limits, one may come across villages in the city and city in the villages. Thus, the phenomenon of 'urban peasants' is not a rare thing. Moreover, the concept of 'Rurban' may also be applied in this situation. In every civilisation, there is a process of cultural continuity that is largely responsible for the justification of the concepts such as **rural–urban continuum**. The advent of the cell phone (now smartphone) is providing more connectivity, automobiles such as bikes more mobility, cheaper and accessible college education (even of indifferent quality) more social equality and caste anonymity in their own ways further strengthening the continuum in Indian society.

Quick Fact

Rural–Urban Continuum

A concept describing the gradual transition and interconnectedness between rural and urban societies in terms of culture, economy, and social structures.

SOCIAL EXCLUSION

Social exclusion is the denial of equal opportunities imposed on some people or groups, which leads to inability of an individual or group of people to participate in basic social, economic and political functioning of the society. In this context, individuals or entire groups or communities are systematically blocked from various rights, opportunities and resources which are normally available to others. When certain groups are systematically disadvantaged because they are discriminated against on the basis of their race/ethnicity, religion, caste, descent and sexual orientation, their social integration with the larger society also suffers. Social exclusion is multidimensional; discrimination occurs in public institutions such as education, health services, employment as well as in day-to-day social life such as denial of housing, shop, office in private spaces. It encompasses social, cultural, economic and political dimensions.

The latest edition of 'Social Science Encyclopedia' says it is flexible and somewhat amorphous in use, yet its core features which separate it from marginalisation and poverty are:

(a) It is multidimensional.

(b) It is conceived as a social, not an individual, problem.

(c) It is regarded not as a particular local problem, but as a development that has global roots.

(d) It suggests the imperative of inclusion.

Social inclusion is the opposite of social exclusion. It is affirmative action to change the circumstances that lead to social exclusion. In the Indian context, the Scheduled Castes and the Scheduled Tribes and to a lesser extent the other backward classes and religious minorities, especially Muslims, may be included in the segment of population suffering from social exclusion in varying degrees. The lesbian, gay, bisexual and transgender and queer (LGBTQ) community is another such category of people. Sometimes the exclusion becomes doubly sharper as in the case of Dalit women who have to suffer on both counts – being Dalit as well as women. Thus, the Dalit women's deprivation and exclusion is further compounded by caste as well as gender.

EMPOWERMENT

The concept of empowerment and other related concepts and ideas such as social empowerment, disadvantaged groups, vulnerable groups and weaker sections has never been more in vogue in the analysis of society, including Indian society, than in the present post-independence period. Empowerment, in general terms, is the process designed to increase the degree of autonomy and self-determination in the lives of people in order to enable them to represent and protect their interests, to overcome their sense of powerlessness and to use their resources and chances. Empowerment has emerged as a key concept for all weaker sections of the society. Obviously, the disempowered or those lacking power in comparison with others need empowerment. In the Indian context, empowerment is the key requirement for Dalits, Adivasi (tribal) communities, women, minorities and any others lacking power and facing discrimination in a variety of ways.

Women's empowerment is now a central concern of the women's movement. It also includes acquiring knowledge of the structures that oppress them and to seek to alter the power imbalance in society.

Social empowerment is largely understood as a process of accessing opportunities and resources in order to make personal choices such as what to eat, wear, where and how to live, etc.

Being disadvantaged and vulnerable are the other key ideas. Disadvantage means an unfavourable circumstance or condition that reduces the chances of success or effectiveness. Thus, a disadvantaged group may be defined by a denial or lack of accessibility to resources and barriers it faces. Overcoming disadvantagement means overcoming or removing barriers to self-sufficiency. A disadvantaged group becomes vulnerable or susceptible to exploitation because of disempowerment and unfavourable conditions. For instance, all the weaker sections mentioned above may also be described as vulnerable groups and also recognised as such by the Government of India. Thus, vulnerability – social, economic or political – shall lead to social exclusion and exploitation.

Questions and Indicative Answers

1. **What are the key causes of social exclusion, and how can it be addressed in contemporary societies?**

   Explain the key causes of social exclusion in points like Economic Inequality, Discrimination, Gaps in Education, Political Marginalisation, Cultural Barriers etc.

   Next, how to address it. Explain the means and ways like Policy Reforms, Empowerment Programs, Anti-Discrimination Laws, Community Initiatives etc.

2. **Evaluate the impact of postmodernism on contemporary cultural practices and media.**

   Explain Postmodernism and how it significantly impacts cultural practices and media – fostering diversity, innovation, and critical engagement while also raising concerns about authenticity and consumerism.

   Impact includes Relativism, Consumerism and media saturation, hyper reality, fragmentation etc. Explain point wise.

3. **How does the rural–urban continuum challenge the traditional rural–urban dichotomy?**

   Start introduction with defining the rural–urban dichotomy and then explain the rural–urban continuum. Then explain the challenges of Dichotomy one by one like Economic Interdependence, Mixed Lifestyle, Peri Urban Areas, Technology and Connectivity, Cultural Blending, Policy and Governance Implications etc.

   Conclude with the interconnected nature of rural and urban areas and emphasize the need for frameworks that address the continuum to promote balanced development.

Previous Years' Questions

1. Discuss the phenomenon of rural-urban continuum with suitable examples.
(UPSC CSE Mains Sociology, Paper II, 2023)

Focus Areas for the Examinations

1. Ethnicity
2. Post modernism
3. Social Exclusion
4. Concept of Globalisation

CHAPTER 18

Changing Indian Society: Social Change in Modern India

Chapter Outline

1. Understanding the concept of Social Change
2. Analysing how modernisation, intertwined with industrialisation and urbanisation, has reshaped India's societal norms while preserving cultural roots
3. Understanding how secularisation has evolved, fostering rational, non-religious perspectives in addressing social, political, and economic issues
4. Examining the Role of Democratisation in India, including universal franchise, minority representation, and the diminishing influence of traditional hierarchies
5. Investigating the Middle Class and Elite Structures, analysing their roles in driving social and economic change
6. Identifying the Agents of Social Change to evaluate the impact of education, mass media, and communication in transforming societal values, increasing awareness, and promoting equity

Social change is any alteration in the cultural, structural, population or ecological characteristics of a social system such as a society. In a basic sense, attention to social change is inherent in all sociological work simply because social systems are always in the process of change. Man and his social institutions have evolved through time. In this course, both man and his social institutions have undergone changes.

Contemporary Indian society is changing rapidly. Due to the surge in technological advancements, the rise of entrepreneurial ventures, and an increasingly global outlook, thereby, empowering individuals and communities alike. While tradition still thrives in India, the society as a whole has been experiencing various transformations on various cultural and social aspects.

India has always been described as a traditional society in which

(i) the status of the person is determined by birth and is fixed, that is, individuals do not strive for social mobility;

(ii) individual behaviour is governed by customs and ways of behaviour of people vary slightly from generation to generation;

(iii) social organisation is based on hierarchy;

(iv) an individual identifies himself or herself with primary groups such as family and kinship relations predominate in interactions;

(v) people are conservative; and

(vi) economy is simple; economic productivity above subsistence is relatively low; and mythical thought predominates in society.

But, this description does not portray the totality. Indian society, like other societies, has also been changing over a period, though the pace of change increased sharply during the last hundred years. Following are some sources of social change also applicable to Indian society.

MODERNISATION

Modernisation has been a dominant theme after the Second World War (especially in the 1950s and 1960s). Modernisation studies typically deal with the effects of economic development on 'traditional' social structures and values. The process of modernisation is related to industrialisation, urbanisation, high standard of living, development of civilisation and broadness of viewpoint. Defining modernisation, Eisenstaedt (1966)[1] says that

> From a historical viewpoint modernisation is the process of change towards those types of social, economic and political systems which were developed in Western Europe and North America from the 17th to 19th century, and after that spread over to South America, Asia and Africa during the 19th and 20th centuries.

Therefore, some scholars considered modernisation to be the child of Westernisation. In a brilliant analysis of the ethical aspect of modernisation, S.C. Dube (1988)[2] says that

> The term *modernisation* was much less value loaded than its predecessor – westernisation. Most countries in the Third World were proud of their cultural heritage and deeply attached to it. While desiring western standards of plenty they had no desire to abandon their own lifestyles and values. The concept of modernisation recognised the strength of roots.

According to Lerner (1958), three features constitute the core of modernised personality – empathy, mobility and high participation. Empathy is the capacity to see things as others see them. All societies possess this capacity in some measure, but to sharpen and strengthen, it can make a qualitative change in human interaction. Such a change is desired in modernised societies. The second attribute, mobility, does not refer only to geographical mobility, but is also used in a more comprehensive sense. The imperatives of change demand a capacity to assume, as occasions demand new statuses and learn to play associated roles. Unlike the traditional society, which had ascribed statuses and roles, the modernised society has an open status system. The third attribute – high participation – refers to the increased role of individuals in realising social goals and objectives in more active ways; high participation requires individuals to visualise new goals or altered objectives and modify their roles accordingly. In traditional societies, social objectives are not open to question. The core of modernisation is, of course, rationality. India, passing through a crucial phase of social change, is adopting all these attributes, though at a tortuously slow pace.

---

[1] Eisenstaedt, S. N. Modrenization, Protest, and Change, Prentice Hall, 1966

[2] Dube, S. C. Modernization and Development, Vistaar Publications, New Delhi, 1988

A modern society is a rational and scientific society. Surrounded by the forces of fundamentalism in neighbouring countries, we have, in recent times, shown signs of succumbing to these pressures. The rising tide of religious revivalism, obscurantism, communalism and fundamentalism in the wake of the Babri Masjid-Ram Janmabhoomi dispute is dangerous. The happening of the fateful day of 6 December 1992 is alarming; it threatens to tear our social fabric apart. The minorities too should shed their tendency of clinging to obscurantism and strengthen the democratic, progressive and secular forces to save the country. Moreover, conditions should be created to ensure increased participation of all sorts of minorities in the nation-building process. During the Ayodhya controversy, enough damage was done to rationalism and scientific temper. We are left with no other option, but to contribute to strengthen rationalism and scientific temper through all available institutional networks. Our failure to achieve this objective will be a fatal setback to modernisation.

As observed by S.C. Dube (1974)[3],

> There is no standard model of modernisation and no fixed path for its attainment. Developing societies can adopt a model of their choice and can chalk out their own path for its realisation.

We have chosen democracy and secularism as the basis of the aspirations for the modernised Indian society. Adoption of modern science and technology shall go a long way in the achievement of India's cultural and technological modernisation.

SECULARISATION

Secularisation got impetus during the British rule in India. The Industrial Revolution and the consequent expansion in the means of transport and communication, spread of education, especially English education, increased the development of towns and cities and various tools of modern science and technology radically affected the thinking and mental horizon of the people. For the first time, Indian people, especially in towns and cities, were exposed to newer ideas and ideologies. Social interaction between the otherwise isolated groups and communities increased tremendously. The ideas of rationalism and humanitarianism gave a new dimension to the thought process of the people. All these factors strengthened the process of secularisation. Many myths were exploded and stereotypes about 'other' people had started changing and moved closer to reality.

The most important consequence of secularisation witnessed in Indian society was that for the first time many Indian people started adopting a non-religious approach for analysing and understanding many social-economic and political problems. Now it was possible for a large segment of society, especially in urban areas, to view many 'worldly' problems in their independent form completely isolated from the trappings of religion. Most significantly, the process of secularisation gave insight to people of the intellectual class to analyse issues of morality and moral values on a purely rational and humanistic ground independent of religion. Previously, ethics and morality could not be seen independent of religion because of the view that it is only the established and normative religions which provide society with guidelines in ethics and morality and religion is the only fountainhead of these virtues.

[3] Dube, S. C. Contemporary India and its Modernization, Vikas Publishing House, New Delhi, 1974

The rise of nationalism and national movement for freedom gave further impetus to secularisation. People of diverse cultural backgrounds, even having conflicting religious ideologies, stood together under the banner of the freedom movement. The Constitution of independent India gave it the ideal form of a republic; the essence and spirit of our Constitution have the moving force of secularisation behind various provisions reconciling diverse socio-religious interests. Though the opposing forces of **religious fanaticism** and revivalism have also been active, the process of secularisation continues to attain roots. What more evidence of it is required than the promulgation of our secular Constitution even after the partition of our country and the formation of a religion-based state in our immediate neighbourhood.

Quick Fact

Religious Fanaticism

It refers to an extreme and rigid adherence to religious beliefs, often accompanied by intolerance toward other faiths or differing interpretations, leading to divisiveness and conflict.

DEMOCRATISATION

Democracy and democratisation have been very important aspects of social change and modernisation in India. India is becoming progressively democratised. The adoption of adult and universal franchise was a revolutionary step forward in the path of democratisation. Adult franchise made it necessary for political parties and candidates to try and reach out the millions of illiterate voters scattered over around six lakh villages and urban slums.

> This seemingly impossible task was achieved through putting to new uses such traditional networks as provided by caste, kinship, ethnicity and patron-client relationship. In the process, even isolated and backward groups became politically mobilised. (M.N. Srinivas, 1992)[4]

The 73rd Amendment to the Constitution in 1992 was a great step forward towards democratisation of Indian society. The abolition of untouchability in all its forms, making its practice a cognisable offence, was a far-reaching, and a necessary step in the fight against inequality. Of course, the 'legal abolition' of untouchability needs to be distinguished from its 'actual disappearance'.

Adult franchise was not, however, the only institution calculated to make democracy meaningful to the common people. The reservation of a certain number of seats in all legislatures and of a percentage of government jobs, to members of the Scheduled Castes (SCs), Scheduled Tribes (STs) and Other Backward Classes (OBCs), ensured that these traditionally underprivileged and exploited sections would improve their lot in independent India. During each election, an increasing number of the poor and underprivileged people got politically mobilised. People who used to get ordered about by the upper castes have now to be approached for their votes. This has given them a new sense of importance, though even now, in several rural areas, the traditional *Jajmani* system (patron–client relations) is somewhat effective in the matter of voting. But, with the declining Jajmani system with its norms getting weakened, more and more political autonomy is coming to the so-called 'service castes'. But, the electoral process has also strengthened caste consciousness.

[4] Srinivas, M. N. On Living in a Revolution, Oxford University Press, New Delhi, 1992

Though whatever success the process of democratisation has achieved over the last 50 years, the fact remains that in a traditional society like India, trust is often placed more in individuals and less on institutions. Talking about India between tradition and modernity, Deepankar Gupta (2000)[5] says that

> Traditional societies function on a diametrically opposite principle - personal trust, personal loyalty and patron-client dependence in all traditional relationships. Once we can go beyond trust at the individual level and can rely on impersonal institutions, the last bastion of tradition has been overwhelmed.

This can also be applied to democratic institutions in whose nurture the process of democratisation plays the pivotal role.

NEW INDIAN ELITE AND EMERGENCE OF MIDDLE CLASS

The role of the elite and the middle class has been an important area of sociological enquiry of Indian society. For the purpose of identification and definition, an elite is any group or category of people in a social system that occupies a position of privilege or dominance. Elites exist within many different social contexts and at different levels of analysis: we may refer to a ruling group as a whole or as an elite, while at another level we may identify the intellectual class as the elite of the society. Elites form and operate within the social and political space accorded to them by a given society. When we try to understand 'middle class', it is found to be theoretically located at the confluence of economy, society and polity.

Antonio Gramsci gave a constructive Marxist analysis of the middle classes and their role in modern capitalist societies. D.P. Mukherji's pioneering work (1948) on middle classes followed by B.B. Misra's (1961) may be the best works on middle classes in India. But, the fact remains that, in India, the every-day term 'middle class' is more of a symbolic than a factual description.

When we look at the process of elite formation and the evolution of the elite in India, the new middle classes prominently figure. Elite structure of a society represents not only its basic values, but also the extent to which these values find a concrete expression in the power structure and the decision-making process of the society.

> Elites represent the standards of value excellence in different domains of life through their roles which are either ascribed to them, as in the traditional society or have been achieved by them by meritorious performance, which is the norm of a relatively modernised society. (Yogendra Singh, 1996)[6]

The social structure of elites in traditional India was based on the principles of hierarchy, holism and continuity – the cardinal values of the Hindu tradition. The king and the priest were the two important elite roles in this tradition. Both roles were derived from the caste system which offered a cultural and moral frame of reference to the elite structure. These two roles were taken by the

[5] Gupta, Deepankar, Interrogating Caste, Penguin Books, Delhi, 2000

[6] Singh, Yogendra, Sociology and the Emerging Challenges of Change, Sociological Bulletin 45:1, 1996

Brahmins and the *Kshatriyas*. With the advent of Muslim rule, the 'feudal pattern of elite structure was further stabilised'. Muslim feudal lords along with their Hindu counterparts continued to assert power and the religious domain manned by the *Qazi* and *Mufti* existed side by side with their Hindu counterparts. Thus, Muslim rule only replaced persons or offices involved in elite status and not the system as such. It was the succession of one class of elites by another in the same system rather than a change in the structure or functions of the elite.

The advent of British rule witnessed the emergency of a new elite. Education was sought to be secularised. A new system of education was introduced, which gave opportunity to all sections of Indian society irrespective of caste, creed or sex.

The new system of education was different in terms of knowledge and content when compared with the traditional system that prevailed in India till about the early nineteenth century. The new system was instrumental in creating a new class of intellectuals.

This new knowledge had two aspects – formal and substantive. I.P. Desai says that the way of looking at the world or the scientific attitude was the formal aspect. The substantive aspect was made up of beliefs, values, views and ideas on technology, economic system, system of government and organisation of society. The new elite, a product of cities rather than villages, belonged to the professions – journalists, lawyers, professors, social workers, etc. This elite constituted a new middle class which grew in India as a result of English education and the expansion of administration, judiciary and teaching professions. The rise of the political elite coincided in India with the growth of a westernised middle class. It emerged as a result of the expansion of higher education among the upper castes. Yogendra Singh says that the early 20th-century Indian elite constituted a composite group. The new elite stood for modernisation of economy, social reforms, policy of egalitarianism, social justice, universal civil rights, removal of caste handicaps and for welfare and equal rights of women and backward classes. These policy exhortations together constituted a value system which was logically distant from the traditional Indian values of hierarchy, holism and continuity. It came closer to the modernised western worldview. Yet, these elites were fascinated by the Indian tradition and wanted to preserve it in its essential forms. Structurally, the new elites were from the middle classes, belonged to various professional groups and had primarily an urban base.

Post-independence India witnessed the emergence of a new form of elite structure. Pinpointing the important trends of change in the elite structure during this period, Singh presents a well-defined scheme:

(i) increasing influence of rural-based political elites and decrease in the influence of the elites drawn from various professions;

(ii) greater differentiation in the elite structure with significant increase in the number of persons belonging to the middle classes;

(iii) greater articulation of regional and interest group-oriented goals in political-cultural ideologies; and

(iv) breakdown in the exclusiveness of upper castes to the elite position and its consequent democratisation.

At the highest levels of the decision-making process, the social composition of decision makers also underwent significant changes. The backward classes, especially OBCs and Scheduled Castes, have now registered their significant presence in bureaucracy and political leadership. Satish Deshpande (2003) rightly comments that the post-independence middle class was entirely a product of the development regime. It is also the major beneficiary of globalisation.

The middle class – the new elite – today is by no account homogenous. It is composed of people of different castes, religious communities and professions. It is spread over urban as well as rural areas. It is caught in the cobweb of consumerism and consumer culture. Its list of 'necessities' is ever growing and the market forces are taking full advantage of it. They aspire and dream to become affluent as quickly as possible and enter the world of the 'upper classes'. In the process, they may resort to any shortcuts. They may not be having strong inhibitions to take up crimes and corrupt means in this endeavour. New economic policy, globalisation and new information technology have opened new avenues for this mobility. These people have no hesitation to make compromises. About three to four decades ago the Indian middle class used to be honest to its duties and tried to find happiness living within its means and acted as an axis of social change. This is no more the ease. The status quoist, western-oriented and paradoxical character of the new middle class ceases to be the vehicle of social change. Even its modernity and 'westernisation' seem to be deceptive. It is rather 'mistaken modernity'. The opportunist, self-centred, corrupt and consumerist middle class of today is entirely different from the middle class of the 1950s and 1960s. Where have all its moral values gone? The politicians and political parties, having dragged caste and religion into politics, are also responsible for diverting the attention of the people from the core issues of nation-building. They have also contributed to 'vulgarisation' of the middle class. Perhaps, that is why, the most 'communalised' segment of Indian population is the urban, educated middle class.

AGENTS OF SOCIAL CHANGE

The process of social change and modernisation does not occur in vacuum. There may be a number of agents of social change. Education, mass media and communication are some of the more important agents of social change. India has been able to achieve a high degree of modernisation, both cultural and technological, during British rule. In terms of technological modernisation, such technological innovations as new means of transport and communication, roadways, railways, waterways, new printing technology and others not only facilitated more spatial mobility but also led to a broadening of the worldview of people. In terms of cultural modernisation, the westernised elite became the harbinger of a new social order. They reinterpreted Hinduism, had a new look at the caste system and other traditional institutions and accepted egalitarianism, gender justice and humanism as key to a new India.

What Do You Think?

How can we ensure that the changes we strive for today remain inclusive, equitable, and sustainable for future generations, even in the face of evolving social, technological, and environmental challenges?

Among the agents of social change, education played a very important role. The system of education as introduced by the British has been, both quantitatively and qualitatively, different. It was liberal in context and steeped in modern scientific worldview. Freedom, equality, humanism and denial of dogmas are the themes of the new system of education. English language was taken up as a medium of instruction from 1835 onwards at the higher levels of education. Exposure to the English language opened up a new worldview based on liberalism and scientific temper. It was also instrumental in opening up the vast store of western knowledge to the educated people of India. When we look at the organisational structure of education, we find that primary education was still being imparted through vernacular languages. English language was introduced at the intermediate tier of secondary education and college/university education was almost totally dependent on English language. Content wise, primary and secondary education was providing only basic or rudimentary knowledge, but not 'enlightenment', which was confined only to college/university education.

In terms of social classes, when education was secularised during British rule, it was taken out from the suffocating environment of sacred/religious places and for the first-time people from all social classes found access to this secular education. This facilitated the entry of new criteria of social stratification in Indian society through which educated people irrespective of caste and social background got new avenues of upward mobility in the traditional rigid hierarchy. Thus, education started playing a significant role in the process of modernisation of Indian society. In the fields of humanities and social sciences, the literary content was primarily drawn from the literature produced in Europe.

The changes in the education system described above led to the growth of a new intelligentsia or intellectual class taking to the path of modernity. Broadly speaking, intellectuals are those who contribute directly to the creation, transmission and criticism of ideas. They include artists, writers, bureaucrats, scientists, philosophers, religious thinkers, social theorists, political commentators and others. Talking about the concerns which have occupied a central place in the cognitive map of modern intellectuals in India, Avijit Pathak (1998) presenting his concerns is of the view that an intense curiosity always exists to understand traditions, religiosity and cultural practices of the past. The dilemma to be resolved is to decide whether our traditions puts a barrier to modernity. Can our traditions develop its own road map to modernity? Another point to be confronted is to decide whether modernity is an elitist goal and how to develop scientific temper in a deeply religious, traditional society?

In science, they saw a great possibility. Raja Ram Mohan Roy wanted it. Akshay Kumar Dutt rejected the traditional system of education. Vidyasagar ridiculed those who believed that the *shastras* contained all scientific truth. For Sir Syed Ahmed Khan, the traditional system of Muslim education was a great stumbling block in the way of progress. Nehru, in Parekh's (1989) words, though valued tradition, but was not a traditionalist. He used the resources of his tradition and with his intense creativity gave birth to an alternate politico-cultural agenda. A major reason behind the popularity of Nehru amongst intellectuals is that they continue to feel that the agenda initiated by him – promoting secular humanism to fight cultural prejudices – has not yet exhausted its possibilities.

Thus, 'education' has always been an important intervening variable in social change and plays a crucial role in the 'socialisation of the younger generation', to use Durkheim's terminology. It paves the way for the development of science and technology. Modern education contains the ability to change the attitude and outlook of people. It has contributed to changes in customs, traditions, morality, religious belief and the whole value system in India. It is contributing to women's empowerment and gender justice. In the domain of social status, it has played its role in occupational mobility. This becomes important under conditions where occupation and social status were traditionally interlinked in Indian society. The spread of education has also contributed to the increase in political awareness among the poor and deprived sections of the Indian society. Though it is true that educated persons are still the most progressive section of our population, it also raises some uncomfortable questions. We also find socially regressive, conservative and orthodox, casteists and communalists among educated people. This at once questions the content of syllabi, a true and correct understanding of social phenomenon and all objective analysis and interpretation by the teachers. And here comes the role of the state too, to promote a particular model of education. What can one expect if the state sponsors the teaching of a 'communalised history' and promotes orthodoxy rather than rationalism and scientific outlook. But, even in such circumstances, the role of education in 'social change' cannot be denied.

The role of mass media and communication as agents of social change has also been a field of sociological enquiry. Mass media is a term popularly used for dissemination of information, ideas and entertainment by the use of technological media such as radio and television, cinema, press and advertising. They continue to coexist with important traditional media such as folk song and dance, drama, puppetry, etc.

The technological innovations of the 20th century have transformed the very face of mass media. If we look at the reach of radio and television, we are really overwhelmed by its reach and impact. The *Peoples of India Project* (1986–1992) done by the Anthropological Survey of India tells us that the radio has reached 96% of the tribal population and the television, 60% of the same population. Tribal regions are considered to be the economically most backward regions of the country and if these two most important popular mass media have registered their presence on such a scale, its reach in rural and urban areas can be very well imagined. Radio programmes are being broadcast in English and all the major languages and dialects of India. Besides providing news and information, programmes related to entertainment include a large area of themes – social, cultural and political. Programmes targeting youth and women have also been promoting social change. But, at the same time, obscure and conservative ideas strengthening status quoism are also being broadcast and telecast. Cinema is also one of the cheapest sources of entertainment and like television being an audiovisual medium, it carries more intense impact than radio. At the micro level, it also promotes culture change, particularly changes in modes of dressing, hair styles, language, mannerism and norms.

The growing desensitisation to violence is also attributed to the impact of cinema. But, the serious and socially concerned cinema, popularly known as 'art cinema' or parallel cinema, has also been promoting the ideas of gender justice, women's empowerment, against corruption and criminalisation, against dowry and other social evils. Tea stalls in rural markets, towns and cities are popular places of dissemination of divergent ideas. These are the places where people, after listening to radio news or reading from newspapers, enter into discussions and debates and take the role of opinion makers for the rest of the masses. Presently, messages are mass produced and distributed to millions of people through the audio and audiovisual media. With the advent of Cable TV, exclusive channels on 'spiritualism' and religion are also promoting obscurantism and religiosity and may also be counterproductive to the process of cultural modernism. Thus, the mass media in India is like a double-edged weapon. Its educative and entertaining role may also be neutralised when it serves as a vehicle of irrationality, superstitions and status quoism. Since mass media has become indispensable, proper and imaginative planning is required to use it as a vehicle of social change.

Taking an overall view of changing Indian society, the following aspects are also worthy of consideration:

1. In the regions witnessing green revolution, we see a departure in authority from older generation to the educated younger generation because of its capability to deal with new agricultural technology as well as new financial transactions and institutions. Moreover, joint family which had almost disappeared from the cities is crumbling and moving towards disintegration in villages too.
2. Emergence of new dominant castes especially in rural areas is a new phenomenon – Yadava and Kurmi in Uttar Pradesh, Bihar etc.; Jat in Haryana, Rajasthan and Western Uttar Pradesh; Maratha in Maharashtra; Patel and Kunbi in Gujarat; Reddy and Khamma in Telangana-Andhra Pradesh; and Vokkaliga and Lingayat in Karnataka are a case in point.
3. Market forces have entered village India in a big way resulting in consumer culture among the rich peasantries. Entry of cell phone and Internet is changing the face of village India. The very nature of the village market is changing.
4. On the one hand, women are now more empowered than ever before. On the other hand, large-scale female foeticide and infanticide have resulted in a highly disturbed sex ratio resulting in 'importing' brides from poverty-stricken areas of Jharkhand, Odisha, West Bengal and Assam to states like Haryana where these girls virtually serve as domestic/sex slaves. Increased domestic violence coupled with the increasing incidence of acid throwing and 'honour' killing of young women present a paradoxical situation.
5. **Casteism** and communalism have emerged as the new face of Indian democracy.
6. Violence in our day-to-day life has increased to an unbearable extent.

Quick Fact

Casteism

Discrimination or prejudice based on caste, impacting social equality and integration.

Questions and Indicative Answers

1. In what way modernisation and democratisation have contributed to the changing Indian society?

   Modernisation-technological as well as cultural has deeply influenced the traditional Indian society in terms of values and institutions.

Adoption of democracy promising equality gave a big blow to the caste-ridden hierarchical Indian society. It not only derecognised caste superiority/inferiority but gave everybody a role in decision making.

2. Discuss the role of mass media in changing Indian society in the post-independence period.

Needless to say mass media-radio, newspapers, television play an important role in moulding opinion of the people and releasing forces of change.

The mass media in traditional societies such as India may be seen as a double-edged weapon. It may also promote revivalism, superstition, obscurantism and irrationality. Currently it is promoting religiosity and also animosity between different communities. The entry of social media has added a new dimension to this problem.

Previous Years' Questions

1. Write a short note on the following:

Modernisation **(UPSC CSE Mains Anthropology, Paper II, 2018)**

Focus Areas for the Examination

1. Modernisation and its impact on Indian Society
2. Role of Mass media in social change
3. Issues in Democratisation in Indian Society

CHAPTER 19

Challenges of Social Transformation

Chapter Outline

1. Concept of social transformation by Karl Marx and its implications in modern society
2. Challenges associated with development-induced displacement and the impact on marginalised communities
3. Evaluating the legal frameworks, and their effectiveness in addressing displacement issues
4. Environmental challenges faced by India, including sustainable development and conservation efforts
5. Exploring the dynamics of ethnic conflicts in India, including the Kuki–Naga, Kuki–Meitei and Bodo–non-Bodo conflicts, and their implications for nation-building
6. Understanding problems related to the role of Traditional Panchayats, Legislative Measures, Ethnic Conflicts, Land Acquisition Act, etc.
7. The socio-political factors behind casteism, caste conflicts and religious revivalism in India
8. Understanding the concept of Honour Killing and exploring the social, cultural, and patriarchal roots of the same
9. Examining patriarchy and gender dynamics to develop an understanding of how patriarchy manifests in Indian society, influencing gender relations, violence, and control over women's behaviour
10. Ongoing issues related to gender-based violence, educational disparities and poverty
11. Interconnections between social exclusion, poverty and empowerment in the context of India's developmental journey

As a concept, 'social transformation' was specifically used by Karl Marx in his book *German Ideology* (1846). It meant social change arising out of contradictions in a society leading to rapid change or revolution. In the process of transformation, society moves from the traditional to modern social structure. Thus, social transformation is linked to social change, that is, change in structure of a society. Rajni Kothari and other scholars are of the view that modernisation and revolution are two models of social transformation. India's path of development is passing through a social upheaval. The State played a crucial role in facilitating the release of forces contributing to major changes. In pursuance of the constitutional provisions, several steps have been taken where the weaker segments of Indian society are getting empowered. However, there are a few challenges of social transformation, some of which are described below.

CRISIS OF DEVELOPMENT: DISPLACEMENT OF PEOPLE

'Development' has become a nightmare for many in the developing third world countries because it continues in such a way that a number of people are being 'victims of progress'. Although it is an established fact that throughout history, rearrangement in human settlement patterns has been a 'companion of development', the process should be just, humane and as voluntary as possible.

Development involves changes in land and water use patterns, and in some instances, these changes require that people be displaced. But, as the well-known expert on displacement Michael Cernea (1985) puts it, involuntary displacement must be avoided or minimised as much as possible. Between 1940 and 1950, most of the countries under colonial rule became independent and took up the task of national reconstruction. Economic development was taken up on top priority.

In a number of such countries problem of displacement and those displaced was seriously and sensitively handled. Unfortunately, it did not happen in India. Here, the largest number of people have been displaced because of hydro-electric and irrigation projects. Among other projects responsible for displacement are mining, thermal and nuclear power plants, test firing range for the army personnel, industrial colonies, military installations, railway lines, highways, expansion of reserved forests, wildlife sanctuaries, mineral-based industries, etc.

Nobody is questioning these projects but displacing people without a suitable rehabilitation plan is criminal and violation of human rights. Further, if there is no other alternative to displacement, it should be done in such a way that the livelihood of the affected people is protected. If this is not done, the development thus intended would be gain for some but pain for others. The resettlement must be 'people oriented'. As Michael Cernea (ibid) puts it, it should be 'putting people first'. Anthropologists and then sociologists and human geographers were the first to document the disruptive social impact forced displacement. Many studies have lately been sponsored by planning agencies. Non-governmental organisations (NGOs) and even social activists have carried out their own studies of the displaced, enriching the existing knowledge on the subject.

In the post-independence period, an estimated 6–8 crore people have been displaced in the name of 'public interest' and 'national interest'. Unfortunately for the governments, both central and state, political parties and policy planners, development-induced displacement is not a serious issue. What better evidence is required of this lack of sensitivity that even the governments do not have definite number of displaced people. Big dams are primarily responsible for the largest number of ousted. Experts such as Walter Fernandes have estimated that around 2.5 crore people have been displaced because of this single reason. No rehabilitation has been done for most of such displaced people and they have been left to fend for themselves. The consequences of such brutal displacement came to the fore in the wake of armed resistance by the tribal people especially of Central India.

The majority of them are either tribal people or Dalits. Ironically, the scheduled tribes constitute only about 8% of our population but are around 40% of the displaced people. These figures amply demonstrate that those displaced are powerless and voiceless people who are being sacrificed in the name of development. The whole process is disempowering especially when nobody is concerned about their resettlement. Perhaps the mindset of the State agencies is based on the axiom 'if you are to suffer you should suffer in the interest of the country'. When the lives of so many people are being disrupted, why is there such deafening silence surrounding the development induced **internally displaced people (IDPs)**? If the displaced are not properly resettled and their capacity to earn a living is not restored, it becomes irrelevant if the project forcing them off their land is of an 'overriding public interest'.

Quick Fact

Internally Displaced People (IDPs)

People who are forced to flee their homes due to development projects, violence or natural disasters but remain within their country's borders.

Studies have shown multiple effects of displacement. Involuntary displacement and resettlement leads to increased stress, both psychological and socio-cultural, and also heightens morbidity and mortality. Another unfortunate outcome is a feeling of alienation, helplessness and powerlessness. Moving away to new places is just unthinkable especially to the tribal communities as they are deeply attached to their ancestral lands. The synonym for the word 'resettlement' does not exist in any tribal language. The widespread consequences of displacement include dismantling of production systems, desecration of ancestral sacred groves and zones or graves and temples' scattering of kinship network and family systems, disorganisation or disintegration of informal social network that provide mutual support in the wake of absence of formal credit agencies, weakening of self-management and social control, disruption of trade and market links, etc. Further, these patterns have been equated with national progress where 'public purpose' and 'national interest' have been used interchangeably. It is this mindset that justifies the labelling of those who criticise the insensitive implementation of such projects as not only anti-project and anti-development but also anti-national. The case of development in Gujarat, Madhya Pradesh, Chhattisgarh, Jharkhand and Andhra Pradesh may be cited of this mindset. It raises a very inconvenient question – are millions of people whose life and livelihood are being destroyed not a part of 'public' or 'nation'? If displacing them from their resource base and disrupting their lives is in 'public interest' or 'national interest', who is going to take responsibility of their rehabilitation and resettlement?

In a landmark ruling in 1984, in the case of a **'public interest litigation'** by an NGO, in the wake of land acquisition by Coal India Ltd. in Giridih district in Jharkhand, the Supreme Court laid out the following guidelines for the project authorities:

Quick Fact

Public Interest Litigation (PIL)

A legal mechanism in India that allows individuals or organisations to file cases in the interest of the public, often used to address social justice issues.

As far as possible, forced displacement should be avoided. If there is no other alternative, then land for land principle should be followed;

(a) Compensation for the acquired land should be in tune of the prevailing market prices and not like peanuts.

(b) At least one member of each displaced family should be provided a job.

It is for everybody to see how far these guidelines were followed.

The most unfortunate part of the story is the case of 'multiple displacement' of people, that is, displacement of the same families and people more than once, even twice or thrice. Several groups after having made the painful transition and settling into a new area and a new life style were again uprooted and displaced for another project. This is height of insensitivity and gross violation of human rights. The displaced people of Rihand Dam in Singrauli in Uttar Pradesh and Hirakund Dam in Odisha are cases in point. In 1960s, people were displaced to make way for coal mining projects and for the third time in 1980s because of setting up of some industries. Are lives of the people, howsoever powerless and voiceless they may be, like a pant or shirt that may be changed at will? Are we really a welfare state?

Land Acquisition Act

The instrument of displacement has been the Land Acquisition Act 1894 (amended twice in 1984 and 1998). This Act is used to acquire land which is privately owned. It also describes the circumstances and purposes for which the Central and State governments acquire land. It involves several stages, from notification to acquisition and determination to disbursement of compensation for the land acquired. The Act was drastically amended in 1984 by the Central Government. Among other things the Act set a time limit for the completion of all proceedings which was two years. All claims and objections could be filed within this period. Later amendment also included some provisions for resettlement and rehabilitation for the namesake. Going by the current trends the amendments, as reviewed by the experts and advocacy groups, are far from being ideal. In the wake of liberalisation the acquisition of land has become easier for the multinational companies through government corporations and this has further marginalised the underprivileged populations.

The issue of 'public purpose' in the Act is perhaps the most contentious, debatable and questionable. The civil society demands a holistic view of public purpose, public good and public interest. Rehabilitation is primarily the process of reconstruction of the livelihood of the affected people. This has never been a guiding principle of this Act promulgated by the selfish colonial rule. In the post-Independence times, the government authorities continued with this approach and mindset. If the Supreme Court is made the only appellate authority, the powerless has no hope because they cannot challenge the governmental action at such a high level through such an expensive process beyond the reach of common man. This definitely makes development and displacement contradictory terms. Under these circumstances, there is no balance between individual rights and the power of the State which is often coercive power.

Issues in Resettlement and Rehabilitation

With the increasing pressure on land due to urbanisation, rapid economic development, increasing infrastructure requirements, etc., the acquisition of land has increased. It requires a comprehensive policy of displacement, resettlement and rehabilitation. The Union Government approved the *National Policy on Rehabilitation and Resettlement* in 2007 and intended to 'suitably' amend the Land Acquisition Act, 1894. The policy aimed at striking a balance between the need for land for developmental activities and, at the same time, protecting the interests of the land owners and others such as tenants, the landless, the agricultural land and non-agricultural labourers, artisans and others whose livelihood depends on the land involved. It also promises no approval to projects without undertaking a social impact assessment.

Under intense pressure of civil society and ongoing armed resistance of tribal people stretching from Srikakulum in Andhra Pradesh to the Sonbhadra region in Uttar Pradesh, the Ministry of Rural Development prepared a Bill called *The Land Acquisition, Rehabilitation and Resettlement Bill* in 2011 with comprehensive provisions regarding acquisition of land and rehabilitation–resettlement of affected people. It became an Act in 2013. Hoping against hope that this law, in implementation, shall be a radical departure from the past shedding the colonial hangover and bring relief to the future 'oustees'. Forget about around 50 million powerless and voiceless people who were sacrificed and made victim of development.

ENVIRONMENTAL PROBLEMS AND SUSTAINABILITY

We live in the time of the worst crisis in the history of humanity. Environmental issues now occupy centre stage of world problems. This is more to say in developing countries such as India. To understand the problems and issues in environmental degradation, one needs to have some idea about the biosphere. In loose and broad terms, the biosphere is the global sum of all ecosystems. It may also be described as the zone of life on the earth, a closed and self-regulating system. From the broadest biophysiological point of view, the biosphere is the global ecological system integrating all living beings and their relationship. An ecosystem is a community of living organisms (plants, animals and microbes) in conjunction with the non-living components of their environment (like air, water and mineral soil) interacting as a system. Though it is not easy to define environment in precise terms, it refers to the physical and biological factors that affect an organism. Natural environment refers to all living and non-living things. In popular usage we also use it as social environment, knowledge environment, etc. The term environmentalism is also very popular. It may refer to any social and political movement with goal to protect natural environment by emphasising importance of nature's role in the protection of the environment in combination with various actions and policies oriented towards conservation of nature. Thus, environmentalism and eco-movement represent, by and large, the similar goals with some overlapping.

Faced with an imminent catastrophe, most of the developing countries including India are concerned about the environmental degradation and its consequences. There is now an increased awareness about the environmental issues. Like other developing countries, India is faced with environmental problems at two levels: one is the impact of high growth-oriented development on environment and the other is the direct impact of the improved standards of living through different lifestyle. 'The protagonists of environmental school argue that the present form of development neither suits nor is necessary for the third world countries (Vyes and Reddy, 1998)'. Their arguments favour low energy, low input intensive production process which would be sustainable in the long run. The sustainable development paradigm is expected to be not only economically viable but also environmentally friendly. Sustainable development is development that meets the needs of the present without compromising the ability of future generations to meet their own needs. Thus, the paradigm of sustainable development incorporates environmental sustainability on the one hand and economic sustainability on the other.

What Do You Think?

Can sustainable development truly address the root causes of environmental degradation, or is it merely a compromise between economic growth and environmental preservation?

Some of the most important goals to be achieved are:

- to reduce consumption of fossil fuels,
- to reduce all sorts of pollution – air and water – with goal of zero pollution,
- emphasis on clean, alternative energy sources that have low carbon emissions,
- sustainable use of water, land and other scarce resources,
- preserving existing endangered species,
- protection of bio-diversity.

India is faced with major environmental issues-air pollution, poor management of waste, growing water scarcity, falling ground water tables, water pollution, preservation and quality of forests, bio-diversity loss and land or soil degradation.

The environmental problems faced by India and other developing countries are more complex than usually understood. The following are the important environmental indicators for India:

- Land
- Forests
- Bio-diversity
- Cropped agricultural area
- Irrigation and Floods
- Input Use
- Livestock
- Water
- Air
- Health and Sanitation

Around 70% of the land area falls used humid regions while the remaining in arid and semi-arid regions and cold regions. Only about 10% of the land is not affected by any inherent soil constraint. A very large area comes under wasteland and affected by salinity, alkalinity and wind and water erosion. The forests have shrunk rapidly because of deforestation. It is estimated that only about 15% of the area has adequate tree cover and if it is not checked we will be heading for disaster. India has been richest in terms of natural biodiversity which is now seriously threatened by the mindless development projects and population explosion. Wells, canals and tanks were in abundance which have now declined alarmingly. Groundwater exploitation has been done without serious attempts to recharge it with the result that the ground water tables are going down in most of the regions. Watershed management and rainwater harvesting, especially in urban areas, has not been done seriously. The people, especially the urban people, lack awareness about conservation of water.

During summers, a number of cities face such severe shortages of water that people fight among themselves to procure and store water. The livestock, a critical factor in agrarian economy, are faced with shrinking grazing areas and are being pushed to forests increasing further pressure on forests. Emissions of air pollutants have crossed the permissible limits in most of the cities. Waters of the Ganga, India's largest river irrigating about 40% of the country's land and providing fresh water to 500 million people is today considered as the most polluted and unfit even for bathing in cities like Kanpur and Varanasi due to industrial effluents and human sewage.

India along with other South Asian countries is likely to face many problems of food scarcity in this century. In the past two decades the urban population has increased alarmingly adding more environmental problems like water shortage and sanitation. Poor waste management is adding to environmental degradation. Hazardous waste dumping in the wake of increasing urbanisation and industrialisation may be ignored at our peril. Unchecked mining is adding more to our woes.

Every human activity has some impact on the environment. The **environmental impact assessment (EIA)** in India was started in 1976 when the Planning Commission asked the Department of Science and Technology to examine the river valley projects from the environmental angle. It integrates the environmental concerns in the developmental activities right at the time of preparing the feasibility report. The EIA is made up of the following phases:

- Screening
- Scoping and consideration of alternatives
- Impact prediction
- Environment Management Plan
- Decision Making
- Monitoring the clearance conditions

Quick Fact

Environmental Impact Assessment (EIA)

A formal process to evaluate the environmental effects of a proposed project to minimise adverse impacts.

The components of EIA are:

(i) Air Environment
(ii) Noise Environment
(iii) Water Environment
(iv) Biological Environment
(v) Land Environment
(vi) Socio-economic and Health Environment
(vii) Risk Assessment and
(viii) Environment Management Plan.

A number of experts and NGOs have expressed concern regarding political interface with EIA administration and the perceived lack of political will and commitment in terms of environmental management. It is widely believed that, under the influence of the corporate sector – often supported by political authorities – EIA processes generally serve to promote activities rather than assess whether those activities should be permitted. Further, it tends to generate mitigation measures rather than assess whether or not activities should be permitted. Corruption charges are also hurled, from time to time, at the decision making authorities especially on the junior or middle level officials.

The Constitution of India clearly states that it is the duty of the state to protect and improve the environment and to safeguard the forests and wildlife of the country. It imposes a duty on every citizen to protect and improve the natural environment. In pursuance of the constitutional provisions, a number of Acts, rules and notifications have been made. As V.K. Agarwal (2005)[1] righty points out, "There is no dearth of legislations on environmental protection in India but their enforcement has been far from satisfactory. The creative role of the judiciary has been significant and laudable. Caring for regulating and protecting the environment is essentially a desire to see that national development should proceed along the rational, sustainable laws."

Inculcating and increasing environmental awareness among the citizens shall also go a long way in the struggle to protect and improve environmental quality. It should begin at the school level among the children and extend to all the universities in the country. General awareness about environment must be an integral part of the school and university curriculum.

ETHNIC CONFLICTS

Ethnic movements and ethnic conflicts, especially in the north-eastern region, have been posing different types of problems in the post-independence period. This is not unusual for multi-ethnic societies.

What Do You Think?

To what extent do globalisation and modern nation-state structures exacerbate or mitigate ethnic conflicts, and how can societies balance cultural diversity with the pursuit of national unity?

Before we take up different ethnic movements and ethnic conflicts, let us have some idea about the concept of ethnicity and ethnic groups. The intellectual history of the term 'ethnicity' is relatively short: prior to1970s there was little mention of it in social science literature and text books contained no definition of the term. Since the mid-1970s, the concept has acquired strategic significance within anthropological theory, and later in sociology, partly as a response to the changing post-colonial geopolitics and the rise of ethnic minorities activism in many industrial states. Etymologically speaking, the term 'ethnic', has been derived from the Greek word '*ethnikos*' referring to (a) a nation or peoples not converted to Christianity; (b) races or large groups of people having common traits and customs; or (c) groups in an 'exotic primitive culture'. Phadnis stated that, in sociological-anthropological terms, an ethnic group could be described as a historically formed collective of people associated, whether actually or imaginatively, with a specific territory, sharing a set of beliefs

[1] Agarwal, V K, Environmental Laws in India: Challenges for Enforcement, Bulletin of the National Institute of Ecology, Vol. 15, 2005

and values that highlight their distinctiveness in comparison to similar groups, and acknowledged as such by others. The definition thus has five components:

(i) A subjective belief in real or assumed historical antecedents;
(ii) A symbolic or real geographical centre;
(iii) Shared cultural emblems, such as race, language, religion, dress and diets, or a combination of some of them which, though variegated and flexible, provide the overt basis of ethnic identity;
(iv) Self-ascribed awareness of distinctiveness and belonging to the group; and,
(v) Recognition by others of the group differentiation; it is thus a self-defined and 'other recognised status'.

Thus, ethnicity involves a number of characteristic features on the basis of which an ethnic group may be identified. Fredrick Barth, a well-known expert on ethnicity, says (1969) that an ethnic group refers to that population which (a) is largely biologically self-perpetuating; (b) shares fundamental cultural values realised in overt unity in cultural forms; (c) makes up a field of communication and interaction; and (d) has a membership which identifies itself and is identified by others as constituting a category distinguishable from other categories of the same order. While race is a biological concept, culture is purely social in nature.

There are three competing approaches to understand ethnicity. They could be roughly categorised as:

(i) **Primordialist**
(ii) **Instrumentalist**
(iii) **Constructivist**

Sokolovski and Tishkov (1996) are of the view that primordialist theories assert that ethnic identification is based on deep, 'primordial' attachment to a group or culture; the instrumentalist approach treats ethnicity as a political instrument exploited by leaders and others in pragmatic pursuit of their own interests; and the constructivist approach emphasises the contingency and fluidity of ethnic identity, treating it as something which is made in specific and historical contexts. It is important to note that all the approaches to understanding ethnicity are not necessarily mutually exclusive and there may be overlappings.

Quick Fact

Primordial Approach

Primordial approach views ethnicity as natural, fixed, and deeply rooted in inherited traits such as kinship, culture, and shared history.

Instrumentalist Approach

Instrumentalist approach sees ethnicity as a strategic tool used by individuals or groups to achieve political, economic, or social advantages.

Constructivist Approach

It views ethnicity as a dynamic and socially constructed identity shaped by historical, political, and social contexts.

Ethnic affiliations are used to designate 'nation' or nationality. As Phadnis (ibid) points out, a nation is not the same as state. The state is primarily a politico-legal concept whereas the nation is a psycho-cultural one.

> A nation may exist without a state and a state may exist without a nation. Strictly speaking, a nation-state referred to a situation in which a nation had its own state. In other words, a nation-state referred to a nation having political sovereignty[2].

[2] Urmila Phadnis, Ethnicity and Nation Building in South Asia, Sage Publications, New Delhi, 1990, p. 14

Since India is considered largely as multi-ethnic nation-state, it is challenging to bring all the ethnic groups coming together in the process of nation building. The north-eastern region having a multiplicity of ethnic groups such as the Naga, Mizo, Ahom, Meitei, Bodo and so on, has erupted in ethnic conflicts from time to time in the absence of just reconciliation of interests of such groups. Ethnic identity is the pivot around which much of the politics of north-east India revolves. Srikanth and Ngaihte (2011) stated that, when taken to an extreme, identity assertions could result in chains of **fratricidal conflicts**, potentially leading to genocide and natural destruction. They also noted that North-East India offers examples of various manifestations of ethnic identity.

Quick Fact

Fratricidal Conflicts

It refers to violent disputes or clashes between closely related groups, such as members of the same family, community, or nation, often resulting in severe divisions and harm.

After several rounds of division and reorganisation in post-independence India, seven states have emerged in the northeast – namely, Arunachal Pradesh, Assam, Manipur, Meghalaya, Mizoram, Nagaland and Tripura – along with the Himalayan state of Sikkim. These states are officially recognised under the North Eastern Council, constituted in 1971 as the coordinating agency for the development of the eight states. However, ethnic aspirations remain largely unfulfilled, and the region continues to experience violence and ethno-political movements. In Manipur, the Kuki–Naga conflict has intensified and now includes the Kuki–Meitei conflict. Meghalaya still exhibits Garo-Khasi rivalry, and violence in Bodoland remains a recurring issue.

The space constraint in this write up does not permit any detailed discussion on Naga and Mizo ethnic movements passing through the phases of secession from India to gradual integration encompassing a variety of ethnic aspirations. However, two such conflicts may be discussed in some detail revolving around the Naga–Kuki conflict and Bodo–non-Bodo conflict giving some idea about the ongoing conflicts in this region and this is not conducive to the nation-building and security concerns as this region shares international borders with Bangladesh, Myanmar and China. 'The accords signed by the Indian State during 1980s with AASU, TNV, MNF or the Bodoland agreement of 2003 were intended to strike reconciliation with conflicting identities in order to subsume them under the state. This democratic arrangement of reconciliation could not provide a permanent solution to the problem. While one block accepts the integration package and tries to use it to its advantage, the other bloc gradually shifts towards a demand for secession from the Indian state' (Roy, 2005).

The Nagas and the Kukis are two distinct ethnic groups who have been coexisting in the north eastern region and Myanmar for centuries. Manipur consists of the majority Hindu Meiteis, who occupy the valley, tribal groups including the Naga and Kuki tribes who are mainly Christians and inhabit the surrounding hill districts, Muslims immigrants known as Pangals are about 8% of the population and a small population of migrants from different parts of India who are called Mayang (outsiders). Manipur is now in a pathetic condition surrounded by militancy and ethnic cauldrons. The main reason of conflict between the Kuki and the Naga is the struggle for control over Manipur's Senapati district. The Kuki want three sub divisions of the Senapati district to be carved out and create a new district called the Sadar Hills where they will be in majority. Control over land in Manipur Hills has been the main reason behind the bloody Naga-Kuki clashes. The Naga opposed it claiming that the land in question is their ancestral land.

They apprehend that it could lead to the creation of a separate Kuki homeland, overlapping with Naga-dominated land. They also suspect that successive governments in Manipur have been lenient toward the Kukis. As a pressure tactic, the Kukis enforce economic blockades on National Highways 2 and 37 (the Imphal-Silchar highway), which are met with counter-blockades by the United Naga Council of Manipur. This often results in violent outbreaks, with hundreds of people – both Kuki and Naga – losing lives and property. In the midst of this, Manipuri Muslims are frequently caught in the crossfire and sometimes become involved in the violence. The conflict between the Nagas and the Kukis in Manipur has led to the formation of several armed groups, such as the Kuki National Army, Kuki National Front and United Kuki Liberation Front. The Nagas receive support from the National Socialist Council of Nagaland-IM, led by Manipuri Naga Thuingleng Muivah. A series of ethnic conflicts in the state – including the Naga–Kuki clash, the Kuki–Paite clash and Meitei–Naga tensions – has severely strained Manipur's social and political landscape. Recently, the Meitei and Kuki communities have been embroiled in unprecedented violence that continues today.

Assam has also been witnessing lot of ethnic tensions resulting in violence. The Bodoland Territorial Autonomous District Area popularly known as Bodoland is now one of the most violence prone areas. Bodo or Boro Kachari are the largest plains tribe in Assam settled mainly on the northern bank of the Brahmaputra River. Since 1990s the Bodos have tried to build movements, insurgents as well as the pressure groups, to assert their rights. Their movement was inspired by the emergence of the United Liberation Front of Asom (ULFA) which was created to 'liberate' Assam from India. Later, several armed groups emerged in Bodoland demanding preservation of their identity and self-rule. They carried several rounds of massacre of non-Bodos. Initially violence against Assamese speaking people was carried out who were considered 'outsiders' but later against the Muslims, accused of being Bangladeshis, and other tribal groups – the Santhals being the main target. According to the *Asian Centre for Human Rights*, more than two lakh people-Muslims and Santhals were displaced during the past two decades who are still living in fear in refugee camps. They are mainly from the Darrang and Udalguri district. The Bodo Accord signed in 1993 attempted to bring end to years of violence and instability by identifying areas where the Bodo population was in majority to be brought under the direct administration of the Bodo Autonomous Council (BAC). Unfortunately it led to the organised '**ethnic cleansing**' in areas where the Bodos were not in majority. The targets of this ethnic cleansing are Assamese and Bengali Muslims as well as the Santhal tribal groups and some other Muslim migrant groups from Bihar.

Quick Fact

Ethnic Cleansing

It is the deliberate and systematic removal of an ethnic or religious group from a particular area through forced displacement, violence, or other means, often with the intent to achieve ethnic homogeneity.

Commenting on the plight of the other tribal groups inhabiting Bodoland, N. G. Mahanta (2013) says that the ruling Bodoland People's Progressive Front (BPPF) and other Bodo organisations argue that the Adivasis are the migrants and thus cannot claim to be indigenous people of the region. Significantly the tribal groups (tea garden tribes) such as Santhal, Oraon and Munda are of Jharkhand origin who were brought to Assam as plantation labour after the rapid growth of the tea industry in 1880s. The Bodo organisations oppose the demand of granting scheduled tribe status to these tribal groups because they may constitute about 50% of the total scheduled tribe population of the state thereby making it the most powerful scheduled tribe group thus diluting the authority of the Bodos.

The ethnic conflict and violence continuing in the North East Region amply demonstrates that the conflicting ethnic interests and competing ethnic identities could not be managed so far. Is anybody concerned about the plight of innocents being killed and uprooted? All of them are Indians and India cannot afford to continue with this situation any longer. It's a serious and complex problem that needs to be addressed on top priority.

ROLE OF TRADITIONAL PANCHAYATS

Numerous studies have shown that traditional panchayats are still playing a strong and important role as a tool of social control in village societies, despite the establishment of statutory panchayats under Panchayati Raj. Of all such traditional panchayats, the *Khap Panchayats* of Haryana have grabbed the greatest attention because of its highly questionable role. For several centuries, Khap and Sarva Khap Panchayats have been characterised for their role in 'social administration'. The term 'Khap' has been known as signifying the social-political aspect in the geographical context. Since ancient times, the social fabric of rural India has been known through village units. The village panchayat has been representing its socio-political system. The Khap Panchayat, even today, may be considered equivalent to the tehsil or district. Several Khaps together constitute the sarva Khap. This whole region has been dominated by the Jats and the Gujjars. Even after the emergence of the statutory, constitutional pachayats, the role of the Khap remained effective in terms of social control. In this entire region, or for that matter in different regions of rural India, the cornerstone of village life is based largely on four points – *Ekta* (unity or solidarity), *Izzat* (honour), *Biradari* (larger kin group) and *Bhaichara* (brotherhood). The Khaps constructed to exercise power because it focused on purely social issues, so important to village India. The main function of the Khap and such other traditional panchayats has been to maintain peace, settle disputes especially with reference to the disputes over property and inheritance, sexual or marital 'misconduct' and a host of others. Significantly, such panchayats have been an all-male institution where women were always kept on the margins in the decision-making process. The main source of their strength has been the local dominant castes and they have been instrumental in enforcing the decisions taken. In this arrangement, Dalits, like the women, have also been on the margins. In the electoral process, right from the panchayats to parliament, their influence is there for everybody to see. Perhaps, that is why all the mainstream political parties, except the left parties, do not challenge its authority openly. Some political parties have, shamelessly, supported the illegal and unconstitutional decisions of Khap Panchayats.

In recent years, the hidden hands of Khap Panchayats may be seen behind the killing of hundreds of women, though its leaders have always denied it. Negating the constitutional rights of citizens, Khap Panchayats have projected themselves as the protector, guardian and saviour of the local culture and doing moral policing at will. Thousands of 'brides' purchased from the poorest regions of Bihar, Jharkhand, Odisha, West Bengal and Chhattisgarh are serving as domestic slaves in this region as a result of the disturbed sex ratio. Where does morality go in such cases?

In the wake of the increasing number of honour killings, the Supreme Court issued notice in 2010 to the Central Government and six State Governments, including Haryana, Punjab and Rajasthan and directed them to take effective measures to prevent such atrocities and killings.

LEGISLATIVE MEASURES

The increasingly combative Khap Panchayats go **scot-free** as the humiliation and killings of women enjoy the tacit approval of the local community. Public lynching of the 'guilty' couples, public beating and humiliation, blackening of faces, murder made to appear as suicide, are regular features of these societies and most of these incidents go unreported. Even in cases which are able to reach courts of law, the rate of conviction is abysmally low as the law enforcement personnel at the lower levels belong to the same social milieu.

Quick Fact

Scot-free

It refers to something or someone that is completely free from penalty or harm. The term is mainly used in discussing a person who has avoided paying taxes.

Under intense pressure from civil society groups, the government is supposed to make some suitable legislation. There is no specific criminal law to deal with the offence of honour crimes. A special law is required along with some specific provisions in the Indian Penal Code. The Constitution of India has ample provisions allowing an individual to exercise his/her choice independent of caste, religion or gender and hence any new legislative measures in this regard would be in conformity with the constitutional rights of Indian citizens. Extrajudicial punishment in Taliban style has no place in India or any civilised society.

Needless to say, without strong political will, neither the humiliation of women nor the role of the illegal and unconstitutional panchayats can be checked. We also have to decide whether we wish to live in an open, liberal, democratic society or live in the dark and dingy caves of the past. This social problem shall continue to play havoc with the lives of millions in the absence of a strong social movement.

CASTEISM AND CASTE CONFLICT

Caste is a major determinant of social, economic and political status in the Indian society. Caste also sets relationships of domination and subordination by different caste groups. This affects the ownership, control and distribution of resources and services in the society, economy and polity. The alien rulers while establishing their supremacy also tended to reinforce the prevailing unequal relations of production and reproduction. Consequently, for a very long time in the country's history the primacy of caste in distribution of awards was not challenged. However, the situation changed a great deal after the departure of the British. Those at the bottom of the caste hierarchy began to fight for their shares in the power and resources. Those dominating the control over them resisted a change. There ensued a duel of conflict of social status. This process resulted in caste conflicts in post-Independent India. Its character, speed, direction, intensity and consequences have varied in different socio-cultural-geographical regions of the country. One unmistakable result is change in the manner in which caste has come to be used in the Indian society at the turn of the first decade of the Twenty First century. This chapter shall examine the caste question and the nature of caste conflicts in the country.

▶▶ India: A Graded and Compartmentalised Society

Scholars such as Louis Dumont and Marc Galanter have described the Indian society as a graded and compartmentalised society. It is a bewildering assembly of groups that possess distinct and diverse styles of life. This diverse group maintains very complicated set of relationships that govern their togetherness and simultaneously their distinctiveness. Social researchers world over have been amazed at the ways in which they accommodate each other while appearing to be distinct. Apart from religious diversity, one of the distinctive and pervasive features of Indian society is its organisation into myriad system of castes. Uninformed scholars attribute it to only the numerically preponderant Hindus, but the ground reality is that adherents of many other Indian religions also have castes. Caste is a very complex empirical phenomenon in India and it is hazardous to specify its universal features that remain valid for the entire length and breadth of the vast country.

▶▶ Casteism: Root Cause of Caste Conflict

Strict enforcement of the rights and duties prescribed under the Hindu code, which offers privileges to one section of the population, and discriminatory treatment to the other, is practice of casteism. Anupama Rao (2009) in fact argues that caste is a specific form of embodiment, universally salient as the process of inequality. The orthodoxy of its enforcement varies from one region to another. Practice of casteism results in a large number and complex varieties of disabilities on those falling in the lower strata of the Hindu order.

Relative positions in the local caste hierarchy are often conceptualised in terms of the theoretical division of Hindu society into four *Varnas* or classes. According to this theory, Indian society is divided into Brahmins, the priestly and scholarly class; Kshatriyas, rulers and soldiers; Vaishyas, merchants and agriculturists; and Sudras, the menial and servant class. The first three Varnas were called the 'twice born' by virtue of investiture with the sacred thread, while the Sudras were subject to numerous disabilities. They were restricted to certain occupations, forbidden to learn the Veda and enjoined to be deferential and subservient to their betters.

The traditional Hindu notions of *dharma* and *karma* justify graded inequality. Each caste group has its specified dharma. Under this ideology, it is surmised that the inequality of statuses and the more onerous duties assigned to some groups is consequence of the karma of previous birth. Similarly, it is argued that others are not responsible for the indignities that the society heaps on him: he himself is responsible for them. He had better accept his fate and get on with it. At the same time, this ideology justifies claims of superiority of other groups. It asks the lowly placed to discharge his ordained duties diligently and earn a 'promotion' in his/her next birth. At the overall structural level, the

Indian society has not been entirely static and the caste system has been changing but the defining principles of purity and pollution have survived over time.

▸▸ Processes and Factors Causing Caste Conflicts

As a unique institution, caste has shown remarkable resilience. It has demonstrated contradictory characteristics of change and continuity at the same time. Its persistence shows itself in continued presence of some characteristics and its change is reflected in modification, or, even substitution of certain other dimensions. The change and persistence of characteristics has not been uniform across the length and breadth of the country. What has changed in one part of the country has survived in another part. The change, of whatever variety, has affected castes both at the top of the ritual ladder as well as the bottom. It is certainly true that the character of change has been more significant in the bottom layer. Explaining the processes involved in this transformation, several scholars have propounded theories. These generally offer explanations around one factor. However, since this change has come about through a combination of several factors, these are unable to satisfactorily explain this **accusatory process**. The changes in the caste have produced both positive as well as negative consequences such as conflicts and violence. A brief discussion of these varied explanations is given here.

Quick Fact

Accusatory Process

In terms of caste conflicts, this process refers to the act of attributing blame or responsibility to individuals or groups based on their caste identity, often escalating tensions and perpetuating social divisions and discrimination.

One, the very composition of caste structures in different states has been a significant factor in caste conflicts there. The composition of the basket of various communities in the Varna order in different socio-cultural – geographical regions of the country is very varied. The Brahmins are present in almost every state excepting perhaps some of the north-eastern states where tribes dominate the social structure. The Kshatriyas are not present in good enough numbers in states like Tamil Nadu, Odisha, West Bengal, Andhra Pradesh, Karnataka, Kerala, Maharashtra, Haryana, Punjab and J & K. It is not that the aggressiveness of the Kshatriyas is totally absent in such states. Earlier on, the Brahmins and Kshatriyas were enforcing the caste rules and practices. What has happened is that some other communities from the middle rung of the ritual order have generally appropriated the mantle of the Kshatriyas, if not that of the Brahmins. The Reddys in Andhra Pradesh, the Vokkaligas in Karnataka, the Marathas in Maharashtra, the Nairs in Kerala and the Jats in Punjab and Haryana are such examples. In many other states, such as Tamil Nadu and Karnataka, this mantle has been taken up by some other castes in the middle tier.

Second, one of the well-known theories on the question of status improvement in the caste order is that of M N Srinivas, who termed the process as Sanskritisation. Stated in simple words, this is emulation of the rituals and practices of the so-called higher castes on the part of so-called low castes to improve their own status in the society. As against Sanskritisation, others have talked about opposing process of *Digitisation* (Kancha Illiaih)/*Arjakisation* (Ram Swarop Verma) which involves inventing a separate identity and ideology under which castes are not ranked inferior to others. In theatres such as Tamil Nadu and Maharashtra, this has taken altogether radical form. In case of Tamil Nadu, this involved rejection of dominance of the north Indian Brahmin led Aryan Hindu ideology, and use of Hindi as national language, creation of a separate Dravidian culture, recognition of dignity and self-respect of different communities, and creation of an independent Dravidian region. This process involved the entire basket of castes/communities present in its social structure. In case of Maharashtra this process covered only the Dalit communities which stated that they were a separate entity from the communities among the Hindu grouping, had their own distinct social, cultural identity and thus needed to be treated as equals, not subordinates, much less untouchable. The *Dalit Panthers* who came in to prominence in the 1970s asserted this identity in more aggressive fashion and as is the case those dominating them retaliated violently in newer ways than they were earlier on. This identity formation and assertion also took the form of 'conversion of religion (into Buddhism)' for quite a large segment of Maharashtrian Dalits. In Punjab, among other things, the Dalits have formed their own sects, established their own Gurudwaras and cremation grounds and practiced a different version of Sikhism, one that does not treat its followers unequally in religious practice.

The reverse process of ritual status change, termed de-Sanskritisation by some scholars, has also been reported. As indicated by Shyam Lal, the most amazing among them has been the adoption of scavenging profession by the Brahmins in Rajasthan. This type of change has not been reported from other parts of the country. Improvement of ritual status of a so called lowly placed caste through gelding of altogether new rituals has been reported by Prema Kurien (2003). She found that the Ezhavas of Kerala, who were treated almost as the untouchables and whose women were in fact not allowed to wear clothing on the upper part of their bodies at one point of time acquired wealth through foreign migration, education and employment in the native state and purchase of landed property coupled with their numerical strength in the political field developed altogether new rituals for themselves. These rituals are now being emulated by the Nairs who once dominated the socio-cultural-economic-political landscape in Kerala. The Ezhavas, helped in no mean part by their demographic strength in Kerala society (over 20% of population), have come to occupy a very prominent position in Kerala polity. This has not been very easily digested by castes such as the Nairs, who along with the Namboodiris, dominated the Kerala society traditionally in earlier period. The animosity of the Nairs to growing Ezhava ascendancy has reflected itself in opposition of the Nair Service Society, a caste association of the Nairs, in stoutly fighting reservation cases in High Court and Supreme Court throughout the post-independence period. In fact, some of landmark cases of reservation issue were raised by NSS of Kerala, and even the appointment of the Narendra Commission, which for the first time in India's history of affirmative action for the deprived assessed the extent of benefits by the SCs, STs and the OBCs in Kerala, also came about due to strident demand of the NSS (H S Verma and Nadeem Hasnain:2006). The Nairs' dissatisfaction with the growing influence of the Ezhavas in Kerala politics was evident when the NSS described V. S. Achuthanandan, the Ezhava Chief Minister of Kerala, as an 'uncouth person' during the 2011 state assembly elections.

Three, progressively there has been a perceptible decline in the importance of caste as an ideology based on purity and pollution in the post-Independence period. This decline has not been uniform in every state or region. In the whole of north India, due to a perceptible change in the political power sharing arrangements, those at the middle and lower rungs of the ritual hierarchy have recovered some of their legitimate place and honour in the society and polity if not entirely in society (Christophe Jaffrelot: 2003). Therefore, overall societal differentiation based strictly on caste norms has ebbed significantly. On the other hand, given the greater religiosity of people in south India, notions of purity and pollution have not declined as much. As a consequence in a state like Tamil Nadu, where Brahmanism has receded to the background but the caste orthodoxy has been propped up by the intermediate castes, especially those that are neo-rich. Increased inter-caste conflict and violence in Tamil Nadu, seen particularly since the 1970s, is the consequence of this factor.

Four, the political scientists like Rajni Kothari have referred to another dimension of change in caste status. Rajni Kothari calls it politicisation and secularisation of caste. Caste had been playing a debilitating role at least for a large part of the Hindu population in India. But practice of Parliamentary democracy offered the opportunity to those from the so-called lower castes to use their numbers in getting representation in the political process and eventually a share in the political power. Thus, caste as a unifying political resource and a powerful mobilizer of political support conferred gains to the less privileged sections of the Indian society. As very cogently argued by Palsikar (2009), this empowering role of caste, referred to as secularisation by Rajni Kothari earlier, has contributed to a perceptible decline of the ritual importance of caste and as a pan Indian political mobilizer and instrument of sharing political power. Now, it is more of a potent instrument at the regional level. Although many instances can be shown where small castes intervene in local process, effective role of caste can be detected only at the state level. At the same time, castes cannot assume all India identities and caste alliances cannot be easily forged at the all-India level. The political salience of caste increased only after castes transcended the 'local' identities and by forging new 'mega' caste identity.

RELIGIOUS REVIVALISM

If we look at various religions of the world, we find at least one thing in common – the tendency to revive its 'past glory' at one point of time or the other. This is largely due to the concerns and frustrations of the followers of religions. Religious revivalism is always accompanied by mass movements. Fundamentalism, another form of mass movement related with religion, is a little different from religious revivalism. While fundamentalism in most of the cases takes on an aggressive form and may not hesitate to use force and compulsion and may be using violence against any resistance, revivalism is generally a peaceful movement run by committed people.

The main factors or causes behind religious revivalism are:

- Sense of insecurity and alienation
- Mass migration to a different place or region
- Widespread sense of victimhood and prevalence of '**siege mentality**'
- Disillusionment with the present state of affairs and search for a new meaning of life through religion.
- Belief that piecemeal reform will not solve the problem and the solution lies in the past glory of the community or religion.

Quick Fact

Siege Mentality

It refers to a collective mindset in which a group feels surrounded, threatened, or under attack by external forces, often leading to heightened defensiveness, suspicion, and a strong in-group solidarity.

In the Indian society *Arya Samaj Movement* and *Tablighi Jamaat Movement* are the most obvious examples of religious revivalism. The Arya Samaj was established in 1875 by Dayanand Saraswati. It emphasised Vedic values and culture and *Sanatan Dharma*. It also established schools to give education to boys and girls separately based on ancient vedic principles. Their main slogan has been 'Back to the Vedas'. The Tablighi Jamaat emerged in 1926 and is believed to be an offshoot of Deoband School, a prominent Islamic seminary. It's founder Moulvi Muhammad Ilyas was concerned and agitated by the Arya Samaj's *Shuddhi* movement trying to reconvert Muslims to the Hindu fold. Going by its name, *tabligh* meaning preaching, its main objective is to purge all 'unislamic' practices prevalent among the Muslims and revive the 'true spirit' of Islam. The main similarity between these two movements is the disillusionment from the present and glory of the past. In this process both goes against key paradigms of modernity and secular life based on rationalism and scientific outlook. This virtual obsession with the past makes them strong votaries of revivalism.

VIOLENCE AGAINST WOMEN

Violence and discrimination against women has always been a salient feature of Indian society. Unfortunately, this violence begins from the stage of foetus and continues throughout her life in various ways. (A detailed account of this state of affairs has been discussed in the book in a separate chapter – Women and Society).

Patriarchy has been the signature hallmark of the Indian society. Consequently, discrimination against women has been practiced with impunity. Historically, Indian women have not been given equality in almost every specific field of society, economy and polity. While it would be empirically incorrect to state that the condition of the Indian women has not changed in the post-Independence, the fact still remains that there is enormous gender discrimination prevailing in the Indian society

The origins of such behaviour can be traced to the rules laid down by Manu in 200 BC in his treatise, *Manusmriti*. It ordained: 'by a young girl, by a young woman, or even by an aged one, nothing must be done independently, even in her own house'. 'In childhood a female must be subject to her father, in youth to her husband, when her lord is dead to her sons; a woman must never be independent'. Women's lives continue to be shaped by customs that are centuries old. Non–Hindu communities also suffer from this in varying degrees.

▶▶ 'Honour Killing' of Young Women

Murder of young girls and women in the name of saving or retrieving the 'honour' of the family, caste or community has assumed serious dimensions in democratic India. Though such killings are not confined to India and may also be seen in other parts of South Asia (Pakistan, Bangladesh, Nepal and Sri Lanka), Middle East, South America and Africa in gross violation of human rights. In US and Europe it is largely confined to the immigrant communities many of whom continue with their archaic traditional notions of 'family honour'. Largely speaking, such killings present the obnoxious face of strongly patriarchal societies. The so called 'honour killing' or 'crimes of honour' may be seen as a part of broader violence against women which is not confined to any particular caste, culture or religion. This is also not limited to the rural areas or uneducated illiterate persons. Though such violence stretching to killings is reported from throughout India except perhaps the tribal regions, the largest number of reports come from Punjab, Haryana, Rajasthan and Western Uttar Pradesh. Many such killings go unreported largely because of its consent from the entire village community.

Most of us agree that the health and moral and political condition of a state should be assessed on the basis of condition and status of women and minority groups. Patriarchy runs deep in Indian society and manifests itself in all forms of violence against women–female foeticide and infanticide, discrimination, domestic violence and killings. The psyche and mindset behind all forms of violence and discrimination against women must be understood to situate honour killings in our social structure. This mindset is rooted in the local culture when women are not regarded as human beings entitled to rights and cultural autonomy but as property representing the honour of the male members of her family. Her body signifies the honour of the family. Hence gender and honour becomes the site of honour killing. Perhaps that is why convicted killers often speak with defiant pride and without regret about their actions.

Shame, dishonour and loss of face accompany the situation in which the daughter violates the normative order. The implications of such a situation are not temporary for it would never be forgotten by the local society. As P.S. Narasimha Judge (2012) points out, non-conformity to normative expectations and exercising choices that are the exclusive prerogatives of the parents and male members of the community poses a serious threat to the existing normative social order. Indeed shame can become a millstone around a family's neck. Even generations later, the event continues to put a family to shame whenever the event is mentioned as a reminder. For most families involved, the only way to defend one's honour is to eliminate the 'source of shame'.

If we analyse the prevailing trends of 'honour killings' we find the perceived dishonour is normally the result of one or more of the following behaviour or even the suspicion of such behaviour:

- Clothing in a manner going against the traditional dress pattern for women. Often this is unacceptable to the family or the community.
- Defying and not accepting or terminating a marriage arranged by the family and going for her own choice or going for divorce.
- Inter-caste marriage or marrying within the village or *gotra*.
- Pre-marital or extra marital intimacy or sexual relation.
- Same sex relation or lesbian relation.
- Going for a profession against the wishes of the parents or brothers.

The feminist explanations of such killings look at 'honour' as power. It helps us to understand how patriarchy perpetuates the right and dominance of males over women and how it justifies the definitions and expectations of males especially with reference to women's behaviour. This 'honour system' may be divided into three broad areas:

(a) control over women's behaviour,
(b) sense of shame in losing this control,
(c) regulation and magnifying this sense of shame by community participation.

Confluence of patriarchy, caste and masculinity is a heady mixture in all the South Asian Societies especially in the Indian sub-continent. Gilbert Sebastian (2013) observed that the semi-feudal, caste-based hierarchy in India traditionally sought to confine women, particularly those from privileged castes, to domestic roles, while capitalist patriarchy expanded their roles to include participation in 'social production' or work outside the home. He noted that semi-feudal caste-based patriarchy guarded the honour of upper-caste women, equating it with the honour of the family and caste, and provided them with 'protection', while prescribing the harshest punishments for men from under-privileged lower castes for even minor offenses or advances toward upper-caste women.

This dynamic, he argued, explains why in states like Haryana, Punjab, Rajasthan, and Uttar Pradesh, any relationship, let alone marriage, between a Dalit man and a woman from a higher caste often results in severe punishment for both individuals. Sebastian argues that the 'violent masculinities' of imperialist patriarchy and semi-feudal caste-based patriarchy intersect in such contexts.

Rigidly, patriarchal societies hardly allow any space to the socio-cultural autonomy for women. In the recent decades, education and economic freedom has empowered substantial sections of women. They are enjoying a bigger role in the decision-making process and they are taking up more responsibilities outside home. All these changes have loosened the grip of patriarchy over women. Religion and caste are not willing to accept these changes. The urban societies unlike the rural ones find it more difficult to restrict the march of women towards greater freedom and autonomy. In villages the space of control of males over women is much wider and the support system against women's rights is always willing to lend a helping hand to the **draconian patriarchy**. It is seen that larger the city, the higher is the flight of women's autonomy. The civil society organisations are also there to support women.

Quick Fact

Draconian Patriarchy

It refers to a system of extreme gender inequality that is oppressive and unjust. It is characterised by the use of harsh laws and rules to maintain male dominance over women.

In the wake of the increasing number of honour killings the Supreme Court issued notice in 2010 to the Central Government and six state governments including Haryana, Punjab and Rajasthan and directed to take effective measures to prevent such atrocities and killings.

Needless to say, without strong political will, neither the humiliation of women can be checked nor the role of the illegal and unconstitutional panchayats. We also have to decide whether we wish to live as an open, liberal, democratic society or live in the dark and dingy caves of the past. This social problem shall continue to play havoc with the lives of the millions in the absence of a strong social movement.

ILLITERACY AND DISPARITIES IN EDUCATION

It is now an established fact that education is a great leveller. It is a great tool towards achieving equality in the society. In a highly hierarchical society such as India an entire section of people were deprived from attaining education. Thus, a whole segment of Indian society has been lagging behind.

▸▸ Consequential Problems in Indian Education

A number of problems afflict the field of education in India. However, the three among them need elaboration These are illiteracy, neo-illiteracy and unemployability.

▸▸ Illiteracy in India

Definition of literacy: The UNESCO has drafted a definition of *literacy* as the 'ability to identify, understand, interpret, create, communicate, compute and use printed and written materials associated with varying contexts. Literacy involves a continuum of learning in enabling individuals to achieve their goals, to develop their knowledge and potential and to participate fully in their community and wider society'.

The National Literacy Mission defines literacy as acquiring the skills of reading, writing and arithmetic and the ability to apply them to one's day-to-day life.

Census definition of literacy rate: The working definition of literacy in the Indian census since 1991 is as follows: 'The total percentage of the population of an area at a particular time aged seven years or above who can read and write with understanding'. Here, the denominator is the population aged seven years or more.

▸▸ Unemployability

India now produces huge numbers of graduates both in all streams of graduate, post graduate general and professional/technical streams of education. However, both public and private sector HR experts indicate that hardly 20% of them possess skills that would be of immediate use to them. In other words, 80% of highly educated Indian human resource is unemployable. This is hurting both the potential employers as well as those who want to be employed. A large number of private corporate sector firms have resorted to two solutions to meet this problem. One, some of them like the IT majors Infosys, TCS, Wipro, have designed their training programmes where they provide the fresh recruits skills that they require taking six to seven months. Others have worked out an arrangement of such training with private sector training outfits that provide such training on a contractual basis. However, these are but a drop in the ocean since the bulk of those coming out of educational institutions do not get benefit of such schemes. This is hurting more of those belonging to the deprived sections of the population. As the recently conducted *Hindustan Times* survey reveals, students from the richest 20% of the society are seventeen times more likely to be studying law than those from the poorest 20%. And a student who does not belong to the other backward class (OBC), scheduled caste (SC) or scheduled tribe (ST) is six times more likely to be studying management than a scheduled tribe (ST) student in India. Girls are less likely to be getting English medium education than boys, and more women take up humanities than men in India.

India's education landscape is extremely unequal. These inequalities manifest themselves in the form of differences based on caste, class and, in some cases, gender. Those at the bottom of the socio-economic ladder are more likely to be studying humanities than a professional course. They are also much less likely to have access to English medium education. Differences in geographical location can increase or decrease these inequalities.

Stereotyping, however, is of little help in understanding India's education landscape. For example, the commonly held belief that most Muslims send their children to Madrasas (religious seminaries) and not proper schools is a myth which is not supported by data.

These findings are based on an HT analysis of unit level data of a nationally representative survey conducted by the National Statistical Office (NSO).

The data points cited above are in keeping with the larger trend of students from privileged sections of the society, who are more likely to be studying professional courses.

The socio-economic have-nots also have a much lower likelihood of receiving English medium education. A student who does not belong to other backward class (OBC), scheduled caste (SC) or scheduled tribe (ST) is almost three times more likely to getting English medium education than a scheduled caste (SC) student. A student from the top 20% of society is ten times more likely to be studying in an English medium school than someone who belongs to the bottom 20%.

As Arun Kumar (2024) says, news that the son of a rickshaw puller cracked the toughest engineering entrance exam or qualified to become an elite-class bureaucrat regularly feature on India's media platforms. Such news represents both the equality and the inequality of India's dynamic education sector. Equality because hard work of such candidates has paid off and education has been empowering for them and their families. Inequality because they represent the exceptional ones among their communities, castes and classes. The sensational reporting of their success does not only show how dreams of a new India are being sold by a highly privatised education and coaching system but also depicts a strange elite world of well-paid, respectable jobs where the entry of a poor labourer's son is a news item, rather than a norm. Such sensationalisation presupposes an education system that has significant learning gaps between students from different classes and social profiles. India's current education system is witnessing a twin phenomenon: greater access to public education by India's socially marginalised castes and classes and a greater privatisation drive of the education sector from bottom to top.

Historically, India has come a long way since its colonial life; in fact, one can say it has undergone a slow education revolution. Today's India boasts a literacy rate of more than 77%, which at the time of Independence in 1947, was below 18.3%. In the 1900s, India was referred to as a nation of illiterates. Now it is the hub of a dynamic education system. However, it is still a society marked by extreme forms of socio-economic inequality that continues to plague its educational achievements.

However, when socially and economically marginalised students enter education, their struggles do not necessarily remain about equal access to education but become about gaining equal opportunities and knowledge like their peers from socially and economically well-off backgrounds. Understanding and recognising this latter issue, both as an educational problem and policy concern, is key to reforming the existing education system.

In today's India, the privatisation of the education sector, which is growing at the expense of increasing educational demands from all sections of society, has the potential to both expand the education sector, but most importantly, sharpen inequalities produced at the site of education.

Huge tuition fees and increased living costs in major urban centers where these desirable educational institutes are located are segregating student bodies along caste and class lines. Unless we recognise that education is a site producing new forms of inequality, we cannot deal with the challenges it poses. The debate on the Indian education system must move on from access to equity of experience.

Strategies to Combat Educational Disparity and for Equitable Resource Allocation: Ensuring that educational resources, including infrastructure and teaching materials, are distributed fairly to all regions and schools.

Inclusive Curriculum: Developing a curriculum that celebrates diversity, incorporates local languages and promotes social inclusivity.

Teacher Training: Providing teachers with the necessary training to teach diverse student populations effectively.

Digital Access: Expanding digital access and bridging the digital divide to ensure all students can participate in online education.

Gender Sensitisation: Implementing programs that challenge gender stereotypes and encourage girls to pursue education.

Affirmative Action: Enforcing policies that provide marginalised communities with educational opportunities and representation.

POVERTY, DEPRIVATION AND INEQUALITIES

People are poor because they are excluded. It is not as if supplies are not available in adequate quantities. For most of the essential items, they are. Yet, about 50% humans live in poverty and 25% live in absolute poverty. Thus, *poverty is a factor of power and exclusion* rather than a factor of production. Poverty, social exclusion, empowerment and development are inter-wined: they affect each other. Cheria et al. (2004) argue that poverty can be seen as a set of relationships in which people are excluded from participation in the normal pattern of social life. Thus, human poverty constitutes denial of human rights to promote social progress and raise standard of living within the wider concept of freedom. In this sense, poverty is a great enemy of human happiness. It certainly destroys liberty. However, poverty is not only lack of material needs. It includes other aspects of life, such as lack of personal security, access to information and ability to influence the political decisions. Poverty reduction would, therefore, must address not only improvement in-livelihoods, but also improvement in access to resources, expansion of knowledge and increased empowerment. To do so, one must understand the process of economic, social and political exclusion. A human rights perspective of poverty enables responses to poverty that promotes rights, growth and empowerment.

Poverty is not so easy to define. It is certainly multi-dimensional in character and diverse in its manifestations. As a concept, poverty has been viewed from:

(i) income (defined poverty line)
(ii) basic needs (i.e., food, health care, education, shelter and other essential services)
(iii) capability (absence of some basic capabilities) and
(iv) human rights perspectives

▶▶ Caste, Gender and Background Still Determine Life Chances

Studies indicate that at least 30% of earning inequality is still determined by caste, gender and family backgrounds. The seriousness of this figure becomes clear when it is compared with rates of the world's most egalitarian countries, such as Finland and Norway, where the respective estimates are below 10% for a similar set of social and family attributes.

▶▶ Causation of Poverty

Several factors have caused poverty in India. Cumulatively; these have not only caused poverty: they have perpetuated it, and prevented the poor from coming out of the web of poverty. We list the principal ones among them.

▶▶ Caste System

While unique, the caste system is not the only source of unfairness. Indeed, it accounts for less than 7% of inequality of opportunity, something that is in itself laudable. We will need to add criteria such as gender and family background differences to explain 30% of inequality.

Caste system is a system that perpetuated compartmentalisation of society into those privileged and those deprived. The Indian Constitution provided certain safeguards to prevent their oppression, and affirmative action initiatives have been undertaken to emancipate their conditions. However, it is conceded by experts that even though their condition has improved quite a bit during the last six decades, at the same time it is a grim reality that most of the Dalits continue to remain poor.

▶▶ Economic Policies

Other countries that were poor have registered dramatic progress and have removed poverty from their society. Some among them – for example, South Korea – have joined the ranks of the developed nations. India has not. Its economic policies are responsible for its agonisingly slow progress.

▶▶ Over-reliance on Agriculture

The Indian economy continues with its over-reliance on agriculture. Farming is not a very remunerative business proposition. Given its structural constraints, while it can continue to be the last bastion of sustenance to the vast majority of Indians, it cannot be fast propeller to poverty removal efforts. While industry and services sectors have registered impressive growths since the 1980s, growth in agriculture has dropped to 2% from an initial 4%. High population growth rate has kept on adding to the absolute numbers of the poor.

▶▶ Adverse Effect of Liberalisation Policies

Leading economists like Jayati Ghosh and Utsa Patnaik, and commentators like Sainath have argued that the economic policies pursued since the 1990s were responsible for the collapse of India's farming economy, and caused an agrarian crisis. These policies encouraged farmers to switch to cash crops. This involved an extraordinary increase in costs. The returns were comparatively not commensurate given the control of the market by the middlemen. Some cash crops (like cotton, ground nut, pulses) are grown in rain -fed areas and there is frequent crop failures. This culminated in large scale farmers' suicides in quite a few states since then, and have not ebbed thereafter despite patchwork solutions offered by the Central and state governments.

▶▶ Outlook on Poverty

Removal of poverty in India would crucially depend on the evolving relationship between social exclusion, development and empowerment. It would also depend on the independent initiatives taken by the deprived communities to empower themselves, not remaining on the mercy of the doles of the governments of the day, a larger part of which does not reach them anyway. Thus, poverty removal would equally be an exercise in creatively actualising development on the one hand and empowerment on the other. This actualisation would have to be genuine from the government's side.

The single largest chunk of absolute poor is that of the tribals. Here the cases of tribal communities of the North-East are different. They obtained their local autonomy through insurgency and struggle. Their lot has certainly improved given increased investment in the infrastructure in that region and domination of governance by their own local elite with considerable minimisation of decisions being foisted from Delhi. Among the tribal communities from the belly part of India, migration of the poor among them to the non-poor categories is limited to just one or two isolated tribal communities from Jharkhand. The rest of the tribal communities continue to suffer from chronic poverty including chronic malnutrition caused by hunger. They also continue to be victims of anti-people policies due to non-passage/non-implementation of Forest Rights, Rehabilitation and Relief, Land Acquisition, Mines and Minerals Acts. Since Naxalism has flourished in most of these parts, they suffer from the atrocities of both the Naxals as well as the paramilitary forces supposedly tackling extremist Naxalism. Development activities that directly benefit these tribals have really not taken off, and therefore, significant reduction of poverty in these parts remains a goal unattained.

The lot of the Dalits continues to be bad even though it has improved somewhat in most parts of the country but more specifically in Uttar Pradesh (UP). The Dalits have sufficient numbers in some states – like UP, West Bengal and Punjab – but have worked out their political line to tackle their all-round deprivation only in UP. The bulk of the Dalit communities in most other states are still groping in the dark. **Sporadic forays** of single segments of these groups in some specific parts of the country have yielded temporary benefits, but have not permanently solved their chronic poverty problems. However, overall the Dalits are moving upwards even though their progress is far from satisfactory.

> **Quick Fact**
>
> **Sporadic Forays**
>
> It refer to occasional or irregular attempts, ventures, or raids into a particular activity, area, or territory.

The one deprived group that has produced mixed and very diverse results in different parts of the country is that of the OBCs. Those holding relatively larger farm holdings among the occupational category of farmers among the OBCs in some states – like Haryana, Punjab, central and western UP, coastal region of Andhra Pradesh and some parts of Kerala – have certainly moved out of poverty, and have in fact also diversified their occupational choices through better education. However, their good enough numbers have not brought commensurate political benefits due to clever political games played by the upper caste/class communities. Even so, they have now gained a better leverage in obtaining benefits – social, economic and political – from the ruling combinations than they were in the late 1990s. This is producing some unheard of results in the Indian polity: state elections have begun to be decided on the basis of performance of the governing dispensations. This is a very heartening political development for the benefit of the absolute poor, something that the inheritors of hereditary democracy had not bargained for.

Among the religious communities, Muslims from the north and south differ fundamentally. That also explains their divergent social-economic-political ground realities. Those from the south are not as backward as their northern colleagues. The south Indian Muslims are better educated, have better occupational opportunities, have moved outside the country, have a much better worldview and are forward looking.

Taking the holistic view, the Sachar Committee Report presents a gloomy picture of the socio-economic condition of the largest minority of India.

Questions and Indicative Answers

1. **Explain the concept of social transformation**

   Start with the definition of Social transformation – It refers to significant changes in the structure, organisation, and functioning of a society, resulting in a shift in its values, norms, and institutions – next explain its key features with examples – Explain the process of change and its impact

   Conclude with how a dynamic process integral to human history, shaping societies and their development over time.

2. **What are reasons for the displacement of millions of people from their land?**

   Introduce the answer with what displacement refers to – the forced or voluntary movement of people from their homeland due to various factors – explain the key factors one by one like Conflict and War, Natural Disasters, Development Projects, Economic Pressures, Environmental Degradation etc.

   Conclude – Displacement is a multifaceted issue, often caused by a combination of economic, social, environmental, and political factors, affecting millions globally.

3. **What are the challenges of environmental degradation in India?**

   Introduction – Environmental degradation refers to the deterioration of the environment through depletion of resources, pollution, and habitat destruction. Explain its key challenges like Air Pollution, Water Scarcity, Deforestation, Soil Degradation, Waste Management, Climate Change etc in details.

Conclusion – Environmental degradation in India poses significant challenges to sustainable development, requiring urgent policy intervention, awareness, and action.

4. **Why the north-eastern region of India is always in the news because of ethnic conflicts?**

   Introduce with the fact that The North-Eastern region of India has been frequently in the news due to ongoing ethnic conflicts rooted in historical, cultural, and political tensions – Explain Key Reasons for Ethnic Conflicts like Ethnic Diversity, Autonomy and Identity Issues, Infiltration and Migration, Political Instability, Neglect by Central Government etc.

   Conclusion – Ethnic conflicts in the North-Eastern region of India are driven by a complex interplay of identity, resource competition, political issues, and historical grievances.

5. **What do you mean by casteism? Why does caste related tensions and conflicts continue in Indian society.**

   Introduction – Explain Casteism – refers to discrimination, prejudice, or social stratification based on the caste system, where individuals are categorised into hierarchical social groups – Key Aspects of Casteism like Social Hierarchy, Untouchability etc. – Reasons for Continued Caste-related Tensions and Conflicts like Deep-rooted Tradition, Economic Disparities, Political Manipulation, Social Inequality, Resistance to Change etc.

   Conclusion – Despite legal measures and social reforms, casteism persists in Indian society due to historical, social, and economic factors, requiring ongoing efforts for true equality.

6. **In what way religious revivalism is harmful and act as barrier to modernisation?**

   Introduction – Explain Religious Revivalism – It refers to the movement aimed at reinstating or reasserting religious beliefs, practices, and values, often in opposition to modern ideas and secularism – Explain the Harmful Effects of Religious Revivalism like Intolerance and Division, Resistance to Scientific Progress, Suppression of Individual Rights, Promotion of Conservatism etc.

   Explain how it is a Barrier to Modernisation (Obstruction to Secularism, Impediment to Social Reforms, Economic Setbacks)

   Conclusion – Religious revivalism acts as a barrier to modernisation by fostering division, impeding scientific and social progress, and promoting regressive values.

7. **Make a short review of status of women in Indian society.**

   Introduction – The status of women in Indian society is shaped by historical, cultural, religious, and socio-economic factors, varying significantly across different regions and communities – Key Aspects of Women's Status like Education and Employment, Health and Well-being, Political Representation, Social Roles and Norms, Violence and Discrimination etc. – A few positive developments in between like Legal Reforms, Empowerment Initiatives etc.

   Conclusion – While progress has been made in improving the status of women in India, significant challenges remain in achieving full gender equality, requiring continued efforts in education, legislation, and social transformation.

8. What are the consequences of illiteracy and disparities in education in Indian society?

Introduction – Illiteracy and disparities in education contribute to socio-economic inequalities and hinder national development – Key Consequences like Economic Impact, Social Inequality, Health and Well-being, Political Marginalisation, Gender Inequality etc. Explain next the long term impact like Cycle of Poverty, Hindrance to National Development etc.

Conclusion – Illiteracy and disparities in education are major obstacles to social and economic progress in India, requiring targeted efforts in policy, infrastructure, and societal change.

9. Discuss the relationship between poverty, deprivation and inequalities.

Introduce with – Poverty, deprivation, and inequalities are interconnected social issues that often reinforce one another, creating cycles of disadvantage in society – Explain

Key Concepts – Poverty, Deprivation, Inequalities etc. – The interconnections between Poverty and Deprivation, Poverty and Inequality, Deprivation and Inequality

Disadvantages – Inequality and deprivation create a cycle, where disadvantaged individuals remain trapped in poverty due to limited access to resources and opportunities. and Intergenerational Effects etc.

Conclusion – Poverty, deprivation, and inequalities are deeply interconnected, reinforcing cycles of disadvantage and hindering social and economic progress. Addressing these issues requires comprehensive policy and societal changes.

10. Analyse the relationship between 'honour' and patriarchy in Indian society.

In Indian society, patriarchy determines the parameters of honour and dishonour. Women not enjoying social-cultural autonomy are subordinated to males. Socialisation moulds women, even the mothers, to legitimise what the patriarchy demands ... Discuss the role of caste panchayats in the so called 'honour killing'.

Khap Panchayats, known by its popular name in Haryana, has become a metaphor for highly arbitrary and strongly patriarchal caste council dominated by upper castes especially the Jats, play the decisive role in taking a decision. It forces the parents and the brothers to surrender and take the decision of killing the 'deviant' girl.

Unfortunately, all the mainstream political parties, except the Communist Party, do not challenge the authority of the leaders of the *Khap* Panchayat because the leaders of the *Khap* mobilise votes for them in elections.

11. Why a large number of people are being displaced from their habitat? Why the largest number of them come from the tribal communities?

Though it is true that displacement and resettlement are unavoidable consequences of development but the principle of 'people first', should always be kept in mind ... Compensation for the acquired land is not rehabilitation ... Fruits of development should also reach those who have lost their land and livelihood.

The tribal communities occupy around 17% of the total geographical area of the country, but it contains around 70% of the mineral wealth and natural resources like forests and